Ideology, Legitimacy
and the
New State

CASS SERIES: NATIONALISM AND ETHNICITY
ISSN 1462-9755
General Editor: William Safran

This new series draws attention to some of the most exciting issues in current world political debate: nation-building, autonomy and self-determination; ethnic identity, conflict and accommodation; pluralism, multiculturalism and the politics of language; ethnonationalism, irredentism and separatism; and immigration, naturalization and citizenship. The series will include monographs as well as edited volumes, and through the use of case studies and comparative analyses will bring together some of the best work to be found in the field.

1. *Ethnicity and Citizenship: The Canadian Case* (NEP 1/3, Autumn 1995)
   Edited by Jean Laponce and William Safran

2. *Nationalism and Ethnoregional Identities in China* (NEP 4 1&2, Spring/ Summer 1998)
   Edited by William Safran

3. *Identity and Territorial Autonomy in Plural Societies* (NEP 5 3/4, Autumn/ Winter 1999)
   Edited by William Safran and Ramon Maíz

4. *Ideology, Legitimacy and the New State: Yugoslavia, Serbia and Croatia*
   Siniša Malešević

IDEOLOGY, LEGITIMACY
and the
NEW STATE

Yugoslavia, Serbia and Croatia

Siniša Malešević

FRANK CASS
LONDON • PORTLAND, OR

First published in 2002 in Great Britain by
FRANK CASS PUBLISHERS
Crown House, 47 Chase Side
Southgate, London N14 5BP

and in the United States of America by
FRANK CASS
c/o ISBS, 5804 N.E. Hassalo Street
Portland, Oregon, 97213-3644

Website: www.frankcass.com

British Library Cataloguing in Publication Data

Malešević, Siniša
  Ideology, legitimacy and the new state: Yugoslavia, Serbia and Croatia. –
  (Cass series. Nationalism and ethnicity; no. 4)
  1. Ideology – Yugoslavia 2. Ideology – Serbia 3. Ideology –
  Croatia 4. Yugoslavia – Politics and government – 1945–1980
  5. Serbia – Politics and government – 1945 6. Croatia –
  Politics and government – 1990–
  I. Title
  320.9′497

ISBN 0-7146-5215-6 (cloth)
ISSN 1462-9755

Library of Congress Cataloging-in-Publication Data

Malešević, Siniša.
  Ideology, legitimacy and the new state: Yugoslavia, Serbia and Croatia /
  Siniša Malešević.
    p. cm. – (Cass series – nationalism and ethnicity, ISSN 1462-9755; 4)
  Includes bibliographical references and index.
  ISBN 0-7146-5215-6
    1. Yugoslavia – Politics and government – 1945–1980. 2. Ideology – Yugoslavia. 3.
  Serbia – Politics and government – 1945–1992. 4. Ideology – Yugoslavia – Serbia. 5.
  Croatia – Politics and government – 1990 – 6. Ideology – Croatia. I. Title. II. Series.
  JN9670.M35 2002
  320.9497–dc21

                                                                    2002020215

Typeset in New Baskerville 10.9 pt/12 pt by Cambridge Photosetting Services,
Cambridge
Printed in Great Britain by MPG Books Ltd, Bodmin, Cornwall

Contents

Series Editor's Preface

The breakup of Yugoslavia and the violence following that event has given rise to a voluminous literature. The present work constitutes a significant and highly original addition to that literature. Rather than treading familiar ground – with its emphasis on civil war, ethnic cleansing, and external intervention – it focuses on the ideology and history on which the two major post-Communist 'successor' states in the Balkans have based their legitimacy. The book is a combination of case study and theoretical-analytical approaches highlighting the reciprocal relationship between the two states. In that sense it fulfils in an almost exemplary fashion the aim of the Frank Cass series on Nationalism and Ethnicity. The research leans heavily on existing sociological, political, and psychological theories; in a final chapter, general theoretical assumptions are reassessed in the light of specific experience.

Siniša Malešević examines the cultural and religious underpinnings of each of the states in heavily documented detail, paying particular attention to the post-World War II period of Titoist consolidation and national-communist experimentation. The author discusses the varied meanings of ideology – including those of Marx, Durkheim, and Parsons, and of the structuralists and postmodernists – and analyzes its normative and operational aspects and its connection with legitimacy. While adopting Weber's concept of legitimacy, the author shows that Serbian and Croatian legitimacy are based only in part on legal-rational criteria, and weighs the place of these criteria relative to charisma, egalitarianism, and selective institutions. The author also deals with the ethnonationalist manipulation of history by politicians who, motivated by the quest for power, seek to reinforce national cohesion by means of the invocation of 'holy traditions,' myths, and heroic events such as 'national liberation'; by the use of slogans such as 'we, the [chosen] people' and 'the working masses'; and by the reference to threats such as imperialism and capitalism. Language plays an important role in this effort: linguistic manipulation is resorted to not only to create and disseminate a desired national ideology, but also to demarcate Serbian and Croatian from each other and show that they are separate languages. Examples from political tracts and other kinds of literature are provided to make this point.

The author is tough-minded and objective, playing no favorites between Serbia and Croatia, and using documentary sources from both countries. Particular attention is devoted to the respective roles of Slobodan Milosevic and Franjo Tudjman and their use of political organizations, clientelistic patterns, the churches, the schools, and the press in order to strengthen their rule. Formerly high communist apparatchiks 'born again' as nationalists, both leaders have attempted to base the legitimacy of their rule in part on post-Communist democratic constitutions, but both have behaved in an unconstitutional manner in the name of national defense and security. And both, while referring to universal principles, have appealed to narrow ethnonational sentiments.

William Safran
University of Colorado

Acknowledgements

This book owes much to the help of other people. I started working on this project in Prague under the guidance of the late Ernest Gellner who will always remain a consistent source of inspiration. Without the unfailing support of John A. Hall and Kieran Keohane this work would not have been completed on time. Their advice, criticism and intellectual support have proved invaluable. I have also greatly benefited from the comments of my friends and colleagues Gordana Uzelac, Sukumar Periwal, Paddy O'Carroll, Iain MacKenzie, Piet Strydom and, especially, my life partner, Vesna.

However, the people who most deserve my gratitude are my father and colleague, Krstan, and my mother, Ljubica, whose encouragement and willingness to help were exceptional. I dedicate this book to them.

Introduction

This study has two aims: theoretical and substantive. The first intends to outline an analytic concept of ideology that is both theoretically and operationally viable. The objective is to develop a new conceptual model of ideology with a framework that is informed by and draws on many different theoretical positions, but which is also empirically well grounded. For that purpose all significant theories of ideology are surveyed, identifying their main structural characteristics as well as their points of dispute. Reviewing these theories of ideology, I have come to the conclusion that their epistemological differences can be brought down to the level of seven main areas of contention: whether ideology should be conceptualised as inclusive or restrictive; be made subject to true/false criteria; be defined in opposition to science; be understood as a universal or particular phenomenon; be regarded as a modern or 'primordial' feature of social life; include values and ideas as well as a material form; and finally, be treated as a rational or an irrational force.

The analytical position developed in this study aims not to resolve these issues in the manner of establishing a new 'grand narrative', but rather to devise an open hypothetical framework that, by concentrating on the form and content of ideology, will indirectly support the theoretical claims in question. Thus, in order to show that ideology can best be approached and studied by applying a loosely formulated inclusive definition of ideology, rejecting true/false and science/non-science criteria and viewing it as a complex but modern, materially shaped and predominantly rational entity, an appropriate operational model of ideology is developed. This operational model is analytical in the sense that by focusing on the form and content of ideology, it aims to 'break down' the structure of ideology into a number of mutually comparable elements.[1] This approach also distinguishes between two deeply related but different ways of how ideology functions in reality, the 'normative' (as postulated and formulated by the official doctrine), and the 'operative' (as it functions in the institutional structures of everyday life). The approach also identifies six conceptual aspects of ideology through which analysis of the form and content of ideology is to be undertaken. These six conceptual elements include ideology's self-perception as well as the perception of ideology's social reality and include the following categories: 'internal organisation of the society' – economy, politics, culture and nation, 'dominant actors', 'type of language and symbols used' and depiction of principal 'counter-ideologies'. In order to test propositions put forward in the theoretical part of this study this conceptual apparatus has been applied to the analysis of the form and content of ideology in three case studies: Yugoslavia (1945–60), Serbia (1987–97) and Croatia (1990–97).

This brings us to the second, substantive, aim of this study, which is to identify dominant ideologies, their form and content, and principal modes of legitimacy in post-World War II Yugoslavia and post-communist Serbia and Croatia. For this purpose a number of theories of legitimacy have been reviewed and critically evaluated. As a result of this evaluation it is obvious that the Weberian concept of legitimacy is still the most effective tool for the comparative analysis of legitimacy formation in differently structured societies. Hence, the Weberian approach is further re-evaluated, applied and tested in the analysis of dominant legitimacy types in these three case studies. Nevertheless, the analysis of political legitimacy in Yugoslavia, Serbia and Croatia aims not only to say something about these three cases, but also to identify some general patterns of legitimacy in more exceptional situations, such as the establishment of a new state.

In terms of structure of presentation this study is divided into three parts. The first part is a theoretical section comprising Chapters 1 and 2 which discusses theories of ideology and legitimacy. The second part is an empirical section that includes Chapters 3, 4 and 5 and deals with the case studies of Yugoslavia, Serbia and Croatia, while the third part, containing Chapters 6 and 7, integrates theoretical propositions developed in the first part with the empirical findings established in the second.

Hence, Chapter 1 contains an extensive review of the most important traditions in the study of ideology (Marxist, Functionalist, Paretian, Psychoanalytic, Neo-Kantian, Weberian, Structuralist, Critical theory, post-Modernist, post-Structuralist and post-Marxist), which demonstrate that ideology is not only to be identified with Marxism as commonly believed, but also with a much wider sociological tradition. The analysis that follows observes significant differences and similarities within these theoretical traditions and also establishes the central standpoint of each tradition. By singling out the main points of difference between various theoretical approaches, a new conceptual model of ideology is proposed. To avoid the hegemonism of another grand theory, the new model has been formulated on a purely hypothetical basis which argues in favour of an inclusive definition of ideology, the rejection of true/false, science/non-science criteria, and the universality, modernity, materiality and rationality of ideology. Seven hypothetical claims are developed to be indirectly tested on the three case studies. This theoretical conceptualisation of ideology has been further operationalised by drawing on Seliger's definition of ideology, which emphasises the crucial distinction between normative and operative ideology, and identifying the six key conceptual elements of ideology structure referred to above.

In Chapter 2, three dominant theoretical traditions in the study of political legitimacy (Weberian, Marxist, and pluralist) are discussed and critically elaborated. The positions are compared and the conceptual superiority of Weberian tradition in the large-scale comparative analysis is demonstrated. However, the Weberian concept of legitimacy is not taken for granted but is further scrutinised, pointing out both its principal qualities and its weaknesses. Taking into account the historical origins and nature of societies that will be under examination in the empirical part of this study, various applications of the Weberian framework, by Rigby, Lane, Pakulski and Gill, to the analysis of political legitimacy of state socialist societies have been reviewed and later critically evaluated. In addition, the relationship between ideology, legitimacy and the establishment of the new state is more closely defined and formulated in this chapter.

The application and testing of a new analytical concept of ideology as well as the Weberian concept of legitimacy on the three case studies have been undertaken in Chapters 3, 4 and 5. In all three chapters these conceptual apparatuses have been applied with the aim of identifying the dominant forms of legitimacy, the form and content of dominant power-keeping ideology, as well as the level of congruence between normative and operative ideologies. The three cases that were examined are post-World War II Yugoslavia and post-communist Serbia and Croatia. Each case study begins with a very brief historical introduction which is then followed by an analysis of political legitimacy. It is argued that while support for traditional and legal–rational types of authority can be found, charismatic and value–rational forms of authority have been decisive for these regimes' claims to legitimacy. However, the relationship between these forms of legitimate authority and the way they operate in reality indicate that the entire process of legitimation has acquired a new and a more complex form, termed here the *ideologisation of charisma*. Once the dominant type of legitimacy has been located, the analysis proceeds to an examination of normative and operative ideologies for all three cases. This is supported by a qualitative content analysis of ruling party manifestos (for normative ideology) and newspaper editorials and school textbooks (for operative ideology) in all three cases. The content analysis was completed along the six segments of ideology structure formulated in the theoretical part of this study (internal organisation of the society – (1) economy, (2) politics, (3) culture and nation, (4) dominant actors, (5) type of language and symbols used and (6) counter-ideologies). The comparison of normative and operative ideologies in all three cases demonstrates that although the two levels of ideology are conceptually very different, their form is similar if not identical: while normative ideologies tend to be scientifically shaped and driven, appealing to some 'higher' reality, operative ideologies are instrumentally driven and formulated, and hence make an appeal primarily to popular interests and emotions.

The final chapters bring together theoretical propositions raised in the first part of the study with the empirical findings of the content analyses applied to the case studies in order indirectly to support the analytical concept of ideology developed here. The results obtained from the three case studies have been commented on, demonstrating the adequacy and applicability of an inclusive definition of ideology. It is argued that such an approach is better suited to the analysis of ideology in differently structured societies. Relying on the results of content analysis, it is also claimed that true/false and science/non-science criteria should be abandoned in the analysis of ideology since this dichotomy is not only often impossible to follow but also appears to be irrelevant for most of the time. Concentrating on the differences that have been identified in the empirical part of the study between normative and operative ideology, on the form and content of language and argumentation used, type of appeal made, issues raised, and institutional mechanisms of ideology dissemination involved, it is argued that ideology is a universal, modern, material and predominantly rational force.

The second part of this section assesses the discussion on ideology and legitimacy, and elaborates on their relationship to the establishment of the new state. The idea of the ideologisation of charisma is more fully developed, explaining how and why this was identified as a dominant form of the regime's legitimation in all three case studies. This section also offers an answer to the question of why differently formed nationalisms have appeared to be a dominant operative ideology in all three cases under examination.

METHODS OF DATA COLLECTION

A traditional perception of quantitative and qualitative techniques of social research is that these two differ in almost every respect. The two are perceived as different in terms of how they view the nature of reality (objective, real vs. subjective, constructed), how they approach this reality (rigorous explanation vs. interpretation, understanding), how they see the position of the researcher (passive, separate from the subject of study vs. active, involved and inseparable from the subject of study), the role of values in the research (value neutral vs. normative) and so on. However, as some have already observed, these are 'two ideal types that are employed only in exceptional circumstances. In concrete cases, research projects employ a methodology that, although predominantly quantitative or qualitative, in essence contains some aspects of the other.'[2] When we engage in the research process we are always forced to rely on elements that are associated with both traditions. For example, even the most loosely formulated and the most simple arguments have to rely on some causal relations (A influences B, C is the result of D, F and G produce E and so on), whereas our 'discoveries' and ways of presentation are always subjectively illuminated and rarely restricted to mathematical formulas. It is really the object of our research which is the crucial element and the determinant of the kind of methods we use. If one intends to find out the gender or ethnic structure in a particular society, it is certainly more sensible and reliable to conduct a large-scale survey using a probability sample or to scrutinise the results of the national census than to conduct several thousand in-depth unstructured interviews. On the other hand, if we intend to find out more about power structure and the organisation of street gangs it would be better to engage in participant observation or ethnographic research than to attempt to bring members of the gang into an institution to run a laboratory experiment using Solomon's four-group design. Nevertheless, it is always better simultaneously to employ a number of different research methods, depending on the object and nature of the research and, most importantly, the accessibility of financial means available for the study.

Starting from this assumption I have decided to choose three different but highly compatible research tools – the analysis of case studies, qualitative content analysis and, occasionally, the use of statistics and other documentary material as a secondary source. The choice of these three sources was determined by the object of my study and by the means available for the study. Therefore, in order to identify the dominant power-keeping normative and operative ideologies as well as the dominant modes of legitimacy in my three case studies, I did not rely on surveys, partly because I am not primarily concerned with the dominant values of the population relevant to the case studies in question, and partly because the results of surveys and public polls are not available or, when available, often unreliable. I also avoided experiments, as many of the issues under study are generally regarded as macrophenomena and therefore not open to experimental testing. Nor did this study's focus on historical events lend itself to experimentation. The same applies to ethnography, grounded theory, observation or in-depth interviewing. None of these research techniques is applicable to study historical events or appropriate for the comparative study of large-scale macrophenomena. Therefore, the use of case studies, content analysis and other secondary sources proved to be the most adequate methods of data collection.

Case studies are employed here because they study 'whole units in their totality and not aspects or variables of these units',[3] they focus on single units and they allow the use of 'multiple sources of evidence'.[4] In other words, case studies are methods of data collection and analysis which, by focusing on single typical units and using a variety of methods of data collection, intend to produce some generalisable findings.

In this study three cases with similar structural features have been analysed with the purpose of developing a broader argument about the characteristics of legitimacy types in regard to the formation of new states. In addition, these three case studies have also been used to support an argument about the universality of some particular features of ideology.

Case studies have also been supplemented with qualitative content analysis. Since the content analysis is 'a documentary method that aims at qualitative and/or quantitative analysis of the content of texts, pictures, film and other forms of verbal, visual, or written communication',[5] it was obvious that this technique would be appropriate for the analysis of the major texts that convey dominant ideology messages. Qualitative content analysis has been chosen over its quantitative counterpart for two reasons. First, as I have demonstrated elsewhere,[6] although quantitative analysis is based on probability theory and its findings are likely to be more reliable and representative it consumes an enormous amount of time and energy but in fact produces similar results. Second, owing to the nature of this study (large-scale macrophenomena, extended historical periods), as well as its theoretical and methodological standpoint (an open hypothetical framework), the use of exclusively quantitative methods would have been incompatible with the analytical concept of ideology. However, the content analysis used was not entirely unstructured and unstandardised. On the contrary, it originated from a rigorously developed conceptualisation and operationalisation. The concepts used (that is, operational definition of ideology, dominant and non-dominant ideologies, power-seeking and power-keeping ideologies, normative and operative ideologies, *ideologem* and so on) are very precisely defined. These strictly defined concepts are then translated into their operational form by developing a certain matrix (consisting of six elements) for the analysis of the form and content of ideology. This matrix has then been applied to the analysis of dominant power-keeping normative and operative ideologies in all three case studies.

The sampling used for the content analyses was a purposive or non-probability sample. The documents used in the analysis were officially accepted and approved ruling party manifestos, government-controlled newspaper editorials and government-approved school textbooks. Along the line of qualitative methodology employed, the analysis of the texts was focused less on the representative and more on the typical units of theoretical and substantive significance. The manifestos analysed include those of the League of Communists of Yugoslavia (LCY), adopted as its official programme at its Seventh Congress in April 1958; the Socialist Party of Serbia (SPS), adopted at its Second Congress in October 1992; and the Croatian Democratic Community (CDC), adopted at its Second General Assembly in October 1993.

The newspapers whose editorials were analysed include *Borba* (1945–60, Yugoslavia), *Dnevnik* (1988–97, Serbia) and *Vjesnik* (1991–97, Croatia). These newspapers were chosen because they were government controlled and had a high circulation.

The school textbooks included in the analysis were history and social science textbooks used in primary and secondary schools in Yugoslavia, Serbia and Croatia during the periods under examination. All the textbooks were recommended and approved by the State ministries for education. The choice of particular textbooks was determined by their accessibility (especially in the case of post-World War II Yugoslavia) and the relevance of their contents for this study.

Apart from the case studies and content analysis, the research also relied on the use of official statistics and other documentary sources for the analysis of political legitimacy types in Yugoslavia, Serbia and Croatia.

The theory and methodology developed and used in this study are certainly far from perfect. On the one hand, the issues of ideology and legitimacy are so complex and vast (not least because of the role of social scientists and philosophers who have contributed to confusion and misunderstanding) that no universal or overarching theory of ideology or legitimacy is possible. On the other hand, as argued in this study, such a grand theory is not even desirable because it would necessarily lead to one more 'hegemonic meta-narrative'. Nevertheless, recognising the pitfalls of essentialist approaches does not necessarily mean abandoning the task of theory-building or negating our ability to say something sociologically, meaning universally, interesting about ideology and legitimacy. After post-modernism, post-structuralism and post-Marxism, our concepts as well as our perceptions of knowledge are unlikely ever to be the same again. However, this does not mean that we should look only for the particular, 'celebrate differences' or give up our comparative analyses of societies and our quest for some general features of social phenomena as many post-modernists claim. Ideology and legitimacy, like other key sociological concepts, are to be sought for and found in every society, and although we are no longer able or allowed to speak in the name of society as a whole, we may still point to some common group patterns of thinking and behaving that are far from being unique and specific to one social group or one society.

NOTES

1 This is the original meaning of the Greek word 'analysis'. According to the *Oxford Advanced Learner's Dictionary*, to analyse means 'to examine the nature or structure of something, *by separating it into its parts*, in order to understand or explain it' and an analysis is 'the study of something *by examining its parts* and their relationships'. See *Oxford Advanced Learner's Dictionary* (Oxford: Oxford University Press, 1995), p. 38 (my italics).
2 S. Sarantakos, *Social Research* (London: Macmillan, 1993), p. 52.
3 Sarantakos, *Social Research*, p. 259.
4 R. Yin, *Case Study Research: Design and Methods* (Newbury Park: Sage, 1991), p. 23.
5 Sarantakos, *Social Research*, p. 210.
6 See S. Malešević, 'Ustashas and Chetniks: Delegitimisation of an Ethnic Enemy in Serbian and Croatian War-Time Cartoons', in C. Lowney (ed.), *Identities: Theoretical Considerations and Case Studies* (Vienna: IWM, 1998). See also S. Malešević and G. Uzelac, 'Ethnic Distance, Power and War: The Case of Croatian Students', *Nations and Nationalism*, 3, 2 (1997), pp. 291–8.

Part I

Theoretical Framework

1

Ideology

THEORIES OF IDEOLOGY

Man is an ideological animal by nature.
L. Althusser

Almost all important reviews on ideology start from one of the two following assumptions: either there is no single acceptable definition of the phenomenon, or the phenomenon itself, as McLellan observes, is 'the most elusive concept in the whole of social science'.[1] Of course, both are true, as they are of any significant social and political concept, for example, culture, class, ethnicity, state. To use Gallie's phrase,[2] ideology is yet another 'essentially contested' concept. However, while some concepts (culture, state, community) are present in social and political theory regardless of particular theoretical traditions, ideology belongs to the group of highly contestable idioms. Part of the explanation for this lies in the fact that the term 'ideology' is of relatively recent origin (appearing first in 1797 in the work of Destutt de Tracy) and, until recently, almost synonymous with the Marxist tradition of thought. This explains why the term 'ideology' was previously contested or neglected by Weberian, Paretian and other non-Marxist traditions, and why it continues to elicit opposition in most post-modernist writings.

I will here, first, review in brief how the concept of ideology was used in classical sociological theory, and how ideology has subsequently been treated in contemporary social and political theory. Second, I will propose a taxonomy that identifies the main differences between various concepts of ideology while simultaneously developing my theoretical position. Finally, I will demonstrate how ideology will be conceptualised and operationally defined in this study.

Marxist tradition

Of three 'founding fathers' of sociology, Durkheim, Marx and Weber, Karl Marx was the only one who developed a relatively coherent theory of ideology.[3] As McLellan[4] has emphasised, there are significant differences between Marx's concept of ideology in the early writings, particularly *The German Ideology*, and in his later work. Thus, Markus[5] identifies three different ways in which ideology is used in Marx's work: polemical, functional and critical–philosophical. In *The German Ideology*, the concept itself has a predominantly negative meaning, applied by Marx to discredit his opponents – 'ideological' was synonymous with idealist, particularly as understood within the Hegelian tradition of thought. Ideologies were treated as illusory world-views, as camera obscura; to criticise them meant to 'unmask' a position that emphasised ideas and spirit as the driving force of history. However, as Giddens[6] points out, ideology was also regarded as necessarily connected to domination. This is clearly stated in the well-known phrase that 'the ideas of the ruling class are in every epoch the ruling ideas'. As Marx demonstrated: 'during the time that the aristocracy was dominant, the concepts of honour, loyalty, etc. were dominant, during the dominance of the bourgeoisie [those became] the concepts [of] freedom, equality, etc'.[7]

In the *Preface to the Contribution to the Critique of Political Economy* Marx further elaborated and proposed a functional argument for this central idea developed in *The German Ideology*. Here the notion of ideology is treated much more widely and all practical ideas are seen as ones that have an ideological dimension. Marx explicitly states:

> a distinction should always be made between the material transformation of the economic conditions of production, which can be determined with the precision of natural science, and the legal, political, religious, aesthetic, or philosophical – in short, ideological forms in which men become conscious of this conflict and fight it out.[8]

Ideology is identified as originating in class structure where the modes of production are seen as determinants of 'the social, political and intellectual processes of life'. As another well-known and often-quoted phrase of Marx tells us, 'it is not the consciousness of men that determines their existence, but on the contrary, their social existence determines their consciousness'.[9]

In *Capital*[10] the concept of ideology is related to Marx's general theory of capitalist society. Here, ideology is analysed as the type of social relations that are determined by the relations of production. This is particularly evident in Marx's analysis of the fetishism of commodities. According to Marx, social relations in capitalism are regulated by autonomous interactions of the commodities produced by human beings. As Eagleton nicely summarises Marx's argument:

> By virtue of this 'commodity fetishism', real human relations appear, mystifyingly, as relations between things; and this has several consequences of an ideological kind. First, the real workings of society are thereby veiled and occluded: the social character of labour is concealed behind the circulation of commodities, which are no longer recognisable as social products. Secondly ... society is fragmented by this commodity logic: it is no longer easy to grasp it as a totality, given the atomising operations of the commodity, which transmutes the collective activity of social labour into relations between dead, discrete things. And by ceasing to appear as a totality, the capitalist order renders itself less vulnerable to political critique. Finally, the fact that social life is dominated by inanimate entities lends it a spurious air of naturalness and inevitability: society is no longer perceptible as a human construct, and therefore as humanly alterable.[11]

Although different, these three distinct meanings of ideology in Marx have one idea in common. That idea comes from his general theory of society and can be stated as follows: those ideas are ideological which have as their function the justification of the unequal distribution of economic and social resources in particular (capitalist) forms of societies.

These three different meanings of ideology had an impact on the development of different Marxist theories of ideology. While Engels adheres to a narrower and more negative concept of ideology, that of 'false consciousness', which was later to become the hallmark of the Marxist approach to the phenomenon, thereby giving it a hard materialist interpretation, Bernstein[12] revises the whole concept, emphasising its more neutral dimension. For Bernstein, ideologies are all socially motivated sets of ideas, and Marxism was not an exception. A third position within Marxism is the one that gave ideology a more functional and positive meaning. In Lenin's works we can see that there were only two competing ideologies: bourgeois and socialist. Since the workers cannot fully develop class consciousness, in Lenin's view, socialist ideology has to be brought to them by 'a body of professional revolutionaries'. Lukacs continued this line of thought but developed a more sophisticated and idealist concept of ideology. For Lukacs[13] the degree of class consciousness inherent in the working class was an indicator of its ideological maturity. The principal difference between the two was that while Lenin relied more on Marx's functional definition of ideology, identifying bourgeois ideology with the control over the institutions needed to disseminate bourgeois views, Lukacs derived his position from Marx's general theory of capitalist society. Thus, Lukacs locates the ideological subjection of the working class in the socio-political and economic organisation of capitalism.

A much more sociological notion of ideology can be seen in Gramsci's work. Gramsci makes a distinction between organic and arbitrary ideologies. Organic ideologies are related to particular social structures and are powerful mechanisms of social change. They provide 'a unity of faith between a conception of the world and a corresponding norm of conduct'.[14] Arbitrary ideologies are only 'arbitrary elucubrations of particular individuals'. Gramsci's work is exclusively concerned with organic ideologies which are defined as 'conception[s] of the world that [are] implicitly manifest in art, in law, in economic activity and in all manifestations of individual and collective life'.[15]

While this emphasis on the 'activist' dimension of ideology, which corresponds to Marx's notion of class consciousness, brings Gramsci closer to Lenin's ideas of the necessity of socialist ideology, the concept of hegemony is Gramsci's original contribution to the debate. Gramsci defines hegemony as the ability of a dominant class to assure the consent of a dominated population by 'preserving the ideological unity of the entire social bloc which that ideology serves to cement and to unify'.[16]

Since this cultural hegemony secured by capitalist ideology is regarded by Gramsci as a powerful tool, he proposes the same strategy for the proletariat by recommending that it uses its ideology in order to achieve proletarian hegemony. To do that it is necessary to rely on the intellectuals that every class 'creates within itself organically'. These organic intellectuals have to spread and socialise (proletarian) ideology not only through philosophy, but also through more practical and applicable means, including religion, common sense and folklore. Gramsci also underlines the importance of institutional frameworks for the dissemination of ruling class ideology. These include the educational system, the media, publishing networks and religious organisations. To achieve its own hegemony, the proletariat would need to use these institutional means of dissemination, with the Party, in particular, concentrating on gaining influence and control over these institutions. Despite Gramsci's strong emphasis on the so-called 'superstructure' and his detailed analysis of ideology, he always held to the traditional Marxist notion of the primacy of matter over idea. In his words, 'it is not ideology that changes the structures but vice versa'.[17]

Drawing on some of Gramsci's ideas, Althusser developed his own original concept of ideology. He concentrated primarily on its functional dimension, where ideology is defined in relation to the State. In

Althusser's writings the State is the principal agent of action. As in classical Marxism, the State is perceived as a repressive apparatus consisting, among other institutions, of the army, police, judicial system and the civil administration. However, the emphasis in his work is neither on the State power nor on the repressive state apparatus, but primarily on what he describes as 'ideological state apparatuses' (ISA). According to Althusser, 'no class can hold State power over a long period without at the same time exercising its hegemony over and in the State Ideological Apparatuses'.[18] ISA include a set of different and specialised institutions: the religious ISA, the educational ISA, the family ISA, the legal ISA, the political ISA (political parties and the political system in general), the trade union ISA, the communication ISA (mass media) and the cultural ISA (literature, arts, sports). While the Repressive State Apparatus (RSA) is a single, organised and centralised whole, the ISA consists of 'multiple, distinct, relatively autonomous' fields which 'express, the effects of the clashes between the capitalist class struggle and the proletarian class struggle'.[19] The key difference between the RSA and ISA is that the RSA belongs completely to the public domain, whereas the ISA is almost exclusively in the private domain. This division leads to the different ways in which these two apparatuses function. As Althusser explains, the RSA functions 'by violence', while the ISA functions by ideology.[20] Ideology is here used as a way in which a person relates to society as whole. As Eagleton points out:

> Ideology for Althusser is a particular organisation of signifying practices which goes to constitute human beings as social subjects, and which produces the lived relations by which such are connected to the dominant relations of production in a society.[21]

The concept of ideology in Althusser is rather complex. On the one hand ideology is based in the material apparatuses that are determined by the relations of production. It is independent of individual subjectivity, it has material existence and is therefore capable of 'producing' subjects. It is a 'cement that holds society together' and operates as a system of representations which do not have much to do with the individual or group consciousness. These representations, as Althusser stresses, 'are usually images and occasionally concepts, but it is above all as structures that they impose on the vast majority of men, not via their consciousness'.[22] Ideology is not a falsified representation of real relations as in the young Marx, but a real, lived relation of human beings in itself.

On the other hand, ideology is also fully unrepresentable, it is 'a will, a hope or a nostalgia', it has no history but (Freudian) eternity,

and it is a representation of the imaginary relationship of individuals
to their real condition of existence. 'What is represented in ideology
is therefore not the system of real relations which govern the existence of individuals, but the imaginary relation of those individuals to
the real relations in which they live.'[23]

Ideology is also opposed to science;[24] ideology being abstract
knowledge and 'raw material', science being more concrete, precise
and ahistoric. Science, which for Althusser also includes Marxism and
psychoanalysis, uses and criticises the ideological products.

While it is possible to discern in Althusser's work a highly rational,
almost mathematical deduction of postulates about ideological state
apparatuses and relations between the State and the dominant class
and its ideology, what is clearly central to his thinking is a deeply affective, almost psychoanalytic concept of ideology.

Among the many ideological state apparatuses, the dominant position in Althusser's theory is occupied by the educational ISA. While in
feudal and other traditional societies the principal ISA was the
Church since it had a monopoly over many different spheres, the
French Revolution led to most of these spheres becoming independent state apparatuses – political ISA, cultural ISA, communicational
ISA, educational ISA. According to Althusser, all of them contribute
to the reproduction of capitalist relations of production and exploitation: the 'communications apparatus by cramming every citizen with
daily doses of nationalism, chauvinism, liberalism, moralism' through
the mass media, the cultural apparatus through nationalism in sport
and literature, and the religious apparatus through ritualism and
ceremonies.[25] However, the most influential ISA in this process,
according to Althusser, is the educational ideological apparatus.
School is the only institution that, on a massive scale,

> takes children from every class at infant-school age, and then for years,
> the years in which the child is most 'vulnerable', squeezed between the
> family State apparatus and the educational State apparatus, it drums
> into them, whether it uses new or old methods, a certain amount of
> 'know-how' wrapped in the ruling ideology (French, arithmetic,
> natural history, science, literature) or simply the ruling ideology in its
> pure state (ethics, civic instruction, philosophy).[26]

Its power lies, on the one hand, in presenting itself as a neutral milieu,
helpful and free of ideology, or, in Althusser's words, as neutral 'as the
Church was "neutral", indispensable and generous for our ancestors
a few centuries ago', and, on the other, in maintaining its position as
the only institution whose members are obliged to attend it 'eight
hours a day for five or six days out of seven'.[27]

The structuralist Marxism that we can recognise in Althusser's work is also a characteristic of several other Marxist theories of ideology, including Hirst's reconceptualisation of Althusser's theory, Goldmann's genetic structuralism, and Godelier's economic structuralism. Although Hirst formally adopts Althusser's framework,[28] his criticism of economism, empiricism, the 'indisputable' unity of ISA and Althusser's opposition of science and ideology, as Thompson points out, 'ends with a concept of ideology which bears little resemblance to the view of Althusser'.[29] The original contribution of Hirst's theory is to be found in his perception of Marxism not as a science opposed to ideology, as for Althusser, but as a political theory that produces a means of 'calculating effects' in political struggles. This position comes close to what one may call academic Leninism.

In Goldmann's theory of genetic structuralism it is possible to recognise the strong influence of his mentor, Lukacs. Interpreting the tragic vision of Jansenism as an ideology of the class in decline (small nobility), Goldmann[30] preserves Lukacs's deterministic view in which cultural products are essentially studied as reflections of class consciousness. This historical determinism is merged with the structuralist view which regards writers (e.g. Pascal, Racine, Kant) as the most effective transmitters of a coherent world-view of their class.

Godelier's concept attempts to extend Marx's analysis of the fetishism of commodities to 'primitive' societies.[31] His position is that kinship structure, having a dominant role in 'primitive' societies, corresponds to the relations of production in capitalist societies. There is, therefore, no significant difference between myths (in 'primitive' societies) and ideology (in modern societies) since both appear as external to consciousness, as a 'reality that misleads the subject'. Ideology is treated by Godelier as a universal representation of social relations, present in all societies.

A completely different line of thought appears among other contemporary Marxist theoreticians such as Therborn and Thompson. While Therborn's concept of ideology moves slowly away from the normative notion of a 'critical' dimension by emphasising conscious actors and their subjectivity, Thompson preserves the classical Marxist theory of ideology with its 'critical edge' by concentrating on the study of language as a source of domination. Therborn's work gives us an inclusive theory of ideology that attempts to include both 'the institutionalised thought-systems and discourses of a given society' and the conscious social actors, but the emphasis is clearly on the actors' subjectivity, since 'to conceive of a text or an utterance as ideology is to focus on the way it operates in the formation and transformation of human subjectivity'.[32] Thompson, however, maintains the idea of structural determination of ideology although the notion of domination is more inclusive than in classical Marxism and extends beyond the class. It also moves towards the study of language, symbols and meanings as key vehicles of ideology. As he explicitly states: 'to study ideology is to study, in part, the ways in which these creative, imaginary activities serve to sustain social relations which are asymmetrical with regard to the organisation of power'.[33]

Eagleton's approach to ideology is probably most representative of the contemporary Marxist view of ideology. It is a sophisticated position that takes into account various criticisms of classical Marxism and thus recognises that ideology can have negative and neutral uses, can have affective and rational effects and representations, and can be composed of true and false statements. In Eagleton's view, ideology 'is neither a set of diffuse discourses nor a seamless whole';[34] it is 'subject-centred' but not reducible to subjectivity; it is modern, but contains traditionalist elements and mythical thinking; it is related to interests but their connection is much more complex than appears in classical mechanistic Marxism. However, what it shares with classical Marxism is its normativism, economic materialism and conflictual position of analysis that is now evidently combined with many eclectic propositions.

As one can see in this extremely brief overview, the Marxist tradition consists of a variety of different and sometimes mutually incompatible approaches to ideology. It ranges from highly speculative, almost metaphysical concepts (Lukacs), to very narrow instrumental 'ready to use' propositions (Lenin). It also varies in its evaluative dimension, progressing from negative and discreditory meanings (the young Marx, Engels), to purely neutral, value-free connotations (Bernstein), before shifting towards an extremely positive (Lenin) or mainly positive definition (Lukacs, Gramsci, Althusser, Goldmann, Hirst). This also points to internal inconsistencies within the body of work associated with a single author.

However, all Marxist concepts have two central ideas in common. The first is an economistic materialist analysis that regards ideology as being in one way or another determined by or strongly related to the economy, or, more precisely, by the modes of production in capitalist society. The second is a conflictual explanatory paradigm, which analyses ideology as an instrument of class struggle (agency-oriented theories) or as originating in the material structure of (capitalist) society as a whole (structure-oriented theories).

Functionalist tradition

As with Marx, Durkheim's works reveal at least two different conceptualisations of ideology. The first, appears in *The Rules of Sociological Method*, the only work where Durkheim clearly operates with the term ideology, and the second, in his main work, *The Elementary Forms of Religious Life.*[35]

When Durkheim speaks about ideology he closely follows a Baconian optimism in science 'where human knowledge and human power meet in one'.[36] Ideology is opposed to science and therefore to sociology. Since social phenomena are treated as social facts and sociology is perceived in the Comtean tradition as positive science, 'ideological method', which goes from ideas to conclude about things and not vice versa, is illusion 'that distort[s] the real aspect of things'.[37] Nevertheless, ideology is not only an illusion but a functional necessity that is, on the one hand, the 'natural bent of the human mind' and a part of human nature, and, on the other, helps humans to adjust their actions to the environment in which they live.

At this stage we are unable to distinguish any connection between ideology and collective consciousness or any other major conceptual idea of Durkheim's general theory of society. As Larrain observes:

> There is no link between ideology and social reality. Ideology is simply an illusion derived from an innate predisposition of the human mind and fixed by habit. Although a crucial phenomenon for the emergence of a science of social facts, ideology is not itself considered as a social fact.[38]

Although there is no direct reference to it, the concept of ideology that appears in *The Elementary Forms of Religious Life* is consistent with Durkheim's general theory, even if it appears to contradict his previous work.[39] Instead of ideology, Durkheim is here occupied with the importance and function of religion in society. Ideology read through the phenomenon of religion is analysed as 'collective representation'. According to Durkheim, it is 'at the school of collective life that the individual has learned to idealise. It is in assimilating the ideals elaborated by society that he has become capable of conceiving the ideal.'[40]

Religion appears not to be different from ideology in *The Rules of Sociological Method* – it is a functional necessity without which society would be impossible. Religion reaffirms collective ideas and collective sentiments that provide the unity of any society. However, while ideology was earlier opposed to science, religion is in keeping with the Comtean positivist–evolutionist tradition, regarded only as a less perfect form of science. They are both social facts and both originate in the collective consciousness, a concept that in Durkheim's work has almost a divine place. Ideology, read again through religion, is an intrinsic part of society. It is a means through which society worships itself. It is the principal element of group solidarity and represents what Durkheim calls 'collective will'. Since society exists and functions as a moral community, religion/ideology is its main cohesive force.

The emphasis on the functional necessity of ideology, on the one hand, and the strict positivist division between science and ideology, on the other, is also present in the works of Durkheim's direct or less direct followers. While Halbwacs follows Durkheim's views emphasising the connection between collective representations and religion, Malinowski[41] and later Mauss analyse ideology/myth principally as a form of the legitimisation of social arrangements. While Mauss focused on the meaning of gift exchange for development of collective ethics and social cohesion, Malinowski concentrated on the analysis of the function of myths in 'primitive societies'. For Malinowski myths are sacred tales and narratives that function mainly as 'sociological charter[s], or ... retrospective moral pattern[s] of behaviour'.[42] In his view, the connection between these sacred tales and existing rituals and social arrangements in a particular society is crucial for our understanding of the function of myths. The mythical story 'comes into play when rite, ceremony, or a social or moral rule demands justification, warrant of antiquity, reality, and sanctity'.[43] Thus, there is no ritual without belief. Myths appear to be practical justifications of relationships and practices existing in the particular society. Myth is not fictitious illusion but rather a strong cultural force and a 'statement of primeval reality which still lives in present-day life and as a justification by precedent, supplies a retrospective pattern of moral values, sociological order and magical belief'.[44]

Parsons follows the functionalist tradition in strongly opposing ideology and science. One could say that in his works ideology is used in three ways. First, like the young Marx though on different grounds, Parsons[45] uses the term ideology to discredit the theoretical concepts of Mills, Fromm and Riesman. He discerns ideological purposes behind their highly critical studies of US society, and regards them as partial insights that pretend to be detailed and complete analyses of that society. Second, in an attempt to distinguish between 'sociological analysis and the ideology of intellectuals' Parsons developed what he termed, a 'value-science integrate'.[46] This concept acknowledges that knowledge can never be free from practical values, but at the same time its independence should be grounded on an empirical basis that can be verified. Nonetheless, Parsons never conducted any significant empirical research. Third, since values and value systems have a central place in his theory of general action,[47] Parsons had to distinguish between ideology and the value system. Therefore, he defines ideology as 'an "evaluative", i.e. "value-loaded" existential statement about the actual or prospective state of a given social system or type or category of social system'.[48] The main difference between ideology and the value system is to be found in ideology's lower 'level of generality' and its 'existential reference'. In order to show that there is always a shared value system in a particular society, he allows for individuals to differ ideologically and at the same time share common values. In his words: 'ideologies may define the values of subtypes and/or subsystems of the main system of reference, but not of the system itself'.[49] In this respect he also argues that ideological changes usually have little or no impact on changes in the fundamental values of the social system. Societies are based on shared value systems that rely on the socialisation and internalisation of group norms. Here we can see that shared value systems, rather than ideology, signify what is understood by religion in Durkheim, or the superstructure in Marxist tradition. A shared value system is the main 'functional pre-requisite' in Parsons's well-known AGIL schema.[50]

Shils's concept of ideology breaks with the positivist tradition of defining ideology in opposition to science. His concept is not based on the criterion of falsehood. Ideology is analysed as a distinctive type of belief system that exists in all societies. Ideology is differentiated on the one hand from world-views which are regarded as more open, flexible and prone to change, and on the other hand, from political programmes which are considered less general and ambitious in their appeal. Ideologies are perceived primarily as normative belief systems that are founded on 'systematic intellectual constructs' that demand total commitment of their followers.

For Shils, ideologies are also recognised by the distinctive dogmatic, sometimes fanatical, nature of their principles, their strong opposition to other belief systems, be they historical or contemporary. Ideologies emphasise irrationality and fanaticism, and appeal to and rely on passion. It is important to notice that Shils sees no scientific ambitions in ideologies: 'no great ideology has ever regarded the disciplined pursuit of truth – by specific procedures and in the mood characteristic of modern science – as part of its obligations'.[51] For Shils, Marxism was the only great ideology with a reasonably persuasive scientific content and terminology which also had scientific ambitions. Like Gramsci and Althusser, Shils also underlined the importance and impact of the institutional frames for the dissemination, reinforcement and reproduction of ideologies.

Not far from Shils is Sartori's theory of ideology. Sartori shares with Shils and other functionalists their perception of ideology as a belief system. He also emphasises the emotional appeal of ideologies as well as their dogmatism and rigidity. However, unlike other functionalists, he conceptualises ideology in a narrower sense. Ideology was not attributed to a belief system but only to 'a political part of a belief system'.

In addition, not all political belief systems are viewed as ideological
because some political belief systems are only pragmatic. Sartori
makes a distinction between ideologism and pragmatism. They are, in
his view, related to different cultural matrixes, ideologies originating
in the cultural context of rationalism and pragmatics originating in
the cultural context of empiricism. Hence, ideology is viewed as a
belief system based on fixed and stable elements, characterised by
strong affect and closed cognitive structure, while pragmatism is
defined as a belief system based on flexible elements characterised by
weak affect and open cognitive structure.[52] From this perspective
Marxism would be more likely to function as ideology since it originated in a rationalist cultural context which is defined as deductive,
doctrinaire, principle oriented and indirect, whereas liberalism
would not be ideology because it developed in a pragmatic cultural
context which is perceived as inductive, evidence oriented and practice driven or where means prevail over ends and where precedent
prevails over principle.

Another important difference in Sartori's position is the distinction between elite and mass belief systems; the first is rich, articulate
and constraining, the second poor, inarticulate and unconstraining.
This difference opens the space for manipulation by elites. As Sartori
explains:

> [a] poorly articulated belief system becomes constraining if and when
> subjected to 'linkage-guidance'. This means that elite rich belief
> systems tend to be self-constraining, whereas poor and poorly articu-
> lated belief systems are basically hetero-constraining. The first provide
> a self-steering, inner-directed system of orientation; the latter require,
> at least for dynamic purposes, other-direction. The implication is that
> elite publics are largely in a position to manipulate mass public.[53]

Furthermore, the more abstract a belief system is, the more space it
opens for manoeuvring and manipulation by the elite.

As evident from this review, the functionalist tradition includes
also a number of different theories of ideology. These theories
exhibit many distinctive features. Some are highly abstract, prone to
different interpretations and difficult to operationalise (Durkheim,
Parsons and, to an extent, Malinowski), while others are concrete,
precisely defined and 'ready to use' (Shils and Sartori). They also
differ in terms of their perceptions of ideology. While Durkheim one,
Parsons and Sartori view ideology in a negative light, Durkheim one
and Parsons opposing it to science and Sartori opposing it to pragmatics, Shils, Durkheim two and Malinowski employ more a neutral
definition of ideology assuming its functional necessity. There are

other specific differences between Shils and Sartori. While Shils emphasises the emotional appeal and fanaticism of ideologies, Sartori highlights the manipulative feature in the elite and mass perception of ideology. Nevertheless, two central ideas are common to all functionalist positions: first, the perception of ideology as a normative value system necessary for social cohesion and the proper functioning of societies, and second, a strong distinction between the closed, dogmatic and stable concepts associated with ideology and the open, flexible and shifting values characteristic of non-ideological systems.

Paretian tradition

It seems that Pareto intentionally avoided the term ideology, since the concept was in a sense already monopolised by Marxists. Instead, he proposed the concept of 'derivations', a term that in many respects resembles what ideology means for Marxists. In order to understand the notion of derivations, it is necessary to locate them in Pareto's general theory. According to Pareto, there are three types of human actions: instinctive, logical (which means rational) and non-logical (irrational, affective) behaviour. The principal difference between logical and non-logical actions is to be found in their openness to verification. Thus, for example, Pareto finds religion and metaphysics to be illogical, and economics and science to be logical. Of the three types of human actions, irrational/non-logical actions are regarded as dominant in human behaviour. These irrational actions are based on deeply rooted sentiments which are manifested in the form of residues. Although residues are not instincts, they are irrational and represent manifestations of 'human impulses and attitudes'. Since human beings aspire to present their acts as rational, they need certain mechanisms to justify them. These mechanisms, which are intellectual constructs that people develop and display to others, appear in Pareto's theory as derivations. Residues are a constant and dominant source of human actions, while derivations are unstable and changeable justifications (reasoning, argumentation) of these deeply emotional residues. Derivations can intensify residues, but cannot manufacture them. Pareto gives the example of newspapers which he regards as influential, not because of their ultimate persuasive potential, but

> due to [their] art ... for working on the residues via the derivations. Strictly speaking the residues have to be there in the first place. That determines the limit of the influence of the newspapers; it cannot run counter to sentiments; it can only utilise them for some purpose or another.[54]

Therefore, the secret of long and successful rule in Pareto's terms is the capacity of ruling elites to utilise residues. To secure the consent of the masses it is necessary for the rulers to mask their interests 'in fictitious derivations which will appeal to their sentiments'.

There are four classes of derivations in Pareto's theory: assertions, authority, accords with sentiments or principles, and verbal proofs.[55] Assertions are general statements that are presented in absolute, dogmatic and axiomatic ways. They are divided into assertions of facts, of sentiments and mixtures of both.

Authority is a derivation that combines a 'mode of proof and a mode of persuasion'. It signifies the authority of one, or a number of individuals, the authority of tradition, usage and custom, and the authority of divine beings or personifications. The authority of the individual includes derivations in which the individual's claim to authority can be verified by experience, but also those claims that originate from misleading evidence or are completely invented and even those where one's mastery is extended to the area where s/he has no competence at all.

Authority of tradition 'may be verbal, written, anonymous, of a real or legendary person'. It is expressed in formulations such as 'wisdom of the ancestors', 'traditions of the party' and so on. Pareto draws special attention to the books of tradition (works by Homer, Virgil and Dante and the Bible) as enormously flexible and therefore subjects of completely different interpretations. The authority of divine beings comes from either one's need for the deity, one's love for the deity or out of fear of punishment.

A third class of derivations are accords with sentiments or principles. Pareto lists six different accords: accords with sentiments, individual interest, collective interest, juridical entities, metaphysical entities and supernatural entities. They all serve as rationalisations, either of interests (individual or collective), sentiments and affects, or of different entities.

Verbal proofs represent 'verbal derivations obtained through the use of terms the meaning of which is indeterminate, doubtful and equivocal and which do not correspond to reality'.[56] These types of derivations include many different terms such as metaphors, allegories, analogies – vague, indefinite terms with a number of meanings, designating a variety of objects and arousing random sentiments.

Pareto's concept of derivations demonstrates another inclusive approach to the phenomenon of ideology. Ideology/derivations are present in all human activities; even science, as Pareto recognises, is a form of derivation. Since human beings are, according to Pareto, primarily affective beings, derivations are both a psychological self-justification as well as a necessity of social life.

A very similar view of 'human nature' and the universality and necessity of the justification of asymmetrical power relationships is evident in Mosca's concept of 'political formulae'. Mosca defines political formulae as the 'legal and moral basis or principles on which the power of the political class rests'.[57] It is an abstract postulate by which the ruling political class justifies its power. He distinguishes between two different types of political formulae: those based on supernatural beliefs such as the divine right of kings, and those rooted in 'rational' beliefs such as popular sovereignty. Neither type has a scientific basis nor, according to Mosca, an authentic foundation. Mosca sees them as basically untrue:

> A conscientious observer would be obliged to confess that, if no one has ever seen the authentic document by which the Lord empowered certain privileged persons or families to rule his people on his behalf, neither can it be maintained that a popular election, however liberal the suffrage may be, is ordinarily the expression of the will of a people, or even of the will of the majority of a people.[58]

Different political systems rely on different political formulae, but every political class has to apply the political formulae necessary to maintain its rule. However, despite its mainly instrumental value, political formulae are not tricks or 'pure and simple mystifications' invented by the ruling class. Rather, as Mosca explains,

> [they] answer a real need in man's social nature; and this need, so universally felt, of governing and knowing that one is governed not on the basis of mere material or intellectual force, but on the basis of a moral principle, has beyond any doubt a practical and real importance.[59]

Since they meet certain human needs, political formulae are universal and inescapable forms of social life. Like Pareto, Mosca sees no difference between pre-modern and modern forms of political formulae/ideology.

What the notion of 'derivations' signified for Pareto and was rendered as 'political formulae' by Mosca is transformed by Sorel into the idea 'political myth'. Sorel follows the Paretian tradition by viewing ideology as an irrational necessity. The principal 'myth' that Sorel analyses is the myth of the general strike. He treats the idea of general strike as a fiction, but a useful fiction that can motivate workers for action and radicalism. The general strike is here perceived as a romantic but powerful symbol that appeals more strongly to ordinary workers than the abstract and distant idea of socialism.[60] A central place is accorded by Sorel to the Bergsonian concept of intuition. It is related to pre-experiential sentiments and emotions that can be provoked by this imaginary plea for a general strike.

The distinctive characteristics of the Paretian tradition are the emphasis on the irrational nature of ideology and the human capacity to use ideology for political manipulation. Pareto, Mosca and Sorel, like Hobbes, share a common psychologistic and deterministic view of human nature as immutable. All political activities demand self-justifications and political elites will always tend to provoke, canalise and instrumentalise mass emotions for their individual ends. The concept of ideology presented here is both inclusive and manipulative.

Psychoanalytic tradition

Like Pareto, Freud very rarely used the term ideology. However, his theory operates with the concepts of illusion, delusion, rationalisation, and justification that all allude to what has traditionally been described as ideological mechanisms. In addition, as with Durkheim, Freud's perception of religion provides us with a clue to his understanding of ideology.

The key idea on which Freud's theory rests is that the individual (ego) and its relationships with other individuals and society is largely formed by unconscious motivation (super-ego) and the need for desire satisfaction (id). Concentrating on this realm of the unconscious, Freud developed two distinct but compatible understandings of ideology. In his early work, *Totem and Taboo*, he traces the origins of civilisation and religious belief in the Oedipus complex. The acceptance of political authority is located in the sons' sexual desire for their mothers and consequently in a sense of guilt towards their fathers. As Freud states: 'Totemic religion arose from the filial sense of guilt, in an attempt to allay that feeling and appease the father by deferred obedience to him'.[61] The structure of paternal authority, according to Freud, is also present in the libidinal relationship between the leader and the group. Indeed, the projection of the father–son relationship is a precondition as well as an ideological justification of power relationships. In this respect, Freud viewed human beings as horde animals always in search of a horde chief.

In *The Future of Illusion*, Freud gives a more rational explanation for religious belief in general and more particularly for the belief in God. He distinguishes between illusion (wish-fulfilment), and delusion (false perception of reality), and categorises religion as illusory wishful thinking.[62] Religious persons are treated as children who project their fears and desires on a father-like figure – God. God and the belief in God are analysed as a projected individual illusion of the external world which has its roots in the need to master the individual's fears, feelings of guilt, and other internal contradictions. This also enables the individual to develop empathic feelings towards superior authority as a defence mechanism. However, the need for protection often leads an individual to identify with the authority or object that itself becomes the source of fear by imitating it or acquiring some of its characteristics.

Like Pareto, Freud also emphasises the need of human beings to rationalise their instincts, desires and motives. This causes them to behave like neurotic patients who unconsciously attempt to rationalise their sickness. Ideology is therefore, in Freud's works, perceived as originating in human nature and in the individual's emotions, fantasies and instincts.

Despite his deeply pessimistic view of civilisation and culture as the forces that restrict human emotions and impulses, and his perception of knowledge as the source of domination and possession, Freud found the answer to ideology in science. Contrary to Pareto who viewed science as a special form of ideology, Freud regarded science in the Enlightenment tradition as the only significant power that can vanquish ideology.

Reich was among the first who applied Freud's psychoanalysis to the study of ideology. His object of study was the origins of fascism. Reich traced these origins in the individuals who grew up in authoritarian families where their sexuality was repressed. These structural influences, he argued, produced sadistic individuals for whom fascist ideology functioned as a political rationalisation of their sadistic impulses and behaviour in conditions of political crisis. Fascism is therefore, in Reich's view, the 'pure biophatic expression of the character structure of the orgiastic impotent man'.[63] Reich accepts the basic Marxist premise about the structural determinants of class relations, but finds it inadequate as the sole explanation of ideology. Since fascist ideology was based on 'all the irrational reactions of the average human character', Reich believed it was necessary to 'decompose' the authoritarian family structure in order to overcome ideology.

Among contemporary psychoanalytic theories, Žižek's is notable for elaborating an original notion of ideology. Žižek follows Lacan in his emphasis on the unconscious (which draws on Freud's early works), and applies a Lacanian definition of the unconscious to the discourse of the Other. Individual desires and passions are analysed as being located in the Other. The principal medium of psychical life for Žižek is enjoyment and, correspondingly, the lack of enjoyment.[64] In order to fulfil this lack of enjoyment, human beings develop fantasies.

It is this enjoyment–lack–fantasy triangle on which ideologies are based. Since the enjoyment is never completely integrated, it functions as a traumatic irrationality. Ideologies are imaginary realms and fantasy scenarios related to symbolic forms of group memberships. According to Žižek:

> Ideology is not a dreamlike illusion that we build to escape insupportable reality; in its basic dimension it is a fantasy-construction which serves as a support for our 'reality' itself: an 'illusion' which structures our effective, real social relations and thereby masks some insupportable, real, impossible kernel.[65]

Ideology is, therefore, a fantasy of enjoyment that aims to fulfil the lack of selfhood. It functions not as a form of escape from reality but, Žižek argues, proposes to 'us the social reality itself as an escape from a traumatic real kernel'. This enables racism, nationalism, sexism and other ideologies to work through the individual's projection of pain onto the Other. Ideologies are passionate; they demand commitment. For Žižek, however, they are not expressed as an Althusserian unconditional zero-sum type of imposed and absorbed image of reality. As Žižek points out:

> in contemporary societies, democratic or totalitarian, that cynical distance, laughter, irony, are, so to speak, part of the game. The ruling ideology is not meant to be taken seriously or literally. Perhaps the greatest danger for totalitarianism is people who take its ideology literally.[66]

Although there are differences between the positions adopted by Freud, Reich and Žižek (Freud's being deeply individualistic and with a firm belief in science, Reich's connecting the human psyche with the Marxist analysis of capitalist society and Žižek's breaking with the Enlightenment faith in reason), the psychoanalytical tradition shares two common features. First, the perception of ideology as a rationalisation of human emotions and instincts, whether or not fully realisable, and second, the conceptualisation of ideology as something outside reality (illusion, wishful thinking, or fantasy).

Neo-Kantian tradition

The distinction between natural and social sciences and historicism are two of the principal features of the neo-Kantian tradition. Windelband and Rickert insist that natural sciences search for universal laws where the principal methodology is causal explanation, while social sciences are concerned with the uniqueness of cultural and historical phenomena that can only be described and interpreted but never explained. The emphasis here is on the multiplicity of meanings and thoughts that are regarded to be situationally and historically conditioned.

Mannheim was not just the only neo-Kantian to propose an original theory of ideology, but was also the only non-Marxist among the classical social theorists to develop a highly influential theory of ideology. There are basically two views of ideology in Mannheim's work: one stresses the distinction between ideology as a 'particular' and 'total' conception, the other relates ideology to utopia. According to Mannheim, from Machiavelli and Bacon to the Enlightenment, there prevailed a mainly 'particular' (meaning particularistic) concept of ideology. The particularity of this conception comes from its emphasis on the psychological and personal motivation in depicting others' views as ideological. Opposed to this is the 'total' conception of ideology which, Mannheim acknowledges, was first formulated by Marx, who specified and analysed it as the entire *Weltanschauung* of different political and historical groups. Ideology is thus related to the concrete historical and political situation. As Mannheim observes:

> When we attribute to one historical epoch one intellectual world and to ourselves another one, or if a certain historically determined social stratum thinks in categories other than our own, we refer not to the isolated cases of thought-content, but to fundamentally divergent thought-systems and to widely differing modes of experience and interpretation.[67]

Ideology is here perceived as a socially and historically determined world-view. As such, any world-view becomes ideological, and Mannheim recognises that his position is not an exception. In order to escape what Merton called an attempt to 'parallel Munchhausen's feat of extricating himself from a swamp by pulling on his whiskers',[68] or what is commonly known today as 'Mannheim's paradox', Mannheim turned his total conception of ideology into 'a method of research in social and intellectual history'. He called this research strategy a sociology of knowledge. This method attempts to study the change and the relations between different world-views and their corresponding historical epochs. He seeks in this way 'to reconstruct the whole outlook of a social group', but 'neither the concrete individuals nor the abstract sum of them can legitimately be considered as bearers of this ideological thought-system as whole'.[69]

However, this neutral, 'non-evaluative general total conception' of ideology is not very practical since it loses its axis points. If one intends to explain (or interpret, as neo-Kantians would prefer) something, one is forced to emphasise some explanatory/interpretative elements over the others. Otherwise, there will be no explanation/ interpretation but merely the pure recording of actions and events. That is why Mannheim had to include the idea of 'evaluative general total conception'. This position, which he termed 'relationism', permits one to make a distinction between ideology and truth, but not on the basis of absolute values, as they are in the functionalist tradition, but rather in their relation to time and space. This enables him to speak of ideological distortions only with reference to the concrete situation and concrete historical period.

According to Mannheim, three types of ideological distortions can be identified: the first insists on ethics that do not correspond to the given historical situation or epoch (to forbid lending with interest is an ideological distortion in capitalist society since such ethics belong to traditional society); the second includes intentions of appealing to some ideals and higher values to hide real relations (to invent and glorify certain ideals while actually seeking self-interest); and the third preserves knowledge that no longer corresponds to the changed social and historical conditions (a capitalist entrepreneur who insists on viewing his relations with employees in a feudal manner).

This narrower and more practical understanding of ideology is also present in Mannheim's later work which distinguishes between ideological and utopian thinking. Ideology is for this purpose defined as 'the situationally transcendent ideas which never succeed *de facto* in the realisation of their project contents'.[70] Ideological thinking is here described as one of the already mentioned distortions that intentionally omits the new realities that have arisen and that 'attempts to conceal them by thinking of them in categories which are inappropriate'. Utopian thinking, on the other hand, represents a different type of distortion, one that exceeds the present and looks towards the future.

Merleau-Ponty's writings show many similarities with Mannheim's initial understanding of ideology. Merleau-Ponty is critical of Marx and of the entire Cartesian tradition which believes in the possibility of non-ideological interpretation of human life and social relations. As Coole explains, for Merleau-Ponty it is intrinsically impossible for one to stand above his own time and concrete social perspective in evaluating what is ideological and what is not.[71] Therefore, Merleau-Ponty sees no escape from an ideological position of analysis.

The attempt to develop a non-evaluative conception of ideology that will solve Mannheim's paradox is most clearly present in the work of Geertz. The significance placed on the distinction between natural and social sciences, on interpretative methodology and the primacy of meanings and symbols in social life, places Geertz's theory of ideology clearly within the neo-Kantian tradition. Geertz's work is influenced by Weber's neo-Kantianism which stresses understanding (*verstehen*) of meanings and ideas in the interpretation of the social world. As he writes:

> Believing, with Max Weber, that man is an animal suspended in webs of significance he himself has spun, I take culture to be those webs, and the analysis of it to be therefore not an experimental science in search of law but an interpretative one in search of meaning.[72]

In addition, Geertz shares Parsons's functionalist view of culture by referring to it as a cultural or symbolic system. Culture is analysed

> purely as a symbolic system ..., by isolating its elements, specifying the internal relationships among those elements, and then characterising the whole system in some general way – according to the core symbols around which it is organised, the underlying structures of which it is a surface expression, or the ideological principles upon which it is based.[73]

The cultural/symbolic system is perceived as an objective group of symbols that invoke meanings which are crucial to the attitude formation and consequently the behaviour of individuals within a certain society.

Ideologies are thus, for Geertz, primarily cultural systems, they are 'maps of problematic social reality and matrices for the creation of collective conscience'.[74] The problem with 'Mannheim's paradox' according to Geertz was not so much in his methodology as it was in his insisting on treating ideology as 'an entity in itself – as an ordered system of cultural symbols, rather than in the destination between its social and psychological contexts'.[75] The problem can be solved, Geertz believes, if we develop a better conceptual apparatus which is capable of dealing with meanings. Starting from the criticism of 'interest theory' (Marxism, elite theory) and 'strain theory' (functionalism, psychoanalysis), Geertz stresses the neglect of the theory of symbols and symbolic formulation in both approaches, but recognises his commitment to 'strain theory'. Thus, he intends to analyse ideologies as 'systems of interacting symbols, as patterns of interworking meanings'. The contents rather than functions of ideologies are in the spotlight in Geertz's theory: the powerful language of metaphor, irony, hyperbole, ambiguity of symbols, analogies and so on. Ideologies are perceived as 'schematic images of social order' through which productions humans become political beings. In addition, since the symbols and symbolic activity serve also as sources and mechanisms of information exchange, their importance increases where such information is missing. As Geertz says: 'It is in a country unfamiliar emotionally or topographically that one needs poems and road maps'.[76] Ideologies are therefore of no importance in 'static', traditional societies. It is a changing, unstable society that needs ideologies. Here, 'the function of ideology is to make an autonomous politics possible by providing the authoritative concepts that render it meaningful, the suasive images by means of which it can be sensibly grasped'.[77] When the traditional view of the world is disappearing, becomes questionable or delegitimised, ideologies appear as systematic explanations of 'otherwise incomprehensible social situations' – they give new meanings and new symbolic frameworks.

Geertz opposes science and ideology, as do most functionalists, but in a different way from Durkheim or Parsons. For Geertz, both ideology and science are forms of symbolic structures that on the one hand give meaning to the new and problematic situation, and on the other provide required information. However, the major difference between these two symbolic structures is to be found in the different aims they espouse: science is disinterested, analytic, non-passionate, whereas ideology is committed, allusive, suggestive and intended to motivate action. As Geertz puts it:

> An ideologist is no more a poor social scientist than a social scientist is a poor ideologist. The two are – or at least they ought to be – in quite different lines of work, lines so different that little is gained and much obscured by measuring the activities of the one against the aims of the other.[78]

Mannheim, Merleau-Ponty and Geertz also differ in many respects among themselves. Thus, Mannheim's theory as a sociology of knowledge and as a theory of ideology basically operates with the two different concepts of ideology: one entirely neutral stressing social and historical determination of world-views, where all coherent value systems are seen as ideologies; and the narrow one, a combination of negative and neutral elements emphasising conscious distortions and falsehood in the actions and doctrines of various interest groups. Merleau-Ponty employs only one vision of ideology: every social and theoretical conception of the human world is inescapably ideologist. Geertz's concept of ideology has three distinctive features: it views ideology as a cultural system that gives meaning to and a summary explanation of a complex and changing social world; it emphasises the modernity of ideology and its necessity in a rapidly changing social environment; and it opposes science and ideology not on the grounds of their contents and outcomes (true–false) but on the basis of their intentions and methodology. However, all three positions share two features: first, an understanding that ideology and ideological practices cannot be causally explained but only interpreted since every social and cultural phenomenon is unique and genuinely different from the natural world; and, second, an emphasis in the analysis of ideology on specific meanings, values, symbols and interpretations that are historically, culturally or situationally shaped.

Weberian tradition

It seems paradoxical to write about a Weberian tradition in the study of ideology as Weber himself only sporadically used the term 'ideology', while his philosophical background might be more appropriately described as neo-Kantian. Indeed, most of Weber's well-known analyses of the concept and meaning of ideology, such as the relationship between Protestantism and capitalism or the belief in charismatic authority, clearly suggest explanations in the spirit of the interpretative tradition.

Weber connects the origins of capitalism with the values of Calvinist ascetic ethics where belief in predestination, 'worldly calling' and asceticism appear not only to be compatible with the spirit of capitalism but also decisive for its development. Although Weber insists that the relationship between the two is not causal, Calvinist moral and work ethics were found to be fertile ground for the development of values oriented towards accumulation, discipline, saving and investment and thus responsible for the success of capitalist entrepreneurship in the West.[79] The emphasis here is clearly on the influence of commonly shared *values* (ideology) on the direction of social change. In other words, values not social structure are identified as crucial for development of a particular form of society. This view is clearly neo-Kantian. A similar type of explanation is to be found in Weber's concept of charismatic authority, which will be extensively dealt with in the next chapter. However, what is important here is to stress that popular devotion to a charismatic leader is interpreted by Weber as highlighting particular *values and beliefs* and the irrationality of devotees. In Weber's *Protestant Ethics and the Spirit of Capitalism*, collective feelings, symbols, sacred objects or authority are the central elements of explanation.

However, Weber's individualist methodology and the emphasis on the rationality of social actors set the terrain for a completely opposed set of concepts, that is, utilitarian theories of ideology. Thus, as Boudon[80] found, Weber's explanations of magic and the cult of

Mithra among Roman soldiers are examples of his more rationalist and individualist approach. In Weber's view, the main reason for the spread of the cult of Mithra among Roman soldiers was not only because it promised benefits in this life and in the afterlife, but also because it was in many ways identical to the bureaucratic structure of Roman military organisation. Mithraism, like a military organisation, was based on a hierarchy of (religious) ranks and ceremonies. It was also deeply ritualistic and as such provided a feeling of order and security for every individual soldier. Therefore, Mithraism was rational religion/ideology because it was based on the belief that it was situationally rational/meaningful for the individual actors.

A similar argument is applied by Weber in his interpretation of magic. Although magic appears to us as irrational, because we define it in such terms, this is not the case since 'acts of magic follow the rules of experience'. Weber explains that for individual tribesmen 'the sparks caused by rubbing the piece of wood are effects which are just as "magic" as the rain caused by the manipulation of the rainmaker'.[81] The aims of magic are considered to be economic (the most rationally known mechanism for achieving certain goals in a particular society) while its actions appear as fully rational in the particular culture (the members of that society see it as rational). The beliefs exhibited by the members of that culture are, in Weber's view, based on false causal relationships and hence are false, but not irrational.

The most influential advocate of Weber's methodological individualism is Boudon. As with other neo-economist models of rational choice,[82] Boudon's theory[83] starts from the assumption that scientific explanation is possible only in terms of individual behaviour analysis. Individuals are perceived as rationally motivated actors and their actions are explained with reference to cost–benefit calculations. However, Boudon's theory applies a much wider notion of rationality than ordinary rational choice theories, since it operates with the notion not only of individual but also of collective rationality. He believes that besides utilitarian rationality (means–ends schema) to which most rational choice theory (RCT) models adhere, there are two other levels of rationality: axiological rationality ('Weberian') and situated rationality. The first is related to the individual actor's 'good reasons' which influence action, and the second to situational determinants of action which outside observers might perceive as irrational. Therefore, in additioin to *Homo economicus* alone there are also *Homo sociologicus*, although sound sociological analysis requires following the principle of methodological individualism and studying social actors and their actions by reducing them to their individual motives and behaviours.

Since the influence of ideologies is often interpreted as a classical example of irrational and non-economic behaviour, Boudon's theory aims to show that this position is misleading and that ideologies have a rational and material basis. Boudon defines ideologies as 'doctrines based on scientific theories, but theories which are false or dubious or have not been properly interpreted, and which are therefore given undeserved credibility'.[84] For Boudon, ideologies consist of propositions of a prescriptive and descriptive nature. Since propositions can be judged according to the criteria of falsity, acceptability or plausibility, they cannot be combined with feelings. In his words:

> The objective correlates of feelings are always objects, whatever their physical or symbolic nature. People like (or dislike) *foie gras*, they respect (or do not respect) the flag; they like (or dislike), or respect (or do not respect) a charismatic leader. As soon as ideology is defined … as a more or less consistent combination of those elements we call descriptive and prescriptive propositions, we cannot see in it a mere show of feelings. Feelings may be behind adherence to a particular ideology, but even here, the affective aspect can only be one instant in the production and spread of ideologies.[85]

Boudon acknowledges that affective acts and emotions are an important part of human personality, but they are seen as important for the actors themselves and not as a source of sociological explanation. Ideologies are consequently always analysed as rational mechanisms of appeal. They are rational in their claims, but they are, at the same time, false. In Boudon's view, all societies rely on ideologies and all of them are related, in one way or another, to science: 'all ideologies, major and minor, right-wing and left-wing, Marxism, Third Worldism, Liberalism and development theory, are based on the authority of science'.[86]

To summarise, utilitarian concepts of ideology represented in the Weberian tradition rest on three principal ideas. First, that ideology can be studied by reducing it to motives and 'good reasons' of individual actors; second, that ideology as defined and analysed in relation to science is a faulty science; and, third, that ideology makes a predominantly rational appeal to social actors since 'social actors often believe in false or dubious ideas for the best reasons'.

Structuralist tradition

De Saussure's distinction between language (*langue*) and speech (*parole*) not only opened a new field of study, socio-linguistics, but also introduced a new methodological strategy in the study of social phenomena – structural analysis. Structural analysis aims to discover 'hidden' structures behind more manifest actions. Among the objects of analysis an important place is given to myths and discourses, concepts that correspond to the notion of ideology used here.

Barthes was among the first to apply structural analysis to the study of myths and mythologies. His concept distinguishes between the denotative (primary, manifest) and connotative (secondary, latent) dimensions of language.[87] His analysis aims to locate these connotative meanings in ordinary, denotative language. The general idea behind this approach is to identify the elementary logical structure on which message, myth, ritual or any other meaningful content is based. Thus, myth is not only concealed structure, but rests on the significations that are changeable and unstable. Myths function also as the 'naturalisators' of historical events and figures. By singling out arbitrary signs and symbols and by giving them connotative meanings, myths produce 'points of reference' and meanings themselves. As Barthes points out:

> Myth does not deny things, on the contrary, its function is to talk about them; simply it purifies them, it makes them innocent, it gives them a natural and eternal justification, it gives them a clarity which is not that of an explanation but of a statement of fact.[88]

In Lévi-Strauss's theory, myth and ideology have the same place: what myth is in 'traditional' societies, political ideology is in modern societies. They are both logical models that aim to overcome a contradiction between nature and culture. Myths have no intention of explaining incomprehensible natural phenomena; rather these phenomena serve as means employed by myths in an attempt to explain elements of empirical reality that are not of a natural but a logical order. Myth functions through the constant reformulation and reorganisation of its elements in new circumstances. Lévi-Strauss aspires to uncover logical structural patterns behind randomness and arbitrary symbols that are present in mythical stories. He searches for the elementary units of myth, *'mythemes'*, with the intention of locating the order behind myth's formal structure. The content of the myth here is of little importance. Like Barthes, he looks not only for the hidden structure of individual myths, but for myth as a variation on a universal theme expressed in the binary opposition of nature vs. society, raw vs. cooked, and so on. In his research on American Indian mythologies, Lévi-Strauss follows several myths from Alaska to Patagonia, identifying the multiplicity of their variations around the single core theme.[89]

For Lévi-Strauss, myth or ideology is primarily an unconscious phenomenon: 'myths operate in men's minds without their being aware of the fact'.[90] They are structures imposed on individuals and their consciousness. Historical circumstances, particular social conditions, and free will of individuals matter little. They are all powerless in the face of structural determinants and eternal and stable logical patterns.

It is also interesting that Lévi-Strauss does not see any significant difference between science and myth/ideology. They differ in procedures and strategies, since myth builds from para-historical 'data' while science produces events and structures in the form of new theories; both operate with the same logic. Both have persuasive effects, coherence, methodological rigour and are, therefore, equally legitimate. A shaman and a psychiatrist play the same role in different societies. The principal difference, as Lévi-Strauss explains, is in the different materials they work with. Since the main aim of science is to collect and classify materials and data, and myth fulfils the same function, Lévi-Strauss finds yet another reason to reject the opposition between myth and science.

In addition to this macro-level structural analysis as pursued by Barthes and Lévi-Strauss, the structuralist tradition is also represented by works that concentrate on a micro-level of inquiry which uses the method of discourse analysis. Among numerous socio-linguistic approaches that employ discourse analysis[91] only a few go beyond the linguistic dimension in the analysis of different discourses. For example, a more sociological type of analysis is to be found in Sacks, Schegloff and Jefferson.[92] They apply Garfinkel's ethnomethodology in order to identify the strategies and procedures applied by actors in everyday conversations. This sociology of everyday life seeks to locate the 'sequential organisation of communication', hierarchies, silent rules, rituals and power-relations in ordinary telephone, street or shop conversations. The intention is not to single out the structural problems of communication, but rather to recognise the lay discourse. In other words, the problems are only those that are regarded as problems by the participants themselves.

Even though one can identify differences between various structuralist positions (especially between the macro theories of Barthes and Lévi-Strauss and numerous micro socio-linguistic positions), two features are central to all structuralist positions: first, there is no significant structural differences between ideological/mythical contents and other contents; they all operate in a similar way, have a similar pattern structure and apply identical logical principles, and, second, ideologies/myths are social phenomena that operate in human societies independent from individual consciousness.

Critical theory

The Frankfurt School of sociologists, particularly Marcuse and Adorno, developed new understandings of ideology that apply, but also go beyond, standard Marxian and Freudian propositions. They offered a 'critical theory' that starts from Marx's critique of political economy but extends it to the entire notion of instrumental reason. From this perspective, ideology is not merely a source of legitimacy for domination within a specific organisation of production, but is itself derived from the concept of reason characteristic of the Enlightenment. As Žižek comments:

> 'instrumental reason' designates an attitude that is not simply func-tional with regard to social domination but, rather, serves as the very foundation of the relationship of domination. An ideology is thus not necessarily 'false': as to its positive content, it can be 'true', quite accu-rate, since what really matters is not the asserted content as such but the way this content is related to the subjective position implied by its own process of enunciation.[93]

For Adorno, ideology is a form of 'identity thinking' expressed as instrumental rationality that constantly aims to reduce the plurality and individuality of things and social reality to a uniform, identical simulation of that reality.[94] Ideology is viewed as an effort to homogenise social life in terms of annihilating all contradictions. State capitalism has managed to achieve this aim by reifying mass culture and society where all cultural (as well as other) needs, and consequently cultural products, look the same. In opposition to this identity homogenisation, Adorno proposes 'negative dialectics' which aspires to the heterogeneity and particularity of objects and social reality. Adorno identifies negative dialectics with the arts since he believes science, together with technology, represents a dominant form of ideology in contemporary society. As it sought to dominate nature, reason became instrumental and manipu-lative, expressing itself in the form of quasi-neutral technology and science.

Marcuse's view was particularly hostile to the status of science and technology in contemporary liberal democracies. Science and tech-nology, he argued, pretended to be value and domination-free means and methods of human activity. Nevertheless, they function as pure ideology. In Marcuse's words: 'domination perpetuates and extends itself not only through technology but as technology, and the latter provides the great legitimation of the expanding political power, which absorbs all spheres of culture'.[95]

It is this technical, instrumental reason with its calculating mechanisms and effects that is the source of ideology. Marcuse argues that liberal capitalist societies no longer rely on force, and that domination changed its form from outright oppression to the control of consumerist needs. The political system legitimises itself through constant growth in the field of production which results in extensive consumption. This leads eventually to the emergence of passive, one-dimensional, consumer-oriented and obedient individuals. Domination is now internalised. Thus, ideology functions as social reality itself: it is as difficult to distinguish where technology ends and domination begins as to determine where science and rationality function as mediums of oppression.

Habermas's theory of ideology retains the main propositions of the early Frankfurt School, but includes new elements of which the most important is the emphasis on language. For Habermas, ideology is communication systematically distorted by power relations. In his view an intensive development of technology in contemporary societies has resulted in the shift of dominant ideology from 'traditional' capitalist ideology which 'masks' market relations making them appear equal, to the new ideology of advanced capitalism which reduces politics to technology. In these new circumstances, there is no longer a direct relationship between labour, on the one hand, and the institutional basis of capitalist society and cultural traditions (what Habermas calls 'interaction'), on the other.

Like Marcuse and Adorno, Habermas sees technology and science as the principal form of ideology in advanced capitalist society. Nevertheless, apart from the enslaving effects of their instrumentality, science and technology also function, in Habermas's view, as progressive forces. The emphasis on the technology used for economic growth and efficiency conceals contradictions that exist in the organisation of capitalist society. Since all discussion is reduced to technology (that is, means not ends), other alternatives are silenced. That is why the new technocratic society functions as a deeply depoliticised society. Since these new forms of ideology are less visible, they are also difficult to oppose. To be able to deal with these contradictory effects, the system has to rely on ideology. As Habermas claims:

> Such forcefully integrated action systems are, of course, in need of an ideological justification to conceal the asymmetrical distribution of chances for the legitimate satisfaction of needs (that is, repression of needs). Communication between participants is then systematically distorted or blocked. Under conditions of forceful integration, the contradiction cannot be identified as a contradiction between the declared intentions of hostile parties and be settled in strategic action.

> Instead, it assumes the ideological form of a contradiction between the
> intentions that subjects believe themselves to be carrying out and their,
> as we say, unconscious motives or fundamental interests.[96]

Therefore, ideology is perceived by Habermas as a form of the rationalisation of asymmetrical power relations that have been restrained
in the process of communication. Unlike Marx and Lukacs who
emphasised (class) consciousness, Habermas regards language as
both the main realm of repression and possibly, an arena for emancipation. Ideology, or what Habermas would describe as the 'legitimat-
ing world-view', is thus a content where 'public meaning' is separated
from its genuine intent by the power of interests. This distortion in
communication can be evaluated, in Habermas's view, by means of
'non-coercive rational argumentation'. Only in an 'ideal speech situation' where domination and power positions are eliminated from
communication activity, and where the 'better (rational) argument
alone will decide' can human beings achieve full emancipation.

Apart from interests, Habermas follows Freud in underlining
unconsciousness as a source of ideology. Just as neurotic patients do
not see the root of their illness, social agents do not see that they are
engaged in pseudo-communication. Freud's idea of rationalisation
also corresponds to Habermas's concept of ideology. According to
Habermas:

> From everyday experience we know that ideas serve often enough to
> furnish our actions with justifying motives in place of the real ones.
> What is called rationalisation at this level is called ideology at the level
> of collective action. In both cases the manifest content of statements is
> falsified by consciousness's unreflected tie to interests, despite its illu-
> sion of autonomy.[97]

Ideology is also for Habermas, as it is for Geertz, a distinctly modern
phenomenon. While in primitive society one can identify an 'externally induced identity crisis' and in traditional society an 'internally
induced identity crisis', in capitalist society, ideology becomes important in concealing the nature of 'system crisis'. Ideologies, as Habermas argues, 'replace traditional legitimations of power by appearing
in the mantle of modern science and by deriving their justification
from the critique of ideology'.[98]

A negative concept of ideology and an emphasis on the modernity
of ideology are also characteristics of Alvin Gouldner's theory of
ideology. Although not a representative of the Frankfurt School,
Gouldner shares many of their ideas. For Gouldner, ideology is a
rational belief system presented in the form of public projects designed

to mobilise the masses. Ideologies are distinguished from science, being, as in Boudon's concept, a form of false science. According to Gouldner, since both ideology and science originated with the Enlightenment, both appeal to reason. Both developed in reaction against traditional authority as new forces of social change and both preferred to be secular and rational explanations of social reality. As Gouldner points out:

> Ideology separated itself from the mythical and religious conscious-ness; it justified the course of action it proposed, by the logic and evidence it summoned on behalf of its views of the social world, rather than by invoking faith, tradition, revelation or the authority of the speaker.[99]

Nevertheless, they are radically different in their aims, since ideology in Gouldner's view intends to present private interests as a public good, while science is perceived in the positivist tradition as a neutral medium.

The modernity of ideology is also, in Gouldner's view, evident from its relationship to the means of communication. As with Habermas, Gouldner finds language to be the most important realm in which ideology operates. Within society individuals have to communicate through symbols that have identical codes. These codes are 'self-reflexive' and often 'independent from the context', and thus prone to manipulation. Since writing is one of the dominant means for the dissemination of ideas through these language codes, the effects of printing and other forms of communication development have had a major impact on the spread of different ideologies. In this respect, Gouldner explicitly identifies the connection between the origins of mass media and the public sphere. Ideologies, in his view, function as the mobilisors of social movements. They are not a primary reality based in the actions of everyday life. They are rather a body of medi-ated, second-order realities expressed through new information, and especially through the interpretation of that information.

The concept of ideology as employed in critical theory has had a mainly negative meaning. Ideology is regarded, as in the Marxist tradition, as a manipulative and mystification-oriented activity. However, the manipulation identified here includes not only capital-ist modes of production, but the entire Enlightenment shaped concept of instrumental reason. While the theories of Marcuse, Adorno and Horkheimer focused on the notions of consciousness, identity and personality, those of Habermas and Gouldner concen-trate on language as the principal object of ideology critique. Nonetheless, all critical theorists share two distinctive characteristics:

the emphasis on science and technology as dominant forms of ideology in contemporary society and the view that individuals and societies can be emancipated from ideology, making possible an ideology-free society.

Post-modernism, post-structuralism and post-Marxism

The principles of universalism, a strong belief in reason, essentialism, commitment to positive methodology and the totalising objectives of classical and contemporary social theory present in Marxism, functionalism, structuralism and other modernist approaches, have recently come under sharp criticism. Post-Marxism, post-structuralism and post-modernism are some of the names used in the description of various approaches that emphasise the impossibility of a single universal truth as promised by the Enlightenment project.

Most of these theories draw on the pessimistic views of human nature propounded by Schopenhauer and Nietzsche. For Schopenhauer human actions are governed principally by will and only secondary by reason.[100] In his theory, reason is a mere instrument of 'blind, unconscious irresistible impulse' – a will. Nietzsche specifies this will as a will to power.[101] In his view it is not knowledge and truth that are the main goals of philosophy and science, but the power 'to control and dominate for the sake of life'. Nietzsche rejects the possibility of objective science, since in his view science, like religion, is based upon faith. He stands strongly in opposition to reason, emphasising that irrational actions and behaviour are important parts of human life. He also relativises the idea of truth as it is presented in modernist and positivist conceptions. In his view, 'truth is not something there, that might be found or discovered but something that must be created'.[102] Truth and falsity are not antipodes, since truths produced and believed by human beings are regularly decisive errors.

Foucault is usually identified as a leading figure of the post-structuralist movement. Originating in the structuralist tradition, Foucault's theory has developed as a critique of structuralist universalism and its scientific ambitions. Foucault shares with structuralists the emphasis on the institutional determination of human actions linking knowledge production with the function of concrete institutions such as prisons and hospitals. He also retains the explanatory primacy of structural factors as sources and mechanisms of domination over individual subjectivity. However, Foucault totally rejects the structuralist ambition of totality and universality in the explanation of social phenomena. Instead, he intends to preserve divergences and discontinuities that exist in social reality. As he would put it,[103] he wishes 'to historicise grand abstractions'. In a Nietzschean spirit,

Foucault opposes the Enlightenment's abstract ideas of justice, liberty, freedom and equality because these concepts were created as 'instrument[s] of a certain political and economic power or as … weapon[s] against that power'.[104] He studies power not as a zero-sum phenomenon, but as a relationship that is all-pervasive. Power is not only totalising state power; it can be located in the family, school, hospital, prison, the sexual act and wherever human beings are engaged in action. Foucault criticises Marxism and other universalist concepts for neglecting techniques, tactics and 'micro relations of power':

> Where Soviet socialist power was in question, its opponents called it totalitarianism; power in Western capitalism was denounced by the Marxists as class domination but the mechanics of power in themselves were never analysed.[105]

Since for him the use of power always produces new information and novel types of knowledge, these two are regularly connected. He believed that since 'no power can be exercised without the extraction, appropriation, distribution or retention of knowledge' it followed that 'power and knowledge directly imply one another'.[106]

Just as power and knowledge function as one, so do ideology and science. In Foucault's view ideology and science cannot be judged by the criteria of a true/false dichotomy. Since truth itself is relational and tied to power, there are no universal criteria to distinguish what is false. These criteria are always in the domain of a particular group, community or society. Rejecting the science/non-science and truth/fiction yardstick, and identifying ideology with its Marxist derivative, Foucault abandons the whole idea of ideology. Instead he proposes the concept of 'discourse'. Discourses have no totalising effects as do ideologies in the theories of Marx and Althusser. They function on a lower level of generality which is neither a priori true or false. They are culturally and socially bound and cannot be regarded as ideological products. This concept, as Foucault explains, attempts to understand how particular ideas, statements and actions correspond to the framework which has 'its own history and conditions of existence'. What is important for Foucault is not the question 'Are the views from particular discourses verifiable?' but rather 'How do views from particular discoveries function in relation to power?'.

In differentiating between discourses and ideologies, therefore, Foucault perceives ideology only in its narrow Marxist sense as open to the application of true/false criteria, emphatic about the role of conscious subjects and categorical about its function as a secondary reality (superstructure) that is regularly determined by society's economic base. It is this concept of ideology that Foucault stands against.

A Nietzschean attack on reason is less emphasised in Foucault than in the works of post-modernist writers such as Lyotard and Baudrillard. For Baudrillard the social world can never be understood and explained as a meaningful totality.[107] All that exists are fragmented realities, incoherent social events and dispersed individual actions. In this respect history has no meaning. In the post-modern world the emphasis is not on production and the economy but on signs, images, information and simulation. These signs and images, having lost their initial meanings, no longer point to anything 'real' behind them. 'Reality' itself has become a grand simulation. Instead of reality there is hyper-reality which is constantly falsified by different representations. Like Foucault, Baudrillard rejects the autonomy of conscious subjects and also opposes the concept of ideology. In the world of signs and images there are only different discourses and no place for ideology. However, unlike Foucault's discourses, those of Baudrillard lack analytical strength; they are empty images – *simulacra.* For Baudrillard ideology

> only corresponds to a betrayal of reality by signs; simulation corresponds to a short-circuit of reality and its reduplication by signs. It is always the aim of ideological analysis to restore the objective process; it is always a false problem to want to restore the truth beneath the *simulacrum.* This is ultimately why power is so in accord with ideological discourses and discourses on ideology, for these are all discourses of truth – always good.[108]

Here again, as in Foucault the concept of ideology is pictured in Marxist terms, that is in a rigid objectivist, true/false light.

Lyotard follows the same line of thought. In the post-modern world there is no place for individual subjects. Since society is perceived in Wittgensteinian terms as a sequence of language games, it is possible only to speak of dissolved social subjects.[109] There is no place here for a single Enlightenment version of Reason, but for many different unprivileged reasons. Lyotard stands firmly against totality and all universalist conceptions that promise full explanation, emancipation or salvation. Concepts that promote class, nation, gender and other entities as the principal agents of social change are denounced as totalitarian meta-narratives. They are all jealous theories (their truth is the only truth) which end in terror as demonstrated by Auschwitz and Stalin's Gulag. For Lyotard, therefore, there is no place for ideology critique: all language games are equal and legitimate.

A less pessimistic, but equally critical tone against absolutist and universalist concepts can be seen in various post-Marxist writings. Drawing on the Gramscian idea of hegemony, the Althusserian emphasis on structure and on Foucault's concept of discursive formation, Laclau and Mouffe launch a sharp attack on the Marxist concept of ideology. Their main idea is that classical Marxism negates plurality and diversity by giving a privileged role to the working class and treating identities as stable and constant features. In their view, identities are basically relational and not necessarily dependent on a subject's position. Like Lyotard, Baudrillard or Foucault, they maintain that there are no privileged subjects of history, nor are there any structural relations between groups and individuals of a universal and constant nature.

Like other 'post-essentialist' authors, they prefer the notion of discourse to that of ideology. However, their definition of discourse has a more totalising meaning than for Foucault and other post-structuralists. Laclau and Mouffe define discourse explicitly as a 'structured totality resulting from the articulatory practice', where an articulatory practice is 'any practice establishing a relation among elements such that their identity is modified as a result of the articulatory practice'.[110]

In their view, every social action and institutional function is discursively constructed. As with identity, discourses are also relational. Individual subjects are dispersed by and within different discursive formations. Subjects can and do change their positions while their relations to the discourse formations are never fixed. There are only 'partial fixations'. As Laclau and Mouffe point out: 'Any discourse is constituted as an attempt to dominate the field of discursivity, to arrest the flow of differences, to construct a centre. We will call the privileged discursive points of this partial fixation, nodal points.'[111]

Since the objects are always constituted as objects of and in a particular discourse, Laclau and Mouffe consider it impossible to make a distinction between discursive and non-discursive practices. In addition, as in Gramsci and Althusser, discourses have a distinctly material form:

> if the so-called non-discursive complexes – institutions, techniques, productive organisation, and so on – are analysed, we will only find more or less complex forms of differential positions among objects, which do not arise from a necessity external to the system structuring them and which can only therefore be conceived as discursive articulations.[112]

As such, the 'practice of articulation' has its material dimension: various institutional frameworks, ritualist practices and other forms of discursive structuration. Nevertheless, this materiality of discourses is not directly connected with the consciousness of the subjects. Rather, the positions of the subjects are 'dispersed within a discursive formation'. For Laclau and Mouffe, society, as a stable articulated entity, does not exist. Instead there are perpetual attempts at discursive articulation. As they argue:

> The practice of articulation, therefore, consists in the construction of nodal points which partially fix meaning; and the partial character of this fixation proceeds from the openness of the social, a result, in its turn, of the constant overflowing of every discourse by the infinitude of the field of discursivity.[113]

A similar criticism of classical Marxist theory is also present in the work of Barrett.[114] She stands against the economic reductionism, functionalist methodology, essentialist explanations and universalist claims of Marxism. Like Laclau and Mouffe, Barrett operates with the notion of discourses, viewing ideology as a Marxist obsession with the illusions of 'the economics of untruth'. Instead she follows Foucault, Laclau and Mouffe in perceiving all theoretical positions, approaches, types of identities as legitimate 'regimes of truth'. She is not interested in their truthfulness, but in the ways they operate and secure their influence. In Foucault's words, she is occupied with the 'politics of truth'. If the concept of ideology is to be preserved, she claims, it can only refer to 'mystification practices' and cannot be 'tied to any particular content, nor to any particular agent or interest.'[115]

Although originally inspired by different traditions of thought, post-structuralism, post-modernism and post-Marxism have arrived at similar conclusions. They all refute the concept of ideology, viewing it as identical to a Marxist position, and operate with the less ambitious notion of discourses. In their common rejection of true/false and science/non-science criteria as ways of distinguishing between different social actions they perceive all knowledge as relational, situational, discursive and, thus, equal. Despite differences between individual authors, there is agreement on the totalising objectives of social science which is demonstrated in the rejection of all essentialist conceptions of the social world, positivist methodology and universalist interpretations of social action and social structure.

TOWARDS A NEW CONCEPTUAL MODEL OF IDEOLOGY:
HYPOTHETICAL FRAMEWORK

If one takes into account the contributions of all these different theoretical positions it is possible to see that the idea of ideology was
conceptualised either in a totalising and overpowering way, as in
Marxism, critical theory, structuralism and other modernist traditions,
or was completely rejected on the grounds of being hegemonic in
itself, as in post-modernism, post-Marxism and post-structuralism. The
central question here is how to preserve the concept of ideology as an
analytic tool (with some of its totalising, meaning explanatory, effects),
while simultaneously avoiding the universalism and epistemological
hegemonism of grand theory. In other words, is it possible to apply
the concept of ideology while accepting the criticism of 'totalitarian
meta-narratives' but without resorting to the self-defeating irrational-
ism and nihilism characteristic of extreme relativist positions?[116]

One possible way would be to pose theoretical claims of a more
general nature as pure hypothetical statements which can then be
tested empirically against several case studies. However, the relationship between theoretical and empirical reality will not be treated in
any causal way, rather the emphasis will be on *the differences in form and
content* of various ideologies. The term 'hypothetical claim' used here
should not be understood in a classical positivist manner as a 'hypoth-
esis' but rather as a heuristic device that enables comparative
research. The various action-oriented systems of beliefs, ideas and
practices would thus be analysed and categorised by breaking them
down into their constitutive elements in order to show their similarities and differences. By identifying common features of ideologies, it
would be possible to make some theoretically interesting generalisations. If the proposed set of statements provided an adequate enough
interpretation of the phenomena under study, then they would
achieve their aim and also simultaneously demonstrate that the
concept of ideology was still theoretically and methodologically
viable. It would give an interpretation of the structure of ideology in
particular societies and also suggest what was sociologically interesting about the concept of ideology. Thus, an inclusive concept of
ideology based on the rejection of true/false and science/non-
science criteria, universality, modernity, materiality and rationality of
ideology will be posed as hypothetical claims that will be empirically
tested on three case studies.

The position adopted here is basically in agreement with post-
structuralism or post-modernism insofar as it maintains the relative
nature of a single universal Truth. I also accept the idea that there are
no universally privileged agents of social change (working class,

nation, gender) and that reality in itself is discursive. However, I disagree with post-modernist, post-structuralist and post-Marxist positions which treat all 'language games' and discourses as equal. Although there are no universally privileged agents and discourses, there are particularly privileged actors of social change whose interpretation of social reality can and does form a hegemonic symbolic frame in particular societies and in certain historical moments which help establish and maintain structurally produced, asymmetrical relations of power. This study will try to show that in particular social and historical circumstances such as the establishment of a new state one can identify wider discursive realities that have powerful and totalising appeals and effects on the broader population. These wider discursive realities are nothing other than ideologies.

I will try, therefore, to show in this study that the concept of ideology should be preserved and distinguished from the currently popular notion of discourse. Although the concepts of 'discourse' and 'discursive practices' have diagnostic relevance as demonstrated in works by Foucault, Laclau and Mouffe, the concepts of 'ideology' and 'ideological practices' as wider and more totalising discursive realities still have decisive analytical power. Political orders, as we will see later on, do not legitimise themselves through discourses but still through ideologies.

The concept of ideology as used here will be tied to power relations, but will not necessarily be treated as having manipulative aims. By the term 'ideology' I understand any politically motivated or action-oriented set of ideas and practices related to the conceptual organisation of society. At the same time, this will not rule out the possibility of some ideologies employing mystification and manipulation. That will be a matter of empirical evidence. Hence, the concept of ideology will be used in a non-Marxist sense: instead of a 'critical edge' approach, the aim will be to develop and work within an analytical position. In opposition to the normativism of Marxist and critical theory, I adopt an analytic approach and reject the idea of critique as a deeply politicised and apriorist concept. As explained earlier the term 'analytic' is used here in its original Greek sense where to analyse means to 'examine the nature of something by separating it into its parts in order to explain it'. Since the criticism is always evaluative (positive vs. negative) and since the position of positivism is deeply reductionist and its principles basically impossible to achieve within social science, a solution may be found in the analytic approach. The analytic position would be somewhere between, on the one hand, not a priori evaluative and political but conscious that positivist principles are impossible to achieve while, on the other hand, it aims to identify as many substantive factors as possible (by focusing primarily on the form and content and only secondarily on the function of ideology). Unlike its aims, the results of such analysis can be, but do not have to be, critical in the political sense.

First hypothetical claim: Inclusive definition of ideology

Ideology is basically defined and then interpreted in social and political theory either in a restrictive or in an inclusive way.[117] Apart from Bernstein, Therborn and, to a certain extent, Godelier, Marxist concepts of ideology typically tend to be restrictive. For Engels and the young Marx, ideology was a 'false consciousness' or illusory worldview. For the mature Marx, Gramsci, Lukacs, Althusser as well as for contemporary Marxist thinkers (Hirst, Thompson, Eagleton), ideology is perceived as intending to 'hide' the domination that results from the capitalist mode of production. Ideology expresses itself as commodity fetishism, as a cultural hegemony, through ideological state apparatuses, or in any other way that is related to the contradictions inherent in the capitalist organisation of society. In their view, non-ideological social action is possible if the conditions of capitalist domination are removed. For classical Marxist-theorists, as well as for Althusser, Marxism is a form of science that has discovered the laws of human history, and therefore cannot be an ideology. For contemporary Marxists, it is not its scientific legacy that matters, but chiefly its critical potential. Thus, the contemporary Marxist theory of ideology insists on the 'critical edge' in the theory of ideology.

The functionalist tradition, as represented in the works of Durkheim and Parsons, also operates with a restrictive definition of ideology where ideological thinking is treated either as illusion or as functional necessity. Ideological views are those that have no scientific essence. In their opinion, science is not ideological, and their theories thus, representing a scientific position, cannot be judged as ideological. Shils is the only author in this tradition who applies an inclusive definition of ideology, perceiving ideology as a belief system present in all societies regardless of their economic or political structure.

Psychoanalytic and Weberian traditions also use restrictive definitions of ideology. For Freud, religion/ideology is illusory wishful thinking; for Reich, ideology is located in the structure of the authoritarian family; for Žižek, ideology is a fantasy scenario that masks a real but impossible essence; for Boudon, ideology is a form of bad science. In critical theory, science and technology themselves are identified as forms of ideology, but Adorno, Marcuse, Habermas and Gouldner also operate with restrictive definitions of ideology. They all see either modern capitalist society or the Enlightenment's concept of reason as a source of ideological thinking.

On the other side, neo-Kantians, Paretians, structuralists and post-modernists employ mainly inclusive definitions of ideology. Mannheim's original position was that any more or less coherent world-view, being socially and historically determined, is to be regarded as ideology. The same line of thought is present in Merleau-Ponty. For Geertz, ideologies are cultural systems, which means that they are present in all contemporary societies. Pareto has also found derivations in all human organised actions including science. In searching for elementary structures, Barthes and Lévi-Strauss analysed all myths and ideologies on the same level as logical models. Since for post-structuralists, post-modernists and post-Marxists there is neither universal truth nor privileged agents of social change, every 'language game' deserves equal treatment and all discourses are intrinsically partial and biased.

Both inclusive and restrictive definitions of ideology, if conceived in terms of logical propositions and if intended to preserve a negative definition of ideology, lead to a dead end. If every socio-political position is perceived as ideological, then on what grounds is it possible to judge what is and what is not ideology? This is the basic problem of Mannheim's paradox.

On the other hand, by grounding it in Marxism, science or, as Adorno would do, in art, would it be possible universally to justify its privileged 'Archimedean point'? All restrictive concepts of ideology start, as Merleau-Ponty noted, from the Cartesian perception of the world which believes that one can 'rise above all particular social perspectives and reach a non-ideological definition of the nature of man'.[118] This approach seems to be even more problematic because of its deeply reductionist nature.

Why look in the capitalist mode of production for the source of ideology and not in the organisation and historical development of the modern bureaucratic nation-state? How can one apply a Marxist concept of ideology to societies where the economy does not function as an autonomous sphere? How can one oppose science and ideology today when even the methodological exactness of the natural sciences is highly questionable? How can one escape the label of intellectual dogmatism when the militant vocabulary is used to discredit opposing theoretical concepts as ideological?[119] And finally, on what basis can one claim that a position is not ideological?

These are some of the questions that one cannot satisfactorily resolve if the concept of ideology is defined in relation to the truth, if ideology is opposed to science, or if ideology is perceived as a non-universal phenomenon, as it is in most of the restrictive approaches to ideology. As the next three sections will show, ideology will not be

defined and used either in relation to truth or in opposition to science
or as a non-universal feature.

This automatically leads us to a concept of ideology that is much
closer to an inclusive rather than a restrictive definition. However, the
inclusive type of definition I will be using here will partially follow
the Geertzian example which seeks to overcome Mannheim's paradox
by concentrating principally on the form and content of ideology.
Focusing on the content and form indicates that ideology will be
conceptualised and then operationalised in a neutral way. The inclusive definition means that ideology will be analysed here, broadly speaking, as any set of more or less coherent action-oriented and politically
(power) motivated group of beliefs and practices related to the conceptual
organisation of a particular society. As we will see later, this approach
will allow us to study the structure and, indirectly, the functioning of
several differently based and opposing dominant ideologies.

Second hypothetical claim: Against true/false criteria

Understanding ideology as something principally false is still a
common feature of everyday social and political life. Describing
somebody's views as ideological often implies that they are untrue.
This line of thought is also evident in the young Marx who criticised
Hegelian idealism as ideological, meaning erroneous. Engels and
many others within the Marxist tradition import the same meaning,
defining ideology as 'false consciousness'. For the mature Marx,
Althusser, Godelier and other contemporary Marxists, this falsity was
not a discreditory feature, a falsified representation, but rather a 'reality that misleads the subject'. It is the structural conditions of capitalism that produce false images in society. Lenin, Lukacs and Gramsci
followed this 'sciencificity' of Marx's 'discoveries' to propose practical
action for the working class. The general idea here is that, as workers
do not know what the true laws of history are, 'professional revolutionaries' have to find the strategy to impose this truth on them.

Not far from this is the understanding of ideology in Durkheim
and Parsons. Instead of the structural contradictions of capitalist
production, we see science as the only true medium of knowledge
and ideologies as false, illusory misconceptions. The aim of the sociologist is to separate the falseness of ideology from the truthfulness of
science. For Pareto and Freud, too, derivations or ideologies were
illusions and fictitious knowledge. The idea of the general strike is
for Sorel also an illusory view. Even Mannheim accepted true/false
criteria, although in historical terms, as relational to time and space.

Shils was the only theorist from the functionalist tradition who
rejected the idea that what distinguishes ideology from science is its

falsity. Neo-Kantians and structuralists also stood against true/false criteria. For Barthes, myths do not deny things, rather they purify them. However, it is the Frankfurt School, and especially the post-structuralists who most fully conceptualised ideology by refuting the true/false dichotomy. Adorno and Horkheimer realised that it is not truth and its structure that matters for ideology but rather how this structure is related to the individual's subjective position as framed by its own process of articulation. In other words, ideology does not have to be built on false statements, it can express itself as methodologically exact, precise and correct, as do science and technology. What is important is their relationship to domination. They serve as mechanisms of domination regardless of their accurate contents. For Foucault, truth is always connected to power and thus when one searches for truth one always finds different 'politics of truth'.

Truth is not a clear-cut entity that can be discovered but it is always socially and historically framed. As Brown observes: 'there is no realm of "pure data" describable either extra-linguistically or in a non-indexical language'.[120] Truth is relational and there are no universally accepted criteria to determine what is false and what is not. For some, such as Hindess and Hirst,[121] the only way in which a theoretical position can be evaluated is in terms of its own internal consistency. As Foucault has rightly argued, each society has its own regime of truth. Each society, as well as each social group, operates within a particular discursive frame that is perceived as being true. All groups, communities and societies develop their own mechanisms, procedures and rules that are accepted as being based on 'the facts'.

In addition, one can observe that most of the statements that compose ideological concepts are given a priori, and therefore cannot be tested. They are normative beliefs which cannot be proved as true or false. Whether one describes members of the Irish Republican Army (IRA) or the Basque Separatist Movement (ETA) as 'terrorists' or 'freedom fighters', both may be regarded as true or false in different social environments. It is the same with concepts on a higher level of generality. How can one prove or disprove, in terms of universally acceptable facts, that imperialism is the highest stage of capitalism, or that there is no other God but Allah? What is important here is not whether these statements are true or false, but what meanings they acquire in a concrete social milieu and how they function in relation to power. It is less crucial to find out whether the terms *Chetniks* and *Ustashas* correspond to war reality in the former Yugoslavia, than to establish what they imply, what kind of emotions they provoke and, most importantly, what types of action they motivate.

All this indicates that the factuality of ideas, concepts and propositions that comprise ideologies often do not matter. Therefore, a true/false criterion to distinguish between ideology and non-ideology has neither heuristic nor empirical value.

Third hypothetical claim: Against science/non-science criteria

The basic problem with all 'grand narratives', as Lyotard would call them, is their self-perception as truth-delivering projects. Marx, Durkheim, Freud and Pareto, among others, understood their theories as scientific ventures in a search for the universal laws of human behaviour and the meaning of history and social life. To be able to discover these laws and meanings, one has to distinguish between facts and values. Since social life is highly dynamic and constantly in motion, it is extremely difficult to 'isolate' social facts from values. For neo-Kantians, and post-modernists that is intrinsically impossible. That is why they oppose social and natural sciences, arguing for hermeneutics instead of positivist methodology or, in other words, for interpretation instead of explanation. Since human and social life is perceived as consisting of meanings that are permanently in the process of recomposition, social actions can never be studied in the same way as that of the natural sciences.

This division between positivist and interpretative methodology is also demonstrated in the theory of ideology. Classical Marxism[122] and Althusser have strongly opposed science and ideology. While in Marx the concept of science represents a mixture of historical interpretative elements of the German philosophical tradition (dialectics and the historical part of historical materialism) and more positivist-oriented endeavours (political economy, functional analysis), for Althusser, science is ahistorical and basically no different from the natural sciences. The Marxist position itself was perceived as a scientific method which Althusser described as 'open', 'counter-intuitive' and theoretically oriented,[123] while ideology was seen as 'closed', 'obvious' and oriented towards practice and concrete political aims. In the works of contemporary Marxists, Marxism is regarded as critical political theory rather than science and the whole issue of science versus ideology is less present.

The strongest distinction between science and ideology is to be found in the functionalist tradition. Both Durkheim and Parsons oppose ideology to science. For Durkheim, ideological method starts from ideas to conclude about phenomena, while scientific method does exactly the opposite.[124] Parsons realised that knowledge and practice are often connected, but still insisted on distinguishing between ideological and sociological knowledge. Freud too shares this belief in the emancipatory power of science against the 'darkness' of ideology. Boudon and Gouldner, on the other hand, stress

the scientific ambitions of ideologies. They are false 'doctrines based
on scientific theories'. For Geertz, it is their separate aims that differentiate science from ideology: science is unprejudiced and analytic,
whereas ideology is committed, suggestive and seeks to motivate
action.

Lévi-Strauss's structuralism sees no fundamental dissimilarity
between science and myth (ideology). Both apply the same mechanisms and logic of operation; what makes them different are only the
different strategies, procedures and materials they work with.

The contribution of the Frankfurt School of sociologists to this
debate is crucial, since they first identified the ways and practices by
which science itself can function as ideology. Enjoying a privileged
status since the Enlightenment, science managed to introduce itself
as a neutral medium. Nevertheless, in the situation of advanced
industrial capitalism, it is exactly this notion of neutrality that gave
science its ideological power. With the victory of instrumental reason,
science (and technology) henceforth functioned as the medium of
oppression. Therefore, the distinction between science as good and
ideology as bad, is deeply misleading.

Post-structuralism and post-modernism are even more radical in
this respect. Since there is no universal truth, but only many different
reasons, and since knowledge is genuinely connected to power, there
can be no scientific truth nor ideology. What we have are only different power-motivated discourses.

As the sociology of knowledge from Mannheim to Kuhn and
Feyerabend has shown,[125] the question of scientific legacy based
only on truth has been questioned for a long time. As Lyotard[126] has
emphasised, Einstein's theory of relativity, Planck's quantum mechan-
ics, Heisenberg's uncertainty principle and Godel's incompleteness
theorem, have all created doubts about a stable and predictable
universe. With chaos theory, the whole idea of linear prediction-
oriented natural science has been undermined. Since the entire positivist tradition in social sciences has developed its methodology in
analogy to natural sciences and physics in particular, this tradition is
even more challenged. As Wallerstein noted, the question of whether
social science should be more like physics is irrelevant because
physics has become more like a social science.[127]

These two arguments, namely that explicated by the Frankfurt
School of sociologists and post-modernists which maintains that
science can easily function as ideology, and that which stresses the
relativity of truth even in the natural sciences, suggest that science/
non-science criteria should be abandoned in the study of ideology.

Since the majority of ideological concepts find their arguments
and legitimisation in the various social and political theories, it is

almost impossible at the level of general concepts to distinguish between ideology and science. As the criteria of fact vs. value usually do not work on the more abstract level of generality, this yardstick is wholly inapplicable. According to Runciman there are four logics of enquiry in social science: reportage, explanation, description and evaluation. While agreement between competing positions at analysis is possible at the level of reportage, all other levels are conflictual, since 'all descriptions are partial, just as all explanations are provisional'.[128]

Geertz's criteria of the different aims of ideology and science are also misleading. Uncommitted, non-apologetic and cold rational language of analysis does not mean that behind this there are no dedicated political motives. As Adorno and Marcuse have demonstrated, this cold rationality can have much stronger ideological bases and effects. One could say that it is exactly the sophisticated terminology and language of neutrality and objectivity that have more powerful ideological effects than 'redneck', vulgar and deliberately suggestive vocabulary. It is not 'White Power' leaflets distributed among villagers in Montana that have profound appeal, but the 'scientific', technical and 'neutral' terminology of school textbooks that have a key impact on the internalisation of certain ideological contents in a modern society.

Fourth hypothetical claim: Universality of ideology

There are two principal approaches to ideology in terms of its presence: for some, ideology is analysed as a universal feature present in all modern societies, for others, ideology is perceived as being specific to particular types of social organisation, group of people or form of political action. Marxist authors tend to tie ideology to the capitalist mode of production or to class relations. Ideology is not a universal phenomenon, and therefore if the political economy of modern capitalist society changes, it is possible to live in a society free of ideology. Althusser is the only classical Marxist writer for whom ideology is an omnipresent phenomenon. He writes:

> [ideology] has no history, or what comes to the same thing – is eternal, i.e. omnipresent in its immutable form throughout history (= the history of social formations containing social classes). For the moment I shall restrict myself to 'class societies' and their history.[129]

For Reich, too, ideology originates in the capitalist organisation of society which creates authoritarian family structures where fascist ideology finds its origins. A non-ideological world is possible if these structural determinants are removed. In critical theory this position is much broader where the source of ideology is located in instrumental reason. While Marcuse and Adorno shift between pessimistic and optimistic views on the possibility of liberation from ideology, Habermas believes in the possibility of the 'ideal speech situation' as a mechanism for emancipation from ideology.

A particularist concept of ideology is also present among so-called 'end of ideology' theorists. Aron, Lipset, Bell and Arendt[130] have all confined the concept of ideology to specific political belief systems. Ideology is identified with extreme-left or extreme-right politics: for Aron and Lipset, Marxism was the last great ideology; for Bell it was Nazism and Soviet communism, while Arendt identified ideology with totalitarianism. They all claim that ideology has lost its influence in post-war politics and that we are approaching 'the end of ideology'. A similar way of thinking is also present in the recent work of F. Fukuyama as demonstrated in his 'the End of History' thesis.[131] Not far from this but on different grounds, is the post-modernist rejection of the universality of ideology. In the writings of Baudrillard, Lyotard and Foucault there are no ideologies in a post-modern world. There are only *simulacra*, language games of different reasons, or power-driven discourses.

At the other extreme, ideology is examined as a universal feature of all contemporary societies. For the 'mature' Durkheim, ideology/ religion is a collective representation that reaffirms collective ideas and provides the unity of society. As such it is an authentic part of society and a cohesive force that every society needs and possesses. Parsons's shared value system and Shils's conceptualisation of ideology as a normative belief system also include all societies and all action-oriented belief systems. The Freudian stress on the primacy of the unconscious and the need for its rationalisation, Žižek's concept of enjoyment and Pareto's residua and derivations, are all defined as universal motives and responses of social life. This universality of ideologies stretches in Mannheim to different historical epochs and is attached to different social groups, whereas Merleau-Ponty found no escape from ideology. In Geertz's theory, ideologies are defined as cultural systems which exist in all modern societies, while in Boudon's theory, ideologies are interpreted through rational mechanisms of appeal which again are characteristic of every society. Structuralists are even more radical. For Lévi-Strauss there is no real difference between the myths of traditional societies and modern ideologies. The same logical patterns are present everywhere.

If ideology is attributed to one type of society, political belief or specific organisation of production, then we leave all other types of politically motivated actions, means of legitimate domination and forms of societal organisation outside this term. This criticism applies equally to Marxist positions and to 'end of ideology' theorists. Traditionally these two are perceived as leftist and rightist approaches to ideology. Simplifying, for those from the left, ideology was everything that ideology was not for those from the right, and vice versa. Marxists would focus on the societies based on the capitalist mode of production and see ideology in the fetishism of commodities, in ideological state apparatuses of the capitalist state or in cultural hegemony that produces one-dimensional individuals. 'End of ideology' theorists would, on the other hand, concentrate exclusively on the study of national socialism, fascism and Soviet communism describing as ideological any view of the organisation of society that differed from the liberal democratic model. These approaches are again restrictive positions that can quickly be labelled as ideological themselves since they both start from normative positions, and are in this way politically motivated and action-oriented. Adopting the so-called optimist stand which maintains that an ideology-free society is possible, Marxists, critical theorists and Reich start from one normative idea and not from an empirical reality. In this way they begin from a priori constructed propositions. The 'end of ideology' position is even more apriorist and normative, since it takes for granted modern capitalist/liberal democratic society as its (universal) point of reference.

In order to avoid this type of labelling and to produce a comprehensive conceptual model of ideology that will not automatically be delegitimised as politically motivated, it is necessary to look for ideological mechanisms in all contemporary societies. This approach does not rule out the possibility of finding some societies, political activities and groups that are more linked to ideological practices than the others. These questions are now a matter of empirical evidence.

Post-modernists and post-structuralists criticise the whole notion of ideology as being a totalising and objectivist concept that is principally oriented towards unmasking the truth. A fundamental problem with all post-modernist, post-structuralist and post-Marxist approaches is that they conceptualise and then criticise ideology exclusively in the Marxist sense. Foucault's intellectual background was rooted in the Althusserian tradition of structural Marxism, while Lyotard and Baudrillard were both originally Marxist philosophers. As disillusioned Marxists they tend, by opposing Marxism, to give up the entire concept of ideology. Standing against the Enlightenment tradition which equalised truth and goodness, they see ideology through the old true/false, science/non-science glasses of classical Marxism. Instead of this Marxist concept of ideology, they prefer the less totalising and less universal concept of discourses.

The problem with the concept of discourse replacing that of ideology is its analytical weakness. As Eagleton rightly stresses:

> the force of the term ideology lies in its capacity to discriminate between those power struggles which are somehow central to a whole form of social life, and those which are not ... It is perfectly possible to agree with Nietzsche and Foucault that power is everywhere, while wanting for certain practical purposes to distinguish between more and less central instances of it.[132]

If one wishes to locate the principal causes of certain social conflicts based on different politically motivated actions, one has to discriminate between dominant views and practices and those which are peripheral to the concrete situation. There is no doubt that the impact of the feminist discourse is relevant for some types of conflictual actions in the former Yugoslavia. However, this discourse in itself has little relevance to the ethnonationalist discourse in the interpretation/explanation of the causes of the war for the simple reason that the latter has been firmly institutionalised in the dominant apparatuses of the State. That is why I wish to preserve the concept of ideology as a wider and more totalising set of ideas and practices that are related to power. In certain periods and in certain societies some ideas can become so dominant and influential that they occupy every segment of social and personal life. It becomes a matter of life and death how you pronounce the word 'coffee',[133] how you dress your children for school, what kind of beard you wear, which newspaper you buy or which jokes you laugh at. At the same time, it may be of no relevance if you beat your wife at home, or if you strongly oppose trade unions. In other words, discourses have analytical strength, but it is also necessary to differentiate between less dominant discourses and more dominant ones – ideologies.

Fifth hypothetical claim: Modernity of ideology

Universality of ideology refers so far only to space and not to the time dimension. Theories of ideology tend to locate the origins of ideology in the Enlightenment and in its practical outcome – the French Revolution. Apart from the structuralist position and its Althusserian and Godelierian Marxist variants, all other concepts see ideology as a distinctly modern phenomenon.[134]

For Marxists, ideology evolved with the Enlightenment but appeared on the 'historical stage' only with the development of capitalist organisation of society. Critical theorists, as well as Gouldner and Geertz, have concentrated particularly on the origins of ideology.

They all oppose ideology to tradition, seeing ideology and science as originating in the same period and appealing to the same audience. For Geertz, ideologies appear when the traditional conceptualisation of the world is questioned; when the divine origin of the monarchs loses its legitimacy, and when religion and myth no longer suffice as ways of conceiving the world. Ideologies, in Geertz's view, offer new interpretations, 'new symbolic frames' for 'incomprehensible social situations' that arise when the 'central organising principle of political life ... is destroyed'. Adorno, Marcuse and Habermas also find the Enlightenment concept of calculative instrumental reason responsible for the appearance and dominance of ideology in contemporary societies. For Habermas, ideologies intend to replace traditional forms of legitimate order by materialising themselves as science and drawing legitimacy from the critique of ideology. Gouldner, too, follows Habermas in connecting the origins and ambitions of science and ideology. Both science and ideology appeal to reason, and both claim a secular and rational perception of social reality. However, Gouldner is less suspicious of science than the Frankfurt School theorists. According to this perspective, religion is not an ideology; only concepts that have scientific aspirations.

The other side of the coin is represented by structuralists, both Marxist and non-Marxist, for whom ideology is infinite. Its content might differ between societies, functioning as myth and religion in traditional societies and as ideology in the modern world, but its structure and the logical patterns on which it is based are basically the same. For Althusser, ideology is simply eternal. His structuralism here is even stronger than his Marxism and he recognises that even the (ideal) communist society of the future will not be free from ideology.

If ideology is defined in relation to power, and that is the way I use this concept, then one may object to the modernity of ideology in terms of how Christianity, Islam and other institutionalised religions have functioned in pre-modern times as sources of the legitimation of power. A similar objection can be applied to the function of myths in earlier periods.

Although myth and religion can both function as ideology, or as in the case of myths more often as a segment of ideological practices, they were not ideologies in pre-modern times. First, as many anthropologists point out, myths and religions are involved in the 'explanation' of more 'existential' questions (birth, death, origins, ancestry), while ideologies are more pragmatic and intrinsically connected to power relationships. Second, and more importantly, myth and religion in pre-modern times were part of a mainly unquestioned tradition that was largely taken for granted. There were no competing 'politics of truth' to challenge Christianity in medieval Europe.

This related not so much to the set of ideas that opposed religion, Christianity or a particular form of Christianity which were always present, but chiefly to religion as a way of life. As Gellner would say: 'In the old days it made no sense to ask whether the peasants loved their own culture: they took it for granted, like the air they breathed, and were not conscious of either'.[135]

Ideologies appear when the entire structure of the pre-modern organisation of life breaks down. It is not only, as Geertz suggests, that 'new symbolic frames' arise as a result of questioning the king's divine origin that traditional religion loses its persuasive potential. More importantly, it is structural reasons that affect individuals and lead them to accept and follow new conceptualisations of the world, that is ideologies. On the one hand, the new structure does not promise security and predictability of serf–nobility relationship as in the 'old times' and thus contributes to the questioning of the entire system of divine origins. On the other hand, the new situation raises new ambitions for liberated peasants in having one's own piece of land, one's own house and consequently being one's own master. These interests arise as a driving force of ideologies.[136]

Ideologies thus emerge with and because of modernity. They also offer their 'stories' which later become tied to particular ways of life, justifying certain more or less coherent principles and ideas of how society should be organised.

Gouldner's connection of ideology and science and his view of religion as having no scientific aspirations do not apply to all forms of ideology. First, one should not define certain sets of ideas and practices as inherently ideological, especially when ideology is conceptualised in a restrictive way as a manipulative force. Every more or less coherent set of socially motivated actions can be formulated as ideology. This includes religion as much as nationalism, feminism or science. There are no a priori defined ideologies, but all those mentioned here can function as ideologies in certain circumstances as they do not have to be ideology in other situations. In this way religion was not an ideology in pre-modern times since it functioned not only as a way of life, but as the only way of life. Nevertheless, with modernity, religious ideas and practices have to compete with other social and political conceptions of the world. In this new environment religion very often functions as ideology. Religion becomes ideology in the same way as conservatism does in Mannheim's theory.[137] In the radically changing world one becomes aware of the tradition and justifies its values through rational means (discussion) by which tradition is secularised and modernised into the ideology of conservatism.

The second point that proceeds from the first, is that some ideologies do not aspire to legitimise themselves in the form of science.

Nationalism and religion are the best examples. They both attempt to justify themselves either in terms of morality or interests. 'Every nation should have its own state' does not appeal to science, but to the interests of a particular group and the 'universal' ethical principle of equality for all. 'Do not kill' is not a statement that can be scientifically proven. It is something that alludes to morality.

Sixth hypothetical claim: Materiality of ideology

Political science theories usually define ideology solely as a belief system. Most inclusive approaches, such as Mannheim's, Geertz's, Pareto's, Sorel's or Lévi-Strauss's also analyse ideologies exclusively as a collection of ideas attached to different systems, groups, cultural traditions and structures. Restrictive approaches of the early Marx, Engels, the entire Functionalist tradition, Freudians and also post-modernists see ideology and discourses as being first and foremost composed of ideas and beliefs. Ideologies are thus defined as symbolic systems, cognitive maps, false consciousness, illusory world-views, fantasy scenarios, identity thinking or distortions.

It is only in the Marxist tradition, the post-Marxism of Laclau and Mouffe, and Weberianism that ideology is perceived primarily as a material force. For the mature Marx it was structural determinants of the capitalist mode of production that generated 'commodity fetishism'. Ideology is not a free-floating set of ideas, but originates in a particular type of social organisation. Under the influence of capitalism real relations between human beings appear in a mystified way as relations between things. For Gramsci the cultural hegemony of the capitalist class originates also in the material structure of the economic system. To fight that hegemony one has to penetrate the institutions of the capitalist state: educational system, mass media, publishers and religious organisations. Following Lenin, he identified the Party as the main generator of proletarian cultural hegemony. However, the strongest statement on the materiality of ideology comes from Althusser. Althusser ties the capitalist state to ideology in the form of ideological state apparatuses. These apparatuses have material shape and express themselves as practices, rituals and in other physical forms. They are determined by relations of production and act as structures imposed on individuals. As in Marx's analysis of 'commodity fetishism', ideology is identified as real lived relations. As Althusser explains:

> The individual in question behaves in such and such a way, adopts such and such a practical attitude, and, what is more, participates in certain regular practices which are those of the ideological apparatus on

which 'depend' the ideas which he has in all consciousness freely chosen as a subject. If he believes in God, he goes to church to attend Mass, kneels, prays, confesses, does penance (once it was material in the ordinary sense of the term) and naturally repents, and so on. If he believes in Duty, he will have the corresponding attitudes, inscribed in ritual practices 'according to the correct principles.' If he believes in Justice, he will submit unconditionally to the rules of the Law, and may even protest when they are violated, sign petitions, take part in a demonstration, etc.[138]

Althusser's materialism goes to extremes where every practice is possible only by and in an ideology. He even rejects the term 'idea', replacing it with the concepts of subject, consciousness, belief and actions.

Among all these material ideological apparatuses, it is the educational one that is dominant in the reproduction of ideology. School is the only institution that individuals are obliged to attend for a very long period of their lives. This emphasis on the 'materiality' of the educational system is also characteristic of Gellner's theory of nationalist ideology. It is universally imposed school-transmitted culture that comes with general literacy and compulsory mass public education, that is at the heart of nationalism. As Gellner puts it nicely:

> At the base of the modern social order stands not the executioner but the professor. Not the guillotine, but the (aptly named) *doctorat d'état* is the main tool and symbol of state power. The monopoly of legitimate education is now more important, more central than is the monopoly of legitimate violence.[139]

For Laclau and Mouffe, discourses are materialised as discursive practices of articulation. As in Gramsci and Althusser, they include institutions and ritual practices, but contrary to classical Marxism they do not stand in direct relation to consciousness of subjects.

A completely different type of materialist explanation is present in Weberianism. Not the structure but (exactly the opposite) agents are here the principal medium of action. According to Weber and Boudon, ideologies are rational mechanisms of appeal based on materially driven individual motivations. Actors attempt to maximise their advantages, and ideologies serve as rationalisations for their individually (egoistically) driven purposes.

Idealism and materialism are traditionally regarded in philosophy to be the starting and opposing points of every interpretation. It is generally considered that idealists view the social world in terms of value-determined actions (mainly symbols and meanings), while materialists analyse social actions which focus primarily on economic and political factors in the explanation of social reality. Whereas materialism states that human actions are determined by economic or political circumstance or are principally utility-oriented, idealism sees social actions mainly as norm-oriented or starting from the position that 'external social reality cannot exist independently of the everyday interactions and subjectivity of social actors'.[140]

Since ideology is inherently related to some set of ideas and ideas are never fully structured and disseminated in a one-way fashion, one cannot reduce it to reflexes of the material world. This type of reductionism is evident in classical Marxism,[141] and has developed to extremes in Althusserian structuralism. There is no place for free will of individual subjects in Althusser's concept. In addition, the Marxist type of materialism as well as Boudon's model of rational actors are of an exclusively economic nature: the relationship to the modes of production or individual self-interest. There is no place for non-economic materialist explanations that include political and other factors such as the institutions of the State or will-power motivated actions.[142]

On the other hand, sets of ideas that are disconnected from material forms of social reality cannot be regarded as ideologies. For a collection of coherent ideas and beliefs to be identified as ideologies it is necessary to include not only the expression of certain ideas and values, but also the means, institutional and other structures through which these ideas are expressed. It is also necessary to connect these ideas to power relations which automatically incorporate organisational and institutional frames such as the State, political system, mass media and party politics.

Since ideas have their material form, they also manifest their influence principally in a material way. For ideas to achieve influence it is necessary for them to be written in books, newspapers, cartoons, pamphlets, shown on TV, heard on radio, distributed through the Internet and so on. Behind these material means one will always find institutions such as the State, party, school and the family. Thus, in order to analyse ideology one has to focus on these material forms of ideology. In this way ideology is often more what one does than what one thinks.

For Manning, ideologies are rooted in different ways of life.[143] They give identity to the groups and 'practical inspiration to those who share a way of life, enabling them to sustain their own identity in political competition with other lifestyles'. Since the majority of people do not have systematic, consistent and very committed belief systems, it is exactly these different ways of life (practices, type of behaviour, rituals, communication) which leads them to support a certain ideology.

Seventh hypothetical claim: Rationality of ideology

The question of whether ideologies are rational or irrational is one where general theories of ideology differ significantly. The emphasis on the irrationality of ideologies is found in the general Marxist position, especially in the young Marx and his metaphor of camera obscura, and in the functionalism of Shils and Sartori as well as and psychoanalysis which view ideologies as illusions and fantasies, whether functional or innate in human nature. Irrational sources of ideology are also stressed by Paretians who see illogical actions dominating human behaviour, by structuralists for whom ideologies operate in human minds regardless of their individual wills, but also by critical theorists, with the exception of Gouldner, who regard the masses as alienated by unknowingly accepting ideas (consumerism) while under the influence of external unconscious structural forces (capitalism or modernity). The Nietzschean spirit of irrationality and the emphasis on blind will and instincts are also characteristics of post-modernist interpretations.

Only a few positions find ideologies to be rationally shaped concepts. Lenin, Gramsci and to a certain extent Althusser see ideologies as practical weapons in the class struggle: ideologies are not irrational, they are world-views of a particular class. Mannheim's concept of ideology as a belief in norms adapted to a particular historical situation as well as Geertz's metaphor of ideology as a road-map, are also examples where ideology is rationally conceptualised. For Gouldner, too, ideologies are perceived as rational belief systems formulated as public projects for the masses. However, the strongest statement of ideology's rationality is present in Weberianism. Both Weber and Boudon highlight individual situational rationality that motivates actors in making their choices.

The question of whether ideologies are rational or irrational cannot be simply answered as it is often erroneously formulated. First, as Boudon himself acknowledged, there are at least three types of rationality: utilitarian rationality, axiological rationality and situated rationality.

Utilitarian (or Weber's *Zweckrationalität*) rationality is the basic form of rationality present in the immediate motives and actions of actors: human behaviour is interpreted as purely economistic and based on cost–benefit calculation. The rationality in question here is the one that can be encountered in rational choice theory: individuals behave rationally to obtain the maximum net advantage. In Weber's words this is 'behaviour oriented to a system of discrete individual ends'.[144]

Axiological (or Weber's *Wertrationalität*) rationality includes a wider definition of rationality where, as Boudon explains, individuals support certain ideas because they feel that these ideas confirm 'values which they consider themselves as espousing material or symbolic rewards'.[145] Thus, a layman will accept the theory of relativity without verifying its mathematical and physical theorems, and an Algerian supporter of the *Groupe Islamique Armée* (GIA) will accept Islamic teachings without extensive reading or understanding of the Koran and other theological writings, not only because these values are promoted by authority but also because they associate some of these values with material and symbolic benefits.

Situated rationality is for Boudon the most important type of individual rationality. It includes a different set of 'good reasons' employed by every individual who pursues certain behaviour. Typical forms of situated rationality are rationality of position where one's social, political, economic, cultural or any other position can determine the way one sees a particular situation or phenomenon, and dispositional rationality where the knowledge that one has about a particular phenomenon can directly influence one's interpretation of it. An example of rationality of position would be the differing perception of the value of glass pearls and golden statues for American Indians and European conquerors in the sixteenth century, where in exchanging these goods, each side was convinced that they had made an excellent deal. An example of dispositional rationality would be a prime minister educated as a neo-liberal economist explaining to parliament the nature of inflation. In this instance, economic knowledge will certainly influence the prime minister's view of the importance of low inflation. In the analysis of ideology one has to take into account all these distinctive forms of rationality.

Second, there are also different levels at which the rationality of ideology can be analysed. One can identify at least three levels in regard to the rationality/irrationality dichotomy: the aims of ideology, the perception of ideology and the way a particular ideology is disseminated.

As far as the aims of ideologies are concerned they include the evaluation of promoted values and ideas, as well as the motives of ideologies and ideologists. Both are clearly rational. The rationality of the motives of ideologists and ideologies is mainly of the utilitarian type, since according to Manning, 'all ideologies have the same objective, which is to win power by persuading as many as possible to subscribe to them'.[146] The principle of actors (promoters of particular ideologies) maximisation of their advantages and interest-driven actions are evident in the motives of every ideology. In fact, the concept of ideology used here defines ideology precisely in these terms as an action-oriented and politically motivated set of ideas, beliefs and practices.

This is similar to the ideas and values promoted by ideologies. Some ideologies apply scientific reasoning, terminology and argumentation (Leninism, economic liberalism, scientific racism), others appeal to universal ethical principles (socialism, ethnonationalism, Christianity) or common interests (ethnonationalism, socialism) but all are shaped as rational projects. Their internal consistency and systematic formulation also confirm this. For an ideology to be fully successful and popular it is necessary to offer some form of blueprint, including: how society should be governed, what kind of economy implemented, which social actors made dominant and which values and ideas fought against. These blueprints or 'rules' are nothing other than rationally conceptualised projects. As Gouldner emphasises: 'the rationality of ideology does not reside in its practice but in the rules, in the grammar of rationality, which is acknowledged as binding'.[147]

Another form of the rationality of ideology is the rationality in the perception and reception of ideology. Although this study does not directly examine the behaviour of actors, an attempt will be made to demonstrate indirectly the relationship between the political elite's conceptualisation and perception of ideology and the popular reception of ideology. The aims of two groups – elites and masses – differ since the political elites are oriented towards acquiring or maintaining the central power positions while masses aspire to realise their immediate everyday interests. For both groups these motives include a utilitarian level of rationality (to realise their interests) but differ in the form of situated and axiological rationality. The differing positions and type of knowledge of elites and masses influences their different perceptions of social reality. It is more likely that elites, whether power-seeking or power-keeping, will have not only different type of and more extensive knowledge about particular political or economic doctrines (liberalism, socialism, conservatism) than the 'ordinary' population but that they would also be more motivated and in a position to collect more information about the social world. A professor of political philosophy, whether a minister in the government or in active or passive opposition to government, will certainly have a different perception of society from a dock worker.

However, the central question for the analysis of ideology is the axiological or value-rational type of rationality. This is the kind of rationality where elites and masses appear to be ideologically united, sharing common values. Thus, in the United States a majority of the public are convinced that 'democracy' is the best form of political system. Similarly, in Iran, where the State is based on the Islamic *Sharia*, a majority see it as the most advanced type of society's organisation. Nevertheless, the majority of the public in the United States have never read Locke, Montesquieu or J. S. Mill, and do not know much or anything at all about the ideology of liberal democratic state, nor are the majority of Iranian citizens completely familiar with the teachings and ideas of Rashid Rida, Muhammad Abduh or Ahmad Lutfi. By instrumentalising axiological rationality, elites manage to mobilise the public around the 'common' political project. In Gouldner's words, the public is nothing other than 'those persons available for political mobilisation, on the basis of a rational appeal to interests they are imputed to share'.[148] In order to maintain and formally neutralise the link between themselves and the rest of society, political elites will rely principally on axiological rationality. Thus, value-rationality will operate whenever elites attempt to present their particular interests as the universal, common interests of the society.

The third level of ideology analysis, the dissemination of ideology, is deeply connected with the reception of ideology. This is the level where axiological and utilitarian rationality are combined with the appeal to emotions. This is also the segment of ideology where possible manipulation can be observed. Ideology is principally disseminated as appealing to utilitarian and axiological rationality as well as to the affectivity of its followers. Ideologies appeal to individual and collective interests and to emotions. The images, symbols and metaphors used in popular discourse in the mass media, school textbooks or posters will provoke already internalised emotions and will connect them to existing interests. As Gouldner points out:

> ideologies can interest readers and convince them in part because they refer to news which some already share and, in part, by providing interpretations that go beyond news accounts, by referring to hitherto publicly unspoken aspects of people's personal interests, experiences, and everyday lives.[149]

FORM AND CONTENT OF IDEOLOGY: OPERATIONALISATION

By reviewing leading theories of ideology and pointing out their constitutive elements, we can see that all of them operate on a very general, macro-level of analysis. They differ over questions of whether ideology originates in the capitalist mode of production, amounts to a fantasy of enjoyment, represents a cultural system or acts as the cement that binds society together. Nevertheless, they do not tell us much about the concrete visible composition and make-up of ideology. We can learn why and how people accept certain ideologies, when and how the State or the ruling class imposes its value system on the rest of society, or why individuals need particular ideologies, but we do not know how precisely to recognise an ideology at work. In other words, we have no empirical criteria to differentiate between ideological and non-ideological contents,[150] or between different types of ideologies in relation to existing power structures, popular acceptance or particular blueprints. This is especially important if we reject, as I do here, normativist and classical positivist criteria in distinguishing what is and what is not ideology.

Apart from some fragments present in the works of Pareto, Mannheim and Geertz, there is no major theory of ideology that examines the form and content of ideology.[151] As Lewins rightly acknowledges, most studies of ideology are functional, that is observe what ideology does, while there are no theories that are content-oriented, that is that focus on what ideology is.[152] Even those theories such as Geertz's which emphasise the importance of ideology contents do not go deeply enough into the analysis of ideology structure but instead 'play' with the meanings of metaphors, ironies and symbols. This is not to say that the language of ideology and symbolism is not important, but only that Geertz's theory does not go beyond the analysis of meanings in symbols and metaphors. As Boudon aptly said:

> It is true that many ideological notions (the exploitation of people by others, the invisible hand, the class struggle) are metaphors, and that many myths are metaphorical systems; but the belief that charging interests on loans is immoral is not based on metaphor.[153]

What is needed is exactly the analysis of the form, content and structure of such a belief. The major problem with Geertz's theory in particular and most anthropological positions in general, is that they treat all individual cultures of particular societies as single homogenous world-views. Hence, Geertz sees no ideological differences within a particular society but treats the whole society as being 'attached' to a single ideology/cultural system. For example, in his analysis of the Indonesian political ideologies there is only one 'exemplary centre pattern' – *Pantjasila* – promoted by Sukarno and replaced later by another single political concept called '*Manipol–USDEK*'.[154] There are no significant competing cultural systems.

Mannheim's 'evaluative general total conception' gives us some empirical criteria to distinguish between ideological and other value systems and practices. However, two out of the three offered criteria (insisting on ethics and knowledge that does not correspond to the given historical situation) are normative and historicist and thus inapplicable in our analysis.

Mannheim takes historical criteria as his 'Archimedean point'. In this way he is in a position to evaluate from a historical distance when and how a certain type of action was ideological. The problem with this perspective is that it views history not only as a teleological project, but also as symmetrical and one-dimensional. Who and by what criteria can the ethics and knowledge of a certain historical period be identified? Let us take just one example: serfdom in medieval France. Was there a single dominant ethics or body of knowledge among the nobility, clergymen and serfs? Was this ethics or body of knowledge shared by 'Frenchmen' and their contemporaries then inhabiting the Ottoman Empire? Hardly so. Furthermore, while Christian morality might have been the only point of congruence for all 'Frenchmen', the gulf separating serfs and nobles in their under-standing and perceptions of Christianity markedly diminish the usefulness of this criterion.

The third criterion proposed by Mannheim which appeals to 'higher' ideals and values that hide self-interested motives and actions, is valuable although very difficult to operationalise.[155] However, what is most worthy in Mannhiem's theory of ideology is its emphasis on the situational dimension in distinguishing between ideological and non-ideological contents. As we will see later in the empirical part of this study, it is exactly this element that will help us to distinguish between value-neutral and power motivated statements.[156]

Pareto's theory of derivations attempts to provide a wider range of empirical criteria to distinguish between, what Lewins calls, 'mundane' and ideological contents. On the micro-level Pareto speaks of assertions (of facts, sentiments and a mixture of the two), verbal proofs (metaphors, allegories, indefinite terms) and accords with sentiments or principles which include a variety of interests as well as juridical, metaphysical and supernatural entities. On the macro-level he proposes derivations of authority: individual, group, tradition or authority of divine beings.

While the derivations of authority resemble Weber's typology of legitimacy, which will be dealt with in the second chapter of this study, assertions, verbal proofs and accords are applicable in the analysis of ideology. Although I reject true/false criteria in distinguishing between ideology and non-ideology, assertions can help in the analy-sis to differentiate between emotional (meaning sentimental) and more rational (though not necessarily factual) statements. Verbal proofs are also helpful in the examination of language forms. They correspond to Geertz's study of meanings, symbols, and metaphors. Accords with sentiments or principles point towards motives that might be behind certain types of reasoning, but also towards logical deceits which omit the mention of individuals or data that would contradict particular arguments. While most theories of ideology are conceptualised as macroprojects, Pareto's theory of derivations suffers from a completely opposite set of symptoms – the syndrome of over-psychologisation. The emphasis is exclusively on the individual's motives and reasons in legitimising certain types of behaviour. Although, similar to Pareto I find individual actors to be the key agents of social change, since ideology is primarily a collective phenomenon it is necessary to identify different collective forms of action and institutional and other types of social organisation. Hence, Pareto's concept does not cover important elements in the analysis of ideology structure: types of ideology, the relationship between ideology and power structures, different levels of ideology, organisational segments of ideology and so on. These are the elements that one has to take into consideration in the operationalisation of the concept of ideology.

Operational definition of ideology

The general definition of ideology that has been used so far indicates that I regard any set of consistent action-oriented and politically motivated set of beliefs and practices related to the conceptual organisation of society as ideologies. It has also been emphasised that ideology is not to be evaluated in terms of true/false and science/non-science criteria. Ideology is conceptualised as a universal feature of all societies and social groups, but also as a materially shaped, modern, and predominantly rationally characterised entity.

This position helps us to theoretically conceptualise ideology, as well as to place it within the world of other social phenomena. This definition, however, cannot help us in differentiating between empirical forms, contents and structures of ideology. That is why we need a corresponding operational definition of ideology. Since there are not many definitions of ideology that have operational potential or adopt an inclusive approach, I have chosen Seliger's definition of ideology as a point of departure. However, since Seliger sees ideology in the traditional political science perspective as a belief system only, I will reformulate and modify this definition to suit my empirical purposes and more fully reflect my theoretical position. The final operational definition as well as the concept of ideology developed here will be tested against the empirical studies which will then enable us to establish the validity of this approach. We start therefore with Seliger who defines ideology as:

> a group of beliefs and disbeliefs (rejections) expressed in value sentences, appeal sentences and explanatory statements. These

sentences refer to moral and technical norms and are related to descriptive and analytical statements of fact which are arranged and together interpreted as a doctrine bearing the imprint of the centrality of morally founded prescriptions. A doctrine, which is to say an ideology, presents a not entirely self-consistent, not fully verified and verifiable, but not merely distorted body of views. These views relate in the main to forms of human relationships and socio-political organisation as they should and could be and refer from this perspective to the existing order and vice versa. Ideologies share with others some morally and factually based views and thus attest to ideological pluralism without thereby losing their distinctiveness. An ideology is a belief system by virtue of being designed to serve on a relatively permanent basis a group of people to justify in reliance on moral norms and a modicum of factual evidence and self-consciously rational coherence the legitimacy of the implements and technical prescriptions which are to ensure concerted action for the preservation, reform, destruction or reconstruction of a given order.[157]

Elements of this definition which satisfy operational criteria are: (a) that ideology consists of, and can be detected in, a group of beliefs and rejections expressed in the form of value sentences, appeal sentences and explanatory statements; (b) that these statements can be descriptive and analytical; (c) that there is a level of consistency between these statements which together form a doctrine 'of morally founded prescriptions'; (d) that this doctrine is not fully verifiable; (e) that this doctrine is related to the social and political organisation of a particular society and to relationships between the members of that society; (f) that there is a certain level of plurality of views within a particular ideology; (g) that this doctrine has the function of justifying certain social actions for a particular group of people whether their aim is 'preservation, reform, destruction or reconstruction of a given order'; and (h) that in the process of justification, this doctrine appeals to moral norms and the segments of 'factual evidence'.

Apart from the already selected elements, one of the qualities of this definition is its emphasis on disbeliefs or rejections in the formation of ideology structure. Rejections or, more accurately, opposing ideas, practices and concepts are exceptionally important in the formation of the ideology. One could say that there is no ideology without counter-ideologies.

> Ideologies are always defined in opposition to others and thus incorporate the denial or rejection of certain principles and beliefs; the separation of powers in constitutional democracy, for example, is premised upon the rejection of the divine right of kings.[158]

To be persuasive every ideology must have morally and 'factually' acceptable answers to challenging ideologies.

Nonetheless, what is missing in this definition is the notion that ideologies are not only composed of beliefs, but also of ideas and practices. Those beliefs, ideas and practices can be detected in particular statements as well as in images and actions such as political caricatures and cartoons, photographs, films, TV programmes and so on, in certain types of activities (demonstrations, riots, terrorist acts, strikes, political meetings, various ritualistic practices) and non-activities or in Pareto's strange terminology 'accords with sentiments' such as those withholding significant information, argument, data or individuals that could seriously damage an ideology's argumentative basis or refraining from certain political manifestations.

This definition also gives us no parameters to distinguish between 'ordinary' and manipulative statements, images, and practices. To avoid the Marxist and post-modernist reduction of ideology to mystification practices, while recognising that there maybe manipulative-oriented aspects of ideology, it is necessary to make a distinction between statements, images and actions that are 'ordinary' parts of the ideology and cannot be judged in terms of true/false criteria (for example, there is no God but Allah) and those that I will call *ideologemes* whose aim is to hide, mislead or justify certain social actions. An *ideologem* is a statement, set of statements, ideas, images or practices which consists of directly manipulative contents. An example of an *ideologem* would be a statement from the manifesto of the Socialist Party of Serbia (SPS) which declares that all forms of ownership should be equally treated and represented whether they are state-run, socially or privately owned.[159] Taken out of its social context, there is nothing unusual about this statement; it is the ordinary view of most reformed socialist or social democratic parties. However, when considered against the fact that 90 per cent of companies in Serbia were at that time state-owned[160] and that the ruling party intended in this way to preserve its monopoly over the economy, the statement emerges with a directly manipulative purpose.

Another problem with this definition is its exclusive emphasis on moral norms. Seliger detects the appeal to moral norms as a principal form of ideology's action (as in Christianity and socialism), while ignoring that some if not the majority of ideologies pose as scientific or truth delivering projects (i.e. Marxism–Leninism, Taylorism, scientific racism), or appeal directly to individual or collective interests (nationalism, ethnicism, European Union project, various forms of liberalism).

Another important element that is missing in Seliger's definition is any criteria to distinguish between motives, levels of influence, position in relation to power structures of different ideologies. Although Seliger rightly perceives all socially or politically motivated and action-oriented projects as ideologies, it is necessary for analysis to make distinctions between them.

First, a distinction should be made between dominant and non-dominant ideologies. Dominant ideology is ideology that can empirically be identified as being supported or 'exercised' in one or another way by the majority of the population within the particular society.[161] Naturally, this does not mean that the majority of the population favours all or most of the dominant ideology's substantive elements, but only that it supports a few key principles, values or practices. Empirically verified examples of the dominant ideology would include, for example, ethnic nationalism as a dominant ideology in Serbia at the beginning of the 1990s, instrumentalism as a segment of contemporary US-dominant ideology or various forms of liberalism as a dominant ideology among Zagreb University students.[162]

Consequently, doctrines, sets of ideas and practices that are supported or 'exercised' in one or another way by minorities of the population constitute non-dominant ideologies. They might range from numerically insignificant action-oriented ideas and practices (i.e. ecological ideology in 1950s Europe, or feminist ideology in nineteenth-century Ireland) to strong opposition ideologies and movements that are close to becoming the dominant ideology (national socialism in early 1930s Germany or political liberalism in 1980s Taiwan).

Second, it is necessary to differentiate between power-keeping and power-seeking ideology. They are both related to power but in a different way. Power-keeping ideology is basically the ideology of the power-holding group. This is usually the only type of ideology to be found as an object of study in Marxist and other instrumentalist approaches.[163] Power-keeping ideology is often referred to as ruling class ideology, power elite ideology or ruling political class ideology. On the other side is power-seeking ideology, which is ideology of the various non-ruling groups. These groups are characterised (for example, in Pareto's theory) as counter-elites, or elites-in-waiting. However, power-seeking ideology is not exclusively tied to elite groups, but possibly to all non-ruling individuals and collectives.

There are four types of relationships between power-seeking/ power-keeping ideologies and dominant/non-dominant ideologies. These are: power-keeping and dominant ideology; power-seeking and dominant ideology; power-keeping non-dominant ideology, and power-seeking non-dominant ideology.

Examples of power-keeping and dominant ideology include Islamic fundamentalism immediately after the Islamic revolution in

Iran, or some broad form of socialism in post-revolutionary Cuba. They were all ideologies of the power-holding groups, as well as ideologies supported in one or another way by the majority of the population.

In times of crisis, power-seeking ideology can be dominant among civil society groups, the majority of the population, as well as cultural and other elites, while absent or not 'exercised' among ruling groups. Good examples are civil rights ideologies and pro-democracy movements which swept through most of East Europe from 1989 to 1991.

Cases of power-keeping and non-dominant ideology cover socialist self-management in 1980s Yugoslavia, as well as most forms of socialism all over pre-1989 Eastern Europe. While the official ideology of the ruling elite included various concepts of socialism, it was not supported by the majority of the population.

Power-seeking and non-dominant ideology is probably the most common and most easily identifiable type. Examples include political liberalism in contemporary Saudi Arabia and Sudan, socialism in present-day United States or Ireland and scientific racism in contemporary Italy. These ideologies are promoted and supported by politically minor groups in these societies.

By including these two criteria of distinction (dominance and power position of ideology) I attempt to widen Seliger's definition and approach. By doing so, ideology will not be treated as directly connected to concrete party politics, as in Seliger, but as the whole set of ideas and practices that often include different groups of actors. If we include these two criteria we can better analyse ideologies at work, for example, in some post-communist societies. On the one hand there is a dominant power-keeping ideology of nationalism (in its various forms), often supported by the ruling party, independent intellectuals not directly related to the ruling group, the Church and other dominant religious institutions and small-scale movements and groups such as anti-abortion or pro-family movements. On the other hand there are a number of different, often mutually exclusive non-dominant and power-seeking ideologies such as various forms of liberalism, feminism, racism, socialism, which often include some opposition parties, a number of independent intellectuals or students.

Another distinction in the analysis of ideology structure that is central for the understanding of the functioning of ideologies is the one between official (normative) ideology and operative ideology.[164] Seliger clearly makes a distinction between fundamental vs. operative ideology, although he does not include it in the definition of ideology. According to Seliger operative and fundamental ideologies are composed of the same elements (description, analysis, moral and technical prescriptions, implements and rejections). What makes them distinct is the emphasis on different elements: at the operative level efficiency and calculation are highlighted, while on the fundamental level the emphasis is on the moral prescriptions. These two forms of ideology are in constant tension. As a result they are permanently in the process of internal change or what Seliger calls 'bifurcation of ideology'. To preserve their coherence, ideologies have regularly to adjust their composing elements to one another.

Since Seliger views ideology largely as connected in one way or another to party politics, the distinction he proposes must be reformulated to include other forms of ideology manifestation. Thus, I will here follow his initial distinction and conceptualisation of fundamental (normative) ideology, while the form of operative ideology, as well as the relationships between them, will significantly differ from Seliger's model.

Fundamental (normative or official) ideology means the 'fundamental principles which determine the final goals and the grand vistas in which they will be realised'.[165] This is a form of ideology that is formulated in the political manifestos, official documents, party programmes, or the works of social scientists, philosophers, theologians or prophets (holy books and scriptures). Here we have clearly defined and consistent views on different matters regarding the organisation of society, relationships between individuals and groups, and other more universally shaped views. These texts contain precise definitions, interpretations and explanations of dominant ideological principles, guiding ethical prescriptions, scientific explanations of social conditions, and a general ideological outlook on the past, present and future. These principles and ideas are used as guidance for social and political action.

Operative ideology, on the other hand, is the type of ideology that is formulated, promoted, shaped and rooted in reality. It is based on the principles, ideas and practices which are differently articulated but are generally conceptualised to justify potential or actual policies and activities. This is an institutionalised mechanism of 'narrative control' which shows how ideology works in everyday life. It is the form of ideology found in the mass media, school textbooks, political and other actions in the case of power-keeping ideology, or in pamphlets, leaflets, posters and activities of power-seeking ideology.

The relationship between the two is more complex than Seliger suggests. They can consist of the same elements as in Seliger, but they can also incorporate completely different sets of values, ideas and practices. For example, the normative or official ideology of the former Soviet Union was Marxism–Leninism. The essentials of this ideology were stated in party documents, official state documents, works by Marx and Lenin or the political speeches of party and state leaders. Operative ideology as observed in the analysis of the mass media, school textbooks, ritual practices and other social and political activities might indicate that the operative ideology, as well as the form of legitimacy, was different: for example, traditionalist, imperialist or nationalist. This is a matter for empirical research.

In general, Seliger's definition of ideology has some operational qualities which, however, require substantive interventions and changes. Let us now see how the final operational definition and concept of ideology looks when all these alterations are taken into account. Taking into account the above mentioned criticism of Seliger's concept and the proposed definition of ideology, we are now in a position to re-conceptualise Seliger's definition.

Ideology is operationally defined and conceptualised here as a set of beliefs/disbeliefs, ideas and practices, expressed in the form of value, explanatory or appeal statements which can assume descriptive and analytical forms as well as appear as images and actions. These statements, images and actions are related to the conceptual organisation of society as well as to the relationships between individuals and collectives within and outside of that society. Their content is usually 'mundane' (ordinary), but can also have manipulative purposes (*ideologemes*). By their contents, ideologies make an appeal to moral norms, individual or group interests, or towards truth/superior knowledge, with the purpose of justifying potential or actual social action. These statements are internally consistent and not fully verifiable.

In regard to their degree of influence, ideologies can be classified as dominant or non-dominant. Their position in relation to power structure can be assessed as power-keeping or power-seeking, whereas their functional position will indicate whether ideology is normative/official or operative.

To be able to apply this operational definition, it is also necessary to identify and specify in more detail conceptual segments of ideology. I have singled out several such elements, the analysis of which will help us to distinguish between the conceptual and functional organisation of the structure, form and content of ideology.[166]

First, as the definition proposed above states, ideology is related to the *conceptual organisation of society*. Therefore, the analysis will focus on the three main segments that are crucial for the organisation of a particular society: *economy* (statements in regard to the production, distribution and consumption of goods and services in society), *politics* (statements in regard to the political system, party politics, power distribution), *culture and the nation* (statements in regard to the dissemination of cultural products, directions of cultural policies, the perceptions of nationhood, issues of minority ethnic groups).

Second, an operational definition of ideology points towards relationships between individuals and groups. Here I will look at how individuals and groups have been described, what kinds of names and images are attached to them, and whether they have been described as positive, negative or neutral *actors*.

Third, an attempt will be made to specify and analyse the *type of language* and images used in the statements and the form of appeal they make. This will also include the analysis of particular symbols, metaphors and descriptions used in the language of normative and operative ideology.

The last segment studied here is related to the depiction and presentation of *counter-ideologies*. The analysis will focus especially on the delegitimising strategies used, highlighting a counter-ideology's weak points and downgrading its strong points.

The ideologies that will be studied here are all dominant and power-keeping ideologies. Since the sources of my data are party documents, newspaper editorials and school textbooks, the analysis will focus on the statements and ideas, and only sporadically on practices. However, before moving on to an analysis of ideology structure in post-World War II Yugoslavia and post-communist Serbia and Croatia, let us examine the meaning and function of the concept of political legitimacy.

NOTES

1 D. McLellan, *Ideology* (London: Open University Press, 1991), p. 1.
2 W. B. Gallie, 'Essentially Contested Concepts', *Proceedings of the Aristotelian Society*, 56 (1956), pp. 167–97.
3 As Larrain, Markus and McLellan point out, Marx had never developed a systematic theory of ideology and the only work which deals extensively with this topic, *The German Ideology*, was not published by Marx himself. Some interpreters (Althusser, Boudon) also stress elements of 'non-Marxist' writings on ideology in the work of the young Marx, while others see no contradiction or significant discrepancies between Marx's early and later writings. See: McLellan, *Ideology*; G. Markus, 'Concepts of Ideology in Marx', in A. Kroker and M. Kroker (eds), *Ideology and Power in the Age of Lenin in Ruins* (New York: St Martin's Press, 1991); J. Larrain, *Marxism and Ideology* (London: Hutchinson, 1983); L. Althusser, *For Marx* (London: Allen Lane, 1969); and R. Boudon, *The Analysis of Ideology* (Cambridge: Polity Press, 1989).
4 See McLellan, *Ideology*, pp. 9–14.
5 Markus, 'Concepts of Ideology in Marx'.
6 A. Giddens, 'Four Theses on Ideology', in A. Kroker and M. Kroker (eds), *Ideology and Power in the Age of Lenin in Ruins* (New York: St Martin's Press, 1991), p. 22.
7 K. Marx, and F. Engels, *The German Ideology* (London: Lawrence and Wishart, 1977), p. 65.
8 K. Marx, *Selected Writings* (Oxford: Oxford University Press, 1977), p. 389ff.
9 Ibid.
10 K. Marx, *Capital: A Critical Analysis of Capitalist Production* (Moscow: Foreign Languages Publishing House, 1954).
11 T. Eagleton, *Ideology: An Introduction* (London: Verso, 1991), p. 85.
12 E. Bernstein, *The Preconditions of Socialism* (Cambridge: Cambridge University Press, 1993).

13 G. Lukacs, *History and Class Consciousness* (London: Merlin Press, 1971).
14 A. Gramsci, *Selections from the Prison Notebooks* (London: Lawrence and Wishart, 1971), p. 326.
15 Ibid., p. 328.
16 Ibid.
17 Ibid., p. 326.
18 L. Althusser, 'Ideology and Ideological State Apparatuses', in S. Žižek (ed.), *Mapping Ideology* (London: Verso, 1994), p. 112.
19 Ibid.
20 This distinction is not as strict as it may seem, since Althusser agrees that all state apparatuses function both by ideology and repression. The difference is that the former relies almost exclusively on repression, while the latter predominantly on ideology.
21 Eagleton, *Ideology*, p. 18.
22 Althusser, 'Ideological State Apparatuses', p. 129.
23 Ibid., p. 125.
24 As Larrain emphasises, this opposition disappears in Althusser's later works, adding however that 'with it the originality of Althusser's contribution has gone, too'. See Larrain, *Marxism and Ideology*, p. 93.
25 Althusser, 'Ideological State Apparatuses', p. 117.
26 Ibid., p. 118.
27 Ibid.
28 P. Hirst, *On Law and Ideology* (London: Macmillan, 1979).
29 J. Thompson, *Studies in the Theory of Ideology* (Cambridge: Polity Press, 1984), p. 94.
30 L. Goldmann, *The Hidden God* (London: Routledge, 1955).
31 M. Godelier, *The Mental and the Material – Thought Economy and Society* (London: Verso, 1986).
32 G. Therborn, *The Ideology of Power and the Power of Ideology* (London: New Left Books, 1980), p. 2.
33 Thompson, *Studies*, p. 6.
34 Eagleton, *Ideology*.
35 It is interesting that commentators who deny the importance of ideology in the functioning of modern societies, rely mainly on Durkheim's *The Division of Labour in Society*, where he is sceptical about the importance of ideology, and almost completely neglect his *The Elementary Forms of Religious Life* and *The Rules of Sociological Method*. See, for example, N. Abercrombie, S. Hill and B. Turner, *Dominant Ideology Thesis* (London: Unwin Hyman, 1980).
36 J. Larrain, *The Concept of Ideology* (London: Hutchinson, 1979).
37 E. Durkheim, *The Elementary Forms of Religious Life* (New York: Macmillan, 1964) and E. Durkheim, *The Rules of Sociological Method* (Chicago, IL: Chicago University Press, 1938).
38 Larrain, *Concept of Ideology*, p. 93.
39 While Hirst argues that Durkheim has tacitly abandoned his position on ideology outlined in *The Rules of Sociological Method* in favour of the one in *The Elementary Forms of Religious Life*, Larrain acknowledges these differences but minimises their importance since ideology in Durkheim 'has effectively become the *a priori* condition of all individuality, even if this happens to be a social individuality'. See Larrain, *Concept of Ideology*, p. 97.
40 Durkheim, *Rules*, p. 423.
41 Like other anthropologists Malinowski analyses 'primitive societies' by employing the term 'myth' instead of ideology.
42 B. Malinowski, *Myth in Primitive Psychology* (Westport, CT: Negro Universities Press, 1926).
43 Ibid., p. 28.
44 Ibid., p. 91.
45 T. Parsons, *Politics and Social Structure* (New York: Free Press, 1969); T. Parsons and W. White, 'Commentary on the Mass Media and the Structure of American Society', *Journal*

of Social Issues, 16, 3 (1960), pp. 67–77; T. Parsons and W. White, 'The Link between Character and Society', in S. M. Lipset and K. Lowenthal (eds), *Culture and Social Character* (New York: Free Press, 1961).

46 Parsons, *Politics and Social Structure*.

47 Parsons's general theory of action explains the structuration of societies through four main systems: the cultural system (values, symbols and meanings), the social system (social roles and interactions between actors), the personality system (motives, needs and attitudes of individuals) and the behavioural organism system (the nervous system and the actor's motor activity). See T. Parsons, *The System of Modern Societies* (Engelwood Cliffs, NJ: Prentice Hall, 1971).

48 T. Parsons, 'A Tentative Outline of American Values', in R. Robertson and B. S. Turner (eds), *Talcot Parsons – Theorist of Modernity* (London: Sage, 1991), p. 39.

49 Parsons, 'Tentative Outline', p. 40.

50 In Parsons's system theory this scheme refers to the four prerequisites every social system must satisfy in order to function properly: adaptation ('the problem of securing sufficient resources from the environment and distributing them through system'), goal attainment ('the system's need to mobilise its resources and energies to attain system goals and to establish priorities among them'), integration ('the need to co-ordinate, adjust, and regulate relationships among various actors or units within the system to keep the system functioning') and latent pattern maintenance–tension management ('the need to make certain that actors are sufficiently motivated to play their parts in the system or maintain the value "pattern" and the need to provide mechanisms for internal tension management'). See T. Parsons, *Social System* (New York: Free Press, 1951).

51 E. Shils, 'The Concept and Function of Ideology', *International Encyclopaedia of the Social Sciences*, 7 (1968), p. 73.

52 G. Sartori, 'Politics, Ideology and Belief Systems', *American Political Science Review*, 63 (1969), p. 405.

53 Ibid., p. 407.

54 V. Pareto, *Sociological Writings* (Oxford: Basil Blackwell, 1966), p. 44.

55 Ibid., pp. 237–47.

56 Ibid., p. 241.

57 G. Mosca, *The Ruling Class* (New York: McGraw Hill, 1939), p. 70.

58 Ibid., p. 71.

59 Ibid.

60 G. Sorel, *Reflections on Violence* (Cambridge: Cambridge University Press, 1999).

61 S. Freud, *Totem and Taboo* (London: Hogarth Press, 1961), p. 145.

62 S. Freud, *The Future of an Illusion* (London: Hogarth Press, 1961).

63 W. Reich, *The Mass Psychology of Fascism* (London: Penguin, 1975), p. 17.

64 S. Žižek, 'How did Marx Invent the Symptom?', in *Mapping Ideology* (London: Verso, 1994). As Keohane makes clear: 'the problem of relationality with the Other is that the Other is always already part of the One. This is so because without the Other there is no One: the One is the original Lack.' See K. Keohane, 'Central Problems in the Philosophy of the Social Sciences after Post-Modernism: Reconciling Consensus and Hegemonic Theories of Epistemology and Political Ethics', *Philosophy and Social Criticism*, 19, 2 (1993), p. 159.

65 Žižek, 'How did Marx Invent the Symptom?', p. 323.

66 Ibid., p. 311.

67 K. Mannheim, *Ideology and Utopia* (London: Routledge & Kegan Paul, 1936), p. 51.

68 R. Merton, *Social Theory and Social Structure* (New York: Free Press, 1957), p. 507.

69 Mannheim, *Ideology and Utopia*, p. 52.

70 K. Mannheim, *Essays on the Sociology of Knowledge* (London: Routledge, 1957), p. 175.

71 D. Coole, 'Phenomenology and Ideology in the Work of Merleau-Ponty', in N. O'Sullivan (ed.), *The Structure of Modern Ideology* (Aldershot: Edward Elgar, 1989).

80   *Ideology, Legitimacy and the New State*

72 C. Geertz, *The Interpretation of Cultures* (New York: Basic Books, 1973), p. 5.
73 Geertz, *Interpretation*, p. 17.
74 C. Geertz, 'Ideology as a Cultural System', in D. Apter (ed.), *Ideology and Discontent* (New York: Free Press, 1964), p. 64.
75 Ibid., p. 49.
76 Ibid., p. 63.
77 Ibid.
78 Ibid., p. 71.
79 M. Weber, *The Protestant Ethic and the Spirit of Capitalism* (London: Allen & Unwin, 1976).
80 R. Boudon, *The Analysis of Ideology* (Cambridge: Polity Press, 1989).
81 M. Weber, *Economy and Society* (New York: Bedminster Press, 1968), Vol. 1, p. 410.
82 See, for example, J. Elster (ed.), *Rational Choice* (Oxford: Basil Blackwell, 1986); J. Elster, *Nuts and Bolts for the Social Science* (Cambridge: Cambridge University Press, 1990); and J. Coleman and T. Fararo (eds), *Rational Choice Theory: Advocacy and Critique* (London: Sage, 1992).
83 R. Boudon, 'The Individualistic Tradition in Sociology', in J. Alexander, B. Giesen, R. Munch and N. Smelser (eds), *The Micro–Macro Link* (Berkeley, CA: University of California Press, 1987).
84 Boudon, *Analysis*, p. 29.
85 Ibid., p. 58.
86 Ibid., p. 67.
87 R. Barthes, *Roland Barthes* (Basingstoke: Macmillan, 1977).
88 R. Barthes, *Mythologies* (London: Vintage, 1993), p. 143.
89 C. Lévi-Strauss, *Strukturalna antropologija 2* (Zagreb: Školska knjiga, 1988).
90 C. Lévi-Strauss, *The Raw and the Cooked* (New York: Harper & Row, 1975), p. 12.
91 See, for example, J. Sinclair and R. Coulthard, *Towards an Analysis of Discourse: The English Used by Teacher and Pupils* (Oxford: Oxford University Press, 1975); and R. Fowler, B. Hodge, G. Kress and T. Trew, *Language and Control* (London: Routledge & Kegan Paul, 1979).
92 Thompson, *Studies*.
93 Žižek, *Mapping Ideology*, p. 8.
94 T. Adorno, *Negative Dialectics* (London: Routledge & Kegan Paul, 1973).
95 H. Marcuse, *One-Dimensional Man* (Boston, MA: Beacon Press, 1971), p. 130.
96 J. Habermas, *Legitimation Crisis* (London: Heinemann, 1976), p. 26.
97 J. Habermas, *Knowledge and Human Interests* (London: Heineman, 1972), p. 311.
98 J. Habermas, *Towards a Rational Society* (London: Heinemann, 1970), p. 99.
99 A. Gouldner, *The Dialectic of Ideology and Technology: The Origins, Grammar and Future of Ideology* (London: Macmillan, 1976).
100 A. Schopenhauer, *The World as Will and Representation* (New York: Dover Publishers, 1969).
101 F. Nietzsche, *The Will to Power* (New York: Vintage Books, 1968).
102 Nietzsche, *Will*, p. 298.
103 M. Foucault, *Discipline and Punish: The Birth of the Prison* (London: Allen Lane, 1977); M. Foucault, *Power/Knowledge* (Brighton: Harvester, 1980).
104 M. Foucault, *The Foucault Reader: An Introduction to Foucault's Thought*, P. Rabinow (ed.) (London: Penguin, 1984), p. 187.
105 Ibid., p. 58.
106 Foucault, *Power/Knowledge*, p. 131, and *Discipline and Punish*, p. 27.
107 J. Baudrillard, *Selected Writings* (Cambridge: Polity Press, 1988).
108 Ibid., p. 182.
109 F. Lyotard, *The Postmodern Condition: A Report on Knowledge* (Manchester: Manchester University Press, 1984).
110 E. Laclau and C. Mouffe, *Hegemony and Socialist Strategy* (London: Verso, 1985).

111 Ibid., p. 112.
112 Ibid. In Laclau and Mouffe the materiality of discourses does not exclude discursiveness of material forms. Thus, 'material' things (modes of production, ideological state apparatuses, state institutions) have themselves a distinctively discursive character.
113 Ibid., p. 113.
114 M. Barrett, *The Politics of Truth: From Marx to Foucault* (Cambridge: Polity Press, 1991).
115 Ibid., p. 167.
116 Taylor and Habermas develop a convincing argument about how the extreme relativisation of truth leads to self-defeating arguments which undermine the epistemological basis of post-structuralist and post-modernist critiques of modern knowledge. See C. Taylor, 'Foucault on Freedom and Truth', in *Philosophy and the Human Sciences* (Cambridge: Cambridge University Press, 1985); and J. Habermas, *The Philosophical Discourse of Modernity* (Cambridge: Polity Press, 1987).
117 This distinction between 'inclusive' and 'restrictive' positions in the study of ideology is also used by Seliger and O'Sullivan. See M. Seliger, *Ideology and Politics* (London: Allen & Unwin, 1976); N. O'Sullivan (ed.), *The Structure of Modern Ideology* (Aldershot: Edward Elgar, 1989).
118 O'Sullivan, *Structure*, p. x.
119 See, for example, the following passage from Habermas:

>   the structural depolitisation itself requires justification, which is supplied either by democratic elite theories (which go back to Schumpeter and Max Weber) or by technocratic system theories (which go back to the institutionalism of the twenties). In the history of bourgeois social science, these theories today have a function similar to that of the classical doctrine of political economy. In earlier phases of capitalist development, the latter doctrine suggested the 'naturalness' of the capitalist economic society.

>   In other words, democratic elite theories and system theories are political agents of the bourgeoisie, and therefore have no scientific value and are ideological, whereas (conveniently!) the author's concept searches for the truth and is not ideologically motivated. Habermas, *Legitimation*, p. 37.

120 R.H. Brown, 'Reconstructing Social Theory after the Postmodern Critique', in H. Simons and M. Billig (eds), *After Postmodernism* (London: Sage, 1994), p. 27.
121 B. Hindenss, and P. Hirst, *Modes of Production and Social Formation: An Auto-Critique of 'Pre-Capitalist Modes of Production'* (London: Macmillan, 1977).
122 For Lenin, Lukacs and to a lesser extent Gramsci, the distinction between science and ideology was of no direct importance since they were more practically oriented. However, they all perceived Marxist propositions as universal truths, and therefore Marxism as a science *par excellence*. Since ideology was a practical means for the dispersion of (Marxist) truth, it is evident that they followed Marx in distinguishing between science and ideology.
123 Althusser, *For Marx*.
124 In *The Elementary Forms of Religious Life* this opposition between science and ideology/religion is more subtle and is similar to Boudon's perception of ideology as an imperfect form of science.
125 T. Kuhn, *The Structure of Scientific Revolutions* (Chicago, IL: University of Chicago Press, 1965); P. Feyerabend, *Against Method* (London: New Left Books, 1975).
126 Lyotard, *Postmodern Condition*.
127 I. Wallerstein, 'The Challenge of Maturity: Whither Social Science?', *Review*, 15, 1 (1992), pp. 1–7.
128 G. McLennan, 'Post-Marxism and the "Four Sins" of Modernist Theorising', *New Left Review*, 218 (1996), p. 74.

129 Althusser, 'Ideological State Apparatuses', pp. 122–3.

130 See, for example, D. Bell, *The End of Ideology* (New York: Free Press, 1962); H. Arendt, *The Origins of Totalitarianism* (New York: HBJ, 1973); R. Aron, *The Opium of the Intellectuals* (London: Greenwood, 1977); S. M. Lipset, *Political Man* (London: Heinemann, 1960).

131 F. Fukuyama, *The End of History and the Last Man* (London: Hamish Hamilton, 1992).

132 Eagleton, *Ideology*, p. 8. To be more precise, I would understand Eagleton's 'certain practical purposes' to be concrete empirical situations where the analysis of the ideology is to be undertaken.

133 This example is related to the case in Bosnia where the pronunciation of the word 'coffee' is one of the rare cultural markers that distinguish the three communities of Serbo-Croat speakers. Thus, ethnonationally conscious Serbs would say *kafa*, Croats would say *kava* and Bosnian Muslims would say *kahva*.

134 It is worth noting that Marx's early statement that 'the ideas of the ruling class are in every epoch the ruling ideas' refers clearly to all 'historical' periods. If this is true, then it is contradictory to the entire Marxist concept of ideology which ties ideology to capitalism. However, one could argue that 'ideas of the ruling class' do not necessarily correspond to the more complex concept of ideology, but only that every rule has to legitimise itself.

135 E. Gellner, *Nations and Nationalism* (Oxford: Basil Blackwell, 1983), p. 61.

136 Abercrombie *et al.* give historical evidence against the so-called 'dominant ideology thesis' in pre-modern times. According to them, dominant ideas of the ruling groups had less to do with the ruled masses than with the rulers themselves. These ideas, among which was religion, have principally functioned as a means of unity for the rulers. N. Abercrombie, S. Hill and B. Turner, *Dominant Ideology Thesis* (London: Unwin Hyman, 1980).

137 Mannheim, *Ideology and Utopia*.

138 Althusser, 'Ideological State Apparatuses', p. 126.

139 Gellner, *Nations*, p. 34.

140 N. Abercrombie, S. Hill and B. Turner, *Dictionary of Sociology* (London: Penguin, 1984), p. 150.

141 Marx's well-known statement that 'it is not the consciousness of men that determines their existence, but on the contrary, their social existence determines their consciousness' is a full expression of this position.

142 On the concept of will-power (a personal conative striving) and its relevance for sociological explanations see C. Campbell, 'Action as Will-Power', *Sociological Review*, 47, 1 (1999), pp. 48–61.

143 D. Manning, 'Ideology and Political Reality', in N. O'Sullivan (ed.), *The Structure of Modern Ideology* (Aldershot: Edward Elgar, 1989), pp. 54–88.

144 Weber, *Economy and Society*.

145 Boudon, *Analysis*, pp. 207–8.

146 Manning, 'Ideology'.

147 Gouldner, *Dialectic*, p. 38.

148 Ibid., p. 56.

149 Ibid., p. 112.

150 To make a distinction here between ideological and non-ideological contents does not mean to distinguish between manipulative and non-manipulative statements, the aim of restrictive theories of ideology, but rather to identify the principal elements and 'building blocks' of ideology from less central, 'ordinary' contents.

151 As a possible exception one can recognise Seliger's and Lewins's emphasis on the content of ideology, but, as we will see later, Seliger's concept is too narrow, tying ideology principally to party politics, whereas Lewins himself recognises that his 'lengthy comment on definitional issues is not presented as a theory of ideology'. See F. Lewins, 'Recasting the Concept of Ideology: A Content Approach,' *British Journal of Sociology*, 40, 4 (1989), p. 691.

152 Lewins, 'Recasting', p. 680.

153 Boudon, *Analysis*, p. 49.

154 Geertz, *Ideology*, p. 68.
155 As it is possible to see later, I have tried to solve this problem by introducing the notion of *ideologem* which helps us to preserve the manipulative and mystificatory elements as (potential) dimensions of ideology, while not destroying the inclusive conception of ideology.
156 It is important again to emphasise that one should not conflate the theory of ideology (macro-level of analysis) with its operationalised form which deals with particular contents (micro-level). In other words, to speak of statements as having manipulative aims does not mean subscribing to a restrictive concept of ideology or seeing ideologies as inherently manipulative.
157 Seliger, *Ideology*, pp. 119–20.
158 Thompson, *Studies*, p. 78.
159 *Korak u novi vek: Osnove programa Socijalističke Partije Srbije* (Belgrade: GO SPS, 1992), p. 36.
160 M. Lazić and L. Sekelj, 'Privatisation in Yugoslavia (Serbia and Montenegro)', *Europe–Asia Studies*, 49, 6 (1997), pp. 1057–71.
161 This could be done through surveys, election results or through mass mobilisation. For an example of such analysis examining desirable forms of an ideal society based on a representative sample of university students see S. Malešević, 'Utopia and Dystopia After Communism: Visions of an Ideal Society among Zagreb University Students', *East European Quarterly*, 30, 2 (1996), pp. 251–69.
162 See S. Mihailović, 'Izbori 90: Mnijenje gradjana Srbije', in S. Mihailović *et al.*, *Od izbornih rituala do slobodnih izbora* (Belgrade: IDN, 1991). See also J. Mirowsky, C. Ross and M. Van Willigen, 'Instrumentalism in the Land of Opportunity: Socio-economic Causes and Emotional Consequences', *Social Psychology Quarterly*, 59, 4 (1996), pp. 322–7; Malešević, 'Utopia and Dystopia'.
163 Marxist approaches regularly equate dominant and power-keeping ideology.
164 Billig and Freeden also make a similar distinction. Billig speaks of intellectual and lived ideologies, while Freeden differentiates between elitist and popular ideologies. M. Billig *et al.*, *Ideological Dilemmas: A Social Psychology of Everyday Thinking* (London: Sage, 1988); M. Freeden, *Ideologies and Political Theory: A Conceptual Approach* (Oxford: Clarendon Press, 1996).
165 Seliger, *Ideology*, p. 109.
166 These elements are by no means the only ones that could be analysed. The reason I have focused on these elements is that they deal with the issues that are most recognisable to the general public and, at the same time, receive the most coverage in political manifestos, school textbooks and the mass media.

2

Political Legitimacy

THEORIES OF POLITICAL LEGITIMACY

The desire to justify one's domination
is as great as the desire to dominate.
R. Barker

If the ruler has the choice of being loved or feared by his subjects, Machiavelli's recommendation was: always choose fear over love.[1] While it may seem that most of human history has followed this pattern, there has rarely been an example of a ruler who relied solely on the fear of subjects. Most rulers and states have depended on a combination of the two, although to different extents. Nevertheless, contemporary states, be they bureaucratic or authoritarian rarely rely on either one. They all have to justify their position by their undisputed right to rule. This might be the 'will of the people' exercised and ritualised through election practices; the scientific legacy of Marxist–Leninist doctrine which having 'discovered' the laws of human history is certain of the path toward an ideal society; the authenticity of a national tradition that follows the 'old ways of our ancestors'; a revolutionary legacy that negates a previous despised regime and even the mystical origins of a royal family that can trace its links back to the Prophet, Mohammed.

All these different ways used by rulers to justify their rule are studied as forms of legitimacy. Just as the concept of ideology has been identified with the Marxist tradition, the idea and concept of legitimacy has been perceived as analogous to the Weberian tradition. Although Weber's theory was and still is highly influential, it is not the only tradition in the study of legitimacy.

This chapter will briefly introduce three main approaches to the study of the relationship between the State and legitimacy. These approaches will then be compared and critically elaborated. The next part of the chapter will concentrate on the relations between the state and legitimacy in state socialist societies. The last part of the chapter will attempt to clarify the relationship between legitimacy and ideology.

Weberian approaches

Weber defined and analysed legitimacy as the subjective belief of individuals and groups in the normative validity of a particular political order. Apart from self-interests, beliefs in the legitimacy of a political system are for Weber the principal forms of an individual's social action. On the other hand, since coercion in itself is insufficient (and often in the long run counter-productive), every state must rely on one or other form of legitimacy to uphold its existence. With regard to the political and cultural organisation of a particular state form, rulers adhere to different legitimacy strategies.

There are three general types of authority or legitimate domination in Weber's theory: rational–legal, traditional, and charismatic.[2] Although Weber often refers to concrete historical and contemporary examples, these three types of legitimate authority are generally treated as ideal types. Rational–legal type of legitimacy rests 'on a belief in the legality of enacted rules and the right of those elevated to authority under such rules to issue commands'.[3] This type of legitimate domination is based on bureaucratic administration and derives its authority from a 'consistent system of abstract rules' and laws. Legal norms are established by agreement or otherwise 'on grounds of expediency or value rationality'. There is an impersonal order to which all persons in authority are subjected and this applies equally, as Weber specifies, to 'officials' and to the elected president of the State. Individuals are obliged to obey this impersonal order usually in the form of 'the law', which means that authority derives from the institutional position in the hierarchy (the office) and not from the will of 'superiors'. Institutions and personnel have specified and separated areas of competence and jurisdiction. They are also organised in hierarchical order. Individuals employed in the institutions have specialised training, and professional relationships between employees are regulated by written technical rules. Administrative staff are separated from the ownership of the means of production, and the 'office' is the 'central focus of all types of modern organised action'. As Weber emphasises, 'bureaucratic administration means fundamentally domination through knowledge'.[4] It is the most rational and economic way of organising society. Therefore, legitimacy lies in epistemic authority. In other words, it is believed that the institutions and personnel responsible for a certain group of activities are the most competent to deal with these activities.

The traditional type of legitimacy is in many respects the opposite of the legal–rational type of authority. In Weber's words it is a type of legal domination that is based on 'an established belief in the sanctity of immemorial traditions and the legitimacy of those exercising authority under them'.[5] Legitimacy is claimed on the basis of the piety of 'age-old rules and powers'. The decisions of the authorities are therefore followed and respected because their right to rule derives from their traditional status. To obey authority simply means to show personal loyalty which, as Weber acknowledges, 'results from common upbringing'.

There are two ways in which traditional authority is legitimised: either by appealing to certain traditions which themselves set the content that should be obeyed, or by the ruler's discretion to interpret the tradition in the light he (rarely she) pleases. Weber distinguishes between several types of traditional legitimacy: gerontocracy and primary patriarchalism, patrimonialism and sultanism, and estate-type domination. Gerontocracy and primary patriarchalism are the simplest forms of traditional authority. These types of rule, as Weber explains, originally referred to the right of 'the eldest in actual years, who are the most familiar with the sacred traditions'. The main characteristic of these types of domination is that authority should be practised as a 'joint right in the interest of all members' and not as a right of possession by the ruler. Patrimonialism and sultanism differ from gerontocracy and patriarchalism in the way that they appear as the personal right of the ruler, and not as a group right. These forms of domination emerge with the development of administration and the military. As a result of this development, the ruled become more subjects or the possession of the ruler. In Weber's words: 'Previously the master's authority appeared as a pre-eminent group right, now it turns into his personal right which he appropriates in the same way as he would any ordinary object of possession'.[6] What differentiates patrimonialism from sultanism is that sultanism is a more extreme form of domination which functions 'on the basis of discretion'. A third form of traditional authority is estate-type domination. Weber defines it as a form of authority 'under which the administrative staff appropriates particular powers and the corresponding economic assets'.[7] These are often hereditary and can include organised groups as well as individuals.

All traditional types of authority include patrimonial recruitment (kinsmen, slaves, *coloni*). Important positions are usually given to the members of one's own clan or family. There are no rationally established hierarchical relationships; there are no impersonal rules to obey; professional training is not an obligatory requirement; there are no clearly defined areas of jurisdiction; and there is no system of appointment on the basis of competence.

Charismatic authority occupies the third and final type of legiti-mate domination in Weber's theory. 'Charisma' or 'the gift of grace' is a form of exceptional quality attached to a certain individual personality. Charismatic authority is therefore perceived as having unique and superior characteristics. These often include magical powers, supernatural heroism, prophetic abilities, superhuman lead-ership qualities, and so on. Thus, the charismatic type of legitimacy originates in the belief of 'the exceptional sanctity, heroism or exem-plary character of an individual person, and of the normative patterns or order revealed or ordained by him'.[8] By charismatic figures Weber meant founders of religious movements, plebiscitary rulers, as well as warlords and party leaders.

Belief in the charismatic figure frequently goes hand in hand with the concrete miracle that functions as 'proof' of the figure's extraor-dinary characteristics. According to Weber, war-like situations and similar aberrant circumstances and more likely to lead to the produc-tion of heroes and belief in their superhuman qualities. Around charismatic authority one can regularly identify a 'charismatic community' of followers who exhibit absolute trust in their leader and develop a cult of hero-worship. Unlike traditional or rational–legal types of authority, charismatic domination has no hierarchical basis. What we have are leaders and masses – followers. There are no mediators between them. The driving force behind this type of authority is usually a spiritual 'calling', a 'mission' or some other form of ideal millenarian target. It is a form of authority that often negates all previous traditions and forms of societal organisation. As such it is a revolutionary force that creates and imposes as divine, new rules and new practices of behaviour. Since charismatic authority is a deeply irrational and non-economic form of domination it cannot last for long. As Weber concludes:

> If proof and success elude the leader for long, if he appears deserted by his god or his magical or heroic powers, above all, if his leadership fails to benefit his followers, it is likely that his charismatic authority will disappear.[9]

In order to prolong this form of authority it is necessary, as Weber explains, to routinise charisma so that charismatic authority 'becomes either traditionalised or rationalised or a combination of both'. It is the material or spiritual interests of the followers and/or leaders, which includes the administration, disciples and party workers, that motivates them to continue this type of affiliation. If the new charis-matic authority is transmitted by a hereditary principle this often leads to traditionalisation or legalisation of the new authority. As

Weber makes precise: 'In the case of hereditary charisma, recognition is no longer paid to the charismatic qualities of the individual, but to the legitimacy of the position he has acquired by hereditary succession'.[10]

To sum up, the main difference between the traditional and legal–rational types of legitimacy on the one hand, and charismatic on the other, is that charisma is related principally to the individual personality, while traditional and legal–rational types of legitimacy are related to the institutional structures.

Friedrich follows Weber in defining legitimacy as a popular belief in the right of the regime to rule. He here formulates legitimacy in the following words: 'the belief that the ruler is legitimate, enhances his authority, that is to say, his capacity to reason effectively when challenged with reference to an action or communication'.[11] Friedrich also follows the Weberian tradition in distinguishing between diverse types of legitimate authority. However, in almost every other way he finds Weber's concept of legitimacy to be insufficient or confusing. First, he criticises Weber for not distinguishing clearly between authority and legitimacy. For Friedrich these two are connected but distinct phenomena. In Friedrich's theory, authority is a central concept based on 'acceptance' and defined as 'the capacity for reasoned elaboration', while legitimacy is a subordinated notion dependent on authority. As he specifies:

> all the different forms of legitimising rule in terms of popular prefer-
> ences, whether broadly defined by ideologies or narrowly by such
> goals as prosperity, security or national freedom, are insufficient, if not
> reinforced by authority.[12]

Second, Friedrich attacks all three types of legitimacy proposed by Weber. He accuses Weber of insensitivity in treating different types of legitimacy under the single category of 'traditional'. According to Friedrich these correspond to three different forms of legitimacy: the magical belief in descent from the gods where rulers have extraordinary powers (as in 'primitive' societies, Imperial China and the later Roman Empire); the belief in blood descent that regards the right to rule as a property right (feudal Europe); and the belief that time as an existence in itself is a proof of a ruler's virtuous qualities and that living traditions provide justification for themselves.[13]

Friedrich also opposes Weber's strong distinction between legal–rational and traditional legitimacy. The argument is simple. The constitution, and more generally the legal system, is a corner-stone of this type of rule and is central for its acceptance. Since the legal system and constitution after some time become a tradition, with the constitution deriving its authority from its duration in time, the legal–rational form of legitimacy is inseparable from the traditional type of authority.

Nonetheless, the most problematic type of legitimacy for Friedrich is the charismatic one. His position is that charismatic leadership as it is developed by Weber refers only to the founders of great religions and to religious leaders in general. As such this concept is in his view of no importance in the analysis of contemporary societies. Since the concept itself is often applied to Soviet-type societies, especially to the 'routinisation' of charisma under Lenin and Stalin, Friedrich attempts to show that this is not the case. In his view, 'Soviet Communism legitimises its rule by the materialistic interpretation of history' and is basically a secular type of legitimacy.[14]

Agreeing with Sternberger that 'each form of government has its particular kind of legitimacy', Friedrich once more emphasises the concept of authority over legitimacy, stressing that 'only where the rulers posses authority ... can they hope to achieve legitimacy in the sense that their rule is seen and accepted as rightful by the governed'.[15] By substituting legitimacy for the concept of authority, Friedrich simply ends up with a concept that not only has little to do with Weber's theory but, more importantly, loses the initial conceptual richness that distinguishes the Weberian approach from other theoretical traditions.

A good part of the criticism put forward by Friederich is his suggestion that Weber's typology does not cover all types of legitimate authority and that he groups distinct types of legitimacy under a single category. The weakness of Friederich's criticism is his extremely narrow understanding of charisma, his neutralisation of the important distinction between traditional and bureaucratic legitimacy and the priority he accords to the concept of authority over legitimation. His claim that the Soviet system drives its legitimacy from the materialist interpretation of history is empirically extremely naive. Friederich confuses official doctrine with the popular belief. The majority of the Soviet citizens certainly did not believe that the regime had the right to rule because it interpreted history in the materialistic way. The majority of the Soviet citizens could hardly conceptualise the abstractness of Marx's materialism vs. Hegel's idealism. The system could derive its legitimacy only on the basis of some familiar and recognisable concepts such as, for example, integral Soviet nationalism, charismatic leadership, a common enemy, war or a revolutionary tradition. Friederich's makes another conceptual error when neutralising the difference between traditional and bureaucratic legitimacy. The distinction between traditional and bureaucratic types of authority, although not perfect by any means, is crucial for Weber's theory;

if this valuable ideal type were to be destroyed in favour of the un-sociological and banal conclusion that each form of government has its own type of legitimacy, it would automatically undermine Weber's integral theoretical model.

Unlike Friedrich's position, Barker's theory of legitimacy stands firmly within the Weberian tradition. Here, too, legitimacy is perceived as a public belief in the regime's right to rule. As with Weber, Barker sees legitimacy not through its policies and outcomes, but principally through the procedures it applies and through the persons engaged in its functioning. Legitimation is analysed as a non-normative concept 'in terms of its success or failure in being acknowledged as legitimate by its subjects'.[16] In addition, Barker accepts Weber's typology of legitimate domination. What distinguishes Barker's position from Weber's is its emphasis on the State, and his expansion of Weber's concept to include a fourth type of legitimate domination: value–rational legitimacy. As we will see, these two ideas are closely related in Barker's theory of legitimacy.

Barker defines legitimacy as a political relationship between the State and its subjects. He stands against the view that government determines or shapes the popular perception of legitimacy, or vice versa, but 'rather that there is an observable relationship between the two'.[17] The State is in Barker an 'author or active possessor of rights, and not a mere lessee, agent, or functionary'.[18] To support this position Barker gives a good example of the State's capacity:

> The State may well be legitimate because it is taken in some way to express or represent concepts of collective identity, whether these are nation, race, faith. But in so far as it articulates these identities, the State also asserts its right and responsibility to interpret and define them, thus being in an important sense the author of the very principles or values by which its power is justified.[19]

The State is largely comprehended as an autonomous agent whose most significant characteristic is the assertion of coercive authority. As such the State attempts to justify its existence through different forms of legitimacy: traditional, legal–rational, charismatic, but also value–rational. As Barker points out, Weber developed the idea of value–rational action, but omitted to include this type of action into his typology of legitimate rule forms. Value–rational legitimacy is, in Barker's theory conceptualised as 'the belief in the absolute validity of the order as the expression of ultimate values of an ethical, aesthetic or of any other type'.[20] It is a form of legitimate rule which is present when the public perceives its rulers as the most competent to articulate and defend the ideology it supports. For Barker this is the most influential justification of obedience because, in this situation, individuals believe that the government they support 'is building communism, or fighting it, or preserving the national way of life, or achieving an Islamic republic'. When value–rational legitimacy is the dominant type of regime's legitimation, the public will

> see the State as 'their' state, not only or not even perhaps principally representing their interests, but representing what it is that distinguishes them. The government must in that sense be like those whom it governs, in terms of its national, racial, religious, or ideological identity. At the same time government must be more than 'ordinary' ... it must seem to be superior to or different from them.[21]

Therefore, a certain political order can be obeyed and supported if it draws its legitimation from the legal–rational organisation of society, from the rule of 'eternal yesterday', from a belief in the exceptional qualities of the charismatic leader, or as Barker suggests, from the belief that the regime correctly interprets the dominant set of political, cultural or other important values by which society functions.

Marxist and critical approaches

Although some scholars find many similarities between Weber's concept of legitimacy and Marx's notion of ideology,[22] there is a stark contrast between these two traditions of thought. The main difference is to be found in their different perceptions of the State. Although Weber did not have a theory of the State, he clearly defined the State in terms of its monopoly of legitimate violence. What interested Weber were the mechanisms of the State's influence on the public and vice versa, as well as a comparative analysis of different types of legitimation. Marx's ambition was of a completely different nature. He conceived of the State as an instrument of class oppression. The State was not autonomous, but partisan. It intends to present itself as a neutral medium, as a guardian of formal rules of democratic contest, while its authority is restricted by its dependence on the means and resources generated by private capital accumulation. In this way, as Marx argues, the State functions simply as a tool of the ruling class. Marx's view on the State was a starting point for several contemporary Marxist positions on legitimacy.

Miliband's theory of legitimacy is a very good example of the Marxist position.[23] His argument is basically Gramscian, although more simplified: the State in capitalist society is an instrument of the ruling capitalist class. Ownership of the means of production includes also control over the 'means of mental production'. Thus, the main 'agencies of legitimation' of the contemporary capitalist state are the mass media and the educational system.

In Miliband's view the mass media appear to be impartial and objective though they are 'both the expression of a system of domination, and a means of reinforcing it'. Freedom of expression that is proclaimed and exists in the capitalist societies must be seen, in Miliband's view,

> in the real economic and political context of these societies: and in that context the free expression of ideas and opinions mainly means the free expression of ideas and opinions which are helpful to the prevailing system of power and privilege.[24]

The capitalist media are especially hostile to political groups on the left. The advertising as well as the entertainment industry are particularly singled out as being instruments of the capitalist class. Emphasis on the entertainment media in the capitalist state encourages apathy, inertia, conformism and apolitisation among the population. In this way their purpose is not only to make profit but also to exercise ideological control over a potentially hostile but now apathetic population. As Miliband concludes:

> given the economic and political context in which they function, they [the mass media] cannot fail to be predominantly, agencies for the dissemination of ideas and values which affirm rather than challenge existing patterns of power and privilege, and thus to be weapons in the arsenal of class domination.[25]

Next to the mass media are educational institutions. In Miliband's view they act primarily as mechanisms for political socialisation. The State legitimises itself through the educational system in three ways: first, education functions as a source of class confirmation (the school system reproduces existing class differences); second, educational programmes are imposed as an alien culture on working-class children (since working-class children are raised and socialised in a different cultural environment they are automatically disadvantaged when they enter an educational system that operates in a culturally distinct milieu); and third, the education system seeks to 'infuse middle-class values' and perceptions of society (dominant views are reproduced by the educational system). Miliband's argument is that 'capitalism as an economic and social system tends to produce in itself, by its very existence, the conditions of its legitimation in the subordinate classes, and in other classes as well'.[26]

Offe outlines a less radical and more analytic Marxist theory of legitimacy.[27] He examines the relationship between legitimacy and efficiency in modern capitalist society and ties legitimacy to the State's ability to maintain economic growth. In his view democratic government rests not on democratic rules and regulations, but on 'the expectations that this form of government will contribute to common and individual welfare'. In this way the rationality of the State differs significantly from the rationality of private corporations. The State has no interest in doing anything efficiently, since it is not possible to determine or measure achieved efficiency. Instead, the capitalist state is motivated to place private actors in a position to increase their efficiency. Consequently, the State's efficiency is observed and measured through 'the extent that it succeeds in the universalisation of the commodity form'. As Offe emphasises, consonance between efficiency and legitimacy is achieved only when:

> 1) the acceptance of the legitimating rules of democratic and constitutional regimes is reinforced by the material outcomes of governmental measures and policies; and 2) if these measures and policies are efficient in successfully providing, restoring and maintaining commodity relationships for all citizens and for the totality of their needs.[28]

This balance between legitimacy and efficiency is often intruded upon by several contradictory processes. According to Offe, the first such contradiction comes from the divergent interests of the monopolistic structure of industry on the one hand and from the rate of growth demanded by the population on the other. Monopolist-oriented industry requires new markets, and when they do not exist 'it becomes more costly for the State to open new investment opportunities for monopoly profits and hence to maintain their rate of growth'. Contradiction arises when the State has to support commodity production, while this manoeuvre at the same time structurally affects the level of unemployment.

Another contradiction arises from the State's intervention to halt the erosion of the commodity form. By introducing different measures (education and training 'to increase the saleability of labour power', flexible frameworks of wage determination), the State might not succeed in maintaining the necessary support from the groups who benefit from the present situation (parts of the capitalist, but also the working class). In all of these cases, as Offe acknowledges, 'the restoration of commodity relationships through the State and its administrative agencies takes place under social arrangements that are themselves external to commodity relationships'.[29]

To sum up, Offe demonstrates the principal contradiction of the capitalist state: state policies are stretched between counter-market measures that appear necessary to maintain economic growth and capitalist (monopolist) industry that can only operate in a market based environment.

Habermas, who developed one of the most influential theories of legitimacy inspired by Marx's original argument, shares much in common with Offe.[30] In his view the economic contradictions of capitalism, especially the relationship between the State intervention and the interests of capital, result in four types of crisis: economic crisis rationality crisis, legitimation crisis, and motivation crisis.[31] Since the economy in capitalist society is inherently unstable and characterised by crisis cycles the State has to intervene in its regulation with the purpose of sustaining political order. These actions make the State's apparatus costly and massive, but also conflict with the free market principle and the interests of capital. These centripetal forces trigger a chronic economic crisis of capitalism. As a result, the State and government are unable to establish standard and coherent policies, which leads to a rationality crisis. These 'systemic limits' and incoherent policies bring about distrust in the political system which then expresses itself in a legitimation crisis. Dissatisfaction with the system ends in the 'erosion of traditions important for continued existence', or a motivation crisis.

Habermas finds Weber's typology useful but opposes the basis of the Weberian concept of legitimacy which regards legitimacy as a popular belief in the rulers' right to govern. In his view Weber made an ethical and logical mistake by concentrating on popular belief as such, and on the rulers' ability to produce that belief. However, the central question for Habermas is the truth and falsity of the beliefs themselves; thus: 'every effective belief in legitimacy is assumed to have an immanent relation to truth that can be tested and criticised'.[32]

Schaar is even more critical of the Weberian approach to the study of legitimacy. In his view legitimacy cannot be dissolved simply into opinion or belief, since the beliefs themselves can be shaped or postulated by institutional frames that in one way or another misguide the subjects who express that belief. If legitimacy is defined as a belief system, then in Schaar's view one can 'examine nothing outside popular opinion in order to decide whether a given regime or institution or command is legitimate'. That is why he wishes to distinguish between legitimacy and consensus. In his view, Weberian definitions of legitimacy fuse legitimacy and acquiescence. To illustrate this, Schaar gives the following example:

> a group or individual refuses consent and obedience to the orders of a regime or institution on the ground that the regime or institution is illegitimate; a regime or institution is acknowledged to be legitimate as

such, but consent is withheld from a particular order on the ground that the regime had no legitimate right to make that order; one consents or acquiesces out of interest or necessity, although he regards a regime or an order as illegitimate. In short, legitimacy and acquiescence, and legitimacy and consensus are not the same.[33]

Schaar also shares Habermas's view of the legitimacy crises. However, his concept extends this crisis to all modern states. It is modernity itself that 'produces' the crisis of legitimate authority because of its strong emphasis on 'rationality, the cult of efficiency and power, ethical relativism, and egalitarianism'. In this situation all modern states are affected by the crisis of legitimacy where obedience results mainly from habit or necessity and rarely from reason, convictions or sentiments.

Schaar is extremely critical of bureaucracy, technology and science and, in a similar vein to the Frankfurt School, stands against the rationality of bureaucracy and the perception of science and technology as value-free tools. He sees liberal democratic ideology as always in collision with expert manipulation and regards the legal–rational type of legitimate authority as nothing other than the outcome of such manipulation. As such he completely rejects the Weberian typology: 'the basic opposition is not between charismatic and rational authority, but between what can only be called personal and human authority on the one side and bureaucratic–rational manipulation and co-ordination on the other'.[34]

Pluralist approaches

While Weberian approaches focus on legitimacy, perceiving the State as an autonomous subject of action and emphasising the diverse forms of political legitimacy, and Marxist approaches emphasise contradictions originating in the nature of the capitalist state, the pluralist tradition tends to see and analyse political legitimacy solely as an expression of the popular will. For pluralists the State is a functional frame for accomplishing the aspirations and ambitions of individual citizens. Legitimacy is essentially identified with liberal democracy and as such is measured only through popular approval. As Barker points out:

> Since liberal pluralism begins with individuals and society rather than with government, so too, when it talks of legitimacy at all, it sees legitimacy as a belief of citizens rather than a relationship between subjects and rulers, an independent attitude of mind whose ebb and flow can be charted, and whose power and volume has consequences for government of the same order as a drop in world oil prices.[35]

The main concern of pluralist theory is the functional stability of liberal democratic societies. In this way legitimacy is often equated with stable liberal democratic governments and reduced to the analysis of party politics, election results and so on.

Lipset is probably the most influential representative of the pluralist approach. He shares with Weber an emphasis on popular belief in the definition of legitimacy which he sees as 'the capacity of the system to engender and maintain the belief that the existing political institutions are the most appropriate ones for the society'.[36] Nevertheless, by perceiving liberal democracy as the only form of legitimate authority, his concept diverges sharply from the Weberian tradition.

Lipset defines legitimate rule (democracy) through 'the existence of a moderate state of conflict'. Groups and individuals might be, and often are, mutually in opposition, but as long as they consider that the values of the political system correspond to their own values, they will perceive the existing system as legitimate. The superiority of liberal democratic rule comes from the fact that the system permits social and political conflicts to find open expression. The system only mediates by moderating the intensity of such conflicts and supplies procedures and 'rules of the game' through which their public outcome is legitimised. At the same time the plurality of regularly cross-cutting groups and interests helps soften the sharp edges of the conflicts.

Lipset also connects efficiency and legitimacy, although in a completely different way from Offe. In his theory, they are linked but not necessarily dependent on each other, since efficiency is instrumental whereas legitimacy is evaluative. He distinguishes four types of possible relations between the two: societies that are high on both categories (the United States, Sweden and the United Kingdom); societies that are high on efficiency and low on legitimacy (Germany and Austria in the late 1920s); societies that are low on efficiency and high on legitimacy (Thailand); and societies that are low both on legitimacy and effectiveness (communist Hungary and the German Democratic Republic). According to Lipset legitimacy is more important than effectiveness for the stability of any political system. However, legitimate rule goes hand in hand with economic prosperity. Crises of legitimacy are, in his view, basically the results of modernity and arise from a crisis of change. As he says:

> Crises of legitimacy occur during a transition to a new social structure, if 1. the status of major conservative institutions is threatened during the period of structural change; 2. all the major groups in the society do not have access to the political system in the transitional period, or at least as soon as they develop political demands.[37]

Good indicators of whether this crisis has been resolved and whether the new society is perceived as legitimate are national rituals and holidays. They verify the existence of the common 'secular political culture'.

Like Lipset, Kateb sees legitimate government as one based only on democratic principles of organisation.[38] However, his position is more liberal–individualist than Lipset's. Kateb intends to show that US society is characterised by a unique sense of individualism. This individualism is reflected in the scepticism towards authority. Individualism and constitutional democracy are linked: 'general or abstract rights and duties must be seen as helping to constitute the individual self'. Citizens of the United States, unlike those of the former Soviet Union who were considered servile and enslaved, have developed a sense of self-ownership. They are aware of their individual powers which exercise through elections and other forms of control over political authority. This consciousness of being self-owned is related to the institutions of capitalism. In Kateb's opinion the legitimate type of rule – meaning here the liberal democratic organisation of society – requires capitalism. Although democracy and the capitalist type of social organisation often proceed in mutually exclusive directions, and are therefore in a permanent state of anxiety, such anxiety is creative. Kateb is aware of the inequalities that arise from the capitalism, but finds all other alternatives worse in regard to the conditions of freedom.

Since legitimation is perceived by Kateb as the process whereby social knowledge explains and justifies dominant social reality, there is no legitimacy crisis in US society. As Kateb specifies: 'there are no deep and widespread feelings and opinions marked by disaffection from and hostility to constitutional representative democracy'.[39] What he does identify are only a few movements and groups of intellectuals on the right and left of the political spectrum who reject these principles and organisation of constitutional democracy.

There are three forms of critique from the right. Each centres on a different type of authoritarianism based on the theory of democratic elitism. First, the authoritarianism of order exemplified in the work of Huntington (the emphasis is on 'the preservation of the established order and of the country's place in international competition'); second, the authoritarianism of expert authority developed by Brzezinski ('democracy must reduce itself in order to expand the role of the knowledgeable elite'); and, finally, the moral elitism (paternalism) demonstrated in the philosophy of Leo Strauss ('officeholders and lawmakers will tend to be wiser in moral knowledge than the people').

The attack from the left is more hostile. It questions the entire economic and political system. Although criticism from the left varies from revolutionary left, reconstructionist left and disappointed left, what unifies it is a common anti-capitalist attitude. It is left theory that speaks of 'legitimacy crisis', locating it into the economic contradictions of capitalism. Although leftist criticism starts with the economy it regularly ends up with a critique of political system – 'attack on the form and spirit of constitutional democracy'.

Kateb stands against both the authoritarian conservatism of the right which intends to reduce free expression and other achievements of liberal democracy, as well as socialism with its fantasy of equal citizenship and focus on centralisation and social control. For Kateb both socialism and authoritarian conservatism are incompatible with legitimate rule, or in other words with constitutional democracy.

American society differs also from European societies since it is based on a Tocquevillian balance of consent where the voluntary principle appears as a substitute for the European sovereign state. What we have therefore, as Kateb concludes, is not the legitimacy crisis of US democracy, but 'a legitimation crisis among numbers of intellectuals and publicists of the right-of-centre and the radical left in the United States'.[40]

Gurr's concept of legitimacy is a genuine representative of classical positivism within the pluralist tradition. Legitimacy is here defined and analysed as 'the extent to which the political unit, its governing institutions, and the incumbents are thought proper and worthy of support'.[41] Legitimacy of the regime is measured through the citizen's support in a mechanical way as 'the proportion of people in the political unit with feelings of legitimacy above some specified threshold'. The legitimacy and illegitimacy of the State are conceived as polar opposites whose relationship is of a causal order:

> If the legitimacy–illegitimacy continuum is related to the magnitude of political violence in its entirety, the relationship is likely to be linear and inverse throughout, but different causal mechanisms are operating on either side of the zero point: positive feelings towards the regime are causally linked with normative inhibitions against political violence.[42]

Positivist methodology and the pluralist theoretical frame are combined in functionalist explanations. Individuals act and behave as rational beings who follow their interests. They attain belief in the validity of a particular political system and develop a perception of the regime as 'an ultimate source of authority' through socialisation. By doing so they internalise the norms which discourage antagonism against the regime. These norms function simultaneously as 'an external surrogate of conscience whose dictates supersede those of conscience'. As interest-oriented beings, individuals will generally abstain from offensive reactions and attacks on the political system and regime 'which they have learned to think of as proper and as acting for their own long-range interests'. As Gurr puts it:

> it is likely that in a country with a legitimate regime, children and youth learn that the deprivations imposed by the regime through its demands for compliance and value sacrifice are 'reasonable' because people are or will be compensated for them by symbolic and material rewards.[43]

Thus, Gurr's main argument is that the intensity and extent of normative justifications for political revolt in any form 'vary strongly and inversely with the intensity and scope of the regime legitimacy'.

Political legitimacy theories observed

As one can see from this brief overview, the three dominant theoretical positions on political legitimacy are strongly opposed to each other. For the Weberian tradition legitimacy is a matter of public belief in the regime's right to rule and as such extends to different forms of state organisation. In contrast to this position, pluralists see only Western-type liberal democracies as a legitimate form of the government's rule. In Marxist and critical approaches it is exactly this type of state organisation, liberal capitalist states, that is regarded as the principal type of illegitimate authority.

Originating in the different socio-political and philosophical traditions these theories also focus on different groups of problems: Weberians are concerned with the variety of political legitimacy types, Marxists concentrate on the legitimacy crises of the capitalist state, and pluralists highlight the relationships between individuals, groups and the political institutions in liberal democracies. There are also significant disagreements and differences between authors who work within the same tradition.

However, what can be identified as a principle element of dispute between Marxists and pluralists on the one side, and Weberians on the other, is their sharp methodological differences. Marxists and pluralists basically operate within a normative framework whereas the Weberian tradition attempts only to give a descriptive and explanatory account of legitimacy.[44] For Weberians there are no a priori illegitimate regimes. All durable and stable political systems are analysed as legitimate. What is important for this tradition is not to question whether particular types of rule are just, honest or lawful from a certain normative stand point. The intention is rather to investigate how different political systems acquire legitimacy. The studies are focused on the forms, mechanisms and procedures that regimes exhibit in the process of achieving broad legitimacy.

For Marxists and pluralists, only some forms of rule are legitimate, while all others that do not conform to the 'ideal normative model' are intrinsically illegitimate; capitalist states are not legitimate in the eyes of Marxists, and liberal democratic states are the only legitimate form of rule for pluralists. In this way both pluralism and Marxism are limiting, since by imposing moral criteria in the analysis the proper sociological questions cannot be posed. Instead of asking how a particular regime manages to secure its legitimacy, they ask how far it is from an ideal model. In the Marxist tradition this is a question of truth and falsehood (as Habermas would argue, 'values and norms in accordance with which motives are formed have an immanent relation to truth'[45]), while in the pluralist tradition this is a question of the system's functionality and the individual's freedom.

Nevertheless, both Marxism and pluralism have their explanatory merits when studying particular problems. Habermas and Offe give a convincing answer to the question of why capitalist states encounter periodic legitimacy crises by locating these crises in the contradictions that are inherent in the capitalist mode of production.[46] Miliband also argues convincingly that the mass media and the educational system are the main devices used by the capitalist state to influence popular perceptions. Schaar is also right when he emphasises the manipulative dimensions of the modern, enlightened, legal and rational state.

The same applies to Lipset and Kateb who acknowledge that a moderate form of conflict and the plurality of individual and group interests provide safe ground for the stable and legitimate organisation of society. Even Gurr's argument about the importance of socialisation and norm-internalisation for the acceptance of regime has its explanatory merits.

However, since these types of analysis are basically reductionist and socio-centric[47] – meaning they concentrate exclusively on one type of society at the expense of all other existing forms of societal organisation – they are not really applicable to societies that have different political and economic structures of organisation. Acknowledging that capitalism influences legitimacy crises should not rule out the possibility that there are other sources of legitimacy for the modern state (protection of human rights, rule of law, gender and minority group equality, national identification), and consequently different types of legitimacy crises within liberal democratic societies (modernity, over-rationality, problems of affluence). At the same time, one should take into account that there are non-capitalist states that also experience temporary or permanent crises of legitimacy which have their origins in different types of legitimacy.

The same criticism applies to Miliband. It is not only the capitalist state that benefits from the cultural hegemony exercised through the mass media and educational system. That is a feature of all modern societies, although their concrete strategies and the level of inten-tionality might differ. In addition, as many studies show, media and educational influences are never one-way processes as Miliband would suggest. By focusing exclusively on capitalism one automati-cally leaves out all other social processes and structures that are taking place and reduces the initial complexity and richness of social phenomena to a single cause.

While one still can try to extend the Marxist type of analysis to non-capitalist societies with greater or lesser success (Wallerstein's world-system theory, Godelier's political economy theory and the depen-dency theories of Cardoso and Faleto), pluralism is theoretically inflexible and unable to go beyond the liberal democratic ideal. Lipset and Kateb's models are essentially US-centric. For a society to function properly it is necessary, in their view, to be based on a plural-ist liberal democracy, preferably of the North American type. In Kateb's theory citizens of the United States are described as excep-tional beings who always behave as conscious self-owned individuals. All other forms of social organisation are illegitimate and individuals living in these type of societies are submissive.

The main problem with this position is that it is fundamentally anti-sociological. If one regards the political systems of Iran or Cuba as ille-gitimate, one cannot explain how it is possible that these regimes have managed to operate for decades, while some liberal democratic soci-eties, such as, the United States during the American Civil War or Weimar Germany, were on the brink of collapse or actually collapsed.

An additional criticism that one can make in regard to the plural-ist approach is that its concepts, especially in Gurr's variant, are solely quantitative. Legitimacy is a matter of plain measurement. The scope and the extent of legitimacy are treated exclusively in a numerical way. A linear and mechanical theory that rests on simple causality is difficult to find today even in the field of physics. Taking into account that the object of my study is the different forms of political legitimacy and that the societies analysed rest on different political and economic organisations, I would put aside Marxism and pluralism as the two traditions that have little heuristic and explanatory potential outside their particular scope of research.

In this way the Weberian tradition emerges as the most applicable sociological tradition within which one can employ a comparative analysis of different types of political legitimacy. Before we go to the analysis of various attempts to apply the Weberian framework to state socialist societies, let us first examine weaknesses and strengths of this tradition.

Weberian concept of legitimacy: strengths and weaknesses

Weber's theory of legitimacy is characterised by an interesting paradox. As Grafstein observes, it is probably one of the concepts most often attacked 'by those political philosophers who have evaluated it', which has also 'proved to be the dominant model for empirical investigations of legitimacy'.[48] One could classify criticisms of Weberian concept of legitimacy into several groups: a critique of its logical foundations that focuses on the epistemological problems of Weber's theory (logical quality of the theory, validity of the ideal type concept, methodological individualism); a critique of its conceptual foundations that either questions the entire idea of legitimacy (emphasis on concepts of authority instead of legitimacy, relationship between legitimacy and consensus, highlighting the psychological features of Weber's concept), or attacks Weber's tradition on normative grounds (the question of truth and falsity, immorality of the theory); and, finally, a critique of empirical foundations that objects to the classification of and the relationships between different types of legitimacy proposed by Weber and the applicability of this typology to specific societies.

Some logicians and political philosophers find Weber's concept of legitimacy circular and empty.[49] It is claimed that Weber infers the legitimacy of a political system from the popular acceptance of that system, while at the same time taking the presence of accepted authority as an explanation for the existence of that political system. As such, they argued, Weber's concept misinterprets the whole idea of legitimacy. As Grafstein points out:

> Weber distorts the essential meaning of legitimacy. The concept should properly signify a normative evaluation of a political regime: the correctness of its procedures, the justification for its decisions, and the fairness with which it treats its subjects. In Weber's hands, however, legitimacy no longer represents an evaluation of a regime; indeed, it no longer refers directly to the regime itself. Rather, it is defined as the belief of citizens that the regime is, to speak in circles, legitimate.[50]

In this way legitimacy is simply identified with obedience. It is deduced from the people's compliance with imposed rules. Since the majority of individuals obey the rules, it is concluded that they treat these rules and existing structural relations as legitimate. In the eyes of critics, the factor of compliance caused by fear and other forms of coercion seems to be neglected.

This, however, is not the case. First, Weber's concept does not identify legitimacy with obedience, because legitimacy is here defined two-dimensionally: as a popular perception of the regime's right to rule and as the power of the State's or the regime to obtain their legitimacy. As Barker explains: 'Legitimacy as used by Weber thus has two aspects: it is both a contributor to domination, and a "justification" of it. It is both a belief held by subjects, or by some subjects, and a claim made by rulers'.[51]

Second and more important, even if legitimacy could be identified with obedience we would still be able to refer to different types of obedience and the concept itself would remain useful. It would still show how different political regimes justify different types of rule and how different populations accept these forms of authority. As Barker rightly concludes:

> Weber does not rely on mere compliance, but takes account of the various ways in which that compliance is justified [and] since it is not legitimacy but the search for legitimacy which characterises states, legitimacy is not a mere empty synonym for government.[52]

It is certainly true that Weber strips legitimacy of its initial legislative meaning. He is not interested in the normative criteria such as the fairness of the regime, the correctness of its procedures and so on, but only in the comparative study of legitimate authority. This however does not show that the concept is circular or empty, but only that Weber's idea of legitimacy differs sharply from conventional, legislative or epistemological understandings of legitimacy.

Another point that is connected to the previous one is related to Weber's ideal type concept. The problem is of a methodological nature: are ideal types intended to have descriptive or explanatory functions? As Grafstein observes:

> The analysis of the ideal type of legitimate domination thus suggests that the descriptive and explanatory functions of the ideal type are in tension. The descriptive aspect of the ideal type leads to a plausible interpretation of the behaviour of any 'typical' individual in a legitimate polity; it loses plausibility as a description of the aggregate of individuals, since legitimacy and stable political order become synonymous. In contrast, the explanatory aspect of the ideal type leads to a plausible and realistic account of political stability by explaining the aggregate of behaviour as the result of a multiplicity of subjective

meanings. At the same time, it sacrifices the possibility of validating any one imputed meaning from this multiplicity. Validation requires the descriptive dimension of the ideal type and that, in turn, eliminates the very multiplicity being validated.[53]

This is a more serious contradiction in Weber's theory. Ideal types, and thus forms, of legitimate authority cannot simultaneously function as explanatory and descriptive, because if they do we end up with a tautological concept. However, the problem lies not so much, as Grafstein insists, in Weber's focusing on the individual behaviour but in the limits of the explanatory potential of the ideal types. Although Weber clearly defined himself as methodological individualist,[54] the concept of an ideal type extends to both individual and collective action. In other words, Weber is not concerned only with the explanation of individual behaviour. As Barker indicates:

> he is engaged in giving as full an account as possible of the various ideal forms of behaviour and relationship which, in real and observable historical situations, constitute domination. In this sense he is concerned with conduct, action infused and informed by values, rather than with mere behaviour.[55]

Ideal types and hence types of legitimate authority are primarily descriptive but 'one-side accentuated' constructs that help us to deal with complex social phenomena.[56] Ideal types are not often found in reality, but function rather as useful research tools of generalisation. They are pure logical types whose purpose is 'to facilitate the analysis of empirical questions'. In Weber's theory they differ from ordinary descriptive concepts for two reasons: they are one-sided accentuations of certain social phenomena and they have explanatory power. In Weber's view it is exactly this move from a descriptive to an explanatory level that differentiates ideal types from ordinary descriptive concepts.

In order to avoid the logical failure of Weber's concept of ideal types of legitimate authority, it is necessary to re-conceptualise the ideal type model. This means that the whole concept, as far as legitimate authority is concerned, should have less ambitious purposes. To achieve this task we have first to give up the explanatory aspiration of the concept in favour of the more descriptive one. As a result of this idea, it is necessary to retain Weber's emphasis on the difference between the ideal type and the ordinary descriptive type. What is possible here is to preserve a distinction between the descriptive type and an ideal type that is descriptive but also includes 'one-sided accentuation'. The ideal type would incorporate the individual researcher's emphasis on the generalisation of certain social phenomena, while still retaining its descriptive ambitions. Second, after identifying different types of authority, the researcher would have to move to the analysis of other social phenomena that have been identified either as a cause, a source of the phenomena under study, as a less general unit of analysis, or as phenomena that are directly related to the phenomenon under consideration. In our particular case, as we will see later, this will be the concept of ideology. After I identify the existing ideal types of legitimate authority for the case studies in question, the study will focus on the structure of particular ideologies and their relationship to concrete legitimacy models. In this way we will satisfactorily resolve the logical problems in Weber's concept of legitimacy while preserving the usefulness of the ideal type concept.

As far as the critique of the conceptual and normative foundations of Weber's theory is concerned, we are already familiar with the ideas of Friedrich, Schaar and Habermas. Friedrich argues that Weber did not properly distinguish between authority and legitimacy. In his view it is authority and not legitimacy that is central to the acceptance of a particular type of rule. Schaar's criticism is centred on the distinction between legitimacy and consensus, since in his view Weber perceives these two as a single item. Habermas attacks the Weberian tradition on ethical grounds: the concept is immoral since it affirms as legitimate whatever is believed to be legitimate.

It is clear that Friedrich and Weber operate with different concepts of authority which arise from their different aims. Friedrich's intention is to discredit the Enlightenment – driven concepts that strongly oppose tradition and authority and that also perceive legitimacy as 'eternally good'. He wants to show that authority plays as powerful a role in the modern enlightened world as it did in the 'dark ages'. Weber, on the other hand, intends to differentiate between different models of legitimate rule. He is determined to show how different types of rule can be justified in the eyes of both the rulers and the ruled.

The main difference here is that Friedrich's understanding of legitimacy is one-dimensional[57] ('the belief that a ruler is legitimate'), while Weber's concept is not, including both the ruler's and the subject's perception of the rule. In Friedrich's theory legitimacy is of secondary importance and in reality a synonym for mere legality. Friedrich's authority is basically what Weber's understands as legitimacy or as Weber frequently described it, legitimate authority. Friedrich is certainly right in pointing out that there are forms of non-legitimate authority, but that is not the object of Weber's interest. Authority might be a wider concept than the kind of legitimacy that includes both legitimate and illegitimate types of rule, but this idea does not essentially disturb Weber's argument. The aim is to locate different forms of legitimate rule and to explain why and under what conditions certain types of rule are considered legitimate and why and when they are not.

Schaar's argument that Weber identifies legitimacy with consensus would not be out of place if Schaar did not have a very narrow view of consensus. The legitimacy of the political order is some form of consensus between rulers or institutional structures and the ruled. The consent of the ruled is acquired by some form of mutual 'agreement' between the two. This, however, as Weber himself emphasised, does not exclude interest, necessity or even fear. It is not to say that the two sides are equal in any way or that ruled subjects, if in a significant minority, have any choices to make.

It seems that Schaar perceives legitimacy in a zero-sum fashion: the ruling authority is either legitimate or it is not. This is never the case. There are no examples of a society where all its members have supported all the rules of the authority. Not every decision or action and moves of the rulers will be considered legitimate or just. Nevertheless, this does not mean that political authority as a whole is considered illegitimate. When that is the case we often have revolutions and wars. As long as a majority of the population supports a certain type of political system, which as Beetham points out may be inferred from electoral procedures, mass mobilisation or a combination of two, it is appropriate to speak about legitimate rule.[58]

Habermas[59] also sees Weber's concept of legitimacy as deeply psychologistic: 'if belief in legitimacy is conceived as an empirical phenomenon without an immanent relation to truth, the grounds upon which it is explicitly based have only psychological significance'.[60]

Weberian theory is accused of concentrating on popular beliefs at the expense of an rationale behind the approval or disapproval of certain forms of rule. Habermas argues that Weber's conceptualisation of legitimacy as a matter of value/belief leaves no room for truth-claims or for the structural determinants of legitimacy creation. The theory is unethical because it 'equates justice with a belief in the existence of justice'. The theory is not sociological since it ignores the questions of how and under what conditions legitimacy is or can be achieved, or when legitimacy becomes a matter of manipulative strategies.

The ethical part of this criticism is largely out of place. As Barker rightly stresses: 'to criticise Weber for not providing a normative theory of legitimacy is not to criticise what he did do, but to wish that he had done something else'.[61] As explained earlier, Weber makes no ethical claims. He is not interested in whether the rule is just and good, but how it operates. By identifying different types of legitimate authority, he has no intention of supporting and denouncing any of these forms of legitimate rule.

Nevertheless, the explanatory criticism laid down by Marxist and critical theory is on the right track, although the train drives in the wrong direction. By focusing on the popular perceptions of the regime and on the regime's own claims (a constantly neglected factor), Weber leaves out several important explanatory 'variables'. These include the question of the internal structural relations within differently organised societies. It is true that Weber's concept does not tell us much about processes of 'internal justification' and the mechanisms applied by rulers and ruled within these processes. Weber gives us the picture from the outside, but not the one from the inside. We know who gives orders, who listens to whom, who carries out decisions, what the relationship is between rulers and the subjects of rule, but we do not know how this relationship is achieved. Weber's concept does not give an answer to the question of why certain people believe in certain forms of authority and not in others. We do not know, for example, where the factor of manipulation comes into play, nor where and when an individual's instrumentality finds its expression in the dominating (hegemonic) world-view.

This is one more argument which shows that Weber's theory of legitimacy should be applied where it works at it's best – as a taxonomic, descriptive 'one-sided accentuation' of social phenomena. The concept of legitimacy as an ideal type should be the first stage in empirical research, with the second stage concentrating on its explanatory aspects which deal with questions of 'why' and 'how'.

An objection that is most often raised in connection with Weber's theory of legitimacy is related to the number of, and relationships between, types of legitimate authority. There is no agreement among scholars working within the Weberian tradition on these questions.

Weber proposed three types of legitimate authority: legal–rational, traditional and charismatic. Friedrich opposed all of these arguing that every political system has its own form of legitimacy. Barker accepted Weber's typology but added one more form of legitimate authority, the value–rational type. Rigby[62] also endorsed Weber's taxonomy but developed another type – goal–rational. Bendix and Murvar[63] identified nine different types of legitimate authority: charismatic, revolutionary, usurpational, oligarchic, patrimonialist, hierocratic, feudal, free city structures and legal–rational. Since my intention here is not to speculate about all possible types of legitimate authority, I will concentrate only on the types that have been singled out as the dominant forms of legitimacy in the State socialist societies.

LEGITIMACY IN STATE SOCIALISM

With the appearance of the Soviet Union and other political systems that adopted Marxist–Leninist doctrine as their official ideology and structural path of development, the Weberian concept of political legitimacy met its first challenge. These societies were quite definitely new. They were built mostly on the ashes of traditional monarchies or empires, but their new form of organisation was clearly anti-traditional. They developed highly bureaucratic and centralised institutional structures, but their purpose was rarely the rationality and functionality that Weber had in mind when he wrote about legal–rational type of rule. They also cultivated cults of personality that in many ways resemble Weber's charismatic authority, but since these lasted for decades and extended to millions of people rather than to the small charismatic community of followers, it is certain that this type of rule does not match Weber's description of charismatic authority. Hence, the question was: what kind of legitimate authority is at work here?

Students of legitimacy generally agree that sources of legitimacy in contemporary industrial societies are multiple, have distinct bases and more than one of them are at work simultaneously. State socialism is not an exception. In Rigby's view the complexity of legitimacy in the Soviet-type societies is characterised by the existence of elements of all three legitimacy types proposed by Weber.[64] Legal–rational legitimacy might be inferred from the scientifically driven organisation of a society that is based on formal written documents (laws, constitutions, party resolutions and programmes), bureaucratic administration with a precise hierarchy of offices, and the existence of staff with fixed salaries, relevant skills and levels of competence. However, since the essential feature of this system, the relationship between the State and the party 'is regulated by discretion and not by law' it is not possible to classify this form of authority as a solely legal–rational legitimacy. As Rigby explains: 'There is rationality here, but it is a substantive rationality rather than the formal rationality essential to rational–legal authority.'[65]

Although state socialist societies have revolutionary origins and thus anti-traditional roots, the extensive usage of traditional symbols from national history as well as the production of new symbols and traditions points toward elements of the Weberian traditional type of authority.

A similar situation prevailed with Lenin's personality cult. In many ways it exhibits elements of charismatic authority: a prophetic leader who spreads 'the word of truth' and who possesses 'the secrets of history and the means to the salvation of humanity' (Marxist–Leninist doctrine); and initially a small group of followers (Bolsheviks) who are inspired by the 'emotional impact of revelation'.

Nevertheless, while both traditional and charismatic elements of authority contribute to the general form of legitimacy in state socialism, neither one constitutes the main source of legitimacy. Rather it is what Rigby calls the goal–rational type of authority that makes up the essence of legitimacy in Soviet-type societies. The justifiable type of rule is one that is drawn from 'the validity of the principal social goals that the authorities claim to represent and promote'. The rationality at work here can only be evaluated in terms of the tasks accomplished in the realisation of the main overall goal. This goal is vaguely defined as 'communism'. As Rigby indicates, this concept differs from similar 'plastic' formulations (freedom, democracy) which allow extensive room for manoeuvre to rulers, because 'it is not seen as an existing quality of the socio-political order but as something to be worked and fought for in the future'.[66] As such it imposes itself as the single overarching aim of the entire society. All other partial and intermediary goals and tasks are deduced from or related to this single overall goal. Hence, the promotions and claims along the social and political ladder are not based on technical competence and quality of outgrowth, 'but from success in a career of task-achieving assignments'.

Pakulski attempts to show that neither Weber's nor Rigby's typology is applicable to the analysis of mass compliance in state socialist societies.[67] The legal–rational type of legitimacy is out of the question because the social structure of state socialist societies contradicts Weber's ideal type. This is because such societies are characterised by systematic violations of the legislative system; clientelism, a 'grey economy', nepotism and other informal organisational activities are not only widespread but society is largely dependent on them. There is no strict division between the official and private spheres, while technical competence is irrelevant to the recruitment and promotion of officials in comparison with ideological 'competence' and political obedience.

Although charismatic authority is often pointed out as typical of state socialism, Pakulski finds no support for such claims. In Weber's theory charisma includes deep and sincere devotion to authority. Since it is unknown whether compliance with authority in communist states was 'a part of engineered ritual and propaganda', fear, the result of blackmail, material rewards or true belief, according to Pakulski, one has to rule out this type of legitimacy. In addition, Weber conceptualised charismatic authority as one that is characterised by a loose and distorted social structure, which stands in opposition to highly centralised and bureaucratised state socialist societies.

Traditional authority is also regarded by Pakulski as insignificant in the explanation of mass compliance. These societies are characterised as genuinely anti-traditional, modernising, industrialised and secular. If traditional symbols are used by the rulers, as in an appeal to nationalism, they are highly selective, rare and basically in tension with communist ideology. As Pakulski says, 'they reflect not so much an accomplishment as desperate attempts by the rulers to use some elements of tradition, especially national symbols and rhetoric, to mobilise the waning support from the ruled'.[68]

The goal–rational type of authority proposed by Rigby has also generated critisism. In Pakulski's view Soviet-type societies had no clearly defined principal goals around which a ruler's validity could be claimed. Most of the principles often mentioned are mutually exclusive, vague, or utopian. There is also a stark discrepancy in the interpretations of the set goals between rulers and ruled. Finally, as some studies show, the general tenets of Marxist–Leninist doctrine were not taken seriously by the majority of the population.

Instead of Weber's and Rigby's typology and explanation, Pakulski offers a new concept that in his view characterises all Soviet-type societies – 'conditional tolerance'. His main point is that in the case of Soviet-type societies we cannot refer to a Weberian type of legitimacy but rather a 'quasi-legitimacy' which is 'artificial in the sense that "substitute" claims are administratively produced and disseminated'. Mass compliance in his view is not the result of popular belief in the regime's right to rule, but is deduced 'from social perceptions of relative costs and benefits of (in)subordination'. As Pakulski makes clear:

> This is based on a belief that the rulers act rationally and in accordance with some known (but not necessarily accepted) 'codes'. It is therefore normally clear which types of behaviour are likely to be rewarded and which increase the risk of punishment. It is also known roughly what may be the nature and extent of the negative and positive sanctions, since both are widely publicised.[69]

However, he himself recognises that his concept is better applied to the satellite states of east and central Europe than societies that arose from the authentic communist revolutions.

Like Pakulski, Lane finds Rigby's concept of goal–rational authority inadequate for the explanation of legitimacy in the State socialist societies in general and Soviet Union in particular.[70] She emphasises the temporal dimension that has been largely neglected in Rigby's theory: sources and types of legitimacy change our time. The overall goal of 'communism', if it ever spread to the masses, has largely disappeared in the more recent period. Rigby has also neglected the fact that there are two competing 'hierarchies of stratification' at work here: a political elite whose actions could be labelled as goal–rational, and a professional or expert elite whose behaviour and motives could be characterised as functional rationality. As Lane argues: 'Striving towards the goal of communism may still be an appropriate device for creating cohesion within the political elite but it no longer suffices to integrate those functional elites basing their position on professional achievement.'[71]

A similar situation prevails with the broader masses. In order to preserve mass compliance the rulers have to rely on other forms of legitimacy. Hence, goal rationality might still exist as an organising principle around which communist society is set up, but 'it is no longer the predominant source of regime legitimacy'.

Like Rigby, Lane finds elements of legal–rational and charismatic authority in state socialism, but differently from both Rigby and Pakulski, identifies the traditional type of authority as the dominant force of legitimation in Soviet-type societies. In the case of the Soviet Union, traditionalism is related less to the pre-Revolutionary period of Tsarist Russia or to Orthodox religion than to the new Soviet traditions established after the revolution. Lane distinguishes between three 'holy Soviet traditions': the revolutionary tradition that draws on the myths and events of the October revolution and the civil war; the patriotic tradition that derives from the events of World War II; and the labour tradition originating with the heavy industrialisation of the Stalin period.

The rulers justify their position in relation to these three traditions. The aim is to demonstrate continuity with the pre-Revolutionary Bolshevik movement, with the victorious results of World War II, and with the successes achieved in the industrialisation and development of the country. Since these traditions must have material form in order to be recognised among the masses, they are mainly exercised through rituals. These ritual practices include initiation into socio-political aggregates and institutions (pioneers, communist youth, army, working class), mass political holidays (May Day, Women's Day, Revolution Day), military parades, holy places, existence of heroes (revolutionary hero, war hero and labour hero), military symbolism and so on. As Lane emphasises, these rituals are primarily intended for the masses,[72] and consequently the stress is on symbolism and the active participation of citizens.

In distinguishing between normative legitimacy ('as postulated by ideology') and real legitimacy ('as empirically measured'), Lane concludes that although official ideology is formulated in the spirit of the Enlightenment, appealing to science and progress, the true sources of legitimacy in Soviet society are deeply conservative and traditionalist.

Gill accepts this evaluation of Soviet-type societies as basically traditionalist and characterised by the intensive presence of myths,

symbols and hero worship.[73] In addition he emphasises underdevel-
opment in the economic and political sphere, low education standards and the peasant form of political culture as being characteristics of all these societies. However, he finds traditionalism in itself as
insufficient for the explanation of dominant legitimacy types. The
traditionalist structure of these societies only appears to be 'fertile
ground' for authoritarian forms of rule; hence it is charismatic
authority that can be singled out as the dominant form of the
regime's legitimacy. What is specific to these societies is the presence
of strong personality cults. Although these cults seem at the first sight
to be in conflict with the collectivist ethos of Marxist–Leninist
doctrine, Gill believes that they are fully compatible. It is his view that
ruling doctrine/theory, including its myths and symbols, had on the
one hand to be articulated in a way understandable and appealing to
the masses, and on the other, to be unique and unquestionable. This
could only be achieved if the ideology is personalised in the form of a
single, strong and infallible leader. In Gill's words: 'because of the
claims for the infallibility of the doctrine, there could be only one line
of theory publicly espoused. This created enormous pressures to
acknowledge one individual as the theoretician of the movement.'[74]
This leader–theoretician is soon perceived as the 'father' or 'teacher',
as the one who performs miracles and who is firm and uncompromising in accomplishing the goals of society. He also establishes a 'mystical union' with his supporters through myths and symbols.[75] Once this
position has been established and a 'special role has been attributed
to the leader in the birth of the regime', as Gill points out, it is 'difficult to deny him a similar role in the post-revolutionary era. The
legitimacy of the leader's position thus came to be rooted in the basic
legitimacy of the system.'[76] What is important here, according to Gill,
is how the rule is perceived by the regime's subjects, because that is
the crucial element in Weber's concept of charisma. The followers
perceive the regime through its leader and it is the leader alone who
appears as 'the sole legitimate figure in the regime's symbolic web'.
The devotion and gratitude is not given to the party but exclusively to
the leader. The leader is seen not only as the interpreter of the
doctrine but also as a source of the doctrine. In his analysis of Stalin's
routinisation of Lenin's personality cult, Gill demonstrates how Stalin
skilfully managed to make a transition from mere a interpreter of
Lenin's works to the main and only source of Soviet ideology. In
contrast to Trotsky and Zinoviev who attempted to establish themselves after Lenin's death as Lenin's comrades and logical successors,
Stalin used intelligent tactics by portraying himself as 'Lenin's most
faithful pupil' and as the only true Leninist, which was much more
appealing to the party membership and later to the masses. Soon

after he acquired power, this portrait was transformed into one of equal partnership (the Lenin–Stalin duo), which ended up in the 1930s as the sole cult of Stalin.

As Gill emphasises this type of authority is also directly connected with the revolutionary nature of these societies. All the societies he analyses have undergone indigenous revolutions (the Soviet Union, China, but also Vietnam, Yugoslavia, Cuba). Therefore the charismatic type of authority had its roots in the negation of the previous political and economic system. The identification with the strong personalities of Lenin, Stalin, Mao, Castro or Ho Chi Minh is, as in Weber's concept of charisma, a form of the rejection of routine structures. These individual's who appear to be in control of society, as both Weber and Gill stress, are also perceived as the ones that can offer security and certainty 'in a changing and uncertain world'.

The point raised indirectly by Gill and Pakulski and directly by Denitch and Tarifa[77] about a distinction between Soviet-type societies which resulted in authentic revolutions as in the Soviet Union, China, Cuba or Yugoslavia, and societies where communist ideas were brought in with the help of Soviet tanks as in Poland, Hungary or Czechoslovakia, is of crucial importance. Although all these societies have many elements in common, the nature of their political legitimacy differs significantly in regard to their revolutionary tradition.

The analyses of legitimacy that follow in chapters three, four and five will attempt to identify the dominant forms of political authority in post-World War II Yugoslavia and in post-communist Serbia and Croatia by applying this Weberian framework and keeping in mind this distinction. As we will see later, all these societies under study have undergone some form of revolutionary change in their political and economic systems. While the second Yugoslavia arose from an indigenous revolution that occurred simultaneously with the liberation of the country after World War II, Serbia went through an 'anti-bureaucratic revolution' in the late 1980s; the change of government and socio-political order in 1990 also led to the radical reorganisation of society in Croatia.

The analysis of case studies will help us not only to test the applicability of the models appropriate are developed by Rigby, Lane, Pakulski and Gill in the cases of Yugoslavia, Serbia and Croatia, but will also establish how adequate and sufficient the general Weberian position is in the study of political legitimacy.

Legitimacy, ideology and the new state

So far I have formulated a theoretical and operational frame for the analysis of ideology and its structure, as well as for the identification of political legitimacy types in state socialist societies. What I have not discussed yet is the relationship between legitimacy and ideology and especially their place within the process of the formation of the new state.

For some authors, such as Abercrombie, Turner and Hill[78] contemporary societies need no ideology to function properly. It is economic efficiency and prosperity that are the principal sources of legitimate rule. For US writers from the early days of the Cold War,[79] force itself was the principal reason for the existence of 'totalitarian dictatorships'.

Although economic prosperity and efficiency are very important sources of legitimacy in every society, material 'reward' alone is rarely a 'winning formula' to be used for potential rulers. With coercion this is almost never the case. There always has to be a set of common beliefs and ideas formulated and exercised through practices shared in one way or another by rulers and their subjects. Neither coercion nor 'reward' provides rulers with the legitimate equipment for governing. In other words, every society has to rely on some form of dominant ideology.

This, however, does not mean that there is a single ideology at work in every society, as Geertz and functionalists would imply. Neither does it mean that individuals and groups in a particular society accept the dominant ideology to a similar extent. It does not mean that dominant ideology operates in the same way at the top and the bottom of the social pyramid, nor that their contents are alike. It also does not mean that some structural determinants, such as a particular form of the organisation of production, shapes the dominant ideology, as Marxists would insist.

What is claimed here is only that every society has to function within some set of commonly accepted ideas and practices regardless of how broadly they might be formulated. When, why and how a certain type of beliefs, ideas and practices replaces the previously dominant set of beliefs, ideas and practices are some of the questions that this study aims to answer.

To be able to detect and analyse a dominant ideology in a particular society, it is necessary firstly to take a look from the outside – to identify the type of political legitimacy at work. For those who operate within the Weberian tradition that means testing against empirical data whether the society under investigation rests on traditional, legal–rational, charismatic, value–rational or any other type of legitimate authority. As already explained, Weberian ideal types of legitimacy will be employed here only for taxonomic purposes. As soon as the form of authority at work has been identified, the analysis will move towards the form and content and the function of a particular dominant ideology. Thus, the relationship between legitimacy and ideology in this study is that of legitimacy being a frame, and ideology being a content of analysis. The analysis of legitimacy will focus on the picture that a particular society displays to the outside world: the relationship between rulers and ruled, the leaders' position, institutional mechanisms of legitimacy achievement such as the relationship between the ruling party, educational system, and the mass media. The analysis of ideology will give us the picture from the inside: a structure and content of normative and operational ideologies, their relationships and level of congruence and dimensions of ideological argumentation.

The three societies analysed in this study share one important common characteristic. They are all 'new societies' appearing as a result of war, revolutionary change and the establishment of a new independent state. As such they are particularly in need of establishing and demonstrating legitimate authority. As the revolution by definition is an illegitimate mechanism of change of regime, the new political structures have to 'explain the revolution' and make new ideas compatible with the already existing essential values of the society in order to justify their dominance. They have somehow to connect the new system of ideas and practices with the values, ideas and practices regarded as the traditions of the particular society. If the new 'symbolic frames' differ significantly from society's traditions, the new rulers will have a more difficult task to achieve. To succeed in their aims new rulers have also to delegitimise the previous political order as well as all other political concepts that could attempt to make a claim on 'throne'. They also have to reformulate the image of the new internal and external enemy.

The new regime, if it stemmed from a revolution, will attempt as long as possible to derive its legitimacy and 'moral authority' from the mass mobilisation achieved during the revolutionary period or civil war. The sacrifices made in that period, especially in the form of human lives, will be shaped as the cults of victimisation and remain as cornerstones of the new political system. The power holders of the new regime are also almost certain to attempt making their rule in the eyes of the public identical to the existence of the new state. In other words, if the power holders are opposed by the counter elite, they will seek to delegitimise it not as opponents of the particular policies of the new regime but as being against the existence of the new state or the new political order, or both. The important questions here are why, when and under what conditions some ruling elites succeed in 'imposing' their picture of social reality on the public as the credible one as opposed to the counter elite's concepts of the same reality, while other regimes are not able to achieve the same goal.

This study will attempt to show that in exceptional situations such as the establishment and formation of the new state, the impact of elite group behaviour on the shape and direction of dominant values can become decisive for the society's ideological organisation. As I will try to demonstrate later with the example of the case studies, in situations such as the construction of the new state with a new authority in power, the role of individual power holding agents can be crucial for the determination and direction of all key social actions.

This study will look at three societies (Yugoslavia 1945–60, Serbia 1987–97 and Croatia 1990–97) where the particular power elite have been successful in articulating the dominant vision of the social reality. This study focuses on the short periods of time immediately after the establishment of the new state and the new political order. In my view this is the period when the ideas, values and practices, in other words, the ideology, of the dominant group makes the strongest appeal to the public and is shared as a dominant ideology in one way or another by the majority of the population.

As far as the relationship between ideology 'disseminated' by the power holders and its reception among the public is concerned, this study will analyse only the first part of that relationship – the structure of official or normative ideology and operative ideology, their congruence and dissimilarities – and not the second part – how, in what form, and whether the masses have accepted the 'offered' ideology. This is because it is extremely difficult to identify and prove empirically, any conclusions, especially in authoritarian types of societies where as Shlapentokh points out, insincere answers by respondents makes it impossible to trust the results of surveys and public polls.[80] Similarly with election results, since, for the most part, no properly democratic elections were held. Hence in the case of post-World War II Yugoslavia, I am in no position directly to prove whether the 'disseminated' ideology functioned as a dominant ideology. However, using indirect ways recommended by Huntington and Beetham,[81] one can look at mass mobilisation to establish how widespread a particular ideology was. To emphasise again, the existence of a dominant ideology does not imply that the majority of the population is familiar with most of the ideas and concepts expressed in the ruling ideology, but only that it clearly shows support for some central principles and values of the 'disseminated' ideology. Since in all three of my case studies the power-keeping ideology was sustained by intensive mass mobilisation and in Serbia and Croatia by popular support through plebiscitary-type election results in favour of the ruling party and referendums held on crucial political issues (independence, the change of constitution), it is obvious that the ideas and values promoted by the power holders were accepted by the majority of the population. It is only in this way that I refer to the dominant ideology.

Therefore the acceptance of the dominant power-keeping ideology among the general public and the impact it made on the masses in this short period of time will here simply be taken for granted.

In the first part of this relationship the central issue is the impact of the dominant power-keeping ideology on the public via the educational and informational system. My aim here is not to focus on the reception of the particular ideology among the public, which is a completely different study, but on the ways in which official or normative and operative ideologies work. I am concentrating here on the relationship between dominant forms of legitimacy and the structure of particular ideology. The intention is to look at the ways in which normative ideology is translated into its operative form through the mass media and the educational system and how this process is related to the dominant form of legitimacy. As we will see in all three case studies the power holders have a monopoly of information, whether in the form of total and direct control of all TV, radio stations and newspapers as in the case of post-World War II Yugoslavia, or through the less direct but also firm control[82] over broadcasting and newspapers read by the majority of the population. As far as the educational system is concerned, the State monopoly here is almost universal in all modern states, since the State's ministries of education are responsible for approving for the textbooks to be published and used in the educational system. As I have already explained in my formulation of the 'materiality of ideology' the monopoly over these two institutions is central for ideology 'dissemination'.

The types of legitimate authority and the process of 'ideology dissemination' will be studied at the three levels. First, I will identify the dominant form of political legitimacy for each of my three case studies by applying the Weberian typology and simultaneously testing the ideas and concepts of Rigby, Lane, Pakulski and Gill. Second, I will content analyse the political manifestos of the three ruling parties (LCY, SPS, CDC) in each of these three cases in order to identify the form and content of the normative ideology. The same procedure of content analysis will then be applied to newspaper editorials and school textbooks published in the three periods under study with the aim of identifying the form and content of the operative ideology. The goal of the analysis at this stage will be to reveal the relationship between the two forms of ideology. Third, I will concentrate on the relationship between the dominant forms of political legitimacy and ideology in each of the three cases. The analysis will look at how dominant forms of legitimacy are sustained by particular operative ideologies and vice versa.

The results of all of these analyses will also simultaneously serve the purpose of testing hypothetical claims on a more general level in regard to the analytical concept of ideology developed here, attempting to demonstrate the advantages of an inclusive definition of ideology and the rejection of true/false and science/non-science criteria in the study of ideology, as well as the plausibility of the conceptualisation of ideology as a universal, modern, material and rational entity.

NOTES

1 N. Machiavelli, *The Prince* (Cambridge: Cambridge University Press, 1988).
2 M. Weber, *Economy and Society* (New York: Bedminster Press, 1968).
3 Ibid., p. 215.
4 Ibid., p. 225.
5 Ibid., p. 215.
6 Ibid., p. 232.
7 Ibid.
8 Ibid., p. 215.
9 Ibid., p. 242.
10 Ibid., p. 248.
11 C. Friedrich, *Tradition and Authority* (London: Macmillan, 1972), p. 94
12 Ibid., p. 94.
13 Ibid., p. 90.
14 Ibid., p. 91.
15 Ibid.
16 R. Barker, *Political Legitimacy and the State* (Oxford: Clarendon Press, 1990).
17 Ibid., p. 2.
18 Ibid., p. 29.
19 Ibid., p. 28.
20 Ibid., p. 51.
21 Ibid.
22 See, for example, Barker, *Political Legitimacy*, pp. 59–60.
23 R. Miliband, *The State in Capitalist Society* (London: Weidenfeld & Nicolson, 1973).
24 Ibid., p. 197.
25 Ibid., p. 211.
26 Ibid., p. 234.
27 C. Offe, *Contradictions of the Welfare State* (London: Hutchinson, 1984).
28 Ibid., p.138.
29 Ibid., p.142.
30 J. Habermas, *Legitimation Crisis* (London: Heinemann, 1976).
31 However, it is worth noting that Habermas sees these legitimacy crises rather as tendencies which are chronic, but not necessarily acute.
32 Habermas, *Legitimation*, p. 97.
33 J. Schaar, 'Legitimacy in the Modern State', in W. Connoly (ed.), *Legitimacy and the State* (Oxford: Basil Blackwell, 1984), p. 109
34 Ibid., p. 123.
35 Barker, *Political Legitimacy*, p. 74.
36 S. M. Lipset, 'Social Conflict, Legitimacy, and Democracy', in W. Connoly (ed.), *Legitimacy and the State* (Oxford: Basil Blackwell, 1984), p. 88.
37 Ibid., p. 89.
38 G. Kateb, 'On the "Legitimation Crisis", *Social Research*, 4 (1979), pp. 695–727.
39 Ibid., p. 696.
40 Ibid., p. 720.
41 T. Gurr, *Why Men Rebel* (Princeton, NJ: Princeton University Press, 1970), p. 186.

42 Ibid., p.187.

43 Ibid., p.189.

44 As Grafstein shows, and I will elaborate more fully later in the text, there is a tension in Weber's theory between descriptive and explanatory conceptualisations of legitimacy as an ideal type. See R. Grafstein, 'The Failure of Weber's Conception of Legitimacy: Its Causes and Implications', *Journal of Politics*, 43 (1981), pp. 456–72.

45 Habermas, *Legitimation*, p. 95.

46 Nevertheless this argument should be brought down to a reasonable, less ambitious level of generality in order not to conflate economic and political legitimacy – a common tendency in Marxist and critical approaches.

47 Schaar's theory might be an exception here since he speaks of modernity instead of capitalism. However, his theory also concentrates on the analysis of modern capitalist states where modernity is often a synonymous with capitalism.

48 Grafstein, 'The Failure', p. 456.

49 See, for example, P. Blau, 'Critical Remarks on Weber's Theory of Authority', *American Political Science Review*, 67 (1963), pp. 305–23; A. DeJasay, *The State* (Oxford: Oxford University Press, 1985); and J. O'Kane, 'Against Legitimacy', *Political Studies*, 16 (1993), pp. 471–87.

50 Grafstein, 'The Failure', p. 456.

51 Barker, *Political Legitimacy*, p. 59.

52 Ibid., p. 57.

53 Grafstein, 'The Failure', p. 466.

54 As S. Lukes points out, although Weber defined himself as a methodological individualist, his historical analyses, stratification theory and explanation of the rationalisation of the modern world, are all based on structural (collectivist) factors. S. Lukes, *Individualism* (Oxford: Basil Blackwell, 1973), pp. 111–12.

55 Barker, *Political Legitimacy*, p. 58.

56 As it is possible to see in Weber and Giddens, ideal types differ from plain descriptive concepts (*Gattungsbegriffe*), since they include 'the one-sided accentuation of one or more points of view', while descriptive types only 'summarise the common features of groupings of empirical phenomena'. See Weber, *Economy and Society*, pp. 23–5 and A. Giddens, *Capitalism and Modern Social Theory: An Analysis of the Writings of Marx, Durkheim and Max Weber* (Cambridge: Cambridge University Press, 1971), pp. 141–4.

57 What also differentiates Friedrich from Weber is Friedrich's perception of authority as an exclusively agency-centred feature ('the loss of authority of a political leader as he ages does not deprive him of legitimacy, although it may eventually deprive him of his power'), whereas Weber speaks of legitimate authority in terms of both rulers (agency) and regimes (political structures). See Friedrich, *Tradition and Authority*, p. 97.

58 D. Beetham, *The Legitimation of Power* (Atlantic Highlands, NJ: Humanities Press International, 1991).

59 See, for example, W. Mommsen, *The Age of Bureaucracy* (Oxford: Blackwell, 1974), and H. Pitkin, *Wittgenstein and Justice* (Berkeley, CA: University of California Press, 1972).

60 Habermas, *Legitimation*, p. 97.

61 Barker, *Political Legitimacy*, p. 25.

62 T. Rigby, 'The Conceptual Approach to Authority, Power and Policy in the Soviet Union', in T. Rigby, A. Brown and P. Reddaway (eds), *Authority, Power and Policy in the USSR* (London: Macmillan, 1980).

63 V. Murvar, *Theory of Liberty, Legitimacy and Power: New Directions in the Intellectual and Scientific Theory of Max Weber* (London: Routledge & Kegan Paul, 1985), and R. Bendix, 'Review Essay: Economy and Society by Max Weber', *American Sociological Review*, 34 (1969), pp. 555–8.

64 T. Rigby, 'Introduction: Political Legitimacy, Weber and Communist Mono-Organisational Systems', in T. Rigby and F. Feher (eds), *Political Legitimation in Communist States* (London: Macmillan, 1982).

65 Rigby, 'The Conceptual Approach', p. 19.
66 Ibid.
67 J. Pakulski, 'Legitimacy and Mass Compliance: Reflections on Max Weber and Soviet-type Societies', *British Journal of Political Science*, 16, 1 (1986) pp. 45–63.
68 Ibid., p. 43.
69 Ibid., p. 48.
70 C. Lane, 'Legitimacy and Power in the Soviet Union Through Socialist Ritual', *British Journal of Political Science*, 14 (1984).
71 Ibid., p. 210.
72 As Lane observes: 'It is no accident that there is no rite of initiation into the Party and no labour ritual for intelligentsia professions.' See Lane, 'Legitimacy', pp. 215–16.
73 See G. Gill, 'Political Myth and Stalin's Quest for Authority in the Party', in T. Rigby, A. Brown and P. Reddaway (eds), *Authority, Power and Policy in the USSR* (London: Macmillan, 1980), and G. Gill, 'Personal Dominance and the Collective Principle: Individual Legitimacy in Marxist–Leninist Systems', in T. Rigby and F. Feher (eds), *Political Legitimation in Communist States* (London: Macmillan, 1982).
74 Gill, 'Personal Dominance', p. 104.
75 The leaders themselves often function as symbols, such as in the case of Lenin after his death. As Gill emphasises, 'the primary point of legitimacy in the system thereby became Lenin and only secondarily the events of October. Lenin was transformed into a symbol.' Gill, 'Political Myth', p. 101.
76 Gill, 'Personal Dominance', p. 99. Analysing the formation of Stalin's cult, Gill (p. 111) gives the following example:

> the saturation of the media and of society in general by the image of Stalin as the perfect leader of genius infallibility guiding the country into the era of communism placed the opposition in an invidious position. If all Stalin's actions could be justified in terms of further advancing the march to communism, any criticism of or opposition to him personally could be interpreted as opposition to communism. Opposition to Stalin based on personal, policy or ideological grounds was thus transformed into treason against the Leninist cause and the fatherland.

77 See B. Denitch, *The Legitimation of a Revolution: The Yugoslav Case* (New Haven, CT: Yale University Press, 1976); B. Denitch (ed.), *The Legitimation of Regimes* (London: Sage, 1979); and F. Tarifa, 'The Quest for Legitimacy and the Withering Away of Utopia', *Social Forces*, 76, 2 (1997), pp. 437–74.
78 See N. Abercrombie, S. Hill, S. and B. Turner, 'The Dominant Ideology Thesis', *British Journal of Sociology*, 29 (1978), pp. 149–70, and N. Abercrombie, S. Hill and B. Turner, *Dominant Ideology Thesis* (London: Unwin Hyman, 1980).
79 Z. Brzeziniski and C. Friedrich, *Totalitarianism, Dictatorship and Autocracy* (New York: Praeger, 1961).
80 V. Shlapentokh, 'The Study of Values as a Social Phenomenon: The Soviet Case', *Social Forces*, 61, 4 (1982), pp. 403–17.
81 See S. Huntington, *Political Order in Changing Societies* (New Haven, CT: Yale University Press, 1968).
82 In the case of post-communist Serbia and Croatia, it was officially the parliament not the ruling party that approved directors and managers of the main newspapers, TV and radio stations. However, since in both these cases the ruling party had an overwhelming majority in parliament, it was in a position to control broadcasting. The other way of controlling the mass media was the sell-off of the State-run media to individuals closely associated with the ruling party (M. Kutle in Croatia and the Karić brothers in Serbia).

Part II

The Case Studies

In the following three chapters, I will, first, very briefly sketch the historical periods under examination (Yugoslavia 1945–60, Serbia 1987–97 and Croatia 1990–97) by focusing on the central events and actors. Second, drawing on the Weberian framework, I will identify the dominant type of legitimacy in all three cases. Finally, I will establish the structure, form and content of the dominant normative and operative ideologies by content analysing the political manifestos of the three ruling parties (LCY, SPS, CDC), as well as school textbooks and newspaper editorials published in the same period. The analysis will also concentrate on the level of congruence between normative ideology and operative ideology.

3

Yugoslavia 1945–60

BRIEF HISTORICAL INTRODUCTION[1]

In contrast to other 'people's democracies' of eastern Europe, and because of numerous and well-organised partisan resistance movements led by Josip Broz Tito and the communists, Yugoslavia was in a position to await the end of World War II as a mainly self-liberated country. Large parts of the country were ruined by war and human casualties were enormous. Most of the population consisted of illiterate and semi-literate peasants working on the land owned by wealthy landlords. There were few big cities and industry was developed only sporadically. In 1945 the government introduced agrarian reform which aimed to expropriate land from large landowners and establish 'peasant working co-operatives'. After questionably free elections in 1946, the communists obtained an overwhelming majority in parliament which enabled them to approve a new constitution modelled on the 1936 Soviet constitution. The country officially became a federation of six republics, while in fact the application of the 'democratic centralism' principle meant that power was in the hands of the central committee of the Yugoslav Communist Party and its leader, Tito. Soon after, more than 80 per cent of industry, mining, transport, banking and trading sectors were nationalised and the first five-year development plan approved. A programme of rapid industrialisation commenced.

In 1947, Yugoslavia still had significant territorial disputes with Italy over Trieste and Austria over the Koruška region which contributed further to the development of antagonistic feelings towards the West, and even closer links with the Soviet Union. As a result of Yugoslavia's pro-Soviet sympathies, the Comintern's information bureau (Cominform) was established in Belgrade.

In 1948, after several ultimatums from Moscow that were rejected by its Central Committee, the Yugoslav Communist Party was expelled from Cominform for 'pursuing a policy of nationalism and Trotskyism', and for 'deviation from Marxism and Leninism'.[2] In 1949 the

Soviet Union, as well as all other Eastern European 'people's democracies' broke off relations with Yugoslavia, describing Tito and the Yugoslav communist leadership as 'an enemy of the Soviet Union' that is 'in the hands of assassins and imperialist spies'.[3]

To respond to these attacks, the Yugoslav government in 1950 started to introduce 'workers' councils in all state economic enterprises with the motto, 'giving the factories to the workers', and developing a new political, economic and ideological order that was officially known as 'socialist self-management'. In addition, military assistance agreements were signed with the US government which secured military equipment and expertise from the US army. The US and Western governments also provided economic and other aid in these grim years so that by 1960, Yugoslavia had received more than US$2 billion worth of non-repayable Western aid.[4]

The period 1953–60 was a time of intensive industrialisation, political liberalisation, moderate decentralisation and dynamic economic development in Yugoslavia with GDP growing at 8.1 per cent annually. As Cohen points out, 'in only two decades, Yugoslavia had been transformed from an underdeveloped agrarian society into a moderately developed industrial country with enhanced economic capacity, research infrastructure, technical competence and participation in international trade'.[5] The Communist Party introduced economic and political reforms and embarked on a policy of international nonalignment. The new 1953 constitution provided for economic, media and education policy to be decided by the republics and not solely on the federal level as before. Soon after Stalin died in 1955, Yugoslavia and the Soviet Union signed the Belgrade agreement under which the Soviet Union recognised an independent Yugoslav 'road to socialism' and normalised its relations with Yugoslavia.

Political legitimacy

If we apply the Weberian typology to an analysis of legitimacy in post-World War II Yugoslavia, we can see that all the proposed types – traditional, legal–rational, charismatic, goal–rational and value–rational – can be supported by data.

Elements of both types of traditional legitimacy, pre-socialist traditions referred to by Rigby and the new socialist traditions emphasised and analysed by Lane, were present in post-war Yugoslavia. The new traditions and new symbols were often simply modelled on the already existing patterns of traditional culture. This was particularly the case with patriotic songs which glorified Tito and the partisans and were based on old folk-songs used to praise national heroes (Marko Kraljević, Hajduk Veljko) who had fought the Ottoman and

Austro-Hungarian conquerors.[6] Existing traditions and myths were also used by preserving their form but changing their content. A good example was the case of the peasant rebel, Matija Gubec, whose revolt against and suffering under the Habsburg (thus foreign) landlords were directed away from their original function as elements of a Croatian national myth and into a socialist-shaped myth that emphasised Gubec's 'class' position and peasant origins against the feudalist 'class' position and aristocratic origins of his torturer, Tahi.

The dominant traditional values such as 'keeping face' (*sačuvati obraz*), heroism and manliness (*junaštvo* and *čojstvo*), as well as hero worship, were also preserved in rituals and popular culture. Thus, instead of *uskoks* and *hajduks* who were traditionally praised as heroic guerrillas invading Ottoman territory in the seventeenth and eighteenth centuries, one found communist partisans in their place as the new heroes and martyrs in epics of everyday life. Dominant collective and egalitarian values which had their roots in the patriarchal culture of traditional extended families typical of southern Slavs who inhabited joint patrilinear households called *zadrugas*,[7] also found expression in the dominant socialist ideology as 'the egalitarian syndrome'.[8]

Although different from its Soviet counterpart, Yugoslav state socialism was not short of holy traditions and corresponding rituals. However, since the 'national liberation war' was fought in parallel with the socialist revolution, both formed a single and important source of traditional legitimacy – the revolutionary–patriotic tradition. Almost all holy places and rituals were related in a direct or indirect way to this tradition. These included initiation into major political organisations, such as the Union of Pioneers or the Socialist Youth Union, and taking a solemn oath when entering compulsory military service. Mass political holidays had a central place in these rituals. These included Republic Day, Army Day, Uprising Day for each Republic and most importantly, Youth Day which also marked the official birthday of Marshal Tito.[9] Military parades accompanied some of these events and student excursions were regularly organised as visits to 'holy' places of revolutionary and patriotic war (Sutjeska, Neretva, Drvar, Jasenovac[10]) or to Tito's birthplace (Kumrovec). In addition, the revolutionary–patriotic tradition relied on a number of heroes among whom the most important were Ivo Lola Ribar,[11] Filip Filipović and Sava Kovačević, who all died very young in the war. However, the most important war hero was the party and state leader himself – Tito.

Although virtually non-existent in the later years of state socialism, the labour tradition had a prominent place in the immediate post-war years. Youth was ritualistically organised into working brigades that participated 'voluntarily' in the rebuilding of the country. They also competed in terms of who set more railway tracks, dug more land, cleared away more bushes or unloaded more coal wagons. There was also the institution of the Labour Hero, the most important of whom was a coalminer, Alija Sirotanović who broke the daily coal-digging record formerly held by Soviet miner, Strakhanov, which became a crucial factor of national pride in the years immediately following the break in relations with the Soviet Union in 1948.[12]

All these examples show that traditions, old and new, played an important role in the process of the regime's legitimation. However, as Gill rightly points out, these traditions in themselves were not enough to serve as sources of legitimacy.[13] They certainly helped sustain the existing political system, but did not in themselves provide sources of legitimacy for state socialism. Rather, the regime had instrumentalised existing traditions in the direction that would fit its interests. As Pakulski stressed, the regime's use of traditionalism in state socialism was selective and most traditional values were in many ways contradictory to Enlightenment-shaped socialist ideology.[14] Additionally, a highly bureaucratised and complex society like communist Yugoslavia with its infinite variety of 'scientifically and theoretically developed' socialist institutions and organisations such as the 'basic organisation of associated labour', 'workers' councils', the 'self-management interest community', the 'independent organisation of associated labour', the 'executive federal council' or the 'contractual organisation of associated labour', could hardly accommodate the idea of traditional communities and authority that Weber had in mind. Finally and most importantly, is the fact that post-war Yugoslavia was a society built after a successful revolution. This meant the implementation of a revolutionary concept of society's organisation that would erase from the collective memory and delegitimise, all previous regimes and political systems that existed on its territory, including the 'feudal and regressive' Ottoman Empire, 'capitalist and exploitative' Austria-Hungary, and 'unjust and undeveloped' monarchist Yugoslavia (all three seen also as the 'prisoners of nations'). Yugoslav communists were striving to build a new, modern, blueprint modelled, rational and just society. So, is Weber's legal–rational model of authority adequate to explain the main source of legitimacy in post-war Yugoslavia?

There are elements that suggest it may be. For example, as in Weber's theory, communist Yugoslavia developed an unusually complex bureaucratic organisation with numerous institutions, esoteric language and concepts which other 'people's democracies' could hardly match. The official leading idea was to develop the most just society possible following the blueprint and 'discoveries' of scientific socialism formulated in the works of Marx and Lenin and further developed by the main LCY ideologist, Edvard Kardelj,[15] and other party theoreticians. In order to justify its independent position in the socialist world and the rightness of its 'own road to socialism', the Communist Party of Yugoslavia developed and introduced the concept of workers' self-management which was expressed through 'workers' councils' in the economy and the 'delegate system' in politics. The system also relied on written documents such as the constitution (federal and constitutions for each federal republic) and laws; all important organisations and institutions had their own statutes and programmes including the Communist Party of Yugoslavia, and all decisions reached during Party meetings and congresses regularly appeared as written party resolutions.

The regime attempted to legitimise its authority through a 'consistent system of abstract rules'. Since most private property was abolished and industry and land nationalised, there was no significant individual ownership; as such the Weberian principle separating administrative staff from the ownership of the means of production was satisfied. As in the legal–rational type, domination through knowledge was established: society was to be organised according to scientific principles of Marxism. There was also a strict hierarchy of offices with the pyramidal structure of power – from the Federal Central Committee of the Yugoslav Communist Party at the top to the 'Basic Organisation of Communist Party' (OOSK), in the town districts and villages at the bottom. As in Weber's concept state employees also had fixed salaries.

However, notwithstanding the existence of these elements of legal–rational type of authority in the post-war Yugoslavia, this type of legitimacy was the least likely to become the principal source of the regime's authority. There are two explanations. First, the relationship between the two central sources of power, the party and the State, was ambiguously defined in the constitution which recognised the Yugoslav Communist Party as 'having a leading role' in the society,[16] and as Rigby points out, the relationship between the two was directed not by law, but by discretion.[17] The contents of state laws were formulated by a narrow circle of the party leadership and then forwarded to lawmakers to frame in a juridical vocabulary. But more importantly, the laws and constitution were not obeyed at all when there was no time to change particular articles that would become an obstacle after periodic changes in the party/state policies. This practice can best be illustrated by Tito's famous and often quoted sentence on one such occasion when he accused those working in jurisprudence in the following way: 'our judges follow the laws as the drunk men who stick to the fence'. Another typical example would be the following argument in *Borba*:

It is really inconceivable that the members of temporary administration of Solicitor's union do not agree with the expulsion of notorious
criminals and traitors justifying that attitude by some 'juridical'
reasons. [They argue] that Ljotić, Vasić and company cannot be inter-
rogated [in their absence] as if their slaughter – oriented and against
people motivated work during the entire period of occupation is not
well known to everybody and especially to those gentlemen.[18]

Second, Yugoslav society was characterised by the extensive practice
of clientelism and nepotism and a very weak division between private
and official spheres that contradicts Weber's model of legal–rational
authority. There was also a huge sector of the black and 'grey' economy in society with more than 2.2 million people involved.[19] Finally,
technical competence was of little importance in comparison with
political competence. This was especially the case in the immediate
post-war years, when highly qualified individuals were forced to work
in the fields and in factories as manual workers. In addition, employment in the State institutions meant that one's 'moral–political character' was assessed as one of the key elements for taking up certain
positions. The fact that Tito was made president for life in 1974 is an
other example of how legal–rational elements were deemed less
important for the regime's legitimacy.

A much more important source of legitimacy in post-war Yugoslavia
was the charismatic authority of Tito. He was perceived as a prophetic
leader who brought and adopted the sacred doctrine of Marxism–
Leninism to Yugoslavia, who successfully conducted a social revolution and set up a millenarian target – communism. But more importantly, he achieved a 'miracle' by liberating and uniting the country
with a handful of devoted followers against the superior military
power of German and Italian forces and their domestic collaborators. It
was emphasised on many occasions that the Yugoslav Communist Party
had only 5,000 members at the beginning of the war and still managed to
organise a large partisan force of 800,000 soldiers by the end of the war.[20]
Tito was regarded as having exceptional qualities such as military and
strategic genius in conducting war operations among which the most
important was his artful and lucid plan to deceive German forces and
successfully transport thousands of wounded partisans over the Neretva
river in 1943, and his masterly escape from his headquarters in Drvar in
1944 against a well-planned German offensive. Tito was also perceived as
an important moral authority and a world-class statesman by establishing himself as a leader of peace and the non-aligned movement
together with Nehru of India and Nasser of Egypt.

His personality cult had enormous dimensions. Just as in the
case of Stalin or Mao, monuments to him were erected all over the

country while he was still alive. Every town and city had a central street or square named after him, and several cities were renamed after him (Titograd, Titov Veles, Titovo Velenje). Postal stamps were issued with his photos and poets dedicated their poems to him. All these elements are fully in accordance with Weber's idea of charismatic personality.

However, what is most important in Weber's concept of charismatic authority is the popular perception of the authority. The devotion to authority has to be deep and sincere. In my opinion this is exactly where Weber's model is most applicable. Although there were no free elections held in Yugoslavia, Tito had all the characteristics of the plebiscitary ruler.

As Beetham points out, in societies where democratic elections do not take place, one can infer the regime's popularity from mass mobilisation.[21] Tito's rule in post-war Yugoslavia had popular appeal. Although support was not spread equally among all strata, nationalities and republics and varied through time, mass attendance of big political rallies in his support, the presence of Tito's name in popular folk-songs and his universally positive image in political jokes leads one to conclude that the majority of the Yugoslav population had a deep and sincere devotion to Tito. Tito's name could just as well mobilise miners such as Alija Sirotanović to set a new record in production, as motivate youth brigades to lay the first railway line after the war (i.e. Šamac–Sarajevo railway), agricultural producers to achieve record harvests or industrial workers to fulfil the first five-year plan ahead of the time. This was much more the case in the post-war period (1945–60) which is the period under examination here, than in the later years of his rule.[22] Some of the numerous songs, sayings and slogans such as 'comrade Tito we swear to you that we will not deviate from the road you set', 'comrade Tito, our white violet, you are loved by the whole youth', 'comrade Tito, our dew-covered flower, the whole people follow you' were often spontaneously shouted at football matches and other non-political gatherings. All these rituals and practices were, of course, also a part of the regime's orchestrated and planned propaganda and this will be more fully analysed later in the text. However, what is crucial here is that the emotions and feelings of people who participated in all these actions and events were real and sincere: they felt excitement when Tito visited their towns and factories, were proud of him as a 'world leader' and cried when he died. These people really worshipped their leader. It is not important whether they were also manipulated and brainwashed, they truly had special feelings of devotion to Tito's charismatic authority.

Like Lenin and Castro, Tito was the leader who achieved a special role in the birth of the new regime and as Gill points out, the legitimacy of this type of system is in many ways equated and identified with the leader. The party was also perceived by the masses as being less important than the leader. For example, the party and its leading officials could be criticised for certain policies, and were often the object of jokes, but this could hardly happen to the leader, because attacking or questioning of the leader was perceived as questioning the dominant value system – 'of our system', 'of our country', and, consequently, 'of us'. Tito was seen by many as a fatherlike figure – a protector, a teacher and a saviour. For example, he was often called 'old man' (*'stari'*), the name used colloquially for the father in Yugoslavia. The firm and uncompromising leader who knows 'where he is going' was particularly needed in this period of radical change, when nothing was predictable. He was perceived by the masses as the only source of security in this rapidly changing world.

Pakulski's criticism that Weber's concept of charismatic authority is related to loose and distorted social structures and is hence inapplicable to complex and bureaucratic systems of state socialism, misses the central point of Weber's theory. First, as Weber himself specifies, the different nature of charismatic organisation does not mean the non-existence of social structure:

> charismatic authority does not imply an amorphous condition; it indicates rather a definite social structure with a staff and an apparatus of services and material means that is adapted to the mission of the leader. The personal staff constitutes a charismatic aristocracy composed of a select group of adherents who are united by discipleship and loyalty and chosen according to personal charismatic qualification.[23]

Second, as I have already emphasised, the most important issues in Weber's theory of legitimacy are both – the perception of the regime by its subjects and the regime's own claim to legitimacy. So, in our case here, what is crucial is that the masses perceived Tito as the source of the regime's legitimacy, and that regime too made a claim to rule on the basis of Tito's charisma and achievements. The social structure and the party/state machine are here of little importance as is the hierarchical organisation of society. What matters is the relationship between the leader and the masses. In this type of society when something goes wrong, the charismatic leader is not to be blamed, because 'he was not informed', 'they did that behind his back' or 'they don't give him the correct information'.[24] The relationship between the leader and the masses is perceived as being direct and uninterrupted and that is also how the leader addresses the masses. Hence, Tito would often address the masses directly (by visiting factories, agricultural co-operatives or by giving speeches in the main city squares) in order to reaffirm and strengthen this relationship. For example, at one of such meeting he said the following:

> Comrades, I have to apologise to you. I did not invite you to give you a speech or lecture, but I wanted to inform you of some things, which I know, are of interest to you. That is why I think that I don't have to convince you that all of what is used against us is a mere lie.[25]

What we have here is a direct relationship between him (Tito, the leader) who comes to inform (to teach, to show the true light) them (people, listeners and followers) about lies that are used against all of them (the leader and his people). He (the leader), also knows (is a superior and has a superior knowledge and thus a right to decide what is important) that this information is of interest to them (meaning that it has to be of interest). This feeling of direct connection between charismatic authority and the masses which is equal and not equal at the same time neutralises the institutional structures and bureaucratic mechanisms of the socialist state and makes charismatic authority an important source of political legitimacy in state socialism. This is clearly formulated in the following paragraph in *Borba*:

> our people are learning, proud of being unhesitatingly loyal to their Party, to their socialist state, to the leadership of their Party and their state and to their Tito in whom are all the best ambitions and insights of the people personified and who gathers enormous strength from them.[26]

However, what is missing in Weber's typology is a connection between charismatic authority and the values and ideas initiated by the charismatic leader. We do not know much about the process of when and how people are introduced to and persuaded of the new value system. We know the answer to the question why (because of the leader's gift of grace), but not to the question how and when particular values and ideas are accepted and believed. In addition, as Weber explains, charismatic authority cannot last for long. If the leader does not deliver the promised millenarian 'miracle' his charisma will disappear. Similarly, if the millenarian target is completed, the leader loses his mission and consequently the magic of charisma disappears.

This is where Barker's fourth concept of legitimacy (value–rational authority) appears to be useful. As Barker points out, value–rational legitimacy is a belief in the total validity of the particular socio-political system 'as the expression of ultimate values of an ethical, aesthetic or any other type'.[27] The system is viewed as legitimate by the population if it is convinced that the rulers promote and fight for values perceived as 'our' values. In this sense the rulers have to be viewed as in some way identical to the ruled subjects, sharing a common religion, nationality or ideology, but also as Barker points out, to be seen as more qualified than or superior to the rest of society.[28]

Therefore, the question is how did Tito and the communist leadership convince the public that they shared the same value system and that they were ideologically identical? My answer would be that in the specific historical and political circumstances of World War II in Yugoslavia, Tito and the communist leadership managed to provide something that was perceived as a miracle. They organised a massive resistance movement which was victorious in war and which liberated the country, they nationalised the property and lands of the already hated former rulers, they provided the impoverished population with jobs and land and they raised the standard of living in the post-war years. All these achievements were associated with the charismatic authority of Tito. He and his closest collaborators were seen as being responsible for these achievements and consequently in such unstable and unpredictable times they became the only source of security.

Having established himself as an authority who possessed this 'gift of grace' and by performing a 'miracle' Tito and the communist party leadership (in Weber's terminology, his disciples) could now use this charisma to initiate the change or rather re-direct dominant values and practices in the way they wanted. In such a situation individuals, Yugoslav citizens, had started to question their existing beliefs and gradually, step by step, came to accept ideas and values promoted by the charismatic authority. Since the system had a monopoly on truth (total control of the media and educational institutions), it could gradually reinforce the new value system and in this way extend the power initially generated from the charisma. However, as Pareto rightly points out, derivations/ideology could not simply be imposed on the population nor could they run against existing emotions.[29] They can operate only through the instrumentalisation of existing sentiments (and interests). And this is exactly where value rationality via ideology comes into play. The regime will present and disseminate its ideology in a way that is acceptable to the masses. Normative and operative ideologies will follow a similar pattern of ideas, but they will operate in completely different ways. While normative ideology will be formulated on a highly theoretical and 'scientific' level making an appeal to abstract rationality, higher values, ethics and similar principles, operative ideology will be framed so as to appeal to emotions, affects and interests. The operative ideology will appeal to familiar symbols, actors and messages.

Hence, in our case, the new regime utilised the leader's charisma in order to disseminate its ideology. So what we have here is not Weber's routinisation of charisma that follows the death of the charismatic leader (and which we will see later on in the study did not work in the Yugoslav case), but the instrumentalisation of charisma. The legitimacy process begins with charismatic authority that relies heavily on traditionalism, introduces some legal–rational elements and operates basically through value rationality, meaning as we will see later, dominant ideology. This complex process of legitimisation will here be called simply the *ideologisation of charisma*.[30]

So far I have described the ways in which charismatic authority functions, but we still do not know how the dominant form of legitimacy (ideologisation of charisma) operates. For values to be dominant it is necessary for them to be shaped in the form of a consistent set of ideas and practices, that is, as ideology. In order to understand this relationship between charismatic, value–rational authority and dominant values, ideas and practices, it is necessary to identify the structure, form and content of the dominant power-keeping ideology in post-war Yugoslavia and understand how this ideology was 'imposed' on the society and to what degree normative or official and operative ideologies were congruent.

Normative and operative ideologies

It is generally considered that the Yugoslav Communist Party moved through several phases and consequently significantly changed its official ideology in the period 1945–60. These changes related especially to two radically different periods, the period before Yugoslavia's break with the Soviet Union in 1948, characterised principally by the imitation of the Soviet model, and the period after 1948, marked by the introduction of more liberal concepts such as workers' self-management, the delegate system and workers' councils. Although these two periods differ in many ways, the basis of normative ideology as laid down in party manifestos, political programmes and other party documentats, did not change significantly. New concepts and principles such as workers self-management in the economy or non-alignment in foreign policy, and others introduced later, were not intended to oppose fundamental principles of the already established ideology. As we will see in the analysis that follows, the core values and practices of Marxism–Leninism continued to be guiding principles of the Yugoslav Communist Party in the post-war period.[31]

The following analysis aims at identifying the dominant normative and operative ideologies of post-war Yugoslavia. The analysis looks at similarities and differences between two levels of ideology by concentrating on the interpretation of the central texts through which this ideology has been disseminated. While a normative ideology has been identified through the content analysis of the manifesto of the League of Communists of Yugoslavia (adopted as the official programme of the party at the seventh congress of the LCY in April 1958), an operative ideology has been reconstructed through the content analysis of school history and social science textbooks and newspaper editorials from one of the most influential newspapers of the period, *Borba.*

Economy

The first striking difference that one comes across in the analysis of the LCY manifesto, school textbooks and editorials, is the very different understanding and interpretation of the central values of economic organisation in society. Normative ideology devotes exceptional attention to economic issues giving extensive and detailed explanations of how an economic system operates in capitalist and socialist society, whereas in operative ideology the economy is of secondary importance. In the presentation and explanation of its arguments normative ideology speaks through the voice of, and appeals to the authority of, Marxism–Lenininism formulated as a pure science with its universalist and highly abstract message, while operative ideology concentrates only on those aspects of the economy that are familiar to the general public and is conveyed through everyday recognisable images and concepts which appeal to individual and collective interests and emotions. Thus, normative ideology operates with the three fundamental ideas or 'grand vistas' around which the economy should be organised: socially owned means of production; socialist planning of the economy; and workers' self-management in the organisation of production and distribution of goods and services. At the operative level these ideas are regularly 'translated' as self-evident and 'normal' principles that one has to apply to build a functional, sustainable and prosperous social community.

Thus, instead of the emphasis on the Marxist–Leninist–Kardeljist theoretical conceptualisations and the realisation of their blueprints, the emphasis of operative ideology is on the practicality, functionality and usefulness of planning in every day life. What is formulated in the manifesto as the centrally planned and directed economy 'based on the scientific analysis of material factors of economic development',[32] reads in a geography textbook for the third grade of elementary school as: '[only] by thoughtful work and according to *plan* did the people overcome many problems and nature [natural obstacles] in the Soviet Union' or 'we have started to work [in our country] according to *planning* in every job'.[33] Instead of invoking the scientific rationale and logic behind socialist planning and self-management of the economy elaborated in normative ideology, the appeal is clearly made to individual and collective interests – it is in our interest to plan the economy so that we can have a better production of goods and services and thus better wages. Instead of highly abstract and popularly incomprehensible formulations such as 'socially owned means of production require society's economy to be ... a consciously organised, homogenous totality, based on a highly developed division of labour',[34] *Borba* contains a number of articles which aim to show that better planning in industry, agriculture or mining brings better results. We read for example that

> one of the main experiences of Slovenian miners in the first half of the
> fourth *plan* year is more comprehensive *planning* of the work in
> general. More dynamics have been introduced in the propositions of
> operative plans which are developed on the basis of main *plans* for the
> individual mines.[35]

The central aim of this ideology 'translation' is to justify the introduction of some highly abstract and normative concepts by showing them as obvious and 'normal'. As Barthes has rightly explained operative ideology does not lie.[36] Rather, it makes the ideas and concepts formulated in normative ideology innocent, giving them 'eternal justification'. Although operative ideology provides simple explanations of why central planning in the distribution of goods and services is better than the chaotic market economy, its aim is not really to explain. Rather, operative ideology pretends to be a statement of fact. Who normal would question the idea that planning in everyday life is better than chaos?

The ideas and concepts that were central to the Marxist–Leninist understanding of economy but which would have been highly unpopular to the masses, such as the almost complete abolition of private property, were again differently formulated on the level of operative ideology. Thus, instead of ideas such as 'to abolish capitalist exploitation of the working class means to abolish private capitalist property over the means of production',[37] one reads in the newspapers that

> the peoples of Yugoslavia celebrate with the enormous successes the
> second anniversary of [their] victory over Hitler's Germany. [This is
> evident from] the process of renewal and gigantic efforts for realisa-
> tion of the five-year plan which will transform our country into an even
> more powerful and progressive homeland of working people which is
> liberated from the exploitation of exploitative class and any form of
> dependence on foreign imperialists.[38]

This statement shows us how operative ideology has to package an idea that in itself is highly unpopular with one that represents

the central point of reference for the masses – the image of the
monstrous enemy that has just been defeated in the war who will
never again raise its ugly head because of the strength of the powerful
Yugoslav state. In this way former landowners and 'capitalists' are
directly connected and equated with 'foreign imperialists'. The introduction of socialist planning in the economy is thus directly related to
the country's independence: '[peoples of Yugoslavia] show their will
to be independent by restless and dedicated work in the realisation of
the five-year plan'.[39] In other words, those who support other types of
economy (namely, capitalist economies) are nothing less than enemies
of society who have already been defeated in the war. To oppose the
socialist economic organisation of the society means to question the
independence of the State for which 'its sons' have sacrificed their
lives. In this case we can clearly see how the normative ideology of
Reason has been transformed and supported by nationalism at the
operative level into the ideology of Affect and Interests in order to
justify the *status quo*.

Even in the cases when it seems that the normative and operative
levels of ideology do not differ significantly, as with the argument for
an economically equal society, it is still possible to see the important
differences between the two. For example, the authors of the manifesto inform us that in socialism 'work has to be a measure of individual economic position' and instead of 'the capitalist race for profit',
socialism is focused on the collective social efforts for maximal satisfaction of individual and collective needs of people'.[40] On the operative level one reads that the 'people's government takes care that all
social wealth, being the property of all people will become the
common good of people and is in service for all working people and
not only for some individuals and even foreigners as it was before'.[41]
At first sight it seems the appeal is made in both cases to a universal
morality in terms of the support for the equal position for all.

However, the arguments used are in fact very different. In the first
case, it is claimed that individual work should be the measure of an
individual's economic position in society with the emphasis on work-
oriented individuals who contribute to 'maximal satisfaction of individual and collective needs of people' living in a particular society. In
the second case, it is not society but the State ('a people's government') which is central for the economic redistribution of goods.
There is no idealist vision of a society where individual and collective
interests are reconciled and where society is freed from the alienating
'capitalist race for profit', but only a paternalist state which will make
sure that all are provided for. In addition, this is not any state, this
is 'our' state which will help only 'us' (not the foreigners). Thus, in
this case we can clearly see how one universalist ethical principle of

equality as a form of individual and collective liberation has been transformed into a simple egoistic and interest-driven idea of being provided for and protected in our own ('people's') state.

This argument is invoked constantly and each time we are in a position to see how some supposedly higher ethical or scientific idea has been reshaped at the level of operative ideology as an appeal to interests and emotions. For example, we can read in the manifesto that 'self-management was introduced as a constitutive principle in the economy (in the form of workers councils) as well as in the political system (in municipalities, counties, republic and federation)' with the aim of 'developing society as a community of producers'.[42] In the operative ideology this statement reads as follows:

> thanks to justly undertaken distribution of land to those who cultivate it, our Republic has during the last year managed to satisfy the hunger of agrarian workers – landless and poor peasants. Thanks to strengthening of state and co-operative sector, the workers of Yugoslavia became the owners of the products they make.[43]

The message is clear and simple – there is no emphasis on abstract ideals about a society of producers but rather on the simple message that 'our' new economic organisation of society will ensure that you will never be hungry again.

Politics
Like those of the economic system, the fundamental values of the political system are differently conceptualised in normative and operative ideology. Whereas normative ideology concentrated on the realisation of some universal tasks and the implementation of the historical laws 'discovered' by the science of Marxism–Leninism, operative ideology focused on the justification of the party's role and position in the postwar period. What we can see in operative ideology is a particularly developed skill of reconciling these two aims so that they appear, selfevidently, as a single and deeply related project to the general public.

Thus, in the opening pages of the manifesto one reads that 'this program attempts to theoretically formulate, with the help of Marxist analysis, general laws of socialist development and specific forms of revolutionary process in Yugoslavia'.[44] This perception of Marxism as a form of science that can and has discovered certain laws of development and whose claims as such are indisputable, unquestionably objective and basically irrefutable is evident in statements and formulations such as: 'contradictions of capitalist organisation of society, its laws and inevitability of its downfall has been discovered, analysed and explained by Marx and Engels';[45] 'Marxist scientificity of particular conception';[46] 'laws of socialist development';[47] 'great scientific discoveries in the works of Marx, Engels and Lenin';[48] 'towards the explanation of laws of directions of socialist society in the transitional phase';[49] and so on. Apart from its scientific legacy Marxism–Leninism is also invoked to give a unilinear evolutionist picture of social development: 'monopolist capitalism emerged on the higher level of development of productive forces of capitalism';[50] 'working class has its historical role';[51] or 'the entire history of development of labour movement consists of the struggle between different opinions. As its final outcome only those views and theories win that were the objective expression of laws of development of social struggles of the particular time.'[52]

By contrast, in operative ideology we find very different formulations and ambitions. There is the emphasis almost exclusively on the particular. Instead of the historical mission of the working class and world revolution of the proletariat, the stress is clearly on the Yugoslav national liberation war and Yugoslav revolution. The contents of history textbooks are not focused that much on the universal and abstract principles of scientific socialism but rather on the successful guidance of the national liberation war by the Yugoslav Communist Party. Thus, for example, one of the general history textbooks uses only six pages to describe the general course of World War II and over 45 pages to describe the battles and victories of Tito's partisans.[53] The same was true with the newspaper editorials. The Yugoslav Communist Party and Tito were not praised as much as those who conducted the socialist revolution but primarily as those who were responsible for the liberation of the country:

> when fascist conquerors enslaved our country in 1941, they started to destroy, rob and kill our people. Peoples of Yugoslavia have raised the uprising under the leadership of the Communist party and its spearhead comrade Tito against German, Italian and Hungarian fascists and their collaborators.[54]

Similarly, 'in time of the terror of fascist occupiers the Communist party started, organised and led the people in the armed uprising which soon after became a national-liberation struggle'.[55] On several occasions it was stressed that the main aim of communists was (not so much the socialist revolution but rather) the liberation of the country.[56]

All these examples demonstrate how and why normative and operative ideologies differ. Scientific discoveries and 'grand vistas' presented in normative ideology are ideal, utopian projects around which, as Gouldner rightly points out, the masses are to be mobilised.[57] They speak in the voice of the public good, making an appeal to reason.

They present themselves through the images of an ideal society, the rational, efficient and moral community where justice and equality for all is to be achieved. Their guarantee lies this time not in religion's promise of a better afterlife, but in the superiority and 'magic' of science that can accomplish heaven on earth. It is Marxist–Leninist science that has discovered this path to earthly heaven and only if we follow its recommendations will we be saved. However, since Marx and Lenin as dead prophets are not recognisable and visible to the masses, and the promise of science is not as persuasive to the general public as it is to party members, it is necessary to look for the guarantee of earthly heaven in the immediate environment. And that guarantee is the party itself. It is the party that liberated 'us' from the monsters of fascism. The party is so strong, big and powerful that it will also save us from capitalists and the Soviet threat. And finally, it is only the party that can rightly interpret the 'laws of history' and thus lead us to happiness.

For the masses to be able to grasp the 'science of Marxism–Leninism', it is necessary to translate it into the familiar images of patriarchal culture. Hence, when reference is made to Marxism–Leninism in operative ideology, it is done in an extremely simplified way, appealing to these images of patriarchy. The authority does not come so much from the scientific discoveries of Marxism as from the exceptional individual personalities of Marx and Engels. So we are informed that 'the laws [of history] are discovered by *great teachers and leaders* of working people Karl Marx and Friedrich Engels',[58] and that '*great men* are great because they have understood better than others historical laws of their time'.[59] So what we have here is not an appeal to superior knowledge and scientific discoveries, but to the patriarchal authority of 'great and wise men'.

This translation is also evident elsewhere. For example, at the normative level the main political principle is derived from the idea that the working class has the leading role in social change and the transformation of world society including Yugoslav society. At the operative level this role is given to 'our peoples', 'our working people' or 'our working masses'. Thus, one reads in the manifesto about the 'leading role of the working class in the State's power structure with the Communist party as its vanguard'[60] and how the privileged position of the working class

> comes from the fact that the working class cannot liberate itself from exploitation if it at the same time does not liberate the entire society from historically surpassed capitalist society and from every form of exploitation.[61]

In addition, the 'people' appear in the manifesto as unconscious and uneducated masses who need to be educated by the party: 'communists have gathered the most revolutionary part of the working masses, *educating* them in the spirit of class consciousness and knowledge about the historical role of the working class'.[62] Similarly, the task of the communists in this new period is to continue

> *to educate* working people so that they could more independently and more directly manage society, think and act socialistically in practice until every individual citizen learns to run the works of social community.[63]

At the operative level the concept of the working class largely disappears and becomes simply the 'people' who are not patronised as in the manifesto but flattered as the true heroes of the war and revolution who now rule themselves in the new Yugoslav state. So one reads that 'the real victory of [the] people [is] demonstrated in the establishment of people's rule in Yugoslavia';[64] or that 'this [idea] does not correspond with the interests of *our country* as understood by *our Party*, *our Party* and state leadership, and *our working masses* gathered in the People's Front';[65] or that

> today *our people's government*, starting from local, county and regional councils to parliaments of *people's republics* and a parliament of Federal Peoples Republic of Yugoslavia, is a real *people's rule*. It is *people's* because the *people* elect it by their free will, it is *people's* because *people* watch over its work, and if it does not work as it should, *people* can replace it by other *people* who will execute the will of the *people*.[66]

Here again, operative ideology has been reformulated in a way that would be comprehensible and appealing to the public by making a clear shift from universalist socialist political ideals to those of particular nationalist content. The mastery and skill of ideology is in achieving this task without recognising that such a shift has taken place. Universalist socialist principles had to be translated into nationalism for two reasons. First, because an abstract and distant ideology like Marxism–Leninism–Kardeljism had to be simplified and brought down to a level that would be generally understandable to everybody. This could be most successfully achieved when these ideas were formulated through simple dichotomies such as rich vs. poor, corrupt vs. morally superior, justice vs. injustice and so on, identifying 'us' with the positive attributes and 'them' with the negative ones. Second, and more importantly, in order to justify the party's monopoly on power and legitimise the new political system, these universalist ideas had to be shaped in a way which was not only familiar and recognisable to the masses but also clearly consistent with their traditional values and ideals. This could be most adequately achieved by invoking and relying on the nationalist appeal which simultaneously tied together three central pillars of individual and group existence: identity, interests and emotions. In addition, to achieve this aim it was necessary to identify the party with those to whom the appeal was made. It is 'we' who are the party. It is 'us' who now rule and decide. Operative ideology represents itself as homogeneous and speaks in a single voice. As Lefort rightly observes:

> State and civil society are assumed to have merged ... A logic of identi-fication is set in motion, and is governed by the representation of power as embodiment. The proletariat and the people are one; the party and the proletariat are one; the politburo and, ultimately, the *egocrat* and the party are one. Whilst there develops a representation of a homogeneous and self-transparent society, of a People-as-One, social division, in all its modes, is denied, and at the same time all signs of difference of opinion, belief or modes are condemned.[67]

Culture and nation

The biggest difference between normative and operative ideologies is in the sphere of 'culture and nation'. At the normative level the emphasis is placed on the concept of the 'brotherhood and unity' of the Yugoslav peoples as a particular form of socialist internationalism and on the scientifically conceptualised ideas of the struggle against class-based culture and 'the liberation of the free human conscious-ness'. At the operative level, however, these concepts have not only been differently articulated but reconciled with the glorification of the particular ethnically defined nations and the emphasis on 'pan-Slavic unity'.

Thus, the cultural policy of the socialist state at the normative level has been formulated as a struggle, on the one hand against its bour-geois forms, and on the other, against blind ignorance towards the culture. An appeal is made to scientific knowledge in the development of cultural policy. As we read in the manifesto, it is important to take

> a Marxist critical attitude towards the cultural creativity of all peoples, towards the cultural heritage of Yugoslav nationalities, the struggle against class–bourgeois mystification of cultural history and cultural values, the struggle against uneducated, primitive and sectarian underestimation of cultural advancements achieved in the past that socialist society, as the natural and historical successor of positive cultural heritage accepts and cultivates as one of the elements for the establishment of classless civilisation.[68]

At the operative level this 'Marxist critical attitude' and the struggle
'against class–bourgeois mystification of cultural history' disappears
and is replaced by the populist concept of culture. The appeal made
is not to some universal value of 'revolutionary Marxism' as a law-
generating science, but rather to popular ('people's') interests.
Hence, one reads about culture in socialism as a people's culture and
the awards given to particular artists as awards to people given by the
people themselves: 'through their people's state these awards are
given by the people themselves, the people–master, people–owner
and producer of culture'.[69] As the owners and producers of their
culture, the people are also masters of their own destiny:

> these first awards are not only first awards given by the State to writers
> and artists, but also the awards in which all people are interested; the
> people who became the master of their destiny through the liberation
> struggle, the people who grew up to become giants with the conscious-
> ness of their struggle led by the Communist Party; the people who
> precisely, because of their victorious liberation struggle, became sover-
> eign subjects, equal and the undisputed owners of their culture.[70]

Here again the shift has been made from ideas shaped by the Enlightenment which advocated an end to superstition, primitivism and
traditionalism and were favoured by normative ideology to their exact
opposites in operative ideology. 'The people' need not to be enlightened and educated, they themselves know the right path. They are
giants, but only as long as they recognise the Yugoslav Communist
Party as their true leader. In this way one can see how the party itself
has in reality no interest in truly educating 'the people'. As long as
they are naïve, primitive and traditional, the party can exploit and
instrumentalise the people's interests and emotions. At the level of
operative ideology simple flattery will always do a better job than any
'critical–Marxist attitude'.

An other important difference between the two levels of ideology
is the articulation of the new 'socialist consciousness'. Whereas
normative ideology poses this aim in the context of universal liberation and the emancipation of human beings from tradition, authority
and exploitation, operative ideology uses and appeals to familiar
images of the morally superior and purified community, images
derived from the popularly well-known and recognisable religious
tradition. In addition, while normative ideology refers to the liberation and formation of the new man as an ideal aim to be achieved,
operative ideology identifies this as a fact already realised in Yugoslav
society. So we read in the manifesto that the new socialist individual
should liberate himself from the different forms of mental repression

by developing 'socialist consciousness', and that this can be only achieved through the struggle 'for new social relationships that free human consciousness from the naïve and untaught belief in religious and mystic narcosis, spiritual slackness, and from the delusion of various fetishisms'.[71] On the other hand, newspaper editorials inform us that

> socialist consciousness and socialist psychology have been developed to extraordinary proportions among the people. Our workers, the builders of socialism, not only are becoming new but are already new men. ... we should be aware of this great and wonderful fact that in [our system] the value and beauty of human beings grow and that the content and meaning of life is upgraded.[72]

Even the nature of the work has been changed:

> in new Yugoslavia work is no longer a slave-like burden for people. On the contrary work is a social responsibility, a matter of honour for every worker, for every righteous and honest patriot who loves his country and struggles for its development and progress.[73]

Here again, the aspect of individual and collective interests is emphasised. It is not so much that 'we' have to change and develop into better human beings but that 'we' are the better and morally superior beings to all those who live in non-socialist societies. Operative ideology here exploits the individual psychological need to identify oneself positively. As Tajfel's social identity theory explains, positive group identification is crucial for individual self-esteem and this positive identification is possible to accomplish 'through the establishment of positive distinctiveness of the in-group from the relevant out-groups'.[74] Group membership gives meaning to individuals and in order to identify themselves positively, out-group members are negatively stereotyped.

However, the most visible difference between the two ideologies is in their conceptualisation of one of the central concepts of post-war Yugoslav ideology – 'brotherhood and unity'. At the normative level this concept is firmly tied to the economic organisation of society and to the socially owned means of production. The policy of 'brotherhood and unity' of the Yugoslav peoples, as it is explained in the manifesto,

> is based on the fact that the means of production are socially owned and that they can be maximally used for the interest of all peoples of Yugoslavia only with their collective efforts and solidarity. In that way

the unity of Yugoslav peoples only in socialism receives its full form
and its strong socio-economic basis.[75]

Thus the manifesto basically suggests that the solution of the 'national
question' in Yugoslavia could successfully be achieved only through
a socialist revolution and through the implementation of socialist
relations of production. This 'socialist Yugoslavism' is, as is explained,
a special form of socialist internationalism. When 'democratic
national consciousness' is influenced by the spirit of internationalism, then the two form an identical process.[76] When this is not the
case, then they are the 'remains of bourgeois nationalism which is
backward, reactionary and extremely harmful for the development of
socialism'.[77]

The textbooks and newspaper editorials make no reference to
the economic organisation of the society in relation to the unity of
Yugoslav nationalities. The concept of 'brotherhood and unity' is rarely
connected to abstract ideas of socially owned means of production as
in normative ideology and more often to the struggle against the
common enemy. Hence we read that 'the brotherhood and unity of
Serbs and Croats has been built by the struggle',[78] that 'the struggle of
our peoples against a superior enemy was difficult and bloody', but
also that 'as the struggle was becoming more difficult the brotherhood and unity of our people, which are based on equality, were
becoming stronger'.[79] This brotherhood and unity achieved in the
war of national liberation have resulted in the situation that 'our
peoples are today connected stronger than ever before in history'.[80]
Therefore, it is not reason and the economic superiority of socialism
that keep us together but blood that we had to spill together that
make us brothers. The unity of the Yugoslav peoples is not derived
from socialist relations of production or from blueprint ideals but
exclusively from the war experience. The message of the operative
ideology is simple, and driven by emotion and interest: only when we
fight together are we strong and powerful.

Unlike normative ideology which presupposes the unity of the
Yugoslav peoples and internationalism via class unity, as explained by
Marx ('classes are real while nations are fictions'), operative ideology
aims to justify the present situation in terms of its historical roots.
Thus, the unity of the Yugoslav peoples has been historically traced
and history textbooks will often emphasise 'age-old aspirations of our
people to unite'. Typical sentences referring to the eighth and nineteenth centuries respectively would be the following: 'although the
rebels did not succeed, this uprising was of enormous importance
because this was the first mass movement of south Slav tribes against
the foreign rule'[81] or 'it was believed that Serbia would ... achieve the

great deed of uniting brotherly Yugoslav peoples'.[82] However, it was
only in the new Yugoslavia that this unification was achieved on equal
terms: the new Constitution 'transformed Yugoslavia from a prisoner
of peoples in the first period of its existence into a brotherly family of
equal free peoples'.[83] Although these peoples went 'from April 1941
to May 1945 … through the painful' period that was also a 'glorious
period',[84] 'the people [now] … truly have power in their hands and
today, in brotherhood and unity of all peoples, they can [successfully]
build their country'.[85]

These examples show how blueprint explanations derived from
Marxist revolutionary science make sense only to party members,
whereas for the masses it is necessary to demonstrate that the unity of
the Yugoslav peoples has deep historical roots. The operative ideology has to justify the present situation in terms of age-old traditions
that are trusted and acceptable to the public.

However, the most striking difference between the two ideologies
is the varying degree of emphasis on individual, ethnically defined
nations. Unlike normative ideology which is firmly universalist and
internationalist, operative ideology gives enormous attention to the
particular histories of Serbs, Croats, Slovenes and other Yugoslav
nationalities. So one reads that

> superior enemies have sometimes managed to overrun and enslave
> Serbia, but never could they destroy the aspiration for freedom in the
> Serbian people who have always valued freedom above anything else.[86]

Another statement declares that the 'Serbian people have shown
great strength and skill in this difficult situation'.[87] There are many
stories about the bravery of Serbian, Croatian and Slovenian soldiers.
Among these is the story about the heroism and skill of the Serbian
king, Vojislav, and his five sons who managed to defeat a Byzantine
army of 40,000 soldiers, or the story about the Croat, Ljudevit
Posavski, and his rebellion against the Franks in the eighth century
which recounts that, 'when Ljudevit Posavski started the uprising
against the Franks, Slovenes joined him. They fought bravely and
defeated the Frankish army on several occasions.'[88]

The importance of national consciousness and patriotism are
constantly pointed out. Thus, the Serbian prince, Mihailo, was given
credit because 'his politics have raised national consciousness to a
higher level and moved Serbs away from the languor into which they
were pushed by the "Constitution-defenders"'.[89] The same applied
to other ethnic nations: 'in that time gradually among Slovenians
the consciousness about the nation and need for national unity
develops'.[90] This attitude equally applies to personalities and social

movements of different historical periods including socialist and workers' movements:

> the workers' movement in Serbia fought with strikes for a better social position. By agitation on workers' meetings and through its press, it fought for political freedom and equality of all citizens without forgetting the real patriotism towards its people and its motherland.[91]

This striking shift from the universalism and internationalism of normative ideology to nationalism, even ethnonationalism of operative ideology needs an adequate explanation. What one sees here is how some new, unknown and very distant idea of class-based internationalism or universalist revolutionary socialism had to be packaged with some commonly accepted ideas and with some flattery in order to be sold successfully. First, to justify its ideas and policies the Yugoslav Communist Party had to demonstrate that communists are true and sincere patriots who will never let their compatriots down. Hence, the workers' movement was not only socialist but also patriotic. The interest-driven appeal is combined with an emotionally shaped appeal: class justice is important, but only if supplemented with ethnic solidarity. For this reason the universalism and internationalism of normative ideology had to be scaled down and articulated through a nationalist rhetoric in the operative ideology.

Second, since nationalism is not only a more powerful and more persuasive ideology but also more understandable and familiar to the public, the party had to be sure that was in control of the direction of nationalist discourses. If the party articulated nationalist feelings in a way acceptable to it's aims and policies, then this space was not open to the oppositional articulations of nationalism. In other words, the nationalist discourse in operative ideology enabled the party to maintain control over this potentially delegitimising force.

Another important idea that does not appear in the normative ideology, and which is connected to the nationalist discourse, is the concept of Slavic unity. This concept is present through the entire 1945–60 period, but is especially emphasised immediately after World War II and before the break with the Soviet Union. Hence, the reader is informed that

> the idea of Slavhood ... has [acquired] a completely new form. It opened up the new road for Slavic kin as a whole and to every Slavic people individually. Isolated, divided and enslaved Slavic peoples could not destroy the door of Hitler's prison, the prison where death was waiting for all of them. It is only when they [the Slavic peoples] have united in the struggle against the common enemy – Hitler's Germany – that they could win.[92]

It often referred to Slavic instead of socialist solidarity: 'Yugoslav delegation together with the delegations of the Soviet Union and other Slavic countries ... has defended the interests of endangered peoples'.[93] Among the all Slavic peoples, the Russians have been singled out as the most important people: 'big and powerful Soviet Russia – queen bee of Slavhood'.[94] Similarly, 'that is why every Slav who feels the meaning and importance of Slavhood has to be infinitely thankful to the Soviet Union for the great act of liberating humanity from the plague of fascism'.[95] It was 'the Hitlerian hordes [that] attacked the strongest bulwark of Slavhood and tower of freedom – the fatherland of Lenin and Stalin'[96] but

> after the defeat of Hitler's Germany there is no power today that can disunite the Slavic peoples with their oldest and most deserving brother, the Russian people, in their ambition to continue to develop their better future.[97]

What we see here is that instead of the appeal to the unity of socialist countries which share similar political systems and common universalist socialist aims, appeal is made only to Slavic kin unity. This presence of Slavic unity instead of socialist unity supports the explanation given above. Socialist ideals are foreign and not understandable to the general public, while the images of our 'Slav brothers', 'our big and powerful mother Russia' or 'queen bee of Slavhood', are easy to understand and connect with recognisable images of the (South Slav) extended family and the traditional related values. To be able to initiate public support for the socialist countries, operative ideology had to translate them into familiar images of 'our Slav brothers'.

Actors
The content analysis of the actors that appear in normative and operative ideologies show us again how and why these two levels of ideology differ. The first important difference is the fact that in normative ideology actors are almost non-existent, while operative ideology gives exceptional attention to the description of various actors. While normative ideology deals mostly with ideas and principles, operative ideology translates these principles into concrete individuals. Operative ideology personalises ideas and principles by locating them in the images of concrete and visible individuals or, more often, in individualised collectives (collectives depicted as having their own personalities and a single will).

Thus, in normative ideology we encounter only a handful of actors: working class and communist party (positive) and bourgeoisie and capitalist (negative). Operative ideology, on the other hand, is extremely rich in its descriptions of various actors. These include positively depicted actors such as working people, communists, the Yugoslav government, the Yugoslav army, peasants, Tito, Stalin (before 1948), and negatively portrayed actors such as the monarchist government of old Yugoslavia, fascists and their collaborators, US and British imperialists with Churchill as their representative, oppositional parties and so on.

The second significant difference is that even when both levels of ideology depict the same actors, they do so in distinct ways. Hence, normative ideology characterises the working class as 'the main force of socialist development in the world' which 'acts consciously for more than a century' and 'using different means, builds new social conditions developing the experience and ideology of socialism'. This is the class that 'becomes objective and is the main vehicle of the interests and progress of human kind'.[98] Its leading social role 'is based on the fact that its class interest is equivalent to the interests of all human progress'.[99] This is the class that acts as an agent 'of conscious socialist action for the liquidation of capitalism'.[100]

A close reading of textbooks and editorials shows us that in operative ideology the notion of the 'working class' largely disappears and is replaced by nouns such as the 'working people', 'people' or, most often, 'our people'. Thus, we come across formulations such as 'working people with all other freedom-loving elements';[101] 'working masses did not want to be exploited';[102] 'great victory of the working people';[103] 'politically conscious people';[104] '[visitors from all over the country] are fascinated with the great victories of the working people of our motherland',[105] and so on. Here again the emphasis has been shifted from some universalist, blueprint-derived and abstract principles of revolutionary science and the idea of the working class as a dominant agent of social change to a particularist and populist glorification of 'our freedom loving people'. Moreover, the full transition has been achieved from the working class as a privileged agent of history as postulated in normative ideology, to the 'people' of Yugoslavia as the bearer possessing of this exceptional position in operative ideology. Thus, it is no longer the working class that is 'the main vehicle of the progress of human kind' but the Yugoslav people who are the chosen ones. Here again we see a clear shift from one universalist idea to its particularist nationalist translation.

A similar difference is noticeable when the Yugoslav Communist Party is discussed. In the manifesto, the party is very often indistinguishable from the working class and when a distinction is made between them, their relationship is described as being of 'an organic nature'. Since the Yugoslav working class is young and newly recruited from the countryside, as stated in the manifesto, this is often reflected in the presence of some 'backward views'.[106] Hence, it is the communist party alone that can correctly articulate the interests and will of the working class: 'the Yugoslav Communist Party has always been the sincere expression of the interests and inclinations of the working class, that also corresponds to the objective interests of all other working strata of Yugoslavia'.[107]

In operative ideology one sees quite different interpretations of the aims of the Yugoslav Communist Party. Instead of the appeal to some higher reality (Marxist–Leninist science) and patronising attitudes toward the 'young working class', we see the party as a strong, united people's front responsible for the liberation of the country. The emphasis is on its historical role and strength as reflected in the following statements:

> the Fifth Congress has shown that YCP has grown from a small but strong illegal party as it was before the war to become a big and powerful revolutionary party ready to overcome all difficulties and victoriously lead our peoples towards communism;[108]

and

> [the Congress] has shown the unbreakable unity and monolith-like strength of the YCP, developed under the leadership of comrade Tito in the stormy years immediately before World War II, in the fire of the national–liberation war and the people's revolution and in the development of our socialist Yugoslavia.[109]

The party has been hailed not only as a liberator of the country and organiser of the socialist revolution but also as 'an initiator and organiser of the struggle for the transformation of our country from undeveloped and primitive … into a modern industrial country'.[110] All these processes, as regularly pointed in the newspapers and textbooks, were achieved with the people. Thus, the 'organic' connection between the party and the working class often referred to in normative ideology, became the connection between the party and the Yugoslav people in operative ideology. The aim of the Yugoslav Communist Party was not to educate the masses who had some 'backward views' nor to articulate the interests of the working class in relation to the world socialist revolution, but rather to present itself as the protector and savior of the Yugoslav people and their country. In this way the relationship between the party and the people is an 'organic' one: 'there is no communist party in the world nor has there ever

been any party that would have such a strong connection with the
masses of working people as in our country'.[111]

Although the manifesto often does not distinguish between the
party and the working class, Lefort's idea of 'People-as-One' is much
more applicable to the analysis of operative ideology. In textbooks
and editorials the Yugoslav Communit Party is indistinguishable from
the Yugoslav government, from socialist Yugoslavia, from the working
class, from the working people or simply from the people. There is an
absolute unity, harmony and identity of all these actors. This is the
discourse of power which, as Lefort stresses, makes no reference to
anything beyond the social.[112] There is nothing beyond this harmonic
and absolutely integrated society.

However, the clearest distinction between the two levels of ideology is visible when individual actors are depicted. Whereas there are
no individual actors in normative ideology, its operative counterpart
devotes exceptional attention to charismatic personalities. For an
idea or principle to be made understandable to the general public it
is necessary to objectivise it by personalising it into concrete individuals. As Gill has already observed, for an ideology to claim to be infallible it is crucial that it be expressed through one superior voice,
through one leader.[113] In the Yugoslav case it was Stalin before 1948
and Tito after 1948. So we read in newspapers of the time about Stalin
as 'a genius leader of the Soviet Union and organiser of the victory
over fascism'.[114] He is also depicted as 'the leader of people in the
struggle for peace and democracy' who 'brilliantly showed the way for
the destruction of fascism'.[115] He was also perceived as a teacher who
'is teaching us how to fight for peace and democracy' and 'whose
intellect goes deep into all complex questions in the world and light-
ens the roads of development and progress of humanity'.[116] However,
the leader is not only a teacher but a dear friend: 'for our people the
words of comrade Stalin are not only wise words of the teacher and
leader but also of a brotherly and close friend who speaks from the
depth of the soul of every one of our men'.[117] Here too, as in the cases
of Marx and Lenin, one notices that an appeal is not made to Stalin's
superior knowledge but principally to patriarchal and paternalist
images of a stern but just father.

After 1948, the role of the father is given to his former and most
dedicated follower and 'eldest son', Tito. So, Tito was now portrayed
as

> the organiser and leader of our liberating struggle, [but] who is also
> the restless leader of our post-war renewal and development, [and
> under whose leadership] our peoples have in a single year of peaceful
> life in their Republic accomplished numerous achievements.[118]

These achievements were so magnificent that 'our country under the leadership of Tito, has achieved in five years what other industrially developed countries have achieved in 50 or 100 years'.[119] Tito was seen as 'a personification of everything that is wise and honourable, brave, talented, noble, everything that the people are and what moves our people forward'.[120] We also read that Tito 'is girdled with the unlimited love of the people, because he is a personification of the people's struggle and the aspirations of the working masses to realise a new, happy life'.[121] He has a brilliant intellect and as such he 'is a symbol and flag, organiser and maker of the new Yugoslavia, the country of heroes and workers, the country that gives everything for independence and independence for nothing'.[122]

The relationship between Tito and the people is again depicted in Lefort's phrase as 'People-as-One'. So we read that: 'in peace time and in war the people and Tito are one – Tito leads people and people follow him [and] Tito leads them on the only possible, only righteous and progressive road'.[123] Tito is not only the leader but like Stalin before him, also the great teacher who sets tasks and directions: 'equality has been guaranteed by our great teacher Marshal Tito';[124] 'by accomplishing the tasks set by Marshal Tito, our peoples achieve victory after victory';[125] 'we go further, without rest, in the direction that Tito has shown us';[126] and 'peasants have also responded to Marshal Tito's invitation'.[127] It is 'his intellect and his thought' that ensures that the transformation of the society goes in the 'the righteous and planned' way.[128]

The difference between normative and operative ideologies is also visible in the depiction of negatively treated actors. Thus, we see that the manifesto's villains are faceless class enemies taken directly from the *Communist Manifesto* (bourgeoisie, capitalists, imperialists) who at the level of operative ideology, are given visible and recognisable faces and images and are depicted as the monarchist government of old Yugoslavia, opposition parties, fascists and their collaborators or US and British imperialists.

So, normative ideology is full of very general and abstract descriptions of the bourgeoisie and capitalists. We read for example that

> the bourgeoisie attempts to keep and develop control over the entire state mechanism and state capitalism to establish itself permanently as its principal and leading force with the aim of conserving capitalist relations and preserving its privileges in national and international spheres[129]

or that

the system of bourgeois democracy is just a special form of political monopoly divided between leaderships of political parties; with a strong division between legislative and executive power which is often in the hands of administrative staff that is tightly connected with the ruling class, political forces of bourgeoisie secure in their rule.[130]

Operative ideology focuses less on the capitalists and bourgeoisie as an abstract class category than on concrete, visible groups and individuals: the representatives of the monarchist government, US and British Imperialists or opposition parties.

The domestic pre-war bourgeoisie are viewed as greedy, egotistic but also as un-patriotic: 'when the Serbian bourgeoisie took power in their hands, they started to use all means to enlarge their wealth';[131] 'Serbian bourgeoisie ... cared not only about exports of agrarian products but also about the interests of domestic capitalists';[132] or

> occupiers have mostly gathered around them bourgeois elements who because of their narrow class interests, and in fear for their capital have joined the foreign conquerors. What separatist chauvinists did because of their blind hatred towards Yugoslavia, the capitalist elements have done because of theirs class interests.[133]

The monarchist government of pre-war Yugoslavia was depicted as a ruthless, non-democratic and non-people's government. Thus it was stated that 'they [the monarchist government] have suffocated people's liberties, persecuted, jailed and killed creditable and honest men who fought for the people and for a better and agreeable life for workers and peasants'.[134] It was also claimed that 'in old Yugoslavia none of peoples had freedom and equality'.[135]

The British and US governments are depicted as hegemonist and imperialist. Hence, we read about 'imperialist rapaciousness',[136] 'imperialist warmongers'[137] and '*agents provocateurs* from the group of American reactionaries and imperialists',[138] and about how 'agricultural workers in the USA are the object of inhumane exploitation'[139] and how

> imperialists did not learn anything from the sad destiny of German, Italian and Japanese aggressors; ... in their blind race for world domination, American imperialism, ... does not miss a single chance to support and strengthen fascism where it still exists.[140]

The same attitude is expressed towards the leaders of 'capitalist states'. US presidents were mentioned in this regard, but among all Western leaders Churchill was most often the object of media depiction in the immediate post-war years. Thus, it was Churchill who 'dreams about the world domination of Western imperialism'[141] and, although 'Winston Churchill and his followers are doing everything they can to stop the further development in Europe',[142] they will not succeed because 'peoples who have liberated themselves from Hitler's tyranny do not want to replace that tyranny with ... Churchill's tyranny'.[143]

The immediate post-war period was also a period of fierce struggle between the ruling party and opposition groups. Consequently, the media and textbooks put maximum effort into delegitimising opposition parties. They are often accused as traitors, war criminals and fascist collaborators:

> behind the 'opposition' there are hidden monsters of treason and crime. Behind the intellectual head of Milan Grol peers Draža Mihajlović [leader of the *Chetnik* movement], peers Ljotić's and Nedić's ideologists ... behind the 'opposition' are hidden defeated Pavelić's *Ustashas* and Pavelić-Maček's *domobranci*.[144]

They are explicitly labelled as 'traitors and political smugglers', 'traders of the motherland', 'eternal vassals and daring traitors', 'hidden *Chetnik* conspirators' or 'tragi-comical figures'.[145] However, their actions will be stopped because 'workers carefully watch the actions of the people's enemies who want to disrupt regular work on the renewal and rebuilding of our country'.[146]

The difference in the depiction and interpretation of actors in normative and operative ideologies indicates again that these two levels of ideology not only have different audiences – normative ideology primarily targeting party members and those who already subscribe to this ideology and operative ideology the masses – but also different aims. Normative ideology paints the picture of an ideal utopian society focusing on the ideas and principles derived from the scientific discoveries of Marx, Lenin or Kardelj. This ideology sees itself as a messenger of the ultimate truth. Its aim is simply to deliver this message and to apply it in the context of the new Yugoslav state. As such normative ideology is not concerned with the specifities of Yugoslav society or about any actors of social change apart from the proletariat and the bourgeoisie. Following its blueprint the existence of these actors is taken for granted. Operative ideology, on the other hand, has a more difficult task. First, it has to connect the theory in normative ideology with the concrete reality of Yugoslav society. It must, therefore, locate capitalists, bourgeoisie and working class in concrete and recognisable actors. Hence, unpopular characters such as former monarchist governments, fascists, foreign occupiers, big powers and all historical enemy nations assume the role of capitalist and bourgeoisie, while the united peoples of Yugoslavia are identified with the working class and proletariat. In this way the public can identify with the ruling ideology. Second, unlike its normative counterpart, operative ideology cannot speak through ideas and principles. To be recognisable to the masses, it has to transform ideas and principles into concrete and visible actors so that the public can project their emotions onto these reified concepts. One can fear or despise Churchill or the Germans more easily than 'capitalist modes of production'. The image of Milan Grol and other opposition leaders who 'whisper from their holes' is something that will always have a stronger appeal than any economistic explanation of inequality in the world.

Language

The differences between normative and operative ideologies identified so far are perhaps most visible in the analysis of the language, symbols and expressions used. What one sees here are two ideologies that speak through two very different mediums of expression. Normative ideology speaks through the voice of reason, using the vocabulary of science, whereas operative ideology functions through representations and images of popular and folk culture.

The careful reading of the manifesto indicates that its authors see the world largely through a single and central dichotomy, derived from the vocabulary of Marxist–Leninist science, that of capitalism vs. socialism. The central metaphor present here is a modernist and evolutionary one. This is the language of the Enlightenment which demonstrates a firm belief in progress. Hence, on the one side we see capitalism as an old and dying system that makes its 'last moves while leaving the historical stage'.[147] This is the system that belongs to the past.[148] Its 'mode of production' and its 'social system are in their final phase'.[149] The attribute most often ascribed to capitalism is 'rotten'. So, we read that 'capitalism is rotting',[150] and that monarchist Yugoslavia was characterised by the 'rottenness of bourgeois socio-political system'.[151]

On the other side of this dichotomy is socialism. This is a young, new system that came with the 'waves of great October'.[152] Socialism is viewed as a 'transitional period'[153] where 'socialist and progressive forces'[154] through a 'socialist chain reaction'[155] work on the 'development of socialist social consciousness'[156] and against 'backward social consciousness' still present among some groups of workers and peasants.[157] What one sees here is a mythology of science, technology and progress at work. The authors of the manifesto regard themselves as carriers of modernity, progress and change. They intend to break the chains of tradition and authority, to get rid of an old, rotten and dying system and to replace it with the new, youthful and progressive one. Their views are strong because they are derived from the authority of (Marxist) science and because they truly believe they are the possessors of ultimate knowledge.

It is precisely because they see themselves as being in possession of knowledge that has discovered the ultimate truth of human existence and the laws of history that they have to be hostile towards all other heretical views. Hence, all concepts and ideas that may, in one way or another, be opposed to ideas of scientific socialism are negatively described and delegitimised unscientific, and thus untrue and insidious.[158] These include small property owner's egoism;[159] blind and destructive anarchism;[160] destructive anarchist undermining of the political basis of socialist society;[161] philistine–anarchist tendencies that have no perspective;[162] pseudo-liberalism or abstract liberalism;[163] pseudo-revolutionary sectarianism;[164] calumny of the enemy of socialism and idle talk of opportunists, *philisters* and *petit-bourgeoisie*;[165] reformist–dogmatist orientation of social democracy;[166] and small property owner and bourgeois mentality.[167] When one encounters the conflicts of ideas and differences of views among 'socialist forces', they are not blind, destructive or abstract as in capitalism but rather the 'expression of dialectical contradictions'.[168] All the language used here is clearly the language of science or scientifically derived theory.

Operative ideology uses much richer and more colourful language than its normative counterpart and employs metaphors and symbols that are not derived from science. The actors, events and actions described are not depicted with reference to some scientific conceptualisation of world history but exclusively by appealing to familiar images of tradition, patriarchy or the family. One does not find here obscure terms such as 'pseudo-liberalism' or 'dialectical contradictions' but rather familiar concepts such as 'pride', 'honour', 'blood', 'mother' and so on. Here again, instead of the reference to ideas, concepts and (counter-) ideologies as in normative ideology, operative ideology makes reference mainly to concrete and recognisable individuals and nations that act as heroes or villains.

The main hero is the people (our people). The people are always brave, heroic, preserve their honour, sacrifice for the common good and never betray their kin. These are all central traditional values for the populations living in this part of the world. The language of operative ideology is couched in this terminology and relies on images that constantly appeal to these values. Hence, one comes across many stories about the heroism of ordinary people who sacrificed themselves for partisans and communists during the war. One such story tells of the bravery of the common people in Vojvodina:

when fascists wanted by force to find out from the mothers where the partisans were they would take their children from their arms and throw them in front of tanks, but the mothers would not say a word. And one boy did not tell them where the hospital of wounded soldiers was even when [fascists] were holding him upside down from the top of the church tower.[169]

Here we see that the central message of the story is that the people (our people) are so heroic and brave that they will sacrifice what is most valuable to them (their children) in order not to betray those who fight for their freedom. The story implies that the goal of the partisans is so noble and sacred that even the sacrifice of our own children is a price worth paying. However, more importantly, the aim of the story is to legitimise the present situation in terms of this sacrifice. If this society that 'we' have built was worth the lives of our children then who could oppose its existence. Here again, operative ideology invokes our emotions to justify the *status quo*.

Sacrifice and bravery are supplemented with the values of honour and pride. So we read how

we stand in defence of *our* unquestionable rights ... and speak about *ours, only ours, and for thousand times ours* Trieste and Julijska Krajina ... we do not do that in the name of the people who have made their history *kneeling on their knees* nor who have got their rights by mercy of others, we do that in the name of the people who had established *their glory, their national pride, their right to life and dignity* among other peoples by *endless streams of blood.*[170]

Hence, we are there to protect the 'honourable socialist flag of our country'.[171] The appeal is made not only to 'our' heroism but also to 'our' dignity and honour. We are as a 'people' superior to all those who 'made their history kneeling on their knees'. Our glory comes from the fact that 'we' did not get our freedom 'by mercy of others' but from 'endless streams of blood'. Thus, one more time we see how the existing political system and the State is justified with reference to the traditional values of honour, sacrifice and bravery. The State and freedom we have today were worth dying for and are, therefore, sacred.

The images invoked in operative ideology are also aimed at provoking an emotional response by using the terminology that refers to actors as family members. So we read about the 'brotherly people of the Soviet Union', 'our brothers in Croatia and Slovenia'; the 'Free Autonomous Region of Vojvodina [which] has been won by its best sons together with the soldiers of our glorious Army';[172] 'the sons of Srem';[173] and 'the best sons of Vojvodina',[174] or recommendations such as 'do not allow the precious blood of the heroic Soviet people to be shed without our participation'.[175] Operative ideology speaks here through a language that is most sensitive and most appealing to the public – the language of family. What kind of individuals and human beings would we be if we were indifferent towards the suffering of our brothers, sons and mothers.

Finally, operative ideology identifies us and defines us directly within the particular historical and geographical areas and actors. The ideology ties us to 'our' ancestors, giving us the fantasy of being part of 'great History'; at the same time it also chains us to this fantasy by making us responsible for the continuation of 'our traditions' and asking us to sacrifice for 'our nation' if 'the nation asks us to'. Hence, it is 'we' who settled in this part of Europe, it is 'we' who fought the Ottoman Empire and so on. Textbooks and editorials are full of formulations that are given in the 'us' form such as: they [the Venetians] wanted to appropriate *our* Adriatic coast;[176] with the help of Byzantium the Venetian Republic has conquered … *our* coast';[177] Romans conquer *our* land;[178] and Roman rule in *our* land.[179]

When heroes appear as individuals, they are as a rule, individuals whose qualities summarise those of 'the people'. One cannot be a hero if one was not born and raised by the people and if one's sacrifice or realisation of heroic deeds is not for the sake of people. Thus we find out that 'only because he is a loyal son of the people, comrade Tito is their leader as well'.[180] It is the same with other true heroes such as Tucović, a leader of socialist movement in early twentieth-century Serbia, who 'remained through all his life close to the people'; who 'when he encountered socialist ideas remained loyal to them from then until his death'; who 'was very diligent and industrious'; and who was also 'wise by nature and physically strong'.[181]

The textbooks and editorials are also full of symbols and metaphors that directly allude to the public's collective memory and traditional – religious knowledge. Thus, for example, the major battles fought by partisans in World War II are interpreted mystically as the 'Seven Offensives' through which Tito and the partisans had to pass with difficulty by relying on their wisdom and bravery in order to achieve the salvation of the country. The structure of this myth resembles in many ways the temptations and sacrifices of Christ and the early Christians.

The colourful language of metaphors is present also in the depiction of villains. They are dehumanised chiefly by giving them animal features and characters. Thus, on the one side, we have the Soviet Union as 'our hope and tower of light',[182] and 'the big and mighty brotherly Red Army [who] came to help us',[183] while on the other, we read about the 'fascist herd who as mad dogs attack the Soviet Union,

our dear socialist country', about 'bloodthirsty fascist rulers', about
the 'unstoppable savagery of occupiers', about the 'bloody orgy of
uncontrolled butcher-like units' or about the 'animalistic killings and
butcher-like murders of *Ustashas* and *Chetniks*'.[184] The occupiers
'poured poison and acid between the peoples of Yugoslavia'[185] while
leaders of the opposition who 'openly collaborate[d] with occupiers'
are now 'whispering from holes'[186] and the Vatican is engaged in
'coyote growling against democracy in Yugoslavia'.[187] The villains are
morally inferior:

> they started to gather small groups of demoralised deserters from the
> vanguard of socialist development and paid careerists to organise
> them to write and publish their counter-revolutionary pamphlets.[188]

They are also traitors[189] and rotten.[190] The villains are shown as
objects. Hence, we read about them as the 'dark elements who
with their hegemonistic policies have tyrannise[d] our people'[191] as
'philistine elements' or 'bourgeois elements'.

The depiction of villains as animals, morally inferior beings and
objects has several functions. First, it helps to integrate society, build
a sense of community in a very heterogeneous milieu and acquire
support for the ruling party's policies by showing how widespread,
dangerous and unscrupulous our enemies are. Since 'we' have so
many enemies we have to stick together behind the party which will
protect us. Demonisation of the 'Other', as Eatwell points out,[192]
helps to crystallise this sentiment. Second, it justifies potential and
actual extreme types of behaviour (imprisonment, execution,
torture) not only against enemies but also against those who would
support their views or as more often, those who might oppose the
party's policies. Third, by depicting villains as objects and animals
they can easily be conceptualised as non-human entities that disrupt
the 'organic harmony' of the (socialist) society, and also easily be
removed from the body (body politic).

Counter-ideologies

The content analysis of counter-ideologies shows again how ideology
operates differently at the normative and operative levels. While in
normative ideology most of the attention is given to 'capitalism' and
'bureaucratism' as economically and politically inferior ideas and
concepts, in operative ideology the two have been reconceptualised
as 'American and Soviet imperialism'. In other words while normative
ideology focuses on ideas and their delegitimisation, operative ideology emphasises the material actions of the enemy, i.e. potential or
actual threat to our territory.

The main counter-ideology of normative ideology is capitalism. The basic feature of capitalism, according to the manifesto, is the exploitation of the working class for the purpose of making profit: 'monopolist capitalism exploits the working class, working people, middle class as well as colonised peoples'.[193] Since this is a contradictory process that periodically produces economic crises and results in the establishment of big monopolies, capitalism itself has no future. As the manifesto tells us, 'with monopolist capitalism the process of the stagnation of capitalist society, as well as its rotting has begun'.[194] The establishment and dominance of huge monopolies has 'reached its last stage – imperialism, and Lenin gave a scientific Marxist analysis of that process'.[195] As a result of this stagnation and crisis, capitalism has caused two World Wars.

In addition, 'capitalist relations of production cannot follow the extremely developed forces of production that are constantly emerging as a result of advances in science and technology'.[196] That is why state intervention is needed: 'Monopolist capitalism uses the mechanism of the State which influences the unification of monopolies, financial oligarchy with the State and its apparatus'.[197] However, as it is stated in the manifesto, 'state intervention cannot save the capitalist system ... these tendencies only show that humanity is, unstoppably and in different ways, entering an era of socialism'.[198] The argument used here clearly makes an appeal to the superior knowledge of the authors of the manifesto. They offer us a scientific explanation of the capitalist economic system and give us theoretically developed arguments about why capitalism has no future.

Operative ideology places less emphasis on the economic explanations and contradictions that arise in capitalist modes of production and more on the imperialist aims of powerful capitalist states. Capitalism is described and presented to the masses in the image of an external power whose aim is the conquest of 'our country'. Hence, we read about the 'expansion of American imperialism'[199] and 'imperialist predators'[200] who intend 'to enslave Western Europe' with the Marshall Plan.[201] A newspaper editorial entitled, 'Independence or Dollars', explained that 'behind American help is hidden [the intention] to leave the country at the mercy of American capital'.[202] It argued that this plan 'shows that American monopolists aim to conquer the peoples of western Europe under the mask of so-called help and to subject them to colonial slavery'.[203] In addition, the United States and Britain were accused of supporting 'monarcho-fascists in Greece' at the expense of democratic forces: 'American and English occupiers and their Athenian quislings cannot resist the heroic struggle of the Greek people'.[204] We do not have here any economic or political explanation of capitalism's inferiority; the appeal is solely to the emotions and interests of the population – the fear from the mighty external power that intends to enslave us and our common interest in resisting such an attack. Here again the actors are not unrecognisable abstract concepts and ideas such as 'capitalism', 'bourgeoisie' but concrete and visible collective actors with their personalities – the United States and Britain.

When reference is made to capitalism and to the bourgeoisie, it is to locate and identify those universalist and abstract ideas within concrete and particular historical actors. The aim is to delegitimise these historical actors by depicting them as 'capitalists' or 'bourgeoisie' but also to give specific meaning to these abstract and popularly unknown terms by associating them with concrete, negatively viewed agents in history. Thus, for example, it was the bourgeoisie that brought 'the bourgeois–democratic Constitution of 1888'[205] which aimed, together with the new civil law, to 'enable the young bourgeoisie to establish their political and economic positions'.[206] Some historical actors were discredited when they changed their socialist policies: 'The Radical party has become now the party of industrial and banker capitalists who left the democratic struggle and moved to reactionary positions'.[207] The pre-war Balkan wars were also explained as being in the 'interests of the large bourgeoisie'[208] who needed economic expansion. The political system of capitalist states was regarded as artificial and thus untrue and inferior: '*AVNOJ* was never a parliament in terms of a traditional bourgeois formal tripartite division of power'[209] or 'pseudo-democratic phrases used by American and British delegations'.[210] It was also commonly believed that the 'bourgeoisie has a stronger class, rather than general and national, interest'.[211]

In addition to capitalism, normative ideology operates with two more counter ideologies – 'bureaucratism' and 'bourgeois ideologies'. They are both attacked and analysed exclusively on theoretical grounds and have been characterised as the 'two ideological tendencies that have been stopping socialist theoretical thought'.[212]

The first group of tendencies lists bureaucratism and *étatism* as special forms of 'dogmatic and conservative-oriented pragmatism', that is, 'a revision of the elementary scientific tenets of Marxism and Leninism'.[213] The tendencies emerged with 'Stalin's authoritative evaluations of all contemporary processes'[214] and was reflected in the overemphasis on the importance of the State and its bureaucracy in the development of socialism and the building of a personality cult. As the manifesto put it: 'Stalin has in his theoretical analyses moved from the methods of materialist dialectics towards subjectivism and metaphysics'.[215] Here again the authors of the manifesto make an appeal to their superior knowledge of political theory and philosophy, presenting their views as unquestionable truths.

The second group of 'tendencies' consists of different 'bourgeois ideologies' which are termed opportunism, reformism, anarchism or bourgeois-liberalism.[216] Anarchism has often been referred to as 'worthless',[217] 'blind and destructive', the result of 'backward social consciousness'[218] or as a 'destructive and philistine' force.[219] Liberalism is viewed as 'abstract',[220] 'pseudo-liberal'[221] or 'bourgeois'.[222] Both anarchism and liberalism are characterised as dependent 'social and ideo-political forces [that] have emerged as the first line of other anti-socialist forces', these being 'bureaucratism or bourgeois counter-revolution'.[223]

Revisionism appears to be the most dangerous force since it represents 'in reality the ideological reflection of deserting the socialist position with the aim of restoring bourgeois society'.[224] It is a tendency that 'uses pseudo-liberalist phrases and sacrifices workers' interests and socialism to the interests of reactionary social forces'.[225] Revisionism is

> a reactionary obstructor of socialist development, a factor that deforms the socialist state in the direction of bourgeois political system, as well as the factor of destructive anarchism that undermines the socialist basis of [our] society.[226]

In operative ideology all these theoretical positions were reduced to imperialism. This time it is Soviet imperialism that appears to be, in addition to 'capitalist imperialism', the central counter-ideology. Instead of Soviet revisionism which is singled out in the normative ideology as the key counter-ideology, it is now Soviet hegemonic tendencies that matter. Although editorials and textbooks make sporadic reference to revisionist ideas of Soviet leadership, it is their threat to the territorial integrity of Yugoslavia that is the central focus of the operative ideology. We are thus informed that 'on the Fifth Congress the YCP has ... stood in defence of the independence of our country',[227] that 'the attempt to impose control from the outside over our people has always provoked even stronger unity as has happened again this time'.[228] The Soviet leadership, often called 'Inform-bureau-people',[229] is accused of spreading 'lies and calumny against our country'[230] with the aim of imposing 'administrative socialism'. The Soviet type of socialism has been defined as a socialism in the 'permitted borders' and with some passive 'made happy people'. As such it is perceived as being 'in contradiction to the entire revolutionary theory and practice'.[231] In this way the visible collective actor, the Soviet Union, is identified as an enemy. We now see it as an imperialist state similar to the United States and Britain.

The difference between the two levels of ideology comes from their different aims. While normative ideology is written mostly for the party membership with the ruling elite explaining the 'grand vistas' of Marxist–Leninist science to its followers and applying these principles to the concrete situation of the Yugoslav state, operative ideology aims to justify the party's position and its 'leading role' in Yugoslav society as well as in foreign policy. The shifts in foreign policy such as the break in relations with the Soviet Union had, at the normative level, to be explained by reference to the Soviet retreat from the true Marxist–Leninist path, while at the operative level, they were explained as a Soviet attack on 'our' territorial integrity. The counter-ideology of capitalism had also to be translated as a territorial threat from the great powers such as the United States or Britain in order to be made understandable and acceptable to the public. The public cannot fear abstract ideas of 'capitalism' and 'revisionism'; however, images of the bloodthirsty and conquest-oriented United States and Soviet Union were definitely something to be afraid of.

CONCLUSION

The content analysis of normative and operative ideologies shows that the two levels of ideology differ sharply in almost every respect. Normative ideology is the ideology of the universal, whereas operative ideology is the ideology of the particular. That is why normative ideology speaks through the voice of reason while operative ideology regularly makes an appeal to the affects and interests of the public. Normative ideology derives its legacy from Marxist–Leninist science which is regarded as an authority on the laws of history; the only aim of normative ideology is to apply this blueprint to the case of Yugoslavia as soon as possible and with as little deviation from the 'holy doctrine' as possible. Operative ideology has a very different aim, which is to justify the party's monopoly on power in the new Yugoslav state. For that reason it derives its legitimation from more visible and direct results of which the most important is the party's role in the liberation of the country in World War II. To be successful in the realisation of this aim, operative ideology has to combine the existing diverse levels of social such as its normative projections, i.e. creation of the new man with the level of family, thus speaking about 'our' fathers, Stalin and Tito, 'our' mothers who sacrificed their children for what we have today, 'our' Slav brothers and so on, and the level of community at which the entire rhetoric is oriented ('the people'). What operative ideology aims to achieve is the absolute integration and unity of the social through what Lefort calls the 'People-as-One' rhetoric.

One could also say that while normative ideology is idealist, projecting the images of an ideal blueprint-developed society, operative ideology is clearly materialist, grounding itself predominantly in the concrete actions and results of its policies. The close reading of the main texts of normative and operative ideology demonstrates how this is the case when the internal organisation of the society is observed, as well as when the main actors, counter-ideologies and the language and expressions used are analysed.

To achieve its aim, operative ideology makes a strong shift from abstract and universalist ideas to those that have a particularist as well as a nationalist content. Hence, instead of the ideas of socialist internationalism and the historical mission of the working class postulated by normative ideology, one ends up with the glorification of the Yugoslav people and their heroic struggle against all enemies. Instead of Enlightenment-shaped ideas of the liberation of the consciousness of the proletariat extensively developed in normative ideology, one finds precisely the opposite appeal to traditional values of the patriarchal and authoritarian community. While normative ideology relies mostly on ideas and insists more on the theoretical and scientific rationalisation of its ideas, operative ideology targets actors and appeals much more to simple, familiar and recognisable images. The actors that appear in normative ideology are also more visible, more clearly defined and often personified in concrete individuals, nations and political groups, historically or immediately familiar to the wider public. In addition, operative ideology packages unpopular ideas with those that have firm public approval in order to sell them to the masses. The language used in operative ideology is much richer in metaphors, symbols and popular fantasies than that used in normative ideology which is full of difficult and popularly incomprehensible pseudo-scientific phrases.

This is also the case with the depiction of counter-ideologies. While normative ideology is concerned with delegitimising the ideas and theoretical concepts of capitalism, bureucratism or revisionism, operative ideology focuses more on what is visible and understandable to the general public – US and Soviet imperialism, meaning a direct territorial treat to 'our nation and state, to us'. The same degree of difference is noticeable when the nation is discussed. Thus, in this case, the appeal is not so much to socialism, 'laws of human development', efficiency and the quality of socialist economy or political justice for all nationalities living in Yugoslavia, but to historical and present glories, prides and victories of 'our people' – 'our' being simultaneously Slavic, Yugoslav, Serb or Croat. Similarly, the affiliation to Soviet Union before 1948 was justified not by highlighting the attractions of the Soviet political system, but by appealing to common Slavic roots and pan-Slavic kin unity.

All these findings suggest the existence of two levels of ideology that are similar in form but different in the content. While normative ideology focuses on developing and justifying the theoretical model of self-management socialism and Leninist ideas and principles, operative ideology translates these ideas through the discourse of nationalism. The nationalism in question here is less ethnic in character (although, as shown, it does include ethnic appeal) with the main emphasis being on Yugoslav state nationalism. Hence, the normative ideology identified in this content analysis will be further elaborated as *self-management socialism*, whereas operative ideology will be labelled *integral nationalist self-management socialism.*

NOTES

1 Since this is not a historical but a sociological study, the intention is not to focus on the historical details of the particular periods that are covered here. The principal aim is historically to locate and situate main events and actors, so that the analyses that follow are more comprehensible. For the same reason the periods analysed here should be treated as approximate.

2 V. Dedijer, I. Božić, S. Ćirković and M. Ekmečić, *The History of Yugoslavia* (New York: McGraw Hill, 1974), p. 704.

3 Ibid., p. 705.

4 D. Dyker, *Yugoslavia: Socialism, Development and Debt* (London: Routledge, 1990).

5 See *Jugoslavija 1945–1985: Statistički prikaz* (Belgrade: Savezni Zavod za Statistiku, 1986), p. 10, and L. Cohen, *Broken Bonds: The Disintegration of Yugoslavia* (Boulder, CO: Westview Press, 1993), p. 30.

6 It is interesting that during World War II these old folk-songs were often reformulated to glorify communist partisans, Croatian *Ustasha* soldiers and Serbian *Chetniks*, depending on the particular audience. Hence, the same structure and form of the song would be used while its content would be slightly changed to praise one or another group such as:

On top of Romanija mountain	Navrh gore Romanije
The Croatian flag is waved.	hrvatski se barjak vije.
It is waved by young lads,	Razvili ga mladi momci,
Francetić's volunteers.	Francetića dobrovoljci.
And the flag finely reads,	I na njemu sitno pise,
that *Chetniks* have disappeared.	da četnika nema više.
On the top of Romanija mountain	Na vr' gore Romanije,
The red flag is waved,	crveni se barjak vije,
And it has two–three symbols,	i na njemu dva-tri znaka,
Sickle, hammer and a red star.	Srp i čekić, petokraka.
On the top of Romanija mountain	Na vrh gore Romanije
The *Chetnik* flag is waved.	četnički se barjak vije.
Let it wave,	Aj, neka ga, nek' se vije,
It is brought to us from Serbia.	Donet nam je iz Srbije.

See I. Žanić, "Navrh gore Romanije …', *Erasmus*, 6 (1994), pp. 14–15.

7 For more on the institution of *zadruga* see N. Davies, *Europe: A History* (Oxford: Oxford University Press, 1996), p. 390.

8 Croatian sociologist Županov used this term to explain the dominant set of values and attitudes in Yugoslav society. His research showed that on many occasions a particular set of egalitarian values was dominant among the Yugoslav public. This 'egalitarian syndrome', according to Županov, was a fertile ground for the hidden alliance between the governing politocracy and a large class of manual workers:

> The political bureaucracy was given total authority in exchange for maintaining the most minimal subsistence level, with social security and the 'right not to work'; that is, the right to a (low) standard of living, a secure position, and the right not to have to work terribly hard.

See J. Županov, *Sociologija i samoupravljanje* (Zagreb: Školska knjiga, 1977), p. 24, and R. Salecl, 'The Crisis of Identity and the Struggle for New Hegemony in the Former Yugoslavia', in E. Laclau (ed.), *The Making of Political Identities* (London: Verso, 1994), pp. 206–7.

9 As Magnusson writes:

> On that day the president would receive delegations of pioneers, accept their gifts, listen to their songs and tell them about the *great tradition* [my italics], encouraging them to follow in the footsteps of earlier generations. There were, later on, similar meetings with students and young workers in the Belgrade House of Youth. And in the evening there was the 'concluding manifestation', a mass rally at the stadium of the Yugoslav People's Army, where Tito would receive the *Štafeta Mladosti*, or 'Relay of Youth', which had been carried through Yugoslavia by youth of different nations and ethnic groups, symbolising the brotherhood and unity of the partisan war.

See K. Magnusson, 'Secularisation of Ideology: The Yugoslav Case', in C. Arvidsson and L. E. Blomqvist (eds), *Symbols of Power: The Esthetics of Political Legitimation in the Soviet Union and Eastern Europe* (Stockholm: Almqvist and Wiksell International, 1987), p. 74.

10 Sutjeska and Neretva are rivers around which most important battles of World War II in Yugoslavia were fought. Drvar is a small town where a failed German offensive was launched to capture Tito and the communist leadership, while Jasenovac was a concentration camp run by the Croatian fascist *Ustasha* regime and where enormous numbers of civilians (mostly Serbian, Jewish and Romany extraction) were killed.

11 Ivo Lola Ribar was a young, educated and handsome partisan leader whose actions resembled those of the Cuban revolutionary leader, Che Guevara. Posters of Ribar circulated in the 1960s and 1970s among the youth, alongside those of Che Guevara.

12 Sirotanović's example and method of work were later followed by other miners with the slogan, 'let's show Inform-bureau how we build socialism'. See 'Miners from Banovici are working on the method of Alija Sirotanović', *Borba*, 20 August 1949, p. 1.

13 G. Gill, 'Personal Dominance and the Collective Principle: Individual Legitimacy in Marxist–Leninist Systems', in T. Rigby and F. Feher (eds), *Political Legitimation in Communist States* (London: Macmillan, 1982).

14 J. Pakulski, 'Legitimacy and Mass Compliance: Reflections on Max Weber and Soviet-type Societies', *British Journal of Political Science*, 16, 1 (1986), pp. 45–63.

15 E. Kardelj, *Problemi naše socialističke izgradnje* (Belgrade: Kultura, 1960) and E. Kardelj, *Izbor iz dela, I–VII* (Belgrade: Komunist, 1979).

16 As stated in the constitution:

> Under conditions of socialist democracy and socialist self-management, the League of Communists of Yugoslavia, with its guiding ideological and political action, shall be the prime mover and exponent of political activity aimed at safeguarding and further developing the socialist revolution and socialist social relations of self-management,

and especially at the strengthening of socialist and democratic consciousness, and shall be responsible thereafter.

The Constitution of the Socialist Federal Republic of Yugoslavia (Belgrade: DDU, 1974), p. 73.

17 T. Rigby, 'Conceptual Approach to Authority, Power and Policy in the Soviet Union', in T. Rigby, A. Brown and P. Reddaway (eds), *Authority, Power and Policy in the USSR* (London: Macmillan, 1980).

18 See *Borba*, 16 May 1945, p. 1.

19 P. Bejaković, 'Procjena veličine neslužbenog gospodarstva u izabranim gospodarstvima', *Financijska praksa*, 21, 1–2 (1997), p. 95. Some economists have argued that this number is much higher and that in the 1980s 60 per cent of the economy was actually a 'grey economy'. See V. Pilić-Rakić, *Siva ekonomija* (Belgrade: Nauka i Drustvo, 1997), p. 137.

20 For example, this fact is mentioned several times in *Šezdeset godina Saveza Komunista Jugoslavije* (Sarajevo: MSCC CK SK BIH, 1979).

21 D. Beetham, *The Legitimation of Power* (Atlantic Highlands, NJ: Humanities Press International, 1991).

22 Nevertheless, Tito's charisma, although slightly damaged among the Croatian public after the 1971 purge of Croatian intellectuals, was strong even after his death. The number of people who cried in the streets and raised the slogan 'after Tito, Tito' when he died, and who attended his funeral, is also a good indicator of his popularity.

23 M. Weber, *Economy and Society* (New York: Bedminster Press, 1968), p. 119.

24 This attitude is all too familiar to medieval historians because it is almost identical to the myth of the good king who is not informed and is deceived by his counsellors about the hardship of peasant population.

25 This sentence comes from the article that describes Tito's meeting with 'the representatives of people from Istria and the Slovenian littoral region' published in *Borba*, 3 April 1949 p. 1.

26 *Borba*, 17 April 1949, p. 1.

27 R. Barker, *Political Legitimacy and the State* (Oxford: Clarendon Press, 1990), p. 51.

28 Ibid. Rigby's model of goal-rationality is partially compatible with this idea, because the regime's validity is claimed on the basis of the principal goals 'that authorities claim to represent and promote'. However, this concept is too narrow, because as we will see further in the study, ideology is not only much more complex than a single goal such as 'communism', but also operates on two different levels.

29 V. Pareto, *Sociological Writings* (Oxford: Basil Blackwell, 1966), p. 44.

30 Although the legitimisation process is initiated by the charismatic force, the sources of power are not solely in the hands of the charismatic leader, but rather in the hands of the ruling elite, or as Weber would say in the hands of 'his disciples'. Charismatic authority functions more, as Gill points out, as a symbol of the regime.

31 At its sixth congress in 1952, the Yugoslav Communist Party changed its name to the League of Communists of Yugoslavia.

32 *Program Saveza Komunista Jugoslavije*, henceforth *Program SKJ* (Belgrade: Komunist, 1st edn 1958, 2nd edn 1977), p. 152.

33 R. Teodosić, M. Stanojević, M. Bajalica and R. Vuković, *Zemljopis za III razred osnovne škole* (Belgrade: Prosveta, 1946), p. 54 (my italics).

34 *Program SKJ*, p. 152.

35 *Borba*, 2 July 1950, p. 1 (my italics).

36 R. Barthes, *Mythologies* (London: Vintage, 1993).

37 *Program SKJ*, p. 26.

38 *Borba*, 8 May 1947, p. 1.

39 Ibid., 25 May 1947, p. 1.

40 *Program SKJ*, p. 27.

41 Teodosić *et al.*, *Zemljopis*, p. 59.
42 *Program SKJ*, p. 158.
43 *Borba*, 28 November 1946, p. 1.
44 *Program SKJ*, p. 7.
45 Ibid., p. 11.
46 Ibid., p. 8.
47 Ibid., p. 32.
48 Ibid., p. 53.
49 Ibid., p. 114.
50 Ibid., p. 11.
51 Ibid., p. 114.
52 Ibid., p. 8.
53 J. Georgeoff, 'Nationalism in the History Textbooks of Yugoslavia and Bulgaria', *Comparative Education Review*, 10 (1966), p. 446.
54 Teodosić *et al.*, *Zemljopis*, p. 62.
55 F. Ćulinović, *Stvaranje nove Jugoslavenske države* (Zagreb: Grafički Zavod Hrvatske, 1959), p. xix.
56 Ibid., p. 53.
57 A. Gouldner, *The Dialectic of Ideology and Technology: The Origins, Grammar and Future of Ideology* (London: Macmillan, 1976).
58 Lj., Ćubrilović, S. Živković and M. Popović, *Istorija za VI razred osmogodišnje škole I II razred gimnazije* (Belgrade: Znanje, 1952), p. 3 (my italics).
59 *Borba*, 25 May 1949, p. 1 (my italics).
60 *Program SKJ*, p. 6.
61 Ibid., p. 113.
62 Ibid., p. 57 (my italics).
63 Ibid., p. 122 (my italics).
64 *Borba*, 8 May 1947, p. 1.
65 Ibid., 22 August 1948 (my italics).
66 Teodosić *et al.*, *Zemljopis*, p. 56 (my italics).
67 C. Lefort, *Democracy and Political Theory* (Oxford: Basil Blackwell, 1988), p. 13.
68 *Program SKJ*, p. 220.
69 *Borba*, 9 February 1947, p. 1.
70 Ibid.
71 *Program SKJ*, pp. 220–1.
72 *Borba*, 17 July 1949, p. 1.
73 Ibid., 11 November 1948, p. 1.
74 H. Tajfel, *Social Identity and Intergroup Relations* (Cambridge: Cambridge University Press, 1982).
75 *Program SKJ*, p. 191.
76 Ibid., p. 192.
77 Ibid., p. 194.
78 Teodosić *et al.*, *Zemljopis*, p. 97.
79 Ibid., p. 62.
80 Ibid., p. 60.
81 Ćubrilović *et al.*, *Istorija*, p. 95.
82 G. Solarić, *Istorija za VIII razred osmogodišnje škole i IV razred gimnazije* (Belgrade: Znanje, 1952), p. 13. Sometimes the statements are written in a clear *ideologem* form such as 'completely independent Serbia would have an even stronger impact on those *Yugoslavs* that were part of … [Austria-Hungary]'. Solarić, *Istorija*, p. 13 (my italics). The statement refers to the mid-nineteenth century when the concept of 'Yugoslav' could not possibly have existed in the minds of the majority of the population.

83 *Borba*, 19 January 1947, p. 1.
84 Čulinović, *Stvaranje*, p. xix.
85 Teodosić *et al.*, *Zemljopis*, p. 94.
86 Ibid., p. 61.
87 Solarić, *Istorija*, p. 87.
88 Čubrilović *et al.*, *Istorija*, pp. 82, 92. Many of the statements that appear in the textbooks
    are written as *ideologems* that treat collective ethnic actors, i.e. Serbs, as individuals whose
    will could easily be known in every historical epoch: 'the great majority of Serbian people
    could not and did not want that rule in Serbia be practised without constitutional law, so
    they continued their struggle for the constitution', or 'the Serbian people in the princi-
    pality were willing to help Serbs in Vojvodina', or 'the Serbian people were for Russia and
    demanded to fight on its side against the Turks', or 'the Serbian people have agreed with
    this government policy since it was resolutely against the imperialist tendencies of
    Germans'. Solarić, *Istorija*, pp. 7, 11, 11, 79.
89 Solarić, *Istorija*, p. 14. 'Constitution-defenders' (*ustavobranitelji*) were the oligarchic group
    ruling Serbia in the mid-nineteenth century.
90 Solarić, *Istorija*, p. 31.
91 Ibid., p. 85.
92 *Borba*, 16 May 1945, p. 1.
93 *Ibid.*, 27 October 1946, p. 1.
94 Ibid., 16 May 1945, p. 1.
95 Ibid.
96 Ibid.
97 Ibid.
98 *Program SKJ*, p. 5.
99 Ibid.
100 Ibid.
101 Čulinović, *Stvaranje*, p. 46.
102 Ibid., p. 82.
103 *Borba*, 16 July 1949, p. 1.
104 Čulinović, *Stvaranje*, p. 80.
105 *Borba*, 21 September 1949, p. 1.
106 *Program SKJ*, p. 140.
107 Ibid., p. 228.
108 *Borba*, 20 July 1950, p. 1.
109 Ibid.
110 Ibid., 21 September 1949, p. 1.
111 Ibid., 20 July 1950, p. 1.
112 Lefort, *Democracy*, p. 13.
113 Gill, 'Personal Dominance'.
114 *Borba*, 22 June 1945, p. 1.
115 *Borba*, 21 December 1946, p. 1.
116 Ibid.
117 Ibid.
118 Ibid., 28 November 1946, p. 1.
119 Ibid., 21 September 1949, p. 1.
120 Ibid., 25 May 1949, p. 1.
121 Ibid., 25 May 1947, p. 1.
122 Ibid.
123 Ibid.
124 Teodosić *et al.*, *Zemljopis*, p. 128.
125 *Borba*, 28 November 1946, p. 1.

126 Ibid., 16 July 1949, p. 1.
127 Teodosić *et al.*, *Zemljopis*, p. 87.
128 *Borba*, 25 May 1947, p. 1.
129 *Program SKJ*, p. 19.
130 Ibid., p. 163.
131 Solarić, *Istorija*, p. 9.
132 Ibid., p. 86.
133 Čulinović, *Stvaranje*, p. 46.
134 Teodosić *et al.*, *Zemljopis*, p. 56.
135 Ibid., p. 95.
136 *Borba*, 27 October 1946, p. 1.
137 Ibid., 8 May 1947, p. 1.
138 Ibid., 13 October 1946, p. 1.
139 Ibid., 25 May 1949, p. 1.
140 Ibid., 8 May 1947, p. 1.
141 Ibid., 13 November 1946, p. 1.
142 Ibid., 8 May 1947, p. 1.
143 Ibid., 21 December 1946, p. 1.
144 Ibid., 22 September 1945, p. 1.
145 Ibid., 1 October 1945, p. 1.
146 Teodosić *et al.*, *Zemljopis*, p. 86.
147 *Program SKJ*, p. 8.
148 Ibid., p. 10.
149 Ibid., p. 30.
150 Ibid., p. 12.
151 Ibid., p. 90.
152 Ibid., p. 26.
153 Ibid., p. 8
154 Ibid., p. 86.
155 Ibid., p. 26.
156 Ibid., p. 5.
157 Ibid., p. 33.
158 As we read in the manifesto: 'the dogma that the working class should accept the system of bourgeois democracy as its own is not only backward, unscientific and shown in practice to be wrong, but is also a serious brake on the development of socialist thought', *Program SKJ*, p. 162.
159 Ibid., p. 33.
160 Ibid., p. 34.
161 Ibid., p. 55.
162 Ibid., p. 111.
163 Ibid., p. 34.
164 Ibid., p. 54.
165 Ibid., p. 58
166 Ibid., p. 62
167 Ibid., p. 145.
168 Ibid., p. 8. When such conflicts occur, the manifesto explains them by employing an oft-used *ideologem*, declaring that they are 'organic parts of a unified and continuous process of socio-economic and political change in the development of socialism', ibid., p. 106.
169 Teodosić *et al.*, *Zemljopis*, p. 96.
170 *Borba*, 4 July 1946, p. 1 (my italics).
171 Ibid., 1 September 1948, p. 1.
172 Teodosić *et al.*, *Zemljopis*, p. 94.

173 Ibid., p. 95.
174 Ibid., p. 117.
175 Čulinović, *Stvaranje*, p. 50.
176 Čubrilović *et al.*, *Istorija*, p. 96.
177 Ibid., p. 99.
178 Ibid., p. 55.
179 Ibid., p. 56 (my italics).
180 *Borba*, 25 May 1947, p. 1.
181 Solarić, *Istorija*, p. 84.
182 Čulinović, *Stvaranje*, p. 54.
183 Teodosić *et al.*, *Zemljopis*, p. 62.
184 Čulinović, *Stvaranje*, p. 54.
185 Ibid.
186 Ibid., p. 79.
187 *Borba*, 28 June 1947, p. 1.
188 Ibid., 28 June 1949, p. 1.
189 Čulinović, *Stvaranje*, p. 57.
190 Ibid., p. 81.
191 *Borba*, 28 November 1946, p. 1.
192 R. Eatwell (ed.), *European Political Cultures: Conflict or Convergence* (London: Routledge, 1997), p. 255.
193 *Program SKJ*, p. 13.
194 Ibid., p. 23.
195 Ibid., p. 12.
196 Ibid., p. 14.
197 Ibid., p. 13.
198 Ibid., p. 25.
199 *Borba*, 12 November 1947, p. 1.
200 Ibid., 27 October 1945, p. 1.
201 Ibid., 12 November 1947, p. 1.
202 Ibid., 3 November 1947, p. 1.
203 Ibid., 12 November 1947, p. 1.
204 Ibid., 3 February 1948, p. 1.
205 Solarić, *Istorija*, p. 78.
206 Ibid., p. 8.
207 Ibid., p. 78.
208 Ibid., p. 89.
209 Čulinović, *Stvaranje*, p. 186. *AVNOJ* stands for the Anti-Fascist Council of People's Defence of Yugoslavia which functioned from 1943 to 1945 as the parliamentary body of the new Yugoslavia state.
210 *Borba*, 8 May 1947, p. 1.
211 Čulinović, *Stvaranje*, p. 46.
212 *Program SKJ*, p. 53.
213 Ibid., p. 54.
214 It is interesting that this manifesto, published in 1958 and again in 1977, finds some of Stalin's ideas inspiring: 'some of these evaluations were correct, whereas some others were surpassed by practice', ibid., p. 54.
215 Ibid.
216 Ibid.
217 Ibid.
218 Ibid., p. 34.
219 Ibid., p. 35.

220 Ibid.
221 Ibid.
222 Ibid., p. 54.
223 Ibid., p. 35.
224 Ibid., p. 55.
225 Ibid.
226 Ibid.
227 *Borba,* 20 July 1950, p. 1.
228 Ibid., 28 July 1949, p. 1.
229 For example, see ibid., 17 April 1949, p. 1.
230 Ibid., 1 September 1948, p. 1.
231 Ibid., 17 July 1949, p. 1.

4

Serbia 1987–97

BRIEF HISTORICAL INTRODUCTION

The 1966 Brioni plenum of the League of Communists of Yugoslavia (LCY) was a culmination of modest liberalisation and economic growth in Yugoslavia. The results of the plenum were the further decentralisation and purge of the secret police, and especially of its hard-line chief, A. Ranković. However, soon after the failure of the economic reforms initiated in 1965, latent conflicts and unresolved problems became more visible. The main issue in this period was a question of the unequal distribution of funds in the federation and the struggle of the republics' party leaders for more independence from the federal centre.

The period 1968–72 was characterised by the first large-scale unrest which began with student demonstrations in 1968 and ended with the removal and imprisonment of party leaders (including the communist party leadership) and prominent figures of the Croatian national movement in 1972. This was also the period when a number of constitutional amendments were brought in which gave more authority to the republics and provinces.

In the same year (1972) the liberal communist leadership of Serbia led by Perović and Nikezić was removed from power and replaced with a more loyal leadership. Nevertheless, Tito and the federal party leadership responded to the claims of the republics' party leaders by approving the new constitution in 1974 which gave all important powers to the republics and the provinces. From 1974 onwards Yugoslavia was a *de facto* confederal state. Serbia's two provinces, Vojvodina and Kosovo, were also given semi-state status.[1]

The death of Tito in 1980 was a sign that the country was about to enter the new stage. This period was marked by a general economic crisis with massive inflation and high unemployment as well as by political and ethnic unrest in Kosovo. Economic stagnation was evident from indicators such as the drop in GDP, which fell from 8.8 per cent in the period 1956–64 to 0.4 per cent in the period 1980–84.[2] The Yugoslav state had also accumulated considerable international debts,[3] and the economic discrepancies between the relatively developed north-west (Slovenia, Croatia and the Serbian province of Vojvodina) and the undeveloped south-east (the rest of the country), continued to intensify. The fact that 65 per cent of all international loans were made not by the federal state but by the individual republics indicates not only the level of the State's decentralisation but also the almost complete economic independence enjoyed by the federal units.[4]

The first significant and relatively vocal criticism of the State's highly decentralised structure was the 'memorandum' drafted in 1986 by a group of academics from the Serbian Academy of Arts and Sciences. The document focused almost exclusively on the position of Serbs in the Yugoslav state and argued that the existing federal state was, from the beginning an anti-Serb project and that 'Yugoslavia, in its present form was no longer an adequate solution to the Serbian question'.[5]

The growing dissatisfaction with the political system, the widening economic crisis and political unrest in Kosovo was used in 1987 by Slobodan Milošević to gain power within the League of Communists of Serbia. His supporters organised 'spontaneous' street demonstrations in Kosovo and Belgrade which signalled the start of the 'anti-bureaucratic revolution'.[6]

From 1987 till 1989 Milošević's supporters organised a number of similar street demonstrations in Vojvodina and Montenegro and managed to replace their party leaders with others loyal to Milošević. A similar attempt was made in Slovenia and Croatia but it failed because the Slovenian and later the Croatian party leadership recognised the potential danger of these demonstrations. This period was also characterised by a constant political struggle between the aggressive Serbian ethnonationalism promoted by the Milošević branch of the federal party and a liberal and pro-Western, but clearly secessionist Slovenian leadership.[7]

At the beginning of 1990 the last federal congress of the League of Communists of Yugoslavia (LCY) was held where, under pressure from the Serbian delegation, the Slovenian deputies left the congress after all their proposals were rejected. The decision of the Croatian delegation to follow the Slovenians was the sign that the party had disintegrated at the federal level. Soon after, free elections were held in Slovenia and Croatia which were won by nationalist-oriented parties. By the end of that year elections were held in each republic. In Serbia, the League of Communists of Serbia changed its name to the Socialist Party of Serbia (SPS) and won the election.

The new governments in Slovenia and Croatia were even less ready to discuss the reorganisation of the federal state. Following Serbia's demand for a more centralised state, they responded with the ideas of 'asymmetrical federation' and confederation. When agreement was not reached in 1991, Slovenia and later Croatia, following successful referendums, decided to proclaim their independence. Serb-populated areas in Croatia simultaneously proclaimed the independent state of 'Serbian Krajina'. This was a prelude to war.

The Yugoslav People's Army (YPA) which initially presented itself as a mediator in the conflict, soon joined the Serbian paramilitaries. In 1992, when the Bosnia and Herzegovinian government, following the referendum boycotted by the majority of the Serbian population, decided to proclaim independence, war spread to the territories of Bosnia and Herzegovina where the YPA openly sided with the Serbian paramilitaries. The Bosnian Serb side proclaimed the independent state of *Republika Srpska* and was supported by the Serbian government of Milošević, both militarily and financially. The war in Bosnia, which lasted three years and killed more than 200,000 people and displaced another two million, ended with the Dayton agreement signed by all sides in 1995.

Although not recognising other independent states, in 1992 Serbia and Montenegro together proclaimed their independence as the Federal Republic of Yugoslavia. Soon after the outbreak of the war in Bosnia, the UN imposed economic and political sanctions on Serbia and Montenegro for their involvement in the Bosnian war. Despite the sanctions and international pressure, Milošević's party won all the elections at the federal and republican levels held between 1989 and 1996.

Political Legitimacy

The Weberian concept of dominant authority appears also to be applicable in the analysis of the principal legitimacy forms in post-communist Serbia. The types of legitimacy already proposed by Weber, Rigby, Lane, Gill and Barker find some empirical backing. 'Classical' traditionalism plays a much more important role in the explanation of legitimacy in post-communist Serbia than was the case with post-World War II Yugoslavia. Whereas the values of the Enlightenment and modernist Marxist–Leninist ideology were in contradiction with traditionalist ideas, the collapse of communism opened the way for legitimisation through traditionalism. The old myths, heroes and political symbols no longer had to be used selectively. Instead of traditions that glorified the unity of the southern Slavs and class wars, the new situation allowed the expression of all national myths, symbols and traditions, especially those previously under strict political taboo.

The central political myth in Serbian tradition is the Kosovo myth. The myth is based on the actual defeat of the Serbian army by the Ottomans in 1389 when the last Serbian tsar was killed and Serbia lost its medieval kingdom which then became an Ottoman province. The myth itself is extremely rich, including, a multi-layered story, numerous characters of which some are historical figures and some completely invented, and a series of events. However, what is important here is that this myth has served as the main point of reference in the political discourse of Serbian society for the last 600 years. Its public presence was scaled down during the communist period but reappeared with the new political leadership in Serbia after 1987. Since Milošević's famous speech in June 1989 which marked the 600th anniversary of the battle of Kosovo on *Kosovo polje* where the actual battle had taken place,[8] the Kosovo tradition has been used extensively in the political legitimacy of the new regime.

According to this myth the last Serbian tsar, Lazar, was given a choice by the Ottomans at the start of the battle to either surrender or fight to his death. However, he refused the generous offer 'choosing the kingdom of heaven over worldly wealth and the betrayal of his nation to a foreign oppressor'.[9] The myth's central message was to become a cornerstone of a new political discourse in Serbia. The excerpts from Milošević's speech on that occasion confirmed this shift in the discourse:

> Kosovan heroism does not allow us to forget that at one time we were brave and dignified and among the few who went into battle undefeated. Six centuries later, we are again in the midst of battles and quarrels. They are not armed battles, though such things should not be excluded yet.[10]

What we have here is a clear appeal to 'a belief in the sanctity of immemorial traditions', meaning the traditionalist type of authority as in Weberian typology. The fact that the new ruler has discretion to interpret traditions in the way he pleases (connecting the Kosovo battle with the present political situation), is an other element that speaks in favour of traditionalism.

The characters from the Kosovo myth such as the 'hero', Obilić, who killed Sultan Murat and the 'traitor', Branković, were also often invoked in the new political discourse. Thus, for example during the war in Bosnia, one newspaper article identified Mirko Pejanović, a Serb member of the Bosnian presidency loyal to the Bosnian government, as a 'Vuk Branković', the traitor from Kosovo. The article entitled, 'What would Serbs do without Branković?' concludes with the following statement: 'History warns Serbs. Vuk Branković has betrayed

Serbs in Kosovo, but even before and after Kosovo unfortunately there were always Brankovićs among the Serbs'.[11]

Other important political myths and characters invoked in the post-1987 period included Saint Sava, the founder of the Serbian Orthodox Church and the character associated with the particular set of moral and religious values termed, *Svetosavlje*; the victimisation myth of Jasenovac, which inflated the number of victims killed in the Jasenovac concentration camp, where the Croatian *Ustasha* regime committed numerous crimes against the civilian, mostly Serbian population;[12] the political myth of an undefeated Serbian army in history (with the famous saying 'Serbs were always winning wars and losing in peace time');[13] and the heroes and events of the Balkan wars and World War I, such as Nikola Pašić, Duke Putnik, Živojin Mišić and Duke Stepa, the Salonika front and the Cer and Kolubara battles. Thus, for example, the match between the Belgrade football team, Red Star, and the Greek team, Panathinaikos, in 1992, in Sofia was interpreted as a continuation of military battles fought by Serbian armies in the fifteenth century and during World War I:

> the army of *Delijas* [Red Star fans] was as numerous as the army of Serbs led by brothers Mrnjavčević in the battle of Marica ... The miracle called FC Red Star ... can be compared only to the Serbian army in World War I. That army was also wretched and abandoned by the allies and forced to leave the fatherland under the invasion of a more powerful enemy. But it survived and won on the front that was always 'abroad' ... We cannot be saved, we must win. It seems that this sentence of Nikola Pašić from 1915 has become the way of life of FC Red Star.[14]

Most of these old traditions, myths and characters were accompanied by the traditional values of the Serbian peasant soldier: manliness, bravery, masculinity and heroism. Thus, Čolović has analysed the rhetoric used in Serbian war propaganda by demonstrating how the mass media, popular songs, advertisements and similar media appealed to these traditional values: 'Who is a male will go with us!', 'Deserters run away to their mammies!' or 'Only those who know what they have between their legs have participated in this war action!'.[15] This appeal to masculinity and heroism is combined with values of sacrifice for the nation:

> And while proud mothers,   I dok ponosne majke,
> sisters and wives   sestre i supruge
> with black tissues wipe their wet eyes   rupcima crnim oči vlažne brisu
> their heroes from twenty second squad   njihove delije iz dvadeset druge

on the Vlašić mountain   na Vlašiću
are writing a new history!   Novu 'učiteljicu života' pišu![16]

'Awakened' old traditions were also supplemented by new ethno-national traditions, heroes and myths. These include the myth of ethnic rapes in Kosovo, the Paraćin barracks and the Martinović incidents before the war and a number of new war-related traditions and warlords who are depicted as national heroes, such as Captain Dragan, Arkan, Giška and Knindjas.[17] The new traditions also include the folk-songs written and sung among the public. Most of these new songs used the established patterns and structures of old epic songs. Hence, instead of Tito and his partisans, the songs were about Slobo (a nickname for Milošević), and the Serbs:

> Come on the terrace and greet a Serbian race.
> From Kosovo to Knin, it is all Serb next to Serb.
> Slobo Serb, Serbia is with you!
> Who is saying, who is lying that Serbia is small,
> It isn't small, it isn't small, it gave us Slobodan!
> Manastirka, manastirka, a Serbian brandy,
> it warms, [dear] Slobodan, the Serbian army.

> Izadjite na terasu, pozdravite srpsku rasu
> Od Kosova, pa do Knina, sve je Srbin do Srbina.
> Slobo, Srbine, Srbija je uz tebe.
> Ko to kaže, ko to laže Srbija je mala,
> Nije mala, nije mala, Slobodana dala!
> Manastirka, manastirka, srpska rakija,
> s njom se greje, Slobodane, srpska armija.[18]

The important feature of this traditionalism is its solely ethnic (Serb) and occasionally religious (Serbian Orthodox) content. Unlike post-World War II Yugoslavia, post-communist Serbia made no attempt to develop a labour tradition and a cult of a labour hero.

Although traditions, and especially ethnically shaped ones were much more important for the legitimisation of the new Serbian regime than it was for post-war Yugoslavia, traditionalism in itself is insufficient to provide the only source of legitimacy. Although this time there are fewer contradictions between the dominant normative ideology and traditional values, the regime is equally selective in its manipulation of particular traditions. While Serbia was still a part of socialist Yugoslavia the new political leadership had to balance between the officially promoted commitment to Yugoslav interna-tionalism and socialist ideals on the one hand and ethnonationalist traditions and values on the other. After the breakup of the federal state and the introduction of the multi-party system the Serbian leadership had to balance ethnonationalist traditionalism and socialism in order to make ideological gain against much more nationalist opposition parties. The Serbian regime had the difficult task of presenting itself as an ideologically new force that would oppose 'bureaucratic and confederate socialism', but would not completely reject the previous political system, its achievements or the idea of socialism. In this way the leadership would portray itself as revolutionary ('anti-bureaucratic revolution') on some occasions and as non-revolutionary on others. However, with the introduction of parliamentary democratic principles, the system was somehow forced to legitimise itself more often in post-revolutionary terms, i.e. as being responsible for the radical social changes that brought about the introduction of pluralist democracy. This post-revolutionary legacy and promotion of the rational, on the model of pluralist democracy build, institutions of the society might indicate the importance of legal–rational type of legitimacy at work here.

Indeed the existence of the bureaucratic state and administration with parliamentary democracy, a tripartite division of power, a legal system with an impersonal order to which all persons in authority are subjected and written technical rules, confirm the existence of Weberian legal–rational authority. As in Weber's concept one can identify a hierarchical order in which the State and its institutions operate, employees have fixed salaries, and technical training and specialised knowledge are deemed important for employment. Since the great majority of the property is still owned by the State, the administrative staff, as in the Weberian concept, are separated from the ownership of the means of production. Since Serbia and Montenegro compose a new Federal Republic of Yugoslavia, there are two sets of bureaucracy at work (federal and one for each republic) and two sets of constitutions and laws. In this way the State organisation is even more than usually complex and hierarchical, resembling Weber's bureaucratic state.

Although some of these elements appear to be more present and influential in the regime's claim to legitimacy than was the case in post-war Yugoslavia, this concept of authority is still a weak source of the regime's legitimacy. First, the relationship between the ruling elite and the State is very ambiguous. This is not a case of the one-party state where the leading role of the party is defined in the constitution as it was in socialist Yugoslavia; rather, the ruling elite around President Milošević still had a decisive influence on the shape and direction of the legislative system. This extends not only to its influence as the parliamentary majority of the SPS in securing the instant passing of new bills and laws, but to its influence on the courts which almost always would decide in favour of the ruling party. This was demonstrated when the opposition, despite winning local elections in major Serbian cities in 1996, was overruled by local and state courts which found the elections to be invalid for procedural reasons.

Before the political changes of 1990, the regime would regularly use non-institutional means to achieve its political goals such as organising 'spontaneous' demonstrations in Serbia, Kosovo, Vojvodina, Montenegro, Bosnia and Croatia to bring down the political leaderships in these republics and provinces or arranging for the arrest of the leader of the League of Communists of Kosovo, Azem Vllasi.[19] The regime also confiscated Slovenian and Croatian property long before these republics proclaimed their independence and committed a huge economic plunder by unilaterally taking money from the federal reserves. After the 1990 changes, the political leadership of Serbia continued with policies that have little to do with the 'rule of law'. These included the proclamation of the new Federal Republic of Yugoslavia without a referendum in Serbia; the summary arrest of war criminals who openly spoke about their crimes committed during the Bosnian war and who showed a willingness to testify in the international war crimes court in The Hague against members of the Serbian leadership (Željko Mišić); and a ban on its own citizens of ethnic Albanian and Muslim origin entering the country.

Second, as in post-war Yugoslavia, the degree of clientelism, nepotism and the extent of the 'black' and 'grey' economy were beyond any 'ordinary' level. Nepotism was evident at the top of the power pyramid where Milošević's wife, Mira Marković, once held the influential position of Belgrade leader of the Communist Party, and after 1990 headed a sister party of the SPS, the Yugoslav United Left (YUL) that was to share power with the SPS. Under the sanctions imposed by the UN in 1992, the 'black' economy and smuggling became the dominant form of trade and money-generation in Serbia. In addition, competence and skills were regarded as less important when applying for job or when career advancement was in question if not accompanied by ethnic (Serbian) and political (membership of the SPS or YUL) qualification. Thus, the great majority of managers and directors in state-run companies, who account for 90 per cent of the Serbian economy, were members of the SPS or YUL.

All this confirms that the legal–rational type of legitimacy was, just as in state-socialist Yugoslavia, the least important source of the regime's authority. Here again, it was the charismatic personality of Slobodan Milošević that appeared to be a more crucial source of the regime's legitimacy.

   With Tito's death in 1980, Yugoslavia was ruled by the eight-member collective presidency which rotated presidents every year. The members of the presidency were typically grey, invisible communist *apparatchiks*, unrecognised and unnoticed by the majority of the population. After Milošević took power in the League of Communists of Serbia in 1987, he introduced a completely new image of the politician in public discourse. Instead of grey *apparatchiks* who would deliver obscure speeches full of pseudo-scientific terms and concepts referring to Marx, Lenin and Tito, as well as to the victories of the partisans in World War II, Milošević would speak clearly and directly using 'fresh' and simple phrases understandable to everybody. His speeches referred to everyday problems and for the first time since 1971 and the 'Croatian spring',[20] he broke a taboo by speaking to an audience consisting solely of one ethnic group (Serbs) and using ethnonational rhetoric. His style of delivering speeches differed from anything seen before. It was a *deus ex machina* type of speech. Like one of the Greek gods or a rock superstar, Milošević would allow the public or demonstrators to wait for a couple of hours, and then arrive from 'Olympus' to deliver a short and direct speech with a single and clear message and leave the podium quickly. During the event marking the 600th anniversary of the Kosovo battle in 1989, which launched him as a charismatic authority, he came like a messiah in a helicopter (as protector and saviour), to deliver a speech to one million people. His speeches were full of short and memorable phrases such as 'Serbia will be united or there will be no Serbia!', 'No one should dare to beat you!' or 'My foot shall not touch the ground in Kosovo as long as Kosovo is not free'. As some political observers rightly noticed, Milošević was the first politician in the former Yugoslavia to realise that Tito was dead.

   As with Tito, we have here a prophetic leader who set up to achieve another millenarian target – to unite all Serbs into single state. Since the target was presented as the dream of all Serbs from the time they settled in the Balkan peninsula to the present, the achievement of this goal would mean the realisation of a miracle. Milošević's success in bringing the two provinces of Kosovo and Vojvodina under Serbian control was a clear sign that the miracle was on the way. Milošević soon established himself as the leader who united Serbia; who had 'solved' the Kosovo problem by protecting the Serbs living there; who, like Tito, had established a direct connection with the people[21] and who had 'returned dignity to Serbian people'. His military victories in Croatia and Bosnia in the period 1991–94 definitely established him as a charismatic figure, while UN sanctions imposed in 1992 contributed even further to the homogenisation of the Serbian public around their leader.

Although Milošević could not rely on the personality cult typical of the communist era, his pictures and posters were all over Serbia, songs were written glorifying his successes and he was permanently present in the mass media. Milošević also had initial support from the Serbian Academy of Arts and Sciences and from many Serbian intellectuals who were in one or another way behind the famous memorandum of 1986.

Although the control of and the manipulation of the mass media was an important device used by the new Serbian ruling elite, Milošević had the support and sincere devotion of the majority of Serbian citizens. As the many elections and referendums held and the indicators of mass mobilizations show, Milošević ruled as a plebiscitary ruler in the period 1989–96.

Like Tito, Milošević achieved a special role in the establishment of the new regime and the new political system, thus introducing an entirely new set of dominant values which the public identified with the new leader. The way the new leader addressed the masses was identical to Tito's. Milošević managed to tailor his leadership to the needs of his followers. Instead of appealing to the working class and working people, he would address his followers as 'the people' or 'the Serbian people', which appeared to be a closer and more direct way of communicating with the masses. The ruling party itself is of even less importance than the LCY was in the former Yugoslavia. As election results show, it is only when the leader's name and photograph appear next to a party candidate's name and photograph that he or she could be assured of victory in the election. The irrelevance of the party in comparison to the leader is exemplified in Milošević's involvement in the establishment of another socialist party headed by his wife.

As in the case of post-war Yugoslavia, the hierarchical social structure of Serbian society does not disturb the existence of the charismatic form of the regime's legitimacy. Here again one finds a relationship between the leader and his followers being presented as direct and uninterrupted. Milošević's speeches resemble those of Tito. The leader portrays himself as being one of the people but at the same time superior to the rest of the crowd. Milošević recognised that it was the 'people who were writing a new Constitution' in 1989 but, like a strict yet just father, he would finish his speeches with the orders: 'Now go home!' or 'Now you all go to fulfil your duties!'. Like Tito he would appeal to the common cause and that justice be done, but what made his speeches different from Tito's was the clear emotional appeal to ethnonational roots. While Tito's use of ethnic nationalism could be strictly limited, Milošević had more room to play this card:

You should stay here. This is your land. These are your houses. Your
meadows and gardens. *Your memories.* You shouldn't abandon your land
just because it's difficult to live in, because you are pressured by injustice and degradation. *It was never part of the Serbian and Montenegrin character* to give up in the face of obstacles, to demobilise when it's time to
fight ... *You should stay here for the sake of your ancestors and descendants.*
Otherwise your ancestors would be defiled and descendants disappointed. But I don't suggest that you stay, endure, and tolerate a
situation you're not satisfied with. On the contrary, you should change
it with the rest of the progressive people here, in Serbia and in
Yugoslavia.[22]

The appeal made in this speech is multi-dimensional. The leader
emphasises to listeners their right to stay (this is their land, houses,
meadows and gardens) simultaneously with their duty to stay (for the
sake of their ancestors and descendents), appealing to their emotions
(this is where their memories are) and their human qualities (to stay
despite hardships of life). However, the central issue is the moral
obligation which arises from the common ethnonational origins
shared by listeners themselves, their ancestors and descendants, and
the leader/speaker himself (it was never part of the Serbian character). In this way the leader reminds his followers what the central
values of their society are, which, shared by all of them and at the
same time, legitimises his position as 'the first among equals' to interpret these values and to lead the masses.

As in the case of post-war Yugoslavia, charismatic authority could
only work in the long run if successfully connected with the dominant
value system. Thus, Barker's idea of value–rational authority here
plays an important role in the regime's process of legitimation.

As with Tito and socialist Yugoslavia, the particular historical and
political environment of the breakup of the State, the change of political and economic system and war had a crucial impact on the dominant attitudes of the public. In this case, too, several of the achievements of Milošević and his collaborators were seen by the Serbian
public as miracles. In the eyes of the Serbian masses Milošević and the
socialists were responsible for the following miracles: the anti-bureaucratic revolution, the unification of Serbia, the protection of Serbs in
Kosovo, the unification of all Serbs into a single state, victories in war,
resistance to sanctions and finally, the peace agreement in Dayton.

Unlike Tito and the communists, Milošević could not provide an
economic miracle or higher living standards; however he and the
socialists were perceived as the only guarantors of existing social
benefits, pensions and jobs. In addition, unlike Tito and the communists who had the difficult task of 'internalising' a completely new,

and in many ways, complex and abstract ideology of Marxism–Leninism, Milošević was free to use the one ideology most easily suited to stir and 'wake-up' – ethnonationalism. Unlike post-war Yugoslavia, the leader and masses were now ethnically, and thus ideologically, congruent.

Milošević's 'gift of grace' and his miracles could be practically used in the canalisation of new dominant values. The new values of ethnonationalism promoted by charismatic authority were much more easy to accept in a situation where they had been taboo for several decades. The monopoly of the mass media and educational system was also decisive in reshaping the new dominant values. One of Milošević's first moves when he took power in 1987 was to appoint the people loyal to him as editors and chiefs of the main newspapers, TV and radio stations. That the manipulation of the mass media was a conscious and predetermined move was confirmed by the words of Dušan Mitević, Deputy Director of the main Serbian TV channel, who said after Milošević's visit to Kosovo: 'We showed Milošević's promise over and over again on the TV. And this is what launched him.'[23]

By appealing to the sentiments of victorious, brave and never enslaved Serbia, Milošević could control the direction and intensity of ethnonationalism for his own political purposes. While offering the fantasy of the resurrection of Tsar Dušan's kingdom to the masses, he and his collaborators could manipulate these masses to further their own power struggle with other party leaderships and acquire real benefits – control over the leaderships of Vojvodina, Kosovo and Montenegro and control over the popular vote at the federal level.

Even more than the government of post-war Yugoslavia, the regime was in a situation to disseminate its ideology by packaging it in a form that the general public could accept. While official and operative ideologies were congruent in their main elements, the way the dominant ideology was shaped and presented differed. The appeal to well-known symbols, agents and language was, as we will see, the main source of ideology dissemination. Relying intensively on traditionalism and partly on legal–rational elements, the regime started with charismatic authority to initiate change in the value system but operated through value rationality. Just as in the case of post-war Yugoslavia, the *ideologisation of charisma* becomes the principal form of the regime's legitimacy.

In order to see the way value rationality works one has to identify the structure and content of the dominant power-keeping ideology in Serbian society in the period 1990–97. This will include the analysis of normative ideology as well as operative ideology for the same period. Normative ideology will be identified through a content analysis of the ruling party's manifesto, whereas operative ideology will be established by a content analysis of school textbooks and newspaper editorials published in this period.

Normative and operative ideologies

Although the actual politics of Serbia and of the Socialist Party of Serbia (SPS) have changed periodically within the period 1990–97, this was not reflected in the party documents. On the contrary, the party leadership has constantly insisted on the continuity of its ideology and political activity. The content analysis that follows has been undertaken on the basis of the manifesto of the Socialist Party of Serbia which was accepted as the party's programme at the second congress of the SPS in October 1992. As in the case of post-war Yugoslavia, the content analysis of this manifesto will help us identify the dominant normative ideology for the period 1990–97.

Taking into account that the mass media and the educational system are the two main pillars of ideology dissemination, I will also content analyse the main textbooks that were, and still are, in use in primary and secondary education in Serbia, as well as the editorials published in a typical government-controlled newspaper, *Dnevnik*, for the period under examination. The analysis of those two will provide the data for the identification of operative ideology.

Economy

Just as in the case of post-war Yugoslavia, the content analysis reveals significant differences between normative ideology and operative ideology. The first striking difference is the fact that while normative ideology devotes enormous attention to the economy, explaining in detail the advantages of the 'mixed type of ownership', operative ideology makes almost no reference to the economic organisation of society.

Hence, we find out that one of the main 'grand vistas' of normative ideology is the idea of the 'mixed economy' which is the central basis for the establishment of a 'mixed society'. One reads in the manifesto that socialists 'want to establish a society where economic processes will be regulated by free competition within specified legal frames and where all types of ownership will be equal'.[24] This type of economic organisation of society is called the *mixed economy* and is characterised as 'an optimal solution for our circumstances'.[25] This mixed economy 'includes market economy' but also 'a certain degree of state regulation, transformed social ownership, and also the possibility of its unimpeded transformation into private, co-operative and state ownership'.[26] All types of ownership are regarded as equal before the law. This ideal of the mixed economy is dependent on the existence of 'mixed type of companies'. According to the manifesto: 'the transformation of socially owned companies into public (state) ownership has as its aim the gradual and controlled privatisation or change into mixed type companies'.[27] Consequently, the main idea is that 'our future is for the most part mixed and not fully private companies'.[28] The emphasis on the mixed economy leads towards the establishment of what is called the 'mixed society'. Thus, we read that

> the Socialist Party of Serbia advocates a modern, mixed society repre-senting a synthesis of those elements of the liberal and socialist models that have so far proved to be successful in the history of modern society and in our own development.[29]

At the operative level there is no reference to the 'mixed economy' or the 'mixed society'. Instead of the insistence on 'mixed type of ownership', school textbooks and newspaper editorials promote either classical socialist views on the economy or single out market economy as the only desirable form of society's organisation. The analysis reflects many contradictions among which the most impor-tant is the Marxist–socialist interpretation of political economy which stresses the exploitative nature of capitalism while unquestionably accepting and emphasising the market-oriented economy. Thus one reads that

> the main causes of crises in capitalism are the contradiction between labour and capital and the unadjusted relationship between produc-tion and consumption. In capitalism production is for the sake of profit only through the extensive exploitation of workers and poor peasants.[30]

This co-exists with the declaration that 'the Federal Republic of Yugoslavia is ... a market-oriented [state]'.[31] How can one explain such a significant difference between the normative and operative levels of ideology? First, to understand this discrepancy between the two levels of ideology, it is necessary to take into account the existing chaotic situation in Serbian society after the introduction of multi-party elections and political and economic changes in eastern Europe. Unlike most other post-communist societies Serbia did not experience a change of ruling elite in the post-1989 period. The ruling League of Communists of Serbia changed its name to the Socialist Party of Serbia but continued to remain in power. How-ever, in the changed economic and political environment of post-communist Europe, the party had to present itself abroad and at home to its opponents as significantly reformed. On the other hand, to demonstrate that it alone was responsible for social benefits established in the communist period, the party had to preserve its 'socialist legacy' in the eyes of the public. Thus, the syntagms 'mixed economy' and 'mixed society' appeared as ideal umbrella concepts that would somehow help to neutralise all existing contradictions in economic policies and show them to be harmonious, theoretically well developed and scientifically elaborated. Hence, normative ideology speaks again through the discourse of science, making an appeal to its superior knowledge in the field of economy. The chaotic and conflict-ridden reality of the post-communist Serbia which expresses itself in operative ideology through the promotion of completely contradictory types of economy, is presented in normative ideology as a well-elaborated and scientifically developed 'mixed society'. Normative ideology aims to explain the existing confusion and chaos as a part of some strategic plan on the part of reason.

At the operative level, such abstract formulations as 'mixed economy' and 'mixed society' have no relevance because the public is not only uninformed about the economic merits of such concepts, but is also deeply divided between those who want to change the former centrally planned economy into a market-oriented one and those who would like to maintain the *status quo*. This is even more so among the party membership. To avoid conflict on these issues, therefore, normative ideology tries to show them as being non-conflictual and attempts to reconcile them through the 'mixed society'.

Second, the 'grand vista' of the 'mixed economy' which appears in normative ideology as an ideal utopian and universalist concept that holds the key for to establishment of the just and equal society, acts simply in operative ideology to justify the monopoly of the ruling party in the field of economy. To maintain the existing *status quo* where 90 per cent of ownership is still in the hands of the State and the State in the hands of the party, and to slow down the transition process, the party has aptly invented the syntagms 'mixed economy' and 'mixed society'. In the situation of the embryonic nature of emerging private and other types of ownership this syntagm also functions as an *ideologem*.

Third, since the two levels of ideology target different audiences (party members and general public) they have to be formulated differently. Since normative ideology speaks to the audience that is either more informed and more knowledgeable about economic issues, or at least demands an answer to these questions, its aim is rhetorically to reconcile socialism and the market economy in a way that will sound satisfactory to that audience. Operative ideology, on the other hand, is aimed at the masses who have already been politically socialised through the education system that has promoted only socialist views and who generally show little interest in theoretical explanations. In that way, through operative ideology, the party preserves the connection between the past and present when it was in power and shows how consistent and positive its policies are in the extremely chaotic situation of the post-communist world. By establishing that consistency the party appears in the eyes of the public as strong and well directed and in this way makes an appeal to the interests and emotions of the masses who need this certainty in a 'world gone mad'. To establish this connection successfully the textbooks criticise the 'centrally planned economy' of the Soviet type but glorify the concept of socialist self-management[32] and see in it the synthesis of the elements of socialist ideas and market-oriented economy. It is regularly claimed, therefore, that institutions of self-management were actually functioning in the pre-1989 period: 'working collectives were electing and displacing the members of working council. The working council was deciding collectively, [and] was adopting important decisions in the company.'[33]

Politics

As with to the economy, the analysis of the political sphere shows how ideology has again been differently articulated at the normative and operative levels. While normative ideology concentrates on promoting two universalist ideas derived from the social and political theory of egalitarianism which appeal to some 'higher' ethical principles and to expert knowledge in this area, operative ideology focuses almost exclusively on the justification of the existing political system again through the appeal to affects and group interests.

The two principal political ideas and values presented in the manifesto might be summarised as follows: 'socialism and democracy are inseparably linked political values' and 'traditional or indirect democracy is not true democracy'. Both these 'grand vistas' are conceptualised as universalist tasks derived from the authority of Enlightenment-shaped political science and theory which are not necessarily related to Serbian society. They carry the message of reason that is intended to address all of humanity. So we read in the manifesto how and why socialism and democracy are inseparable qualities:

> the socialists of Serbia believe that the ideas of socialism and democracy in their true meaning are inseparably linked. A truly just society is impossible unless the citizens have the equal right to participate in decision-making where they live and work, and in the election of their representatives to state institutions. And conversely, true democracy is impossible unless certain material prerequisites exist, which enable citizens to enjoy their legally guaranteed rights and freedoms.

> Socialism as a social system which ensures freedom, equality and justice,
> enables democracy to develop further in relation to its elementary,
> liberal forms.[34]

The discourse used here is clearly a universalist one. The manifesto
speaks about an ideal just society where true democracy is to be established. This is an inclusive society for all and everybody.

The same attitude and language is used in when the other central
'grand vista' (the insufficiency of indirect democracy) is discussed. As
the manifesto suggests:

> for the people truly to be able to govern – directly, in local communities
> and enterprises and indirectly, through their elected representatives
> in the political institutions of society as a whole – all monopoly on
> power must be abolished.[35]

It is argued that 'democracy is indispensable not only in politics but
also in the domains of economy and culture, both as an indirect
(representative) and direct (participatory) one'.[36] The representative
form of democracy is characterised as insufficient and should therefore be supplemented by different forms of direct democracy. That is
why the Socialist Party of Serbia intends to build a new society on this
idea. The goal is to develop a society where

> employees participate through their representatives in decision-making
> in their enterprise. The administrative boards of firms which supervise
> the work of the manager and his staff should include not only the
> representatives of the owners but also the representatives of the
> employed workers. With the right of participation in decision-making
> and self-management in socialism, employees no longer have the
> status of hired labour.[37]

Here again the appeal is a firmly universalist one. At the level of operative ideology we do not encounter these ideas. First of all, the political organisation of society is very rarely mentioned in the textbooks
and editorials. When the political system is referred to then the
emphasis is, just as in the Yugoslav case, on the particular. Thus,
instead of an elaboration and application of the ideas of direct
democracy or democratic socialism, the main emphasis of textbooks
and editorials in the domain of politics is on the legacy of 'anti-
bureaucratic revolution'. Textbooks and editorials clearly indicate
that the Eighth Plenum of the Central Committee of the League of
Communists of Serbia (CCLCS) was the breaking point in contemporary history: 'the Republic of Serbia, after the Eighth Plenum of

the Central Committee of League of Communists of Serbia (1987) took adequate measures to correct the injustice done with the Constitution of 1974'.[38] Or again:

> At the Eighth Plenum of CC LCS, the conception that promoted democratisation of society, revision of the existing Constitution, protection of Serbs and Montenegrins in Kosovo and Metohija, and the establishment of united Serbia on its entire territory had won.[39]

Instead of the inclusive universalist utopian projects of a harmonious and egalitarian society extensively dealt with in the normative ideology, operative ideology again makes a shift to traditionalist, patriarchal and nationalist values which appeal to emotions and interests. Thus, textbooks and editorials of the time depict the political leadership in control before the Eighth Plenum as 'subjugated and bureaucratised structures on the political scene of Serbia [that] have without argument accepted the 1974 Constitution'.[40] The representatives of the *ancien régime* are delegitimised as being cowards who could not stand for the rights of Serbian people. By doing so they appealed to exclusivist traditionalist values of heroism and sacrifice and to 'our' group interests as a members of Serbian nation.

Moreover, the results of an 'anti-bureaucratic revolution' were also interpreted as a renewal of the Serbian nation, initiated and led by the president of Serbia:

> the Serbian renewal of the last years has started in the spirit of the president of the Serbian state, moving along the lines of the entire Serbian people. Serbs in Serbian Krajinas are protected from the new *Ustasha* genocide and their national question is for the first time internationalised.[41]

In this way operative ideology also makes an appeal not only to ethnonationalism but also to the images of patriarchal culture where the strong father-like figure of the president of Serbia serves as a guarantee for stability and self-direction.

What one sees here is the same pattern already identified in the analysis of Yugoslav ideologies. Operative ideology transforms and translates two universalist and inclusive principles into exclusivist and particularist ideas that promote ethnonationalism and traditionalist values in order to justify and legitimise the existing political order.

Culture and nation
Just as in the case of Yugoslavia's dominant ideology, the greatest difference between normative and operative levels of ideology is in

the different articulation of the 'culture and nation'. Thus, normative ideology sets as its central cultural value the 'elevation of the civilisational level of the people' while operative ideology abandons this value in favour of the glorification of 'authentic' ethnonational Serbian culture. This difference is even more visible when the 'nation' is discussed. Here one can see how the shift has been made from a universalist ethical and legal principle of equality for all to the particularist practices of ethnonationalism.

Normative ideology speaks again in the voice of reason, explaining that 'elevation of the civilisation level of people' means full emancipation from the remains of a patriarchal civilisation, based on the dependence of women on men and the young on the old'. The new order will also 'surpass the traditional liberal civilisation with its outdated political and economic institutions, egotism, and class distinctions.[42]

Many different types of behaviour are listed as ones that should be brought to the higher 'civilisational level'. Among them are: 'a responsible attitude towards public property', 'respect for certain rules of proper conduct in communication with people', 'the overcoming of provincialism which at present finds compensation in the irresponsible passing of judgement on everything that is more or less superficially known' and so on.

Operative ideology ignores these Enlightenment-shaped ideas and the implicit paternalism present in normative ideology, focusing instead on 'authentic' praise of the Serbian culture. Serbian culture is depicted as stable, persistent and basically unchanged from the eighth century to the present. Special emphasis is placed on the importance of the Serbian Orthodox Church in safeguarding the Serbian nation. A typical paragraph would be the following:

> in far overseas countries our people are mostly gathering around the Church … the Church has an enormous role in the life of our people. Of great importance are also [national] cultural–educational and sport clubs … [people] meet there, listen to [Serbian] radio and watch [Serbian] Television. And in this way they protect and keep from forgetting their origins, faith, customs and language.[43]

The difference between the two levels of ideology is further revealed when the 'nation' is discussed. The first important difference is that while the Serbian nation is an issue which is modestly present in the SPS manifesto, it appears to be a central aspect of operative ideology where it fills almost every chapter of textbooks and almost every newspaper editorial. Another difference is in the conceptualisation of the nation. Whereas normative ideology simultaneously employs a territorial (inclusive) and an ethnic (exclusive) concept of the nation, editorials and textbooks always operate with an ethnic definition of the Serbian nation. In operative ideology the nation is depicted as an eternal, timeless community of people who share a common past, present and future and hence, a common destiny.

Thus, while normative ideology focuses on the legal and ethical issues such as the right of self-determination in the event of a break-up of the federal state, the legal definitions of a national minority or the establishment of institutional mechanisms for the equality of all citizens, operative ideology moves from these issues in two ways. First, it ignores any reference to 'empathy' with the other ethnonational groups other than Serbs, and second, it 'translates' some of these abstract and universalist concepts into concrete and particular practices of ethnonationalism and the collective worship of the Serbian nation through history.

Thus, we see in the manifesto that an appeal is made to higher ethical principles and to superior knowledge in the domain of legislation:

> in the circumstances of the disintegration of the former Yugoslav state, the Socialist Party of Serbia has opted for the principle that all its peoples and citizens must be equal, and that on the grounds of the same right of national self-determination according to which the Slovenes, Croats, Bosnian Muslims and Macedonians decided to secede from Yugoslavia, the Serbian nation on the territories where it constitutes the majority population can also decide to remain in a common Yugoslav state.[44]

The knowledge of the international law is also alluded to:

> the Socialist Party of Serbia is convinced that the principles of international law have been violated when the Serbs in Croatia and in Bosnia-Herzegovina, who spent seven decades united with their brothers, were prevented from remaining in a common Yugoslav state on the basis of the right of nations to self-determination.[45]

The same principles are invoked when establishing the difference between the 'constitutive peoples' of the new Yugoslavia and 'national minorities'. An institutional division of nationalities that live in the new Yugoslav federation is made according to whether they have their national state within the Yugoslav federation. Thus, only Serbs and Montenegrins are regarded as 'constitutive peoples' while all other ethnic groups are defined as national minorities. So we read that 'what defines a national minority is not its size but the fact that this concept refers to citizens whose people possess a national state outside the borders of Yugoslavia'.[46] One of the main differences between 'constitutive peoples' and 'national minorities' is that minorities have no right of self-determination, whereas constitutive peoples who 'are associated in the common federal state, that is Serbian and Montenegrin people as well as the peoples that eventually in the future join Yugoslavia', have that right.[47] The manifesto insists that

> it was only with the constitution of Serbia of 1989 that the ground was laid for the rule of law to function effectively, to live and work in freedom, for the safety of persons and property for Albanians, Serbs, Montenegrins, Muslims, Croats, Turks, Romanies, Gorani and the members of all the other ethnic groups.[48]

In operative ideology some of these principles have simply disappeared while others have been articulated in reference to some mystical and special position of Serbs in history. As in the Yugoslav case, operative ideology relies on descriptions of 'its people' as victims of history but who are, at the same time, enormously brave. They are regularly depicted as suffering and sacrificing for the ideas of freedom and justice. There are a number of sentences that glorify Serbs in this way. For example, we read that 'in the difficult times of slavery under foreigners, the freedom-loving spirit of Serbian people that could not come to terms with the slavery was growing',[49] or that 'the people that have such monuments [as monstrous *Ćele kula*] cannot ever be destroyed',[50] or that

> this choice ... Serbian people cannot accept. Not only because it humiliates and insults the entire people, but also because we cannot [again] escape the role ... of the one who should be sacrificed as an example to others.[51]

This bravery and sacrifice is historically traced to the Kosovo battle and resistance to Ottoman conquerors, the wars and uprisings of the nineteenth century, the Balkan wars, and the two World Wars, as well as to the recent wars of 1991–95 in the former Yugoslavia. Thus, one is informed that 'the bravery of Kosovo heroes and their death have been sung of in the popular poems encouraging the spirit of Serbian people in the long and difficult struggle against the Turks';[52] that 'Serbian people who with their first victories in the First Serbian Uprising tasted freedom, could not stand Turkish terror any more';[53] that it was Serbs who 'came to help them [Bulgarians] and the Turks were then defeated';[54] or that in comparison with other Yugoslav peoples, 'the contribution of Serbs to the liberation war was the greatest'.[55]

Victimisation and heroism are also central attitudes when the position of Serbs living outside of Serbia is described. We read in textbooks and newspapers that

> Serbian people who live on the territories of, until recently, Croatia, have been proclaimed to be a national minority and stripped of their rights. It was the same with the Serbs in Bosnia and Herzegovina. Because of all these reasons, Serbian people had to stand up in defence of their national rights.[56]

Or again that 'Serbian people in Croatia and in Bosnia were only defending their right to preserve their lives and age-old homelands'.[57] Their right to have independent states in these areas is historically and ethnically traced: 'their descendants remained in these areas but today, after many centuries of living in these areas, have to defend their national rights';[58] and 'Serbs from former Bosnia and Herzegovina have proclaimed Republika Srpska on the territories where Serbian people are in the majority'.[59] Nonetheless, it is their moral right that appears to be crucial:

> Serbs had to protect themselves from new sufferings and destruction. They accepted the struggle imposed on them, convinced that like other people, they too have the right to be independent and decide their destiny.[60]

What one observes here is a very striking shift between the two levels of ideology. How can one explain this clear shift from the Enlightenment-inspired secularism of normative ideology to the religious Orthodox traditionalism and ethnonationalism of operative ideology? Why does normative ideology affirm a rationalist concept of the nation that emphasises universalist solidarity and equality for all, using legal arguments and appealing to empathy and the discourse of rights, while operative ideology employs an exclusivist, affective and egotist concept of the nation that ignores empathy and ethical arguments? The answer lies in the party's need to justify its policies and thus to legitimise its political monopoly of the State. To be able to present itself as the 'voice of the people', the party has to translate the universalist message of normative ideology into one that makes a direct appeal to the masses. This can be successfully achieved when the images of Reason are transformed into images of Affect and Interests. In the chaotic political circumstances of the period 1990–97, with no articulated ideological forces at the political stage and the war situation, the party attempted to mobilise as many voters and potential supports as it could. Hence, in order to assure 'everybody's' support it could only rely on the widest possible ideological force – nationalism.

In addition, being responsible for Serbia's international isolation and for sanctions imposed by the UN, the party had to use ethnonationalism and traditionalism in order to establish a certain level of continuity between the prevailing mythology and traditional values which cherished the image of Serbs as victims where 'they have to resist the same injustice again', thus transferring the blame on to the shoulders of the 'nation'. It is not Milošević and SPS policies that are responsible for the war and international isolation, but 'us', 'the people' who made the decision to resist the world. Hence, the appeal to values of sacrifice, heroism and victimisation that already existed and were strong among the masses were simply 'awakened' and related directly to the new political circumstances. Thus, instead of the Ottoman and Habsburg emperors who wanted to enslave 'us' in the last century, we now have US emperors with the same ambition. Instead of the Third Reich soldiers of Hitler's Germany 'we' have today to fight the force of Helmut Kohl's Fourth Reich. The message is simple and direct: as a nation we have always suffered for our freedom, and what is happening today is the same as that which happened five hundred years ago – we are the victims of injustice. The strength of such an appeal to the values of victimisation comes also, as Eatwell observes, from the Orthodox Church's teachings which stresses the importance of obedience and celebrate suffering.[61] Given that the great majority of Serbian population was in one way or another socialised within this value system, it is understandable why the appeal to suffering and sacrifice has had a such a powerful effect.

Actors

As in the case of Yugoslavia's dominant ideology, the dominant normative and operative ideologies of Serbia differ sharply in their description of actors. While normative ideology gives very little attention to actors, operative ideology relies extensively on the depiction of different actors. Only a few actors appear in the SPS manifesto and they are all very vaguely defined. The actors that one encounters in textbooks and editorials are numerous and very precisely described. This fact demonstrates again that while normative ideology operates predominantly with ideas and concepts, operative ideology translates these concepts into the familiar images of concrete individuals and collectives.

The main positively depicted actors in normative ideology are socialists and Serbs. Although Serbs are mentioned on several occasions there are no direct references to their qualities. Indirectly, we find out that they are victims of the new international order,[62] that they are forced again to fight for their existence,[63] and that their main characteristics are 'advocating truth, justice, solidarity, resistance to all tyranny, [and] courage at critical moments'.[64] Socialists are described mainly as a progressive, democratic and stabilising force. Hence, we read that the 'SPS ... enjoys the massive support of the citizens of Serbia because of its stabilising, dynamic and progressive role';[65] that 'the Socialist Party of Serbia has proved that it is a party of democratic and progressive reforms';[66] or that 'the socialists of Serbia remain what they are: a party of the democratic Left that relies on the world of labour and is open to the future'.[67] We are also told that

> if the essence of democratic socialism is a commitment to a society of political, economic and cultural democracy, a rational economy, care for the natural environment, civic, national and religious equality and social security, then the future of Serbia belongs to the Socialist Party of Serbia.[68]

At the operative level these two actors are not only much more extensively described but are also differently articulated. Thus, instead of vague and imprecise formulations that interpret actors only with reference to ideas and principles where they appear to be of secondary importance, operative ideology regards them as the primary subjects of action. In other words, while normative ideology ignores actors seeing them only as carriers of ideas, operative ideology works in the opposite way – it derives ideas and principles from actors and their personalities. For example, in the SPS manifesto democratic socialism is the central idea and socialists and Serbs are there only to implement that idea, whereas in textbooks and editorials the Serbs are the central point of reference and socialism and other ideas are there to help the Serbs achieve certain (national) goals more practically, more justly or more rationally.

Serbs and socialists are also differently represented in operative ideology. While normative ideology gives almost no description of Serbian qualities and justifies the political actions of Serbs by relying on universalist principles such as a Serb's right to live in a single state, operative ideology is almost exclusively focused on the depiction of Serbian qualities and derives its justification for the actions of Serbs from their qualities and from their collective historical experience. In other words, in operative ideology Serbs have the right to certain territories because they were always brave, have suffered for their state and thus have acquired that right through blood sacrifice. Hence, we read in normative ideology how the case of SPS policies is made through an appeal to the party's expert knowledge of international law and to reason:

the right to self-determination is not interpreted [by the European Union and the United States] as the right of the people [as it should be] but of territories, and the inviolability of internal administrative borders is elevated to the level of a principle, yet the violation of external state borders is permissible.[69]

At the operative ideology the shift has been made to group collective memory and to extensive description of Serbian group qualities: 'Frightened by the bitter experience from the Independent State of Croatia in World War II, the Serbian people armed themselves'.[70] Thus, because Serbs were always victims who have suffered for their freedom, 'truth and justice are on their side'.[71]

While in textbooks and editorials Serbs exhibit all positive characteristics, two of them are more pronounced than others: heroism and victimisation. So we read regularly about Serbs as experienced and brave soldiers, who have 'successfully protected Austria from the Turkish attacks';[72] who 'although poorly armed ... under the command of Stepa Stepanović defeated the enemy and threw them out of the country';[73] whose help was crucial for Bulgarians to defeat Turks;[74] who have heroic traditions,[75] or whose army regularly 'completely defeat[s] the enemy [who usually] retreat[s] in panic'.[76]

We are also informed that 'the largest Slavic tribe that moved to the south [in the sixth century] were Serbs';[77] that the contribution of Serbs to liberation during World War II was the greatest,[78] or that at the time of the Byzantine empire Serbs were 'gentle towards foreigners', 'not wicked and mean' and '[gave] freedom even to war prisoners'.[79] The textbooks and the editorials give special attention to Serbian war heroes and the victories of various princesses and kings (Vlastimir, Stefan Nemanja, Stefan Prvovenčani[80]) including the medieval kingdoms, and Balkan wars and World War I heroes (Stepanović, Mišić, Putnik among others).[81] A special place is given here to Tsar Dušan because during his rule 'the Serbian state was the biggest power and had the largest territory' compris[ing] two-thirds of the Balkan peninsula'.[82]

Unlike normative ideology which declares itself to be strictly anti-fascist and critical of the *Chetnik* movement that openly collaborated with Nazi troops and was responsible for crimes committed on Muslim and Croatian civilians, operative ideology views all nationalist programmes and ambitions as positive, including the *Chetnik* movement itself: 'The movement of Draža Mihailović that was established and started as anti-Occupation, [and] freedom-loving, because of its anti-communism, ended as anti-Allies and had to be defeated'.[83] This fact indicates once again that unlike normative ideology which has to remain within the externally 'imposed' ethical code of

Enlightenment rationality and morality and the discourse of justice for all members of the human race, operative ideology is free to appeal to individual and group desires and egoism through ethnonationalism. The *Chetnik* movement was perhaps fascist, but since it was 'ours' it could not be wrong. The discourse of ethnonationalism can never accept the idea that the members of the 'nation' can do anything wrong in the name of the nation. Since the 'nation' has a holy status, everything done in its name acquires a sacred dimension. 'We', as Serbs were and are always right.

Not only Serbs but also socialists are differently articulated in operative ideology. So instead of a description of socialists as 'progressive', 'reformist' or 'democratic', and who aim to establish democratic socialist order inspired by a universalist idea, one finds that the emphasis is absolutely particular. The aim of operative ideology is historically to trace and identify actors who will help to justify the SPS's position by legitimising it through the particular history of Serbia. Thus, history textbooks devote special chapters to leftist parties, movements and influential individuals in the history of Serbia, aiming to project in a certain 'normal' (as in Barthes and Althusser[84]) sense a continuity between past and present. Thus, one is informed that 'bourgeoisie and workers lived in towns. In the 1880s and 1890s workers' associations and social democratic parties that fought for the realisation of workers rights appeared [in Serbia].'[85] There are also entire chapters and sections on Svetozar Marković, 'the initiator of socialist ideas in Serbia in the nineteenth century',[86] and 'the development of the workers' movement among Serbs at the end of the nineteenth and beginning of the twentieth century'.[87] At the same time, no other political movements, parties or social groups have received such attention. This strategy of omitting actors and ideas whose presence could be damaging for the dominant power-keeping ideology is exactly what Pareto had in mind when he spoke of 'accords with sentiments'.[88]

Unlike normative ideology which makes no reference to individual actors at all, operative ideology gives a prominent place to individuals among whom one in particular receives the most attention – the charismatic personality of Milošević. He is the individual who often appears most often in newspaper editorials. Thus, we read about the 'far-reaching, wise and consistent politics of Slobodan Milošević',[89] or about how crucial for the Dayton peace treaty was 'the consistency, unhesitation, wisdom and bravery of the politics of our president, Slobodan Milošević',[90] or how 'the peace [agreement] achieved in Dayton is the crown of the statesmanship, wisdom, continuity and bravery of Serbian President Slobodan Milošević'.[91] As with Stalin and Tito, the appeal is made not to Milošević's knowledge but exclusively to his authoritative and patriarchal image. He is the new father of Serbs. He is praised as the defender of Serbian interests and also as the saviour of Serbs in Bosnia: 'it is a fact that with this just peace in Dayton our delegation, especially President Milošević, has defended the interests of the entire Serbian people, our state and all citizens equally'.[92] Similarly, 'the big question is what would happen to the Serbian people over the Drina river, whether they would survive at all if there was no homeland state and Slobodan Milošević'.[93]

Nevertheless, the most obvious difference between the two levels of ideology is in their depiction of negatively described actors. Here again normative ideology is indifferent towards enemy actors. These actors are invisible, rarely referred to, and if referred to then especially vaguely defined. Thus, in normative ideology instead of concrete actors we come across terms such as 'new world order', 'great powers', 'the West', 'imperialism', 'liberal imperialism' and only sporadically are these identified directly with the United States and Germany.[94] In addition, all enemy actors and their ideologies are world-class agents. They represent well-developed ideas, concepts and doctrines to which normative ideology responds argumentatively through a knowledge of economics, political science or law.

By contrast, in operative ideology enemy actors are extensively present. In fact, the great majority of all actors that are depicted in textbooks and editorials are negatively treated actors. In operative ideology they are all depicted as visible, familiar and recognisable collective actors, usually described as entire nations: Croats, Bosnian Muslims, Albanians, Germans, Turks or Austrians. Additionally, the actors that appear in operative ideology are rarely world-class agents who are delegitimised through their wrong doctrines. As a rule they are all historically familiar enemies drawn from the Serbian 'micro-cosmos' – Serbia's neighbours and nations that Serbia had fought with throughout history. They are also delegitimised primarily through the descriptions of their 'personalities and characters'.

Croats are the actors that are most often pictured in a negative light, whether individually or together with the Catholic Church. They are shown as traitors, murderers, Serb-haters or those who have always intended to Croatise and convert Serbs to Catholicism. The textbooks and editorials attempt to show that these features of Croats were present in all historical periods. So, one reads that, in the seventeenth and eighteenth centuries,

> Croatian feudalists and the Catholic Church could not come to terms with the free status of Krajina [Serb] people. Feudalists wanted to make serfs out of them and the Catholic Church wanted through the Uniatism to convert them to Catholicism.[95]

Similarly, 'if this idea were to be accepted and realised, Serbs would as a people be Croatised'.[96] Croats were also accused of being hostile and obstructive to the first Yugoslav state and Croatian extremist organisations are emphasised in that respect: 'Croats have especially singled themselves out with their demands for the recognition of national authenticity behind which were hidden separatist intentions and the desire for the break up of Yugoslavia.'[97]

Croats are also shown as treacherous at the start of World War II: 'the capitulation of the Yugoslav army [in 1941] surprised many officers. At the same time there were some, first of all Croats, who openly took the side of the enemy',[98] or 'there was a lot of treason, especially in Croatia',[99] or 'when German forces entered Zagreb they were greeted with admiration and joy and with flowers'.[100] The crimes committed by the *Ustasha* regime in World War II are discussed in detail. Thus, textbooks devote special sections and chapters to the nature and functioning of the puppet 'Independent State of Croatia' (NDH) regime. For example, a history textbook for secondary school devotes six pages to crimes committed in the NDH with extensive descriptions of the methods of torture and killings undertaken by this regime.[101]

The post-war period does not lack descriptions of Croats as nationalists and chauvinists. The emphasis this time is on the so-called '*Maspok*' (mass movement) and we are informed that '[i]n the period of *Maspok* (1970–71) in Croatia, nationalist feelings and hatred against Serbs in Croatia and against Yugoslavia in general achieved dangerous dimensions'.[102] The election of the CDC to the government of Croatia brought new accusations and animosity against the new regime which was often identified with the Nazi-sponsored NDH state. Hence, one reads that 'the democratic mortar which had been put up in a rush started to fall from the national–fascist facade of the "new Croatian state"';[103] that Croatian television propaganda satanised the Serbian people;[104] or that

> Tudjman's regime ... even with its legal acts follows its model – Pavelić's NDH. Croatia cleansed of Serbs was the same dream for one [Tudjman] as for the other [Pavelić] and in the realisation [of this dream] they equally did not care about the means [used for its realisation].[105]

Albanians are also portrayed in a very negative way. In this period they are not even called Albanians but 'Shiptars' which although derived from the word used by Albanians themselves (in Albanian *Shqiptare* equals Albanian), has a clear pejorative meaning. So one comes across the following terms: 'the representatives of Shiptars' 'the leaders of Shiptar parties';[106] 'Shiptars';[107] 'Shiptar youth from Kosovo and

Metohija'; 'Shiptar children'; 'Shiptar masses'[108] and so on. Albanians are constantly accused of being separatists and aggressive:

> With the aim of realising the idea 'Kosovo Republic' and joining Albania, Albanian separatists were pressuring Serbian and Montenegrin inhabitants to leave their property and to emigrate so to make Kosovo and Metohija ethnically clean.[109]

Germans represent another negatively depicted collective actor. A distinction is almost never made between the Nazi regime and Germans as an ethnonational group. Thus, Germans not Nazis are accused of atrocities committed during World War II: 'Germans have without the declaration of war bombarded Belgrade';[110] or 'as soon as they occupied our country, the enemy [Germans] started unprecedented terror over the population; in their hands were mines and factories that were robbed by them';[111] or 'Germans while withdrawing were burning everything they could and leaving a desolate region behind them'.[112]

The same attitude is present when Turks are mentioned and evaluated. The textbooks are full of torture descriptions committed not by subjects and soldiers of the Ottoman Empire but by Turks. Thus, one reads that 'during their rule Turks conducted unprecedented terror over the Serbian population';[113] that 'Turks crushed all rebellions and then took extreme revenge against people who rebelled: they robbed entire regions, burned villages and towns, killed the people or took them into slavery';[114] or that 'Turks continued with the robbery, abuse and killings of innocent people'.[115] Emphasis is placed on the so-called 'blood tax' (*danak u krvi*): 'Andrić has nicely described this blood tax – taking Serbian children to Turkey, where they have made them enemies of the Serbian people – Janissaries'.[116]

Not dissimilar descriptions of Austrians and Hungarians are to be found in textbooks. Austria-Hungary is typically shown as 'a prison of peoples' and plotting against Serbs and the Serbian state. Thus, it was Austria-Hungary which 'attempted to cause the allies [Bulgarians and Serbs] to squabble and to destroy this alliance';[117] and it was Austro-Hungarian soldiers who 'as soon as they had crossed the Drina river started robbing and killing innocent and unarmed people'.[118] The same soldiers were responsible for 'committing the unprecedented slaughter of women and children'.[119] Later we find the Austro-Hungarians together with 'Bulgarian and German soldiers committing mass crimes against people'.[120] Here again the authors give extremely detailed descriptions of killings and massacres, especially of women and children.

The difference between the description and presence of actors in normative and operative ideologies can be explained, as in the case of Yugoslav ideology, through the different aims exposed by the two levels of ideology. Since normative ideology targets those who already share the main ideas of this doctrine (party members and its sympathisers), it is not necessary to present these ideas in a way that would be more appealing to them. On the contrary, the party has to demonstrate to this audience that its ideas and policies are not strategically made up, but that they truly follow the blueprint of democratic socialism. The ideas that one encounters in normative ideology had to be shown as originating from universalist, scientifically derived concepts that are only applied to Serbian society. To justify its position externally (internationally) and internally (within the party membership), the 'grand vistas' of normative ideology have to be fully congruent with the ideals of other democratic socialist movements and parties world-wide and their message must in that way be a universalist one. That is why normative ideology makes no reference to actors.

The aims of operative ideology are completely different. Here, official ideology has to gain the support of the public which has little knowledge and interest in the universalist message of democratic socialism. Hence, to mobilise the public behind its ideas, the party has to articulate the message of normative ideology through its ethno-nationalist translation in operative ideology by making an appeal to individual and group interests, emotions and traditionalism. Since affects and interest-driven behaviour can be most appropriately directed through a projection of the images of concrete, familiar and visible actors, operative ideology has to rely on this translation. Here again, it is easier to hate or fear Turks and Croats than it is to hate or fear 'imperialist liberalism' or the 'new world order'.

Language

Just as in the Yugoslav case, we can see that the language of the dominant ideology points to sharp differences between normative and operative ideologies. While the main characteristics of the language and expressions used in the SPS manifesto are the absence of any reference to heroes and the very rare use of metaphors and symbols, language, symbols and expressions appear to be central elements of operative ideology. Whereas the main form of expression in normative ideology are pseudo-scientific terms and explanations, operative ideology speaks through popularly recognisable metaphors and symbols.

The feature of pseudo-scientific terminology and explanations offered in the manifesto is a strong belief in the economic and historical laws of development. These views are sometimes combined with elements of an esoteric language such as the formulation 'modern

mixed society'[121] or 'the identity of the socialists – unity in differences'.[122] Thus, we are informed that the 'production of goods for the
market is the basic form of material production in modern civilisation';[123] or that 'it turned out that one of the most powerful weapons
to suppress political voluntarism was a certain automatism in the
regulation of economic relations';[124] or that 'since they uphold the
belief in historical progress, socialists are making preparations for
future economic growth'.[125] This view is most elaborately developed
in the following statement:

> The young people of Serbia should find the strength to overcome the
> confusion in which the entire world finds itself today and in which
> many panic-stricken intellectuals and young people look for salvation
> in long-outmoded, medieval ideas. By persevering with the ideas of
> democratic socialism, young people would avoid going astray and, in
> the years to come, would find themselves at the very centre of the
> mainstream of world history.[126]

This is clearly the evolutionary language of reason, science and
progress associated with the Enlightenment. The manifesto writers
still see themselves as the possessors of ultimate knowledge.

The language of operative ideology is, as in the Yugoslav case, very
far from being the language of science and reason. On the contrary,
operative ideology speaks again through hero-worship, conspiracy
theories, traditional values and the images of patriarchy. The appeal
made here is not to some 'higher reality', but rather to individual and
group egoism, to fears, passions and traditions.

The form of argumentation is very often a conspiracy theory. The
break up of the federal Yugoslav state is thus explained in these terms:
'the conditions were set up for the realisation of already prepared and
masterly thoughtful scenario (inspired and helped by some foreign
actors as well) for the destruction of the Yugoslav community';[127] or

> protagonists of Yugoslav destruction were well aware that on the
> federal level there were only two cohesive factors left: LCY and YPA.
> That is why they have with a well prepared plan in advance, decided
> to destroy the first one (LCY) and then the other (YPA) factor of
> cohesion.[128]

Similarly, 'the plan for the destruction of Yugoslavia into a number of
small states came to realisation stage',[129] and

> the shadow of one horrifying civil war that was consciously thrown to us
> in the dark AVNOJ *vilajet* has covered their heads too, filling insolent

Europeans with the dramatic fear that the door of Balkan madness could easily turn into a big fire which could burn them as well.[130]

An identical argument is used for the explanation of the intentions of Albanians in Kosovo and of the international community for the destruction of Serbia and the creation of a new federal Yugoslavia: 'this is a decades-long strategy organised by Albanians, but it has now received full support and affirmation from some foreign, order-giving groups, primarily from the USA, France and Germany';[131] and 'it looks like everything is [done] for the purpose of dividing Montenegro and Serbia, but a few of them act from personal convictions. Most of them act following orders given by foreigners.'[132]

Operative ideology relies on conspiracy theories in order to collect the diverse layers of a politically heterogeneous society under the single idiom of 'the nation in danger'. By stressing that 'our' enemies are strong, powerful and well organised, and have thoughtfully mastered the plan to destroy 'us' as a nation, the party can again manage to mobilise the public behind it by offering the image of itself as a protector who is strong enough to organise and lead 'the nation' as well as to resist such powerful enemies. In this way the potential conflict within the society has also been displaced outside of society. By relying on conspiracies, operative ideology, as Billig points out, 'offers the chance of hidden, important and immediate knowledge, so that the believer can become an expert, possessed of a knowledge not held even by the so-called experts'.[133] With these simple and instant explanations individuals acquire the feeling of security and control over unpredictable events. The conspiracy theories are focused on the intentionality of certain events where contingency is regularly interpreted as destiny and where 'the cause is danger, and danger is a cause. The conspiracy mentality reveals it in order to eliminate it, not in order to understand it.'[134]

Hero-worship, appeal to masculinity, militarism and patriarchalism are all extensively present in the textbooks and editorials. The textbooks for example speak often about 'Serbian uprising heroism'.[135] There are many epic songs about heroism referring to *hajduks* and *uskoks* who bravely fought against Ottoman conquerors. One such example is the following song where Old Vujadin encourages his sons:

Oh sons, my falcons,	O sinovi, moji soklovi,
don't be with the heart of the girl,	ne budite srca udovička,
but be with the heart of the hero,	no budite srca junačkoga,
don't betray any of your friends,	ne odajte druga ni jednoga,
don't betray our concealers	ne odajte vi jatake naše

| where we spent our winters, | kod kojih smo zime zimovali |
| and where we kept our treasures. | Zimovali, blago ostavljali.[136] |

There are also many stories that glorify the self-sacrifice of individuals for the good of the Serbian nation. One such story which appears in several textbooks recounts how Major Gavrilović and his regiment were heroically sacrificed in the defence of Belgrade in 1915.[137] Gavrilović's last command to his soldiers was regularly cited:

> Heroes! Exactly at 15:00 hours the enemy has to be broken down with your powerful storm and destroyed with your bombs and bayonets. *The face of Belgrade, our capital, has to be bright.* Soldiers! Heroes! The supreme command has deleted our regiment from its list, our regiment has been sacrificed *for the honour of Belgrade and our fatherland.* Thus, you don't have to worry for your lives because they do not exist anymore. So, go ahead into glory! Long live the king! Long live Belgrade! For the king and fatherland!

Just as with Yugoslav operative ideology, here again we find the appeal to individuals to make a sacrifice for the nation. The heroic deeds of Major Gavrilović and his regiment indicate that the 'nation' has sacred features and represents the ultimate good. The nation is not only 'us', it is the most valuable and most pure articulation of 'us'. The nation is truly a Durkheimian collective will, it is an object of worship that has noble and clean features. To give your life for the nation means both to acquire the sacred aura of a saint or a god and to contribute to the purity and sacredness of the nation.

This example also shows how the language of operative ideology connects this call to self-sacrifice with the appeal to traditional values of honour. The soldiers have sacrificed their lives to save the honour of Belgrade and the fatherland; both, Belgrade and the fatherland, are thus objectivised and humanised. They have faces that need to stay bright. They are our mothers and fathers. To remain honourable the soldiers have to preserve the clean face of Belgrade and the fatherland. In other words, they have to protect the honour of their mothers and fathers.

The face-saving values and honour are also accompanied with patriarchal terminology and militarism. Thus, we read about Russians who did not object to some American proposed resolution as 'let them be in their honour' (*na čast im*),[138] as well as about 'prominent masters of the house' (*vidjeniji domaćini*) who should 'feed the son[s] and send [them] into the army, [because] Serbia cannot rest'.[139]

On the other side, the enemy is also related to these values. So we see how the enemy lacks honour, pride and heroism and is devoid of real substance. His very existence is denied. So we see that references to 'Bosnian Muslim' are written with the small letter 'm' as in muslim instead of with a capital letter 'M', which in Serbian indicates that they are considered only as a religious group and not as an ethnic nation.[140] Similarly, the name 'Albanian' was dropped in favour of the pejorative 'Shiptar',[141] while Bosnian Croats and Bosnian Muslims are reduced to religious groups – 'the Croatian–Muslim federation ... is a result of only one aim – defeating the common enemy Serbs, but many things show *that federation of Catholics and Muslims* does not function from the beginning'.[142] Bosnian Muslims are also treated only as converted Serbs and Croats – 'it is well known that Bosnian Muslims are converted Serbs and Croats'.[143] The aim of the language used here is to humiliate the enemy by insisting that his claims are false, because he is not real, he is completely made up.

The enemies (Croats and Bosnian Muslims) are also depicted as 'nationalist, chauvinist and genocidal';[144] as 'ultra-chauvinist';[145] as Tudjman's *Ustasha soldatesk*;[146] as spreading 'beggar–cringer types of lies';[147] and as 'blood-thirsty allies'. Bosnian Muslims are also shown as 'Muhammedans'[148] who intend to establish '*jamahiria* Bosnia and Herzegovina'[149] and who are 'in the war against Serbs for [their] green *transversal* [which is supposed to link Islamic countries with Europe over Kosovo and Bosnia]'.[150] Here again one can see how the language of reason has been replaced with the language of affect.

The affectivity of the language present in operative ideology is also visible when the images and the metaphors of the 'old fireplaces' that Serbs had to leave in World War II, as well as in the most recent wars, are invoked. So we read about the 'mass emigration of Serbs from their age-old fireplaces'.[151] Traditionally, the old fireplaces are associated with the large families of the joint patrilineal house-holds of South Slavic *zadrugas*. Images of being forced to leave these age-old warm fireplaces and go to a cold and unknown destination, elicits deep emotions from the public. The images of fire and warmth are also emotionally related to the traditional values of courage, honour and pride. Thus, leaving the old fireplaces means nothing less than being deprived of courage and honour. Without this honour and pride in a world of tradition an individual's existence is meaningless.

These values are followed further by the victimisation strategy which depicts Serbs as those who have always suffered in history and paid their price for freedom with enormous human casualties. This attitude is present also in the explanation of contemporary events. The Jasenovac myth is here of central importance.[152] Detailed descriptions of killings are given and extensive attention is paid to victims of *Ustasha* state crime.[153] We read, for example, how prisoners in the Jasenovac concentration camp were slaughtered with knives, killed with hatchets, axes, hammers, mallets and iron bars, shot and burned in the crematoria, cooked alive in kettles, hanged and starved to death by hunger, thirst and cold.[154]

We are also informed that the Croatian communist authorities wanted to hide the truth about the camp, but they failed because

the Jasenovac camp will always stay in the historical memory of the Serbian people as our biggest suffering and our biggest mass grave from the time we came to the Balkan peninsula to the present.[155]

What one sees here is an extremely detailed description of killings and modes of torture. These descriptions appear in operative ideology for three reasons. First, in order to make an impact on the masses, normative ideology has to be translated in its operative form through images that will shock, hold the attention of and, most important, be remembered by those among whom these images are disseminated. Thus, the detailed picture of torture and modes of killing and the images of people cooked alive will remain for ever in the memory of students exposed to the contents of these textbooks. The facts of World War II, the statistics and numbers of casualties, the mass destruction and the delegitimisation of ideas and reasons behind the establishment of an independent Croatian state, which appear in normative ideology, will never have such an impact as the picture of people slaughtered with knives, killed with hatchets, axes, hammers, mallets and iron bars, shot and burned in the crematoria, or cooked alive in kettles. And this is indeed how operative ideology functions. It animates the principles of normative ideology by providing familiar, emotionally or interest shaped details that are not only more recognisable, but also more direct and affective. The language of blood will always be better and longer remembered than the language of reason.

Second, the aim of these descriptions is to dehumanise the enemy, to show that the enemy's behaviour and actions do not belong to those of the human race. By demonstrating that the enemy, on the evidence of its characteristics and behaviour, does not belong to the human species, it is easier to justify one's own behaviour and actions. Since the enemy is sub-human we have every right to treat it in the way that sub-humans are treated – to isolate, to torture or to remove them physically from our environment.

In this way operative ideology also justifies its own policies during the most recent war in the former Yugoslavia. The images of torture and suffering are 'awakened' to legitimise the present situation and directly to connect the behaviour and actions of the *Ustasha* regime with the new democratically elected government in Croatia. This is how the connection has been made:

> The situation is almost identical to 1941. Serbian people from Croatia have been forced to leave their homes. Serbs have been tortured and the bestial conduct towards innocent civilians is similar to that fifty years ago. Entire Serbian villages are set on fire and robbed, Orthodox churches are destroyed, cemeteries and sacred places are polluted.[156]

The message is that these people are the same ones that tortured 'us' in the last war. They deny our substance by destroying our churches and by polluting our sacred places. The message aims to show that Croats are predestined to be killers, and that 'we' as a nation can never trust them.

Third, the image of Jasenovac as the biggest Serbian mass grave, 'the scene of our greatest suffering since we came to the Balkan peninsula', aims to remind students what their duties and responsibilities are as members of the Serbian nation. They have to remember this suffering and pass on its memory to further generations. By giving them this responsibility, operative ideology simultaneously defines them (the students) as Serbs and imposes certain forms of behaviour on them. If they do not remember this horrific tragedy in the way required by the ideology, they are not only imperfect Serbs but are not even true human beings. By defining them as Serbs and human beings simultaneously, operative ideology is in a position to control them as individuals.

Counter-ideologies

Although at first sight it may seem that the counter-ideologies to normative and operative ideologies in Serbia are identical, this is certainly not the case. While both levels of ideology operate with concepts such as imperialism, bureaucratism and clericalism, viewing them as the main 'forces of darkness', the three are very differently conceptualised and articulated. While normative ideology focuses on the scientific, i.e. economistic, and ethical reasons in the delegitimisation of the main counter-ideologies, operative ideology locates the enemy in recognisable collective actors, appealing to collective interests and emotions.

The first counter-ideology is liberal imperialism which is the main external enemy in normative ideology. This is identified as standing behind the 'new world order'. The SPS manifesto defines liberal imperialism in the following way:

> In contrast to imperialism of a totalitarian type for which the invasion and occupation of a territory was characteristic, a specific feature of

> this [imperialism], of liberalist origin, is that economic interests (the
> supply of oil, taking over the markets, the recovery of debts and
> control of the indebted countries) are achieved primarily by political
> means. However, the ultimate argument is the argument of force.[157]

Although relatively precisely defined, this counter-ideology is almost
never identified in concrete visible actors.[158] The arguments are
always kept at an abstract level.

This ideology is accused of having primarily economic hegemonist
tendencies but, in order to fulfil this task, it has firstly to establish
cultural hegemony. This can be achieved, according to the SPS manifesto, most successfully through the mass media and information
sphere. Thus, the manifesto reads:

> A colossal concentration of capital in the sphere of information has
> come about in the world. There is an evident tendency among the
> leading industrial powers and multinational corporations to take over
> a dominant role in an increasingly large number of countries.[159]

This type of influence is depicted as an attack on national freedom:

> foreign domination of the mass media would mean a direct threat to
> national independence. However, the most conservative forces, which
> control a considerable section of the press, direct their efforts towards
> taking over the remaining, most significant mass media. This will be a
> struggle for survival and it will continue during the coming years.[160]

Whereas normative ideology makes almost no reference to the classical definition of imperialism, operative ideology and especially textbooks make a direct link between 'old' capitalist imperialism and
'new' liberal imperialism. Thus, we still read about 'imperialism as
the final stage in the development of capitalism'[161] whose main
features are the establishment of monopolies and the 'beginning of
the struggle for a new division of the world'.[162]

However, unlike the classical Leninist interpretation of imperialism
as exploitative of the working class, the new interpretation focuses
primarily on imperialism as a threat to individual nation states: 'with
the support of Austria-Hungary and Italy, the Albanian state has been
formed which will become the weapon of imperialist states for further
expansion in the Balkans';[163] or 'the biggest problem of newly liberated countries was their economic undevelopment. Their problems
were used by economically wealthy states to impose political, cultural
and economic dependence. The new form of colonialism is called
neo-colonialism.'[164] This newly interpreted 'old' imperialism is then

directly related to the new liberal imperialism referred to in normative ideology. Nevertheless, instead of an attack on the abstract ideas
and concepts of this counter-ideology, the attack here is directly on
personalised, concrete actors. New liberal imperialism is thus
associated with the European Union (especially with Germany) and
the United States. Their motives are regularly shown as exclusively
interest-driven. Thus, one reads in textbooks and editorials that

> the attempts to destroy Yugoslavia evidently confirm the fact that the
> appetites of the great powers, especially the economically mighty
> Germany, are so big that they do not choose the means in the realisa-
> tion of their interests.[165]

Similarly,

> the EC under the pressure from united Germany ... has unprecedent-
> edly supported the secession of Slovenia and Croatia. With this it
> showed that its interests are beyond international law, truth and justice
> for the endangered people.[166]

Imperialism, personified in the form of 'international community'
and the 'new world order', is described as unscrupulous, bloodthirsty
and inhumane:

> those who have blood-thirstily butchered us in two world wars for
> their empires and who now in the name of their new European and
> world order are threatening us with expulsion and force ... should
> know that *we will not be anybody's servants* and that we were never
> stronger, more experienced and ready to decide about our destiny
> than today.[167]

Similarly, 'the world was hesitating, playing, taking sides, mostly not
the Serbian side, pursuing their interests through somebody else's
tragedy'.[168] Here again an appeal is made to collective memory, the
affects and common interests of Serbs. The phrase 'we will not be
anybody's servants' is almost identical to the one we encountered in
the Yugoslav case ('we did not make our history kneeling on our
knees'), and indicates one more time that the traditional values of
honour, pride and heroism stand as the central ones in operative
ideology. Unlike normative ideology which aims to delegitimise liberal
imperialism by demystifying its economic and political rationale,
operative ideology invokes images of powerful empires whose only
aim is to deprive us of our pride and glory, making us their servants
and slaves. Thus, as Serbs we have both a collective responsibility (not

to betray our ancestors) and a collective interest (to resist the 'new world order').

The second important counter-ideology present at the normative and operative levels is bureaucratism/confederalism. This ideology is mainly treated as being defeated but 'always ready to reappear' as an internal enemy. Unlike the LCY manifesto in which bureaucratism was regularly accompanied by *étatism* and as such was often identical to the centralisation and concentration of power in the hands of the State and its officials, the SPS manifesto gives us a picture of a different type of bureaucratism. This bureaucratism is identified with highly decentralised policies of the State, and with the arrogance and wilfulness of the State authorities. As such, this bureaucratism is typically associated with confederalism. Hence, the manifesto gives the following descriptions: 'In the bureaucratic system of administration which we have had throughout most of our history, the authorities behaved arrogantly and scornfully towards the people';[169] or 'the anti-market definition of human needs was not achieved by some supposed "scientific methodology", but in most cases arbitrarily, and in a bureaucratic manner';[170] or the '[p]olitical self-will of leaders has produced many erroneous systemic solutions such as ... confederalisation of the State and formation of independent states and [separate] national economies'.[171]

The Socialist Party of Serbia stands against this 'dogmatic ideology and the authoritarian system, as well as the bureaucratic style of rule and cadre policy-management'[172] that had been practised most intensively before the 'anti-bureaucratic revolution'. The 1974 constitution has been singled out as the final and disastrous outcome of bureaucratic and confederative ideologies:

> The 1974 constitution of Yugoslavia definitively destroyed Yugoslavia by proclaiming the republics sovereign states, by giving the veto power to each one of them, and by permitting republican laws to take precedence over federal laws.[173]

At the operative level the argument against confederalism and bureaucratism takes a different form. First, 'the authorities' are personalised and we read that in order to keep themselves in power, Tito and the State leadership undertook a reform of the federal state that resulted in the new constitution of 1974, which was a prelude to the State's break up. As stated in the manifesto:

> the party and state leadership with Josip Broz [Tito] were interested only in keeping themselves in power. That is why they decided to reform the federation and bring in a new Constitution ... With the

reform of the federation, Yugoslavia was practically destroyed as a single state.[174]

Second, the attack has shifted from the 'authoritarian system' as a whole to the level of the federal units. We now read that individual republics, i.e. Croatia, Slovenia, and their leaderships are responsible for the policies of bureaucratism and confederalism. It is argued that it is only 'under the mantle of the struggle against the unitary state and dictatorship that many republican and provincial leaders ... have prepared themselves to take over power'[175] and that, in fact, 'the constitution of 1974 was a victory for nationalist and separatist forces from the republics and provinces' and, as such, this constitution is regarded 'as the most disastrous document in the recent history of the Yugoslav peoples'.[176]

This particular translation of normative ideology into its operative form is important because it suggests to the public that 'our' present-day enemies were always 'our' enemies. So the animosities towards Croatia and Slovenia are historically traced by developing the same old argument about the conspiratory nature of the enemy: while 'we' were blind and trusted them completely, 'they' were working behind our backs to destroy 'us'.

The third counter-ideology one can identify while analysing these texts is clericalism. The difference between normative and operative ideologies in this case is the most striking. While clericalism in normative ideology is conceptualised as an internal enemy that aims for a stronger connection between the State and the Church in Serbian society, operative ideology identifies clericalism only with the non-Serbian Orthodox religious denominations.

The content analysis of the manifesto indicates that clericalism stands as an important internal counter-ideology. The manifesto clearly states that socialists 'contest clericalism, i.e. the aspiration of certain church circles to acquire greater spiritual and political power over the people'.[177] The influence of the Church and religion in politics has been regarded as inappropriate in a modern secular state: 'any dogmatic approach to religion or ideology is incompatible with the spirit of the secular culture of the modern age'.[178] The Party stands for 'a lay state and a lay political culture as opposed to a clerical state and a theological political culture'.[179] As we read in the manifesto:

> Any form of clericalism is extremely intolerant and dogmatic. A political system may be considered democratic to the extent that it has separated the secular from the religious and the State from the Church.[180]

The strong pressure from the Church and clerical political parties for the inclusion of catechism in the school curriculum has been identified as the most important danger. Thus, we read: 'To nurture this spirit of equality, breadth of mind and tolerance is the basic reason why schools should not be places for ideological or religious indoctrination.'[181] Similarly,

> the school must not impose religious convictions on any pupil because this would violate the principle of freedom of conscience and religion. For this reason the socialists consider that the study of religious dogma (religious instruction) should not be part of the curriculum in public educational institutions.[182]

At the operative level, clericalism is articulated in a completely different way. Operative ideology sees clericalism as a counter-ideology only when it comes from Roman Catholicism or Islam. Both denominations are depicted as a threat to the Serbian nation and the Orthodox Church. At the same time, the Serbian Orthodox Church is always defended. Religious denominations other then Serbian Orthodoxy are all condemned as proselytising, highly politicised, aggressive and even collaborators in crime. This includes their teachings as well as their institutional forms.

Unlike normative ideology, operative ideology glorifies and praises the Serbian Orthodox Church. Thus, special sections are given to Saint Sava who established the Serbian autocephalous Church and who 'is celebrated as the one of the most important saints by the Serbian people'.[183] We are also informed that

> the Serbian Orthodox Church has from its establishment (1219) to the present been a completely independent religious organisation of Serbian people. Its activity always coincided with the main interests and needs of the Serbian people.[184]

On the other hand, Roman Catholicism is interpreted as a fundamentalist religion that demands the total submission of its followers: 'The Roman Catholic Church ... demanded absolute loyalty and behaviour in accordance with its teaching which is very extreme, especially towards the Orthodox religion.'[185] The idea that the Catholic Church is extremely hostile to Orthodoxy is repeated on many occasions. One such declaration is as follows: 'through the Catholic Church and its fanatical believers the struggle is fought against the Orthodox religion and Serbs'.[186] Unlike the Serbian Orthodox religion, Roman Catholicism is viewed as a regressive and dark force: 'Roman Catholic clericalism was very active in the Kingdom of

Yugoslavia in the struggle against progressive forces through clerical political parties and the formation of unions as militaristic organisations'.[187] These aggressive tendencies have been again historically traced by appealing to collective memory and emotions. We read, for example, that during World War II 'clericalism wanted, through the NDH, to realise the idea of a strong Catholic state in the Balkans, which was to open the door for the spread of Catholicism and ensure the return of "renegades" from the [true] religion'.[188]

However, the most severe accusation against the Catholic Church relates to its collaboration with the *Ustasha* regime during World War II. It is emphasised that Catholic priests were 'among those who ran the concentration camp [at] Jasenovac'[189] and that 'many of them inspired slaughter and were spiritual leaders of religious fanaticism'.[190] On one occasion there is a detailed description of a priest who instructed his flock on how to slaughter Serbs. The words of the Catholic priest were as follows:

> Brother Croats, go and slaughter all Serbs. First, kill my sister who married a Serb and then all other Serbs. As soon as you finish this job, come to me in church for confession, where I will give you blessing and communion so that all your sins will be redeemed.[191]

This description of the Catholic priest who calls upon his flock to kill Serbs shows again how operative ideology articulates the principles of normative ideology by providing particular details. The teachings of Catholicism or any other religion which are opposed in normative ideology by relying on arguments derived from science are articulated by operative ideology in a way that the masses can comprehend them. Thus, what we see here is not the delegitimisation of the Church's teachings by showing them to be 'dogmatic' and 'doctrinaire' but rather examples that confirm that this is a diaboliical and monstrous Church whose clergy is not only morally corrupt for giving its blessing for the mass execution of Serbs, but also the main instigators of genocide. More importantly, by identifying the actual priest (Fr Srećko Perić), operative ideology personalises the principle and evokes deep emotions of fear and hatred. Operative ideology tells us: look at the Catholic priest in your village, street or town! He looks innocent but under his mantle there is a murderer who only wants to eradicate you and your family from the earth.

In a similar vein, Islam is equated with Islamic fundamentalism. The emphasis is mainly on some radical teachings in Islam and its cultural differences with Christianity. Thus, we are instructed in a number of editorials that Turkish secularism is only 'a passing "illness", while Islam is eternal'[192] and that the aim of Islam 'is to renew the Islamic empire as a world-wide Islamic caliphate that intends to return all former Balkan territories to the rule of Istanbul'.[193] Islam is viewed negatively, mostly in connection with the Bosnian Muslims and the war in Bosnia and Herzegovina. The message is that Islam as a religion cannot live side by side with Christianity because its aim is to conquer the world and spread its teachings.[194] Islam is often identified with radical groups and militant policies, especially with the holy war (*jihad*) and holy warriors (*mujahedin*) who are described as 'fanatical volunteers from various Islamic countries'.[195]

This transformation of the main counter-ideologies from normative ideology to operative ideology can be explained by reference to the party's need to justify its policies and to mobilise popular support in the extremely turbulent period of post-1989 Serbia. Faced with the biggest external challenge to the party's policies, such as the EU- and US-backed international blockade of Serbia, the party had to legitimise its policies at the top (among party members) and the bottom (the public) of the power pyramid. Thus, it formulated the ideas and principles of the EU and the United States as a main counter-ideology of liberal imperialism which was understandable and would also appeal to the Leninist educated party membership. However, at the level of operative ideology the task was much more difficult since the public had little knowledge and interest in Leninist ideas and concepts. More importantly, these new foes were for the most part popularly unrecognisable as enemies. Therefore, the operative ideology had to make these new enemies appear as much as possible like Serbia's old enemies.

This was achieved in the operative ideology in three ways. First, the existing Leninist interpretations of imperialism and capitalism have been reformulated in the textbooks to sound much more nationalist by emphasising the 'capitalist and imperialist threat', not to the workers but to individual ethnically defined nation states. Second, to delegitimise the enemy ideologies it was necessary to establish a very strong connection between the images of the new enemies and the old and familiar ones. Thus, the emphasis in operative ideology has shifted from the United States and new world order to the microcosmos of the former Yugoslavia where the enemies have been given the familiar faces of Catholicism and Islam which are popularly associated with old foes such as the Ottoman and Austro-Hungarian Empires and even Nazi Germany. Thus, Croats and Bosnian Muslims have simply replaced Austrians, Germans and Turks as already familiar and recognisable collective enemies. Continuity has been established and old and new enemies have become one. This has even been explicitly stated:

> this time as well, an attack on Serbia and the Serbian people has originated from the same German–Austrian–Vatican sources. Their aim in

history was always the same – to destroy the Serbian people. This time, however, their tactics were more villainous and dangerous. As in 1914 and 1941, they did not succeed in their aims. The [Serbian] people [today] are the same as they were back then, deciding with whom, where and whose side they will take. And whenever it moved them, the Serbian people were certain of what to do and where to go.[196]

Third, to acquire as much support as possible, the secularist and universalist ideas of normative ideology have been replaced at the operative level by the glorification of the Serbian Orthodox religion. Secularism has disappeared in operative ideology and traditionalist, religious and nationalist ideas are invoked to gain the popular support. Thus, we see again how the message of normative ideology is always idealist (the message of reason), whereas the message of operative ideology is materialist (the message of affect and interest). The skill of ideology is to reconcile these two levels and to 'translate' them in a way that they never appear as two contradictory or unrelated projects to the public.

CONCLUSION

As one can see from the analysis undertaken above, the pattern identified in the case of post-World War II Yugoslavia applies here as well. There is a strong and striking degree of difference between normative and operative ideologies. Here, too, normative ideology focuses on the more abstract values of democratic socialism, the elevation of a people's level of civilisation or the economic laws of development, while operative ideology is formulated to appeal to interests, emotions and fictional or real collective memory, of which the most important appears to be a common ethnic ancestry. Whereas the authority of normative ideology is derived from the superior knowledge of economics and political science, operative ideology grounds itself in the authority of tradition.

Thus, while normative ideology explicates in detail the qualities and advantages of 'mixed economy and mixed ownership', economic democracy or theoretically developed alternatives to classical parliamentary democracy, operative ideology completely ignores the economic and political system. Operative ideology is principally shaped to promote ethnonational unity by glorifying national history and the values of heroism and sacrifice for the ethnonational collective. While normative ideology is more concerned with ideas and concepts and less with actors, operative ideology constantly repeats a few of the same ideas and emphasises recognisable actors and events that are historically and currently familiar. Hence, operative ideology attempts to locate ideological threats and enemies not so much in ideas and concepts but primarily in concrete, personified collectives. As I have shown, most of these were depicted as historically familiar ethnonational collectives – the neighbours of Serbia – Croats, Germans or Turks.

The appeal to universal ethics or superior knowledge is also to be encountered as a source of the regime's justification at the normative level, while operative ideology stresses pragmatic successes such as the results of the 'anti-bureaucratic revolution' and socialist legacy. This attitude is also evident in the structure of the language used: normative ideology operates with pseudo-scientific terminology, while operative ideology appeals to symbols, mythologies, conspiracy theories and fantasies. While normative ideology is rich in principles, ideas and explanations, operative ideology is rich in details, metaphors and popularly recognisable images. A big difference is also noticed in the depiction of counter-ideologies. Whereas normative ideology, defining itself as socialist and secular, is opposed to clericalism and basically treats all religions in the same way, mostly by ignoring them, operative ideology clearly glorifies and defends Serbian Orthodoxy and unhesitatingly condemns and attacks other religious denominations.

As in the case of post-war Yugoslavia, normative ideology is firmly universalist, whereas operative ideology articulates this universalist message through the particularist ideas of ethnonationalism with the aim of justifying its monopolistic and hegemonistic political position in society. If operative ideology is successful in this process of the translation and articulation of its normative principles (considering that the SPS had won all the elections in the period under examination, it is clear that this ideological reconciliation was successful), it is able to collect the diverse layers of society under the single idiom of the 'nation'. The 'nation' is the widest possible umbrella one can use to bring together heterogeneous aspects and actors of Serbian society. The unity of the social has again been achieved through the rhetoric and practice of 'People-as-One'. In this case, however, unlike Yugoslavia, unity is not achieved through integral, state-centred nationalism that aimed to assemble different identities and nationalities of multi-ethnic Yugoslavia, but solely through appealing to egoisms and to the attractions of ethnonationalism. The old normative ideology of integral nationalist self-management socialism has disintegrated together with the common (Yugoslav) public to which this ideology used to be disseminated. The new (Serbian only) public needs a new operative ideology that will integrate only the different layers of Serbian society – an ideology that will subjugate regional, educational, urban and rural, gender, class and other differences. It is this that is the particularly articulated operative ideology of ethnona-tionalism. The content analysis indicates again that although similar in terms of form, normative and operative ideologies are functionally and conceptually very different. Since the core values and ideas expressed in normative ideology are formulated as being socialist and reformist, I have termed this ideology as a *reformed democratic socialism.* In operative ideology these key values of socialism are supplemented with another group of core values – ethnonationalism. Hence, the appropriate name for the operative ideology that existed in Serbia in the period under consideration would be *ethnonationalist socialism.*

NOTES

1 Every republic had the right to a central bank, separate police, educational and judicial system. For more on the features of Yugoslav federalism see S. Malešević, 'Ethnicity and Federalism in Communist Yugoslavia and its Successor States', in Y. Ghai (ed.), *Autonomy and Ethnicity: Negotiating Competing Claims in Multi-Ethnic States* (Cambridge: Cambridge University Press, 2000).

2 L. Cohen, *Broken Bonds: The Disintegration of Yugoslavia* (Boulder, CO: Westview Press, 1993), p. 31.

3 The sharp rise in oil prices in 1973 devastated Yugoslavia's balance of trade. Instead of following the recommendations of the IMF to limit domestic consumption, the Yugoslavian government continued borrowing. As a result of its dreadful economic policy, the country's foreign debt rocketed from under US$3.5 billion in 1973 to more than US$20.5 billion in 1981. See C. Bennett, *Yugoslavia's Bloody Collapse* (London: Hurst, 1995).

4 D. Dyker, *Yugoslavia: Socialism, Development and Debt* (London: Routledge, 1990).

5 L. Silber and A. Little, *The Death of Yugoslavia* (London: Penguin and BBC Books, 1995), p. 30.

6 The movement led by Milošević and his followers from the LCS insisted that it would fight bureaucratism in Yugoslav federal and republic structures; soon it became known to its supporters and its opponents as the 'anti-bureaucratic revolution'.

7 According to Silber and Little:

> In the early eighties, the tiny northwestern republic [Slovenia] embarked on a period of liberalism unprecedented in the Communist world. Alternative groups were tolerated and even flourished, functioning almost as political parties. They covered a wide spectrum, from ecology to gay rights. Slovenia was the most accustomed to plural-ism of all the republics when multi-party elections were called. (*Death of Yugoslavia*, p. 49)

8 It was estimated that one million Serbs gathered to hear Milošević's speech. Ibid., p. 75.

9 Tsar Lazar had the following dilemma:

> 'What kingdom shall I choose? Shall I choose a heavenly kingdom? Shall I choose an earthly kingdom? If I choose an earthly kingdom, an earthly kingdom lasts only a little time, but a heavenly kingdom will last for eternity and its centuries', and according to myth he chose the heavenly kingdom and all the Serbian aristocracy died in the battle. (Ibid., pp. 75–6)

10 Ibid., p. 77.

11 *Dnevnik*, 12 August 1993, p. 7. Although the Kosovo myth portrays Vuk Branković as a 'traitor', the actual historical figure, Vuk Branković, was not a 'traitor' but the only survivor of the battle.
12 The phrase derived from this political myth and coined by the Serbian nationalist poet, Matija Bećković, 'the remnants of a Slaughtered people', was later to be used constantly to accuse Croats of being a 'genocidal nation'. See *Književne Novine*, 15 September 1989, p. 3.
13 This phrase which became a motto of the Serbian nationalist movement in the 1980s was first formulated in the novel by D. Popović. See D. Popović, *Knjiga o Milutinu* (Belgrade: Prosveta, 1986).
14 I. Čolović, *Politika simbola* (Belgrade: Radio B92, 1997). Because of political and economic sanctions, the Belgrade team was forced to play its home match in Bulgaria.
15 I. Čolović, 'Društvo mrtvih ratnika', *Republika*, 145/146 (1996).
16 Ibid., p. 4.
17 *Ethnic rapes*: In the second half of 1980s there was an intensive propaganda campaign in the Serbian media about numerous rapes committed by ethnic Albanians on Serbian women. However, research conducted later showed that the percentage of rapes in Kosovo was much lower than in the rest of the former Yugoslavia, while there were only two cases of inter-ethnic rape in the year when the rape propaganda was strongest. *Paraćin barracs incident*: In 1987 an ethnic Albanian recruit killed a number of other recruits while they were sleeping. The incident was widely publicised as an Albanian attack on Serbs. In reality the soldier was mentally deranged and of the four dead soldiers only one was Serb. *Martinović incident*: In 1986 a Serb peasant, M. Martinović, was raped with a glass bottle by an unidentified man. The media, however, depicted the incident as an ethnic attack by an Albanian on an ethnic Serb. See S. Mežnarić, 'The Rapist's Progress: Ethnicity, Gender and Violence', *Revija za Sociologiju*, 24, 3–4 (1993), pp. 119–26. See also Silber and Little, *Death of Yugoslavia*, p. 40.
18 Čolović, *Politika Simbola*, pp. 158–61.
19 In 1989, after demonstrations in Belgrade where protesters shouted 'Arrest Vllasi!', Milošević addressed them with the statement: 'We will arrest those who have to be arrested! No matter what function they hold.' Vllasi was arrested the next day. See Silber and Little, *Death of Yugoslavia*, p. 72.
20 The term 'Croatian spring' was used to describe the Croatian national(ist) movement in the late 1960s and early 1970s. For more about this see the next chapter.
21 Although Milošević had initially praised Tito, attempting to routinise his charisma, it soon became obvious that owing to changing political circumstances and the nature of Milošević's target, that attempt would fail. By 1989, therefore, an appeal to Tito's charisma had disappeared from Milošević's speeches.
22 Silber and Little, *Death of Yugoslavia*, p. 37 (my italics).
23 Ibid., p. 38.
24 *Korak u novi vek: Osnove programa Socijalističke Partije Srbije* (Belgrade: GO SPS, 1992), p. 3.
25 *Program SPS*, p. 31.
26 Ibid.
27 Ibid., p. 38.
28 Ibid., p. 40.
29 Ibid., p. 31.
30 N. Gaćesa, Lj. Mladenović-Maksimović and D. Živković, *Istorija za 8. razred osnovne škole* (Belgrade: Zavod za udzbenike i nastavna sredstva, 1997), p. 80.
31 *Dnevnik*, 1 May 1992, p. 1.
32 See, for example, N. Gaćeša, D. Živković and Lj. Radović, *Istorija za III razred gimnazije prirodno-matematičkog smera i IV razred gimnazije opšteg i društveno-jezičkog smera* (Belgrade: Zavod za udzbenike i nastavna sredstva, 1996).
33 Gaćeša *et al.*, *Istorija za 8. razred*, p. 152.

34 *Program SPS*, p. 13.
35 Ibid.
36 Ibid., p. 14.
37 Ibid., p. 18.
38 Gaćeša *et al.*, *Istorija za 8. razred*, p. 154.
39 *Ibid.*, p. 156.
40 *Ibid.*, p. 154.
41 *Dnevnik*, 1 May 1992, p. 1.
42 *Program SPS*, p. 69.
43 D. Danilović and B. Danilović, *Poznavanje društva za 4. razred osnovne škole* (Belgrade: Zavod za udzbenike i nastavna sredstva, 1993), p. 13.
44 *Program SPS*, p. 75.
45 Ibid., p. 85.
46 Ibid., p. 82.
47 Ibid., p. 27.
48 Ibid., p. 83.
49 Danilović and Danilović, *Poznavanje društva*, p. 54.
50 Ibid., p. 60. *Ćele kula* is a castle built by the Ottomans with the skulls of Serbs who participated in the uprising against the Ottoman Empire.
51 *Dnevnik*, 20 April 1993, p. 5.
52 Danilović and Danilović, *Poznavanje društva*, p. 53.
53 *Ibid.*, p. 61.
54 *Ibid.*, p. 66.
55 Gaćeša *et al.*, *Istorija za 8. razred*, p. 138.
56 Danilović and Danilović, *Poznavanje društva*, p. 12.
57 *Dnevnik*, 23 November 1995, p. 1.
58 Danilović and Danilović, *Poznavanje društva*, p. 14.
59 Ibid., p. 12. This second statement is obviously an *ideologem* because *Republika Srpska* includes many parts where Bosnian Muslims or Croats were in an overwhelming majority before the war.
60 Ibid.
61 R. Eatwell (ed.), *European Political Cultures: Conflict or Convergence* (London: Routledge, 1997), p. 253. The importance of different articulation of Christian teachings is also indirectly identified by Humphreys who has studied Irish society in the 1960s and found its dominant (operative) ideology to be Augustinianism, where the emphasis is placed on 'the weakness and evil to which human nature is prone as a result of original sin'. A. J. Humphreys, *New Dubliners: Urbanization and the Irish Family* (London: Routledge, 1966), p. 26. Thus, in the Irish case the central traditional value derived from Christian teaching is the idea of sin, while in the Serbian case it is the idea of suffering.
62 *Program SPS*, p. 84.
63 Ibid., p. 85.
64 Ibid., p. 70.
65 Ibid., p. 86.
66 Ibid.
67 Ibid., p. 87.
68 Ibid., p. 86.
69 Ibid., p. 74.
70 Danilović and Danilović, *Poznavanje društva*, p. 87.
71 *Dnevnik*, 1 May 1992, p. 1.
72 Danilović and Danilović, *Poznavanje društva*, p. 13.
73 Ibid., p. 69.
73. Ibid., p. 66.

75 Gaćeša *et al.*, *Istorija za 8. razred*, p. 83.
76 Danilović and Danilović, *Poznavanje društva*, p. 70.
77 Ibid., p. 44.
78 Gaćeša *et al.*, *Istorija za 8. razred*, p. 138.
79 V. Simonović, 'Ratni udar na čitanke', *Vreme*, 9 May 1994, p. 26.
80 Danilović and Danilović, *Poznavanje društva*, pp. 45–6.
81 Gaćeša *et al.*, *Istorija za 8. razred*, p. 64.
82 Danilović and Danilović, *Poznavanje društva*, p. 49.
83 Gaćeša *et al.*, *Istorija za III razred gimnazije*, p. 185.
84 R. Barthes, *Roland Barthes* (London: Macmillan, 1977). See also L. Althusser, 'Ideology
    and Ideological State Apparatuses', in S. Žižek (ed.), *Mapping Ideology* (London: Verso,
    1994).
85 Gaćeša *et al.*, *Istorija za 8. razred*, p. 12.
86 Ibid., p. 15.
87 Ibid., p. 52.
88 V. Pareto, *Sociological Writings* (Oxford: Basil Blackwell, 1966).
89 *Dnevnik*, 10 September 1995, p. 1.
90 Ibid., 23 November 1995, p. 1.
91 Ibid.
92 Ibid.
93 Ibid.
94 *Program SPS*, p. 73.
95 Gaćeša *et al.*, *Istorija za 8. razred*, p. 37.
96 Ibid., p. 38.
97 Ibid., p. 85.
98 Danilović and Danilović, *Poznavanje društva*, p. 81.
99 Gaćeša *et al.*, *Istorija za 8. razred*, p. 103.
100 Gaćeša *et al.*, *Istorija za III razred gimnazije*, p. 162.
101 Ibid., pp. 162–7. The NDH was established in 1941 by *Ustashas* with the help of Nazi
    Germany.
102 Ibid., p. 246.
103 *Dnevnik*, 4 August 1991, p. 1.
104 Ibid., p. 7.
105 Ibid.
106 Ibid., 23 January 1996, p. 5.
107 Gaćeša *et al.*, *Istorija za 8. razred*, p. 83.
108 Ibid., p. 155.
109 Ibid., p. 153.
110 Danilović and Danilović, *Poznavanje društva*, p. 17.
111 Ibid., p. 79.
112 Gaćeša *et al.*, *Istorija za 8. razred*, p. 130.
113 Danilović and Danilović, *Poznavanje društva*, p. 53.
114 Ibid., p. 56.
115 Ibid., p. 61.
116 Ibid., p. 57.
117 Ibid., p. 68.
118 Ibid., p. 69.
119 Ibid.
120 Gaćeša *et al.*, *Istorija za 8. razred*, p. 70.
121 *Program SPS*, p. 31.
122 Ibid., p. 87.
123 Ibid., p. 32.

124 Ibid., p. 33.
125 Ibid., p. 42.
126 Ibid., p. 96.
127 Gaćeša *et al.*, *Istorija za 8. razred*, p. 155.
128 Ibid.
129 Gaćeša *et al.*, *Istorija za III razred gimnazije*, p. 252.
130 *Dnevnik*, 1 May 1992, p. 1. The name AVNOJ Yugoslavia is synonymous with socialist Yugoslavia. *Vilajet* is a Turkish word for a territorial unit, associated in the public mind with the grim period of Ottoman rule (hence 'dark vilajet').
131 *Dnevnik*, 18 April 1993, p. 3.
132 Ibid., 6 July 1994, p. 5.
133 M. Billig, *et al.*, *Ideological Dilemmas: A Social Psychology of Everyday Thinking* (London: Sage, 1988), p. 132.
134 C. F. Graumann and S. Moscovici (eds.), *Changing Concepts of Conspiracy* (New York: Springer, 1986), p. 157.
135 Gaćeša *et al.*, *Istorija za III razred gimnazije*, p. 34.
136 Danilović and Danilović, *Poznavanje drustva*, p. 55.
137 See, for example, ibid., p. 72, and Gaćeša *et al.*, *Istorija za III razred gimnazije*, p. 101 (my italics).
138 *Dnevnik*, 20 April 1993, p. 5.
139 Danilović and Danilović, *Poznavanje društva*, p. 59.
140 Ibid., p. 87, and Gaćeša *et al.*, *Istorija za 8. razred*, p. 43.
141 Gaćeša *et al.*, *Istorija za 8. razred*, p. 83.
142 *Dnevnik*, 4 December 1994, p. 3.
143 Gaćeša *et al.*, *Istorija za III razred gimnazije*, p. 235.
144 Ibid., p. 162.
145 Ibid.
146 *Dnevnik*, 4 December 1994, p. 3.
147 Ibid., 4 August 1991, p. 1.
148 Ibid., 12 March 1995, p. 3.
149 Ibid., 12 August 1993, p. 7.
150 Ibid.
151 Ibid., 18 April 1993, p. 3.
152 The use of the term 'myth' here is not intended to minimise the crimes committed against the civilian population in the concentration camp at Jasenovac. However, it does emphasise the use and manipulation of this historical tragedy in the context of contemporary political struggles.
153 Danilović and Danilović, *Poznavanje društva*, p. 80, and Gaćeša *et al.*, *Istorija za 8. razred*, pp. 127, 157.
154 Gaćeša *et al.*, *Istorija za 8. razred*, p. 120.
155 *Ibid.*, p. 121.
156 *Ibid.*, p. 157.
157 *Program SPS*, p. 74.
158 It is only once in the 98-page-long manifesto that the main protagonists of the 'new world order' are identified as the United States and Germany. However, even there the claim is made indirectly: 'The break up of the Soviet Union and the collapse of the real socialism … made the domination of the United States of America in the world and of a united Germany on a European scale possible'. See *Program SPS*, p. 73.
159 Ibid., p. 67.
160 Ibid., p. 68.
161 Gaćeša *et al.*, *Istorija za III razred gimnazije*, p. 14.
162 Gaćeša *et al.*, *Istorija za 8. razred*, p. 6.

163 Ibid., p. 29.
164 Ibid., p. 142.
165 Ibid., p. 157.
166 Gaćeša *et al.*, *Istorija za III razred gimnazije*, p. 232.
167 *Dnevnik*, 1 May 1992, p. 1 (my italics).
168 Ibid., 23 November 1995, p. 1.
169 *Program SPS*, p. 19.
170 Ibid., p. 33.
171 Ibid., p. 8.
172 Ibid., p. 9.
173 Ibid., p. 8.
174 Gaćeša *et al.*, *Istorija za 8. razred*, p. 153.
175 Gaćeša *et al.*, *Istorija za III razred gimnazije*, p. 246.
176 Gaćeša *et al.*, *Istorija za 8. razred*, p. 153.
177 *Program SPS*, p. 93.
178 Ibid., p. 62.
179 Ibid., p. 21.
180 Ibid.
181 Ibid., p. 62.
182 Ibid., p. 93.
183 Danilović and Danilović, *Poznavanje društva*, p. 49.
184 Gaćeša *et al.*, *Istorija za 8. razred*, p. 94.
185 Ibid., p. 95.
186 Ibid., p. 157.
187 Gaćeša *et al.*, *Istorija za III razred gimnazije*, p. 162.
188 Ibid., p. 165.
189 Danilović and Danilović, *Poznavanje društva*, p. 80.
190 Gaćeša *et al.*, *Istorija za III razred gimnazije*, p. 165.
191 Ibid., pp. 165–6.
192 *Dnevnik*, 8 January 1995, p. 9.
193 Ibid.
194 Ibid.
195 Gaćeša *et al.*, *Istorija za III razred gimnazije*, p. 2.
196 *Dnevnik*, 1 May 1992, p. 1.

5

CROATIA 1990–97

BRIEF HISTORICAL INTRODUCTION

Although the partisan resistance movement in Croatia was strong and widespread, a great number of people including the Catholic Church in Croatia sympathised initially with the establishment of the Nazi-sponsored Independent State of Croatia. This resulted later in the communist government's distrust of many Croats and especially antagonism towards the Catholic Church for collaboration with the Nazi regime. This legacy was important in the general distrust of the Croatian population towards the new communist government.[1] However, Tito's charisma and his Croatian origins helped to 'integrate' the Croatian population into the new Yugoslav state. This was achieved mainly through the gradual federalisation of the State and granting the party leadership of each republic more powers within their republics. Nevertheless, a clear difference in the level of economic development between the north and south of Yugoslavia provoked conflict between the leaders of different republics. The richer republics were opposed to contributions to the fund for under-developed republics. In the mid-1960s the Slovenian and Croatian leadership started opposing the policies of centralisation and territorial redistribution of economic resources. While the Slovenian leadership soon obtained some concessions, the Croatian opposition to redistribution developed into an ethnonational movement consisting of intellectuals and students who stood for cultural nationalism and ethnic purity, i.e. the firm separation of the Croatian and Serbian languages, separatist economists who wanted to see an independent and economically viable Croatian state, and minority liberals who demanded a change in the political system. Nevertheless, the leadership of the movement (which its opponents called the mass movement (*Maspok*) and its supporters, 'Croatian spring') was under the control of the Croatian branch of the LCY and its most prominent figures – Mika Tripalo and Savka Dapčević-Kučar. The movement, launched in 1967 with a declaration about the status and name of the Croatian language, was crushed by Tito and the federal LCY in December 1971. The leading members of the movement were removed from power and some of them were imprisoned. Newspapers and magazines published by the members of the movement were also banned.

Although the new constitution of 1974 basically accepted most of the demands made by the Croatian leadership, the period 1972–89 in Croatia was later termed the period of 'Croatian silence'. Advocates of the opposition movement, especially those seen as nationalist, were persecuted, jailed or forced to emigrate.

With Tito's death in 1980 and changes in the political leadership in Serbia and Slovenia, a shift began in Croatia as well. Opposition groups and parties were established in 1989, most of which emphasised ethnonational issues as crucial. While the leadership of the Croatian League of Communists supported the Slovenian League of Communists in its struggle against the Serbian League of Communists under Milošević and the reform of LCY, the Croatian Democratic Community (CDC) was building the strongest political movement. Within a couple of months the CDC, with the financial backing of Croatian émigrés living abroad, developed a wide network of its organisations all over Croatia, and Bosnia and Herzegovina, which made it the only political force ready for the forthcoming elections.

In the first democratic elections, held in the spring of 1990, the CDC won the largest number of parliamentary seats in the Croatian parliament. As soon as it was in power, the new government introduced discriminatory policies against its ethnic Serb population. The new state was defined exclusively as a polity of ethnic Croats. The government launched policies to secure the summary removal of ethnic Serbs from all important state institutions and introduced the Latin script as the only officially recognised script (hence virtually banning the Serbian Cyrillic script). Furthermore, the immediate change of political symbols (some of which were perceived as a continuation of the Nazi-sponsored 'Independent State of Croatia') and street names stirred ethnonationalism among Serbs in Croatia, many of whom had already received encouragement from Belgrade. In the rural parts of the country where the Serbs had a provisional majority, many did not recognise the new Croatian government and started establishing their own institutions. In 1991, when agreement was not reached on the constitutional transformation of the Yugoslav federation, Slovenia and, soon after, Croatia proclaimed their independence from Yugoslavia. At the same time, the territories of Croatia where Serbs were in a majority proclaimed their independent state of 'Serbian Krajina', and, with the backing of the Yugoslav Army, succeeded in establishing their own institutions. The second half of 1991 was characterised by an intensive war on Croatian territory that was partially stopped by UN intervention that confirmed the *status quo*. The period 1992–94 was a situation of relative peace in Croatia, while in 1995 the Croatian army conducted two military offensives, crushing the 'Serbian Krajina' state and establishing the authority of the Croatian state on these territories. All the elections held in the period 1990–97 were victories for Tudjman and his Croatian Democratic Community.

Political Legitimacy

As in the cases of Yugoslavia and Serbia, the Weberian concept of legitimate authority appears to be fully applicable to the study of the dominant form of political legitimacy in post-communist Croatia. Traditional, legal–rational, value–rational and charismatic types of authority all contribute to the overall legitimacy of the new political order. However, as in the previous two cases, there is a clear difference in the extent to which each type of authority is decisive for the entire process of legitimisation.

The use of old traditions and traditionalism in general appears to be an even more important source of the regime's legitimacy in post-communist Croatia than it was in the case of Serbia. As we will see later, a new official ideology which is traditionalist in character is in many ways an antipode to modernist and Enlightenment-shaped ideas of socialism. This means that traditional symbols, myths and practices become the cornerstone of the regime's political activity. The traditions used are exclusively ethnonational in their scope and content.

The most important historical reference in Croatian political discourse is the idea of an independent Croatian state. While commentators often mention the fact that Croatia lost its independence in 1102 to the Hungarian king, Koloman, they also emphasise that the agreement signed at that time guaranteed a statehood to Croatia.[2] This idea of preserved statehood has been repeatedly invoked in Croatian political discourse from the twelfth century to the present. However, owing to the establishment of a Nazi-sponsored Independent State of Croatia during World War II, which was later held responsible for numerous war crimes against the Serbian population during the communist period, the notion of Croatian independence was a political taboo. In 1990 with the new government in power this taboo was broken and, with the establishment of the new independent Croatia in 1991, the whole idea of Croatian statehood became the most important element in the political discourse of the new regime. By invoking the fact of the 'Croatian right to an independent state' as the central political aim of society, the new regime managed to manipulate this tradition in order to depict itself as the realiser of a 900-year-old Croatian dream. An example of the public reception of this political myth appears in one of the typical statements published in the newspapers of this period: 'Croatia did not have its own sovereign for nine hundred years. And now, instead of being happy and proud that we have again and finally our own Croatian sovereign, some are trying to resist him.'[3] Another declared:

> We all know that there is no perfect government, so this Croatian government is not perfect either. But I am ready to be loyal and even meek because this is the Croatian government that we were waiting 900 years for.[4]

The new political regime relied heavily on traditionalism. Old heroes such as the medieval Croatian kings, Tomislav and Zvonimir, *uskoks* and traditional folk heroes such as Mijat Tomić and Ivo Senjanin, and Croatian historical political figures such as A. Starčević and S. Radić were intensively revived in the media, public speeches and the education system. Traditional national and political symbols such as a flag and coat-of-arms were immediately changed as soon as the new government was established. The use of Roman Catholic symbols, such as the cross and rosary beads, became widespread. Even in the arts the emphasis was placed on folk music such as the Herzegovinian Croat *ganga*, Slavonian *bećarac*, or Dalmatian *klapas*, as well as on authentic Croatian naïve painters from Zagorje and traditional Croatian knitting crafts (*pleter*).

Traditional values of masculinity, militarism and heroism were, just as in the Serbian case, invoked in everyday parlance. This is well illustrated in common images on the street such as Croatian army posters which read: 'A tiger, join us if you are a male!', or in the new recruits' phrase, 'We are soldiers and not mama's boys'.[5] These values are supplemented with ethnonationalist values and the cult of Croatianhood as clearly demonstrated in the interview with the Croatian parliamentary speaker at that time, N. Mihanović:

> in the educational system from the first grade of elementary school onwards, we should introduce the cult of Croatianhood and noble patriotism. Our children should be educated in the spirit of Croatian state-building [and] love for their country.[6]

These old traditions went hand in hand with newly invented traditions[7] and political myths such as the victimisation myth of Bleiburg,[8] which became the equivalent of the Serbian myth of Jasenovac. This is shown in the following song:

Thousands of Croatian soldiers	Na tisuće Hrvatskih Vojnika
call their mother 'Our Dear Mother',	Zovu Majku 'Draga naša Mati',
the voice is heard from the grave:	Glas se čuje ispod Spomenika:
'Slaughtered Croats pray to you'	'Poklani te sad mole Hrvati'.[9]

Other new traditions include the mythologisation of the 'Croatian spring' and Croatian political émigrés, among which the most important is the Bruno Bušić myth.[10] Other myths centre on 1991–95 war heroes, notably M. Dedaković-Jastreb, S. Glavašević, who was killed in Vukovar, J. Jović, who was one of the first victims of the war, and the town of Vukovar itself, which was completely destroyed in the Serbian offensive and which was later proclaimed a 'town-hero'. New traditions include the introduction of holidays such 'the day of thankfulness' established in 1995 to commemorate the victory of the Croatian army in the war offensives codenamed 'Storm' and 'Lightning', and the 'train of freedom' in which Tudjman and his collaborators travelled for the first time through 'liberated territories'. In addition, as in post-World War II Yugoslavia and post-communist Serbia, the presence of popular epics that glorified Tudjman and the new Croatian leadership became widespread, especially in the rural areas of Croatia and Croatian-populated Herzegovina. All these examples demonstrate the importance of traditions and the sanctity of ancient rituals and rulers. Traditional authority operates here in both the ways proposed by Weber: new rulers appealed to 'certain traditions that themselves set the content that should be obeyed' (mostly ethnonationalist traditions) and, at the same time, these new rulers shaped the content of these traditions and interpreted them as they pleased (mostly by interpreting current political events and their relationship to one another in the light of old traditions).

However, despite this extensive appeal to old and new traditions, traditionalism could not be regarded as the regime's dominant type of legitimacy. As in the two previous cases, we do not have a small traditional community, but rather a complex modernising society. Although there is an obvious difference between the dominant normative ideologies of communist Yugoslavia and socialist Serbia in comparison with demo-Christian Croatia, all these societies aim to build a modern bureaucratic and industrial society. Traditionalism is certainly more compatible with demo-Christian ideology than with revolutionary communism or reformist socialism, but traditional values are used only as an appealing content whereas, at the same time, the direction of the development of the society's organisational structure remains unchanged: to build a rationalised, functional and economically viable society. As Gellner observes: 'nationalism is a phenomenon of *Gesellschaft* using the idiom of *Gemeinschaft*: a mobile anonymous society, simulating a closed cosy community'.[11] Thus, Croatian society continues to be highly bureaucratised and complex, as it was under communist Yugoslavia. Instead of the scientifically shaped institutions and terminology of the communist period ('self-management interest community', 'independent organisation of associated labour'), Croatian society now operates with a new esoteric language, most of which has been derived from archaic Croatian and is largely untranslatable (*državotvornost* or *vrhovnik*, for example), whose function is the same as it was in communist Yugoslavia.

Finally, the new political order in Croatia is also in many ways revolutionary. Since it came to power, the regime has been committed to delegitimise and 'erase from collective memory' everything related to the previous political order: whatever was connected to socialism and Yugoslavism has become a political taboo. However, the new political order has defined its own political ideal. The new society was again to be built on a blueprint. Instead of the most just and most rational ideal of communism, the new blueprint envisaged the most rational and most functional Western-like democratic nation state.

All these facts lead us to investigate how important legal–rational authority is for the legitimacy of the new Croatian political order. Since in Weber's theory the legal–rational type of legitimacy is based on a belief in the legality of rules and in the authority of those in a position to give orders, one might find many elements that would support this type of legitimacy in the new Croatia. First, Croatian society was organised according to a 'consistent system of abstract rules' such as the constitution adopted in 1990 and state laws which have largely been adapted from the constitutions and laws of different western European countries. Second, personnel and institutions have separate realms of jurisdiction and competence, have fixed salaries and are organised hierarchically, starting from the State ministries over regional governments (*županija*) to local government. Third, without a specialised training one cannot officially be employed in professional institutions. Fourth, since the process of ownership transformation was extremely slow, the State continued to control most property, thus ensuring that administrative staff were still separated from ownership of the means of production. Finally, regular elections for political posts indicate that all persons in authority are officials subjected to impersonal rules.

Since the Croatian government saw its state as developing along the lines of a Western liberal democracy and was eager to show the progress achieved in that direction, the official emphasis on the elements of legal–rational authority was much stronger than in the cases of Yugoslavia and Serbia. In order to join the Council of Europe and the European Union, Croatian society is obliged to transform itself in a direction where the 'rule of the law' will replace the 'will of the authorities'. However, despite the regime's intention to present Croatia abroad as a society where 'the rule of the law' had been established, many indicators show that legal–rational elements were very far from being a principal source of the regime's legitimacy.

Even though the legal system is nominally established on the model of a Western liberal democracy, President Tudjman's and the CDC's influence on the functioning of the political and legislative systems have been decisive. The president formed an unconstitutional body, the 'Council of Defence and National Security' (VONS), which in many ways resembled a politburo and took over the functions of the parliament, and which included him and his closest collaborators. To illustrate the power of this institution let us take a look at some incidents. In 1996 a group of Bosnian citizens were arrested in Croatia on suspicion of being involved in the organisation of the planned assassination of a pro-Croat Bosnian politician living in Croatia, F. Abdić. The Council of Defence and National Security discussed the case and identified these Bosnian citizens as international terrorists. Shortly afterwards the charge of attempted manslaughter which had been brought against the Bosnians was changed and they were indicted by the State attorney on charges of international terrorism.[12] The degree of influence exercised by President Tudjman and his collaborators over the legal system[13] can also be illustrated by the case of the president of the Supreme Court, K. Olujić, a member of the ruling party, who was replaced as soon as he opposed the CDC's policy of interfering in the legislative system.[14] Since as a president of the Supreme Court he was also the president of the election commission, he was perceived as not loyal enough for the forthcoming elections.[15] Other examples include charges against journalists from the independent media who were taken to court for 'insulting the President', 'publicising the State's top secret documents' or 'offending public morality'; the summary arrests of the self-confessed war criminals, M. Bajramović and M. Naletilić-Tuta, whose actions might have implicated the State leadership; and refusing to allow Croatian citizens of the Serbian origin who had left Croatia with the offensive of the Croatian army in 1995 to re-enter the State.

There are other indicators that deny the legal–rational form of legitimacy as the dominant type of authority in Croatian society. Of these, the most evident were the levels of nepotism, clientelism and the 'grey' economy. As some recent research shows,[16] more than 25 per cent of GDP in Croatia comes from the 'black' and 'grey' economy.

The majority of the population was involved in some kind of informal economy whether it be a second, unregistered job, smuggling, profiting from the currency exchange or renting property. Nepotism and cleintelism were also widespread among the ruling elite. Thus, President Tudjman appointed his son, Miroslav, to several important positions including chief of the Croatian secret service and member of the 'Council of Defence and National Security'. His daughter, Nevenka, and grandson, Dejan, became overnight owners of several banks, chains of supermarket stores and other profit-making properties. Similarly, the relatives of the highly influential Croatian Minister of Defence, G. Šušak, were given many influential posts in various ministries and the State administration. Furthermore, when applying for a job or seeking promotion, it was necessary not only to possess a certificate of Croatian citizenship (*Domovnica*) which was extremely difficult for non-ethnic Croats to obtain, but also to be of Croatian ethnic origin and, preferably, a member of the ruling party. The list of these and similar activities is huge and it is not necessary to identify each individual case in order to demonstrate that legal–rational type of authority was in reality very weak and a less important source of the regime's legitimacy. As in the cases of Yugoslavia and Serbia, the charismatic authority of the leader contributed significantly more to the overall legitimacy of the political order.

Even before he was elected president, Tudjman had the features of a charismatic personality. He would gather around himself a small group of devoted followers who were ready to sacrifice their freedom for the ideals promoted by their leader.[17] His image as a person who had devoted all his life and 'sacrificed for Croatian-hood'[18] also appealed to the masses. In the well-funded and well-organised election campaign of 1990, his charisma definitely inspired a majority of the Croatian population. With the proclamation of the State's independence and the successfully conducted war of liberation in 1995, Tudjman acquired all the characteristics of the plebiscitary ruler. Like Tito, he was seen by his followers as a prophetic leader who promoted the idea of Croatian-hood and set up a millenarian target – to realise the 1,000-year-old dream of establishing an independent Croatian state. In addition, he achieved a 'miracle' by accomplishing that task. Tudjman's actions were compared to Tito's miracle; under Tudjman's leadership, unarmed Croatian people successfully defended their country against 'the fourth military force in Europe'.[19]

As a historian and an academic Tudjman was also perceived and would present himself as an epistemic authority, as a person who knew the past and consequently the future of Croatian people. He himself had a 'personal conviction that he had a mission to rule'.[20] In his speeches he would regularly utilise his knowledge of history.[21] Like

Milošević, Tudjman's pictures and posters were to be found in every corner of the new Croatia, songs were written depicting him as a prince or king and celebrating his successes, as in the epic song by the Croatian peasant-poet Ž. Šimić, from Herzegovina, who sings about 'the enthronement of Doctor Franjo Tudjman',[22] or in this verse from a long epic song from the region of Imotski:

Naš Tudjmanu, kneže i viteže	Our Tudjman, you prince and knight
na tebe se oružje poteže,	they are threatening you with the guns,
u Benkovcu spremni na ubistva	in Benkovac they are ready for the murders
kod našega bratstva i jedinstva!	despite our brotherhood and unity![23]

In the media, Tudjman's relationship with the people and the new Croatian state is often mystically depicted as being one:

> In that expression of togetherness it became clear that Tudjman was not making decisions alone, but it was the history and people in Tudjman; that one man [Tudjman] is not an accident of free will but of collective identification and a thousand-year-old ambition with which an individual Tudjman is not an individual Tudjman any more but Croatian destiny. In that way his decisions are the decisions of the Croatian people.[24]

Tudjman was often depicted as the father of the nation:

The voice is heard from the sky,	Glas se čuje do nebeskih visina
Over the sea and Croatian mountains,	Preko mora i hrvatskih planina
Motherland you are our mother,	Domovino, ti si naša majka
A wise father is our president.	Mudri otac vrhovnik je naš.[25]

At other times he was depicted as God's representative on Earth: 'It was only God that brought you to this land , Mr President'.[26]

The power resulting from this devotion was enormous. Hence, Tudjman would decide who was to be a new minister, who was to be given priority in the sell-off of state companies to be privatised and who was to play on the national football team. To illustrate how powerful Tudjman was, one need only look at the case of the main Zagreb football team. The team was known in the communist period to its supporters as *Dinamo,* but when Tudjman came to power he himself decided to rename the club *Croatia.* Most of the teenage supporters (known as 'Bad Blue Boys') were against the change of name; they protested and sent petitions to the president and boycotted the team's matches. Despite all of this pressure, Tudjman did not give up and periodically accused the teenagers of being 'Communists and Yugoslavs'.[27] Another example of his power was the occasion when Tudjman opened a new post office and mentioned that in each post office there should be a yellow line of discretion as he had seen in Germany. Next day, all post offices in Croatia had yellow lines of discretion.

Like Tito and Milošević, Tudjman and his party had control over the most important sections of the media, including TV, radio and daily newspapers, that had an influence on popular attitudes. However, as the results of all elections held in the period 1990–97 show, Tudjman was admired by the majority of the population. Like Tito and Milošević, Tudjman had the sincere devotion of his followers.

Gill's point about the popular tendency to equate the leader with the new political system in order to consolidate the leader's position and the new regime, is plausible in this case too.[28] This has been explicitly stated by leading CDC politicians on many occasions such as: 'If this Croatia, established by the CDC, this Tudjman's Croatia would fall through, I am sure that would be the end of Croatian people';[29] or 'In my opinion one can put a symbol of equality between [new] Croatia and Tudjman'.[30] Like Tito and Milošević, Tudjman succeeded in establishing a direct relationship with his followers. His appeal to a common Croatian ethnic ancestry was identical to Milošević's appeal to the common ethnic roots of all Serbs. Tudjman would often visit different places in Croatia, give regular monthly press conferences and all his speeches were broadcast on the main TV channels. His style of addressing the public was in many ways similar to Tito's and Milošević's. He would also attempt to give the impression of being equal with the public (on the ethnonational level – 'we are all Croats and we finally have our own state') and, at the same time, demonstrate his superiority to the rest ('it is I who knows best what the Croatian state should look like'). The only difference was that he would also make an appeal through his extensive knowledge of the history of southern Slav relations and on that basis would patronise his followers. Uzelac gives a typical example of Tudjman's attitude towards the public by quoting Tudjman:

> Those who are raising questions about the building of the Presidential Palace or the yacht or buying the presidential plane belong to the Yugo-unitarists, in other words, to remnants of the Yugo-communist ideology, who cannot accept the fact that Croatia has became a sovereign state which has its own Head of State, who had settled in the Ban's Palace until it was attacked and destroyed, trying to decapitate Croatia …

such questions are asked by *politikanti* and those who cannot deeply understand historical changes.[31]

Tudjman, as a father-like figure, would also promise benefits for loyal and 'patriotic' behaviour while threatening all those who were not loyal to him: 'This election has shown that all enemies of the CDC are also the enemies of the sovereign Croatian state'.[32]

The importance of the ruling party was, as in the cases of Tito and Milošević, based primarily on the leader's charisma. It was Tudjman's name next to that of a CDC candidate that would guarantee the candidate a seat in parliament.

All this evidence confirms that Tudjman's charismatic authority was of exceptional importance for the legitimisation of the new political order. However, as in the cases of Yugoslavia and Serbia, charismatic authority cannot be sustained for long if it is not incorporated in the broader framework of dominant values. In order to sustain its privileged position the system has to reformulate the dominant set of values in the direction that fits its own interests. What has happened here is similar to the cases of Yugoslavia and Serbia. In the circumstances of the breakup of the federal state, war and radical change in the political and economic order, Tudjman's authority was needed to provide a feeling of security and certainty. As soon as Tudjman succeeded in presenting himself as a messiah who could accomplish the miracle of realising the 1,000-year-old dream of an independent Croatian state and defend that state with a handful of unarmed supporters, he was in the position to use this power to promote new values. Since the new values were ethnonationalist in their content, Tudjman like Milošević, had less difficulty in evoking these already present feelings. As in Barker's concept of value–rationality the leader was now ethnically and, by definition, ideologically identical to his followers. With the help of charismatic authority, the new regime was able to introduce a new dominant 'symbolic frame', a new ideology, and then regularly demonstrate itself to be the only authentic interpreter of the dominant values. In other words, the system would bring in a new set of values and practices and then, after establishing hegemony, would legitimise itself within these new values. Since the new regime was the one that introduced these values into the public arena, and since these values were now seen by the majority of the population as the crucial values for the functioning of society, it became almost impossible to oppose the legitimacy of the new regime without also opposing the dominant values of society. Through this *ideologisation of charisma* the new regime has successfully established hegemony over other ideologies and political discourses. As in the cases of Yugoslavia and Serbia, the process of legitimation started with a charismatic authority that depended heavily on traditionalist values, was officially shaped as legal–rational and in reality sustained by value–rationality. The monopoly on truth through the education system and the mass media, just as in the cases of Yugoslavia and Serbia, has been exceptionally important for the dissemination of new values. The new values are to be again presented in ways acceptable to the general public. Normative and operative ideologies will mostly consist of similar elements, but while normative ideology will be formulated by appealing to ethics and some 'higher values', operative ideology will use symbols and language already known to the public. Its appeal will be primarily to emotions and interests.

Let us now identify how value rationality operates. This will be done by analysing the content and structure of the dominant power-keeping ideology in Croatia for the period 1990–97. The content analysis of the CDC's manifesto will give us information about the dominant normative ideology, while the content analysis of school textbooks and newspaper editorials published in the same period will help us to identify the structure and content of operative ideology.

Normative and operative ideologies

As in the cases of Yugoslavia and Serbia, the analysis that follows will identify the form and content of the dominant normative and opera-tive ideologies. Normative ideology will be reconstructed through the content analysis of the manifesto of the Croatian Democratic Commu-nity, while operative ideology will be identified by content analysing editorials published in the government-controlled newspaper, *Vjesnik*, as well as school textbooks that were in use in the period 1990–97. The content analysis that follows has been undertaken on the basis of the manifesto of the Croatian Democratic Community that was accepted as the party's official programme at its second general assembly in October 1993.

Economy

The important difference between normative and operative ideologies which has been identified in the analysis of the dominant ideologies of Yugoslavia and Serbia is highly visible in this case as well. Here also one recognises a stark discrepancy between the official understand-ing of the economic system as described in the manifesto and the one present in operative ideology.

The first and most striking difference, already identified in the two other two cases, is the amount of attention given to economic issues in the two ideologies. While normative ideology devotes an entire chapter to the economy, giving detailed and precise explanations of how the Croatian economy ought to function, operative ideology largely ignores these issues and the economy appears to be of little interest. As in other two cases, the main reason for this difference is to be found in the different audience to which the two ideologies are addressed. Whereas normative ideology targets individuals who already subscribe to the main principles of this ideology and who only need further confirmation of these ideas in the all-important spheres of social life including the economy, operative ideology is aimed at an audience that has little knowledge or interest in economic issues. In other words, since the economy is not the main issue around which the masses can be mobilised, operative ideology levels mostly to ignore it.

A second significant difference is the way in which the economy is conceptualised at the two levels of ideology. Thus, while normative ideology concentrates on arguing for the 'social-market economy' as the ideal form of society's organisation, operative ideology does not use this concept at all. The 'grand vista' of the 'social-market economy' has been derived from the universalist principles of Christian teachings. So we are informed that 'social-market economy finds its basis in the Christian understanding of Man and the idea of responsible freedom',[33] and that its main principles are 'efficiency and social justice, competition and solidarity and individual responsibility and social security'.[34] The appeal made here is obviously based on universalist principles.

In contrast to the previous type of social ownership, the manifesto sees private property as the basis of the economic system.[35] However, since the introduction of private property and an unregulated market economy may lead to social inequalities in the process of transition, the CDC also supports the existence of public ownership and a certain degree of state influence. All these elements are articulated in to CDC's economic programme known as 'the system of social-market economy'. Thus, the manifesto reads:

> CDC believes that overwhelming progress can be achieved by the transformation of the inherited economic system into the system of social-market economy on the principles of pluralist and private ownership, free entrepreneurship and fair competition by giving equal chances [to everybody] and [introducing] humane principles of work which are the main prerequisites for the self-realisation of the individual.[36]

In contrast to the socialist form of economy but also in contrast to pure market relations, the party finds the system of social-market economy 'the most efficient and socially acceptable economic system'.[37]

As explained by the manifesto: 'This system most fully reconciles the free initiative of citizens, entrepreneurship, private property with the principles of solidarity, justice and interdependence'.[38]

At the level of operative ideology, there is no reference to a social-market economy or to the 'main prerequisites for the self-realisation of the individual'. The economy promoted in textbooks and editorials is far from being related to the ethical principles of Christian universalism. On the contrary, when reference is made to the economic system, the emphasis is on the full market economy, while the social-market economy present in normative ideology does not appear as a phrase at all. Hence we are informed that 'the basis of economic order in the Republic of Croatia is the entrepreneur and market freedom',[39] or that Prime Minister Valentić's government has demonstrated to the IMF that it knows its job and that in its turn towards a market economy, it is fully in accordance with the main recommendations of IMF.[40]

There are several reasons why the economy is articulated differently at the two levels of ideology. First, the idea of the 'social-market economy' has a similar function to that of the 'mixed economy' in Serbian normative ideology. It aims to overcome all the differences and contradictions that exist within the party membership by avoiding the potential conflict between those who are eager supporters of economic change and those who prefer the strong influence of the State. The idea of the 'social-market economy' functions therefore as a 'magical' concept that can conceal existing differences and also function as a new master key to achieve the ideal of an economically viable and socially just society.

Second, the 'social-market economy', like the 'mixed economy', has every feature of being an *ideologem*. In the situation where the ruling party virtually controls the entire economy and where very few large and influential companies have been privatised, the party's support for different types of economy means nothing other than the justification of its monopolist position.

Third, while normative ideology appeals to universalist (ethical) principles and ideas derived not from Marxist–Leninist science or expert knowledge of economics but from the knowledge of Christian teachings, operative ideology grounds its influence in appealing to the emotions of the general public. This is achieved through the existing contradiction between the two levels of ideology. Whereas normative ideology must refer to the social aspects of the economy and a just society in accordance with Christian doctrine because of the dominant ideology's exceptionally strong opposition to the *ancien régime*, operative ideology cannot use the rhetoric associated with the previous political order which is defined as oppressive and illegitimate.

That is why operative ideology is forced to speak of and glorify the market economy in terms of it being firmly opposed to socialism and Yugoslavism. Any reference to 'social' or 'socialist' would evoke the *ancien régime* and thus soften the image of this officially despised and doomed political order. While Reason acknowledges that there are good and bad sides to the market economy, Affect only sees the good sides.

Politics

The analysis of the political system indicates again how and why the two levels of ideology differ. As in Yugoslavia and Serbia, normative ideology in Croatia operates with some universalist principles, such as the right of self-determination and the equality of nations and states in the world-system and the values of Christian democracy, while operative ideology focuses on the particular, appeals to instrumentally articulated traditionalism which aims to justify the *status quo* and the dominant position of the ruling party.

Hence, one reads in the CDC manifesto about 'equality and understanding between the peoples and especially on the inalienable right of every people independently to decide about themselves in their own state'.[41] This idea is further formulated as being in support of global integration, but only that which would not question the national sovereignty of states. So, as we are informed by the manifesto, 'CDC supports civilisational integrations, but insists on the preservation of national uniqueness and sovereignty in decision-making about the destiny of peoples'.[42] The principal values and political aims of the party are given with clear reference to these universalist ethical principles:

> the Croatian Democratic Community is an all-Croatian and all-people's party that came into existence in the last decade of the twentieth century as the most authentic expression of [the] centuries-old aspirations of Croatian people for the realisation of their freedom and independence and as a promoter of their entire national, historical, political and cultural traditions.[43]

The manifesto often emphasises that the party's membership includes people from different layers of society; as such it is a people's party 'whose main task is to secure the betterment of the Croatian people, [and] Croatian state in co-operation with the countries and states of the entire international community'.[44] The ideas of sovereignty and self-determination to which normative ideology appeals here are the ones developed by Enlightenment thinkers including Locke and Rousseau, and are clearly shaped as universalist concepts.

Apart from values that insist on the right to self-determination and national sovereignty, the political system also includes a reference to Christian democratic values. Thus, it is underlined that the CDC bases its programme and activity on 'the principles of [the] Christian civilisation of the Western world to which the Croatian people have always belonged'.[45] The CDC is defined as a 'people's party that gathers together a wide range of strata of Croatian people and other citizens of Croatia, by building its programme on democratic-Christian principles'.[46] It also stated that

> [the CDC's] task is the democratic integration of all people that are ready in public and political action to apply the principles and human values of Christian civilisation and morality with the aim of establishing a new spiritual and material renaissance of Croatia.[47]

Defining itself as a democratic-Christian party means, as we see in the manifesto, that the CDC stands for 'a Christian understanding of life' which is based on the 'non-contravention of personal integrity and honour, dignity and freedom, true love towards fellow-creatures and conceptualisation of the family as the untouchable basis of human community'.[48] Both these 'grand vistas' (the right of self-determination and the values of Christian democracy) are derived from principles that originate from and make an appeal to universalist reason and a corresponding universalist ethics.

However, at the level of operative ideology these two central values of normative ideology have been reformulated differently. In operative ideology the right of self-determination is deduced from, and related only to, the particularist content. The focus of operative ideology is not on the 'equality and understanding between peoples' and 'civilisational integrations' but exclusively on the justification of the role of the party and the president in the establishment of an independent Croatian state.

Operative ideology ignores universalist principles that justify and explain the establishment of the independent Croatian state in relation to the norms of reason and universal ethics and locates Croatian independence only in the exceptional qualities of President Tudjman and his party. In other words, the realisation of the independence is not depicted as an outcome of global social and historical changes such as the end of the Cold War but rather as a result of the strong will, determination and sacrifice of the CDC and its leader. As in the cases of Yugoslavia and Serbia, operative ideology appeals to the interests and emotions which relate to patriarchal images of the strong and uncompromising father-like leader. The image of the leader is invoked to provide assurance and control over unpredictable events.

According to the authors of editorials and textbooks, it was only because of the personality of President Tudjman and the dedication of the CDC that independence was achieved:

After the elections in the spring of 1990 Croatia got a strong and skilful president and a parliament with the overwhelming majority of the one party ... whose MPs have shown themselves to be uncompromising in the most important thing – preservation of the Croatian state. Taking into account the threats that the Republic faced immediately after its birth, one does not have to be a genius to imagine what would happen if there was a parliament divided between many small parties and if there was a weak formal head of state: it [the State] would certainly not exist today.[49]

The role of President Tudjman and the CDC in the realisation of an independent Croatian state and the success of Croatia military resistance to the Yugoslav army is also clearly acknowledged in the textbooks. So, we read how,

of all political parties, the Croatian Democratic Community (CDC) under the leadership of Dr Franjo Tudjman had the fullest, and for a majority of Croats, the most acceptable political programme. It supported an independent and sovereign state, free economic enterprise, various types of ownership (private, stocks, state), multi-party democracy, full equality for all citizens of Croatia, all civic freedoms, reconciliation between all Croats (because they have all, although from different positions, fought for Croatia), and for the strong and permanent inclusion of Croatia into [the] western European civilisational circle where it [Croatia] has always belonged. With this programme, which was a synthesis of Croatian state-building thought and the contemporary aspirations and wishes of the Croatian people, the CDC has won.[50]

Since all these successes were achieved through the 'firm guidance of the Croatian President', he is expected, like a father, to have the right to demand further sacrifices: 'however, as the Croatian president would say, one should be aware that stability and cohesion of the constitutional order will demand new [and] continuous efforts and perhaps sacrifices'.[51] Furthermore, as already demonstrated, the presence of a charismatic leader is believed to be accompanied by the realisation of miracles. Therefore, editorials and textbooks refer to two Croatian miracles, the first miracle being the victorious armed resistance of Croatia and the second miracle being 'the unbelievable democratic transition in the last two and half years'.[52] It is argued that 'Croatia has in the two and a half years of its political life made an enormous step from the completely inefficient "self-managing socialism" to mature functional and stable democracy'.[53]

The discrepancy between the two levels of ideology is even more visible when the other 'grand vista' is discussed. Thus, another central value of normative ideology, that of Christian democracy, has been 'translated' at the operative level solely as the glorification of the Roman Catholic Church and its values. Instead of an appeal to universalist Christian messages, operative ideology has reduced and narrowed it down to represent only ideas that stand for the Roman Catholic Church.

Hence, there are separate sections in the textbooks on the Catholic Church's position on various issues. It is the Catholic Church and not Christian doctrine that is invoked as a source of authority in explaining various issues. It is the authority of the traditional institution that matters and not the authority of ideas. So, the evaluation of the 1864 *Syllabus* of Pope Pius IX on the 'delusions of the contemporary world', which details the Church's stand on socialism, rationalism and other ideas of the time, are presented as the only right interpretation of these ideas. We read, for example, that the '*Syllabus* [contained] directions not dogmas that were rejected by liberal circles which attacked the Pope and Catholic Church as the enemies of culture and truth'.[54] Socialism is also attacked in line with the teachings of the Catholic Church: 'realising the possible clashes between workers and owners as a result of growing inequalities and the danger of propaganda by socialists who spread envy among poor against rich, the Pope brings *Rerum Novarum*',[55] or 'it is established that what socialists offer for the solution of workers' questions is unacceptable because it is unjust'.[56]

In both these cases, one sees how the ideas and principles of normative ideology have been translated and articulated at the operative level by relying on traditionalist values that are directly related to individual and group emotions and interests. In operative ideology, authority is regularly derived from particularistically conceptualised traditional institutions (the Church, the father-like leader, the party) and not from universalist ideas and concepts (Christian universalism, the Enlightenment ideas of sovereignty and self-determination) as in normative ideology. Here again we see that if ideology wants to be dominant it has to make a shift from the Idealism of normative ideology to the Materialism of operative ideology. To be acceptable to the masses the normative ideology of Reason must make a transition to the ideology of Interests and Affects at the operative level. Nevertheless, the aim of such a transformation is the same as in the cases of Yugoslavia and Serbia. The appeal to traditionally comprehensible values helps to justify the dominant power-keeping ideology.

Culture and nation
Taking into account the fact that the official ideology of Croatia differs sharply from those of Yugoslavia and Serbia, it being already normatively formulated as nation-centred, one would expect that

normative ideology and operative ideology would be fully congruent when 'culture and nation' are discussed. Although it seems that one finds less difference between the two levels of ideology when compared to the Serbian and Yugoslav cases, the way 'culture and nation' have been articulated in operative and normative ideologies demonstrates that even in this case the difference is significant.

Normative ideology even here speaks in the language of universalism by making reference to wider 'civilisational' circles and positioning Croatian culture in that world. Hence, in the view of the manifesto's authors the cultural policy of Croatia 'should be based on our 13-centuries-old civilisational heritage that has its roots in the Christian–Mediterranean–West European cultural circle'.[57] The legacy of Croatian culture here is derived from some more universal state. Croatian culture is not superior *per se*, but because it belongs to some wider 'civilisational' circle which is already defined and acknowledged as superior. At the same time, a strong need to ground this culture into some 'firm' higher reality means that there is some uncertainty and ambiguity about the position of 'Croatian culture'. This means that it is not self-evident or certain that this culture belongs to this 'civilisational' circle.

This uncertainty is present not only outside, but also 'within' the culture. Along the same line of thinking is a wish expressed in the manifesto to 'promote and develop a united Croatian national culture by adjusting programmes of cultural activities in all Croatian regions'.[58] Here again one sees that even internally 'Croatian culture' in itself is far from being identical and 'united'. It is precisely because this culture is not 'unified' that it is necessary to homogenise it. According to the authors of the manifesto, this 'unified' culture can be achieved by, among other things, the educational system which is 'an important element in the development of consciousness about the authenticity of the creative values of our own civilisation and a proof of our national identity and historic existence'.[59]

Croatian culture also has to be shaped along the lines of Christian ethical principles where

> all members of the community are obliged, according to their capacities, to fulfil their responsibilities towards the community. The community is responsible for showing solidarity and care towards the families and individuals that cannot provide for themselves.[60]

This principle is equally applied to families, children, war victims, refugees and the elderly. For example, we read in the manifesto that 'concern for the elderly has to be based on the Christian principle of love towards fellow creatures'.[61]

At the level of operative ideology Croatian culture is defined more externally than internally. Hence, instead of an appeal to universal principles, the emphasis is on the markers of non-Croatian culture. In other words, textbooks and editorials contribute to the articulation of the Croatian culture by identifying what Croatian culture is not. Thus, Croatian culture is opposed to Balkan culture: 'Croatian people have followed the road of [the] peoples of Europe as its constitutive part';[62] or 'as an old European people of Catholic faith, Croats have their saints'[63] in opposition to 'the synthesis of primitive politics and war crimes in the Balkan way'[64] or 'the discrepancy between the Balkan-like and European-like behaviour in the Croatian state apparatus'.[65] By identifying and emphasising the markers of 'non-Croatian culture', operative ideology is in a position to define and impose a singular concept of Croatian culture. If the operative ideology is successful in this task then it can practically control the attitudes and behaviour of its subjects. Since the ideology has the last word on what is Croatian and what is not, any behaviour that would oppose the policies and actions of the ruling group could easily be delegitimised as 'non-Croatian' and thus subversive.

Another difference between the normative and operative levels is that while in the manifesto we read that Croatian culture has to become standardised and united, in textbooks and editorials this has already been achieved; Croatian culture, it is argued, was always unified. Here again we are in position to see how normative ideology focuses on the potential whereas operative ideology presents itself as a statement of fact. Hence, one reads that

> development of education, promotion of practical Catholic books and strengthening of literacy have contributed to the development of a united Croatian culture that will later on become one of the cornerstones of [the] people's [national] consciousness.[66]

Similarly, 'his [Andrija Kačić Miočić] poems and a popular history book ... have contributed to [the] people's consciousness at every level of Croatian society'.[67]

In operative ideology Christian universalim is again reduced to Catholicism and to the authority of the Catholic Church. So we read how the Church provides the solution to social problems at the theoretical and ethical levels:

> an epistle to workers establishes the right of association through which one should bring a solution to the workers' questions; epistle *Rerum Novarum* appeals to the desire for social justice and invites all Catholics

to participate in the public life of society in the form of political and union associations.[68]

At a more practical level, 'The Church turns to new social problems, organises different charity and spiritual societies that help the poor'.[69]

The difference between normative and operative ideologies is again clearly visible when the 'nation' is discussed. While at the normative level we read about the necessity of Croatian unity and paternalist claims about the CDC's aim spiritually, morally and physically to rebuild and reintegrate the Croatian nation, at the operative level we are reminded that Croats were always united, superior and glorious.

Reading the manifesto we find out that the party's main goals are an independent Croatian state and the political and cultural well-being of the Croatian people. As explained in the manifesto, the establishment of the independent state was necessary for the survival of the Croatian people.[70] Apart from the establishment of an independent Croatian state, the party finds it particularly important to promote and strengthen the unity of all Croats regardless of their political views and economic or social positions. Therefore, the manifesto states that 'on the basis of [the] historical experience of the Croatian people and the Croatian state, the CDC sees it as particularly important to continue to work on the preservation of a Croatian national accord'.[71] This unity has to be achieved

> on the basis of a critical and objective attitude to the evaluation of the past for the purpose of [ensuring a] free, human and decent life for all Croats in the world and as a fundamental pre-condition of the survival and development of the Croatian people and their state.[72]

Since the imposed communist system had negative effects on the Croatian people, among the most important being their political and cultural degradation, depopulation caused by political emigrations, and political and territorial divisions, the CDC intends to undertake a 'moral and spiritual renewal of Croatian people'[73] and 'to strengthen the spiritual and territorial integration of the Croatian people'.[74] That also includes 'the expression of spiritual togetherness and unity of Croatia proper and Croats who live abroad' and calls for the reconciliation 'of all strata of Croatian people'.[75] The Croats who live in Croatia and Croats in neighbouring Bosnia and Herzegovina, as well as Croats living all over the world are thus characterised as 'inseparable parts of integral Croatian national being'.[76] All these examples show how the party sees itself as a force that is responsible for the 'right' articulation of the Croatian national idea. Through normative ideology the party addresses its followers and sympathisers by setting a theoretically well-formulated and developed agenda (a blueprint) that will be followed in the realisation of the Croatian national question. The party has a monopoly on this nation-articulation and is well aware of this fact.

At the operative level, however, these paternalist claims have disappeared, to be replaced by the ideas that glorify the (Croatian) people. What one sees here is populism and flattery that intends to identify the aims of the party and the people as one. Thus, here too we can apply Lefort's 'People-as-One' idea. The party aims to demonstrate that its interests and those of the 'people' are identical; the CDC and the Croats are one, just as the LCY and Yugoslavs and the SPS and Serbs were one. They share the same interests and the same destiny. There is an absolute 'organic' harmony between the party and the people. According to operative ideology, there is really nothing beyond the social.

Thus, operative ideology aims to show that Croats were always brave, glorious, superior and, most importantly, united and conscious of their ethnonational identity. School books attempt to show that there has been an uninterrupted Croatian statehood and Croatian political identity dating from the earliest medieval Croatian states to the present. Indeed, the emphasis in all textbooks is on the unity of all Croats regardless of their economic, social and political status, regardless of them living under different foreign rulers and States, and regardless of different historical periods and epochs. The authors of these textbooks are eager to prove that through the ages there was a constant awareness among Croatians of every social group of being members of a Croatian nation. Thus, one reads about 'the thousand-year-old history of Croats',[77] about how 'Croats [managed to] preserve their independence and statehood [in the eighteenth century],[78] about Croats belonging to 'those European peoples who fought for the unification of their national territory and the realisation of full national and state sovereignty',[79] about the 'continuity of the Croatian people',[80] or about various Croatian heroes and thinkers who have managed to express and preserve the idea of a Croatian state throughout history: 'One could say that Croatian political thought, even in a such wise man and thinker as was Križanić, preserves the State and that will remain thereafter the feature of people's ideas and politics'.[81]

The Croats are the central focus of all history books and the main points of reference in newspaper editorials. Thus, one history book explains to students that its purpose is to 'inform you about the history of Croats and other peoples in the eighteenth and nineteenth centuries'.[82] The books are full of stories that demonstrate the uniqueness and bravery of Croats. The heroes depicted in the books, including Zrinski and Frankopan, Luka Imbrišović, Josip Vukasović, duke Jelačić, Aleksa Tomo Dundić, Andrija Hebrang, lived in different periods of time, supported different political ideals, had different social origins but they all shared the common characteristic of fighting, in one way or another, for the Croatian motherland. Croats are often presented as always having a single will, a will that is also well known to the authors of the history textbook. Thus, we are informed that the 'Croatian people were struggling for the preservation of their entire national territory';[83] that 'by finding themselves in the Kingdom of Serbs, Croats and Slovenes [the first Yugoslav state] and losing their statehood, Croats could not cope with that fact';[84] that Croats aspired 'to unite with their brothers from the other side of the Velebit mountain';[85] or that the 'great majority of population did not know the Italian language and called their language Croatian and were conscious of, as foreigners have noticed, belonging to a Croatian people'.[86] This organic concept of the nation often ends in a certain reification of the group; so we read about the 'bordering parts of the Croatian people'.[87] Sometimes the authors speak about 'us' or 'our people', such as 'our people under Venetian rule',[88] appealing directly to collective emotions and identifying with their readership. The rhetoric also attempts to show that Croats as a collective entity were victimised and always deprived of their rights – by Habsburgs, Venetians, Ottomans, Austro-Hungarians, Serbs or the communist government, as indicated in the following titles of separate chapters: 'The Position of Croats under the Burden of Centralism and Great Serbian Hegemony';[89] 'Regime's Crimes and the Resistance of Croats'[90] or 'Croatia in the Chains of the System of Second Yugoslavia'.[91]

The way normative and operative ideologies differ in their interpretation of Croatian 'nation and culture' shows again that the two levels of ideology have different aims. Normative ideology is (consciously or not) aware of the fact that Croatian culture is very far from being single and unified and that Croatian historical unity and consciousness is of very recent date. Its main aim or its main 'grand vista', therefore, is to establish this unity and singularity in relation to other 'fully fledged nations' – the Croats must have a single and recognisable culture and polity as the French or Germans do. Regardless of its nationalism, normative ideology is truly universalist, grounding its ideas and concepts in the tradition shaped by the Enlightenment and Romanticism which see the world as divided into civilisational circles and nation-states. Its only aim is to develop the Croatian nation state according to this blueprint as soon as possible. Like the LCY and the SPS in Yugoslavia and Serbia, the CDC sees itself as the possessor of ultimate knowledge and the only true interpreter of this grand idea.

That is why the party has also developed an elaborate plan of how to achieve the unity of Croatian culture and nation.

Operative ideology, on the other hand, has a different aim, which is practically to justify the party's monopolistic position in the new Croatian state. The nationalism that one encounters here is a firmly particularist one. To realise this aim successfully, operative ideology relies on flattery and egoism, describing the people (Croats) as true heroes and historical victims. The people are, again as in Yugoslav ideology, giants but it is only the party that can rightly articulate and recognise their heroism and force. In this way operative ideology demonstrates to the masses that there has always been an interrupted Croatian national consciousness and a singular culture in which the policies and historical importance of the CDC play the most significant role. The CDC appears 'at the historical stage' as a force that will give to this already mature and conscious nation its last element of unity and national maturity – statehood. The message of operative ideology is the following: It is you people who have always been loyal members of your nation and who were always aware of your true collective self, so what is asked of you today is nothing more that what was asked of your ancestors. If you are a true human being/Croat you will not betray your ancestors, you will have a common and singular culture and be one nation in our new state under the leadership of the CDC.

Actors
As with normative ideology in the cases of Yugoslavia and Serbia, there is very little reference to concrete actors in the CDC manifesto. Instead of actors, the emphasis is placed on ideas and concepts as well as on their justification or delegitimisation.

The only significant actors in the manifesto are Croats. We see them as 'the old European people with democratic traditions'[92] who can be proud of their '13-centuries-old civilisational heritage'[93] and whose right for independence and freedom has been 'interwoven in the consciousness of Croatian man'.[94] However, even this actor is not represented in the manifesto as an independent agent of social change. It is only sporadically that this actor is depicted as acting of its own free will. It is rather that the manifesto speaks in the name of this actor from the position of some universalist and rationalist principles. In other words, Croats presented in normative ideology are neither like self-governing individuals nor collective actors, but passive objects in need of guidance and direction.

That direction and leadership is provided by another actor which appears in the manifesto as an important agent of the social change – the CDC. Thus, one reads that the CDC is the only force able to lead the Croatian people: 'The foundational assembly of the CDC was the first public convention of a Croatian democratic party after fifty years of communist totalitarianism'[95] or that 'it was only the CDC among all Croatian parties which came up with a clear programme for the establishment of a democratic, independent and sovereign state of Croatia'[96] or that the 'CDC [alone] leads Croatian people in the struggle for freedom'.[97]

Unlike its normative counterpart, operative ideology focuses much more intensively on the depiction of actors. There are many actors that appear in textbooks and editorials but only a few could be regarded as dominant actors present in all history books and editorials. An important characteristic of operative ideology is its emphasis on actors and not ideas. Whereas the actions of the actors who appear in operative ideology are derived from their personalities and characters and not from the ideas they stand for, actors in normative ideology are presented only as a representatives and carriers of particular ideas and principles.

The actors who appear most often in operative ideology are Croats. However, unlike their depiction in normative ideology, they are shown here as self-confident, strong-willed collective actors who are always presented as subjects of the change. We do not see Croats any more as passive entities in need of guidance and leadership, but as conscious and self-directed actors who have always been aware of their historical maturity and strength. Thus, we learn about the bravery and sacrifice for freedom of Croats through history. One textbook starts with a two-page-long story about the Croatian pursuit of freedom written by a French historian. There we read about Croats as being 'never calm but always free', about how 'there are so many scars on Croatian land' or about how 'they have made sacrifices for justice. They have died bloodied for freedom.'[98] The history books list examples of Croatian bravery from medieval times to the war of 1991. So we read that 'Croats gained the title of the best of Napoleon's soldiers',[99] that 'although Croats were the most numerous in the anti-fascist struggle 1941–1945, that fact was regularly undermined'[100] or that

> in the long and violent battle for Vukovar [in the autumn of 1991] the Croatian army demonstrated bravery that will be remembered for ever in Croatian war history … in this war for the defence of their fatherland, Croats have shown exceptional bravery and the highest degree of unity.[101]

However, Croats are not only brave and freedom-loving soldiers, they are also, according to textbooks and editorials, diligent, intelligent and hardworking:

> Some Croatian emigrants won recognition for their diligence, thriftiness and intelligence and are individually mentioned in the works of

some publicists and writers. Thus, for example, an American writer, Jack London, in his novel *Moon's Valley*, mentions some Croatian immigrants from the Dubrovnik region as good, diligent and skilful people.[102]

Another description is as follows: 'Working outside their homeland on various manual jobs (as workers and craftsmen), but also in highly skilled jobs (as engineers, doctors, scientists), Croats have everywhere shown themselves to be diligent workers and honest people'.[103]

The way operative ideology depicts Croats is almost identical to the way the Yugoslav people and Serbs were depicted in the other two case studies. The appeal is made to the interests and emotions of the public that consumes operative ideology. Instead of the patronising views characteristic of normative ideology, operative ideology uses flattery and ethnocentric descriptions of Croats. The textbooks and editorials are full of examples of Croatian traditional qualities, among which the most important are heroism and bravery. In this way operative ideology affirms the positive social identity of its public[104] and simultaneously provides it with the fantasy of having a significant role in dramatic moments and battles in national history. By insisting that Croats were always brave, heroic, diligent and intelligent, operative ideology basically says, it is you who are brave, heroic and intelligent. However, operative ideology also implies that in order to have all these positive features, you as an individual have to carry the responsibility of your ancestors, which means you have to be a good Croat. As noted earlier, to be a good Croat means to follow without question the articulation and definition of Croathood formulated by the dominant ideology.

Unlike normative ideology which grounds some of its key ideas in Christian-democratic doctrine but which largely ignores the institution of the Church, operative ideology gives a special place to the Catholic Church. While textbooks devote special sections and chapters to the Catholic Church and its stand on different issues, editorials comment regularly on important Church sermons[105] and the Church's views on different social matters. All attitudes present in the Catholic Church are positively oriented. Thus one reads that the Church organised various charity organisations and helped the poor 'in times when there was no workers' legislative' and that the Church was the only institution that took care of 'the problems of socially deprived groups'[106] but that unlike other institutions, the Church 'put stronger emphasis on the people and "lasting values"'.[107] We are also informed that 'the Catholic Church is a supporter of peace in the world'[108] and that popes 'as the first priests devoted to God and people' have always 'done everything they could in the interest of religion and peace in the world'.[109]

The authors of editorials and textbooks regularly sympathise with the difficult times experienced by the Catholic Church in history, such as during the French Revolution when the Catholic Church was deprived of its estates;[110] or at the beginning of nineteenth century when 'the position of the Catholic Church was the worst in Germany';[111] or under the communist regime in the former Yugoslavia:

> [O]perating in the difficult times of the Communist regime in Croatia, the Catholic Church has shown its durability and strength because it had stubborn and skilful priests grown up within (or brought up by) the Croatian being and had loyal believers.[112]

Here again we see how the Ideas of (Christian-democracy) at the normative level are translated at the operative level into an appeal to recognisable Institutions (the Catholic Church). For the ideas present in normative ideology to be comprehensible to the wider masses, they have to be articulated through familiar traditional images such as the Church. Instead of the abstract and rational concepts of Christian ethical universalism, operative ideology invokes a particular and popularly recognisable actor – the Catholic Church. Ideas can have meaning only if personalised in concrete, visible and material actors.

The importance of actors for the operative ideology is also visible when the principal individual actor is discussed – the charismatic personality of Tudjman. Regardless of his academic merits, the Croatian leader, like Tito and Milošević, has been portrayed mainly as a firm and just father. The appeal made is not so much to his expert knowledge but to his firmness, individual suffering, life experience or strong personality, in other words to his particular patriarchal qualities. Hence we read that

> Dr Franjo Tudjman, President of the Republic, has contributed much to the strength and international reputation of the Republic of Croatia. As a man for whom a free and independent Croatia was a life preoccupation, who *has worked and suffered for such a Croatia* and also as *a man of great knowledge and experience, as well as strong personality*, Dr Franjo Tudjman has *firmly held the political sail in his hands by not allowing any retreat or deviation*. His *authority* has been *respected* in Croatia and he is respected abroad. With his speeches, press conferences and interviews he is always, at the right time and in the right way, *giving directions* and answers on all important questions that are crucial at that moment and, in the long run, for Croatia and its interests. Working for the good of Croatia, he also acted outside the fatherland, by making a number of official visits abroad'.[113]

Another important difference between normative and operative ideologies is the fact that while negatively treated actors are almost non-existent in the manifesto, textbooks and editorials give enormous attention to the depiction of an enemy. The enemy is a familiar one. It is Serbs and their Orthodox Church as well as the communists.

The main aim of operative ideology is to demonstrate that our current enemies were always our enemies. That is why operative ideology often relies on conspiracy theories trying to show how the Serbs had always planned to enslave the Croats. Thus, history books intentionally devote chapters and special sections to Serbian history in order to trace historically the causes of the most recent war in the former Yugoslavia. The idea of Greater Serbia appears in the Ilija Garašanin programme, *Načertanije*, at the beginning of the nineteenth century, where the idea of the unification of all Serbs living in the Balkans was first proposed. However, the textbooks attempt to show that throughout history Serbs always had aggressive motives and were bent on conquest. Thus, we read that 'Serbia and Montenegro went to war with the Ottoman Empire in 1876 to conquer Bosnia and Herzegovina';[114] or that 'Serbia, Montenegro, Bulgaria and Greece had their expansionist goals ... in the Balkan wars';[115] or that '[even] after achieving their independence, the advocates of Greater Serbia did not stop. In the domestic and international press they have aspired to foreign territories. Oppressed with the spirit of *Načertanije*, they untruthfully and mythomaniacally glorify their history.'[116]

We are also informed about the character of Serbs: 'in order to establish Greater Serbia, [the advocats of] Greater Serbia did not hesitate to use terror and were engaged in the establishment of terrorist organisations';[117] or 'on the territories they [the Serbs] conquered in the war of 1877–78, they tortured Albanians and committed genocide against them'.[118] There are numerous descriptions of how Serbs insulted, tortured and killed their Croatian prisoners,[119] all of which highlight the Croats as their victims: 'these killings of prisoners bitterly remained in the mind of every Croat'.[120] There are detailed descriptions of Serbian misdeeds during monarchist rule in Yugoslavia,[121] a special section on *Chetniks* in World War II that includes extensive descriptions of the killing of Croats and the burning of Catholic churches,[122] and especially detailed descriptions of crimes committed by Serbs in the most recent war in Croatia. The terms Serb and *Chetnik* are used interchangeably; we read about 'Serbian masters of war', the 'terrorist clique from Pale' and '*Chetniks*';[123] the '*Chetnik* siege' or '*Chetniks* from the former Republic of Yugoslavia';[124] the '*Chetnik* brotherhood';[125] and the 'Serbia rebel (*Chetnik*) forces'.[126] A typical paragraph is the following:

> [The a]ggressors committed horrible crimes: they stole, burnt houses, took the non-Serbian population into camps on the occupied territories of Croatia or on the territories of Serbia, massacring and killing Croats ... Their 'ethnic cleansing' was a typical genocide ... By destroying Vukovar, Dubrovnik ... and other Croatian cities and villages they have shown themselves to be the most cruel and delirious barbarians. They wanted to destroy everything that is Croatian and Catholic, including monuments of the Croatian and Catholic past on this more than 13-centuries-old Croatian territory.[127]

Apart from the cruelty and inhumanity of the Serbs, we are also informed about their 'Byzantism' and their deceitful character:

> using tricks in order to deceive and avoid duties already agreed upon is typical of Serbian politicians who do not hesitate to use the most obvious lies. Pašić's models of such uncivilised behaviour in public conduct remind us of an ideal common to almost all generations of Serbian politicians.[128]

Similarly, 'it is typical for the Serbian side to accept an agreement and even sign its acceptance and then not to feel obliged to honour it'.[129] Serbs are also depicted as cowards, their military victories are omitted and their defeats in war emphasised, as in their war with Bulgaria in 1885.[130] One such example is the following passage relating to the rapid defeat of monarchist Yugoslavia by German forces in 1941:

> [the] Serbian people, who were always boasting about their military skills and their patriotism, did not show either their military bravery or their loyalty to their fatherland; they avoided war battles and escaped from their units not hesitating from cowardice and treason; in this non-heroic behaviour their leaders lost face, [including] their king, generals and ministers.[131]

The Serbian Orthodox Church is also painted in the same colours. Hence, we read that it was acting in the best tradition of Byzantism[132] or that the

> Serbian Orthodox Church was developing a basis for aggression, directly participated in it and erected its temples on the ruins of the churches and mosques and in the places where the blood of the massacred was not yet dry, as in Dalj.[133]

The Orthodox Church is also accused of proselytism and hatred against Catholics: 'in the resistance of the Orthodox Church (to ratification of the Concordat with the Vatican), there was its intention to have as much space as possible to convert Catholics to Orthodoxy and to promote its hatred of Catholics'.[134]

Although communists are not often mentioned, the attitude towards them, with the exception of a Croatian nationalist communist leader, Andrija Hebrang, who was removed from the political scene in the late 1940s,[135] is always negative. Thus, it was communists who 'in reality were exercising their party single-mindness'[136] or who

> were saying one thing and at the same time thinking and doing another. They spoke about freedom and democracy but were strangling freedom and acting undemocratically. Demagogy and violence were their methods of action.[137]

Elsewhere it was the

> communists [who] were constantly emphasising that in the process of recruitment for employment and career advance one has to honour the principle of 'moral–political aptness'. That communist principle has enabled and kept in place permanent discrimination. It was sad to see how, always and everywhere, the advantage was given to those who were politically apt instead of those with skills and the potential for work.[138]

As in the cases of Yugoslav and Serbian dominant ideology, the use and depiction of actors at the normative and operative levels differ significantly. While normative ideology mostly ignores actors or presents them as a passive objects whose only function is to be guided by a blueprint of ideas and principles, operative ideology depends chiefly on actors and tries to personalise the principles of normative ideology by giving them familiar and recognisable faces. While in normative ideology the central idea is the realisation of the universalist principle of nationalist ideology according to which every nation should have its own state (the establishment of this idea in the Croatian case being just a step further towards the achievement of the grand historical project where agents of change are, for the most part, irrelevant), operative ideology does exactly the opposite. In operative ideology actors have the central place for two reasons. First, to disseminate ideas of normative ideology successfully they are located in the familiar images of the enemy. The Yugoslav state/Serbs have opposed the principle that every nation must have its own state, so they are depicted not as being against this universalist principle but as being against Croats *per se*; operative ideology has aptly traced this hostility through history. What we encounter in operative ideology is not the clash of ideas such as unitarism and federalism vs. confederalism and self-determination, but rather the conflict of genocidal *Chetniks* vs. brave and honest Croats. Second, the importance given to positively depicted actors such as Tudjman in operative ideology has the function of justifying their privileged position in the realisation of an independent Croatian state, which is here formulated in a very particularist way. It is Tudjman's individual qualities that have determined the outcome of the war. The independence of the Croatian state is not viewed in relation to the wider socio-historical environment, such as the collapse of the State socialism world-wide and the disintegration of all socialist federations (the Soviet Union, Czechoslovakia and Yugoslavia), but as a miracle achieved by the determination, strong will and sacrifice of President Tudjman.

Language

The analysis of the language, symbols and expressions used in normative and operative ideologies indicate again that the two levels of ideology differ sharply. Just as in the cases of Serbia and Yugoslavia, one recognises that the language of normative ideology is mostly dry and difficult to understand, whereas operative ideology works through familiar images, metaphors, mythologies and symbols.

The language of the CDC manifesto is distant, complicated and abstractly formulated. This is not the language of Marxism–Leninism or pseudo-science, as in the cases of Yugoslavia and Serbia, but it still has the same features. This is the language that exhibits the elements of an esoteric, almost semi-feudal, terminology which derives its vocabulary from archaic Croatian and Slavic terms. Sometimes it is difficult to understand the full meaning of a particular sentence and some terms, as previously explained, are literally untranslatable. One such term is *državotvornost* which has a crucial place in the new Croatian political discourse. The term literally means 'state building' but its meaning is much stronger and more mystical than that. While it includes patriotism, devotion to the ethnonation and the State, it is not common patriotism (that is, 'the CDC will support the development and cherishing of *državotvornog* patriotism').[139] Rather, the term *državotvoran* functions as a symbol of political identification that invokes on the one hand support for the independence of the new state and, on the other, serves as a mean of self-legitimisation in the new political order. He who is not *državotvoran* is a potential enemy of the new state.

The function of this newspeak introduced in normative ideology is similar to the one present in Yugoslav and Serbian normative ideologies. Its aim is not only to differentiate Croatian from the Serbian language and in this way to delete the common history but also to codify the concepts of the new dominant ideology in a mystical way that will differentiate the rulers from the masses. Linguists have a very appropriate term to describe this phenomena – diglossia. Diglossia exists when there are two languages which are stratified according to the social position of those using them. Thus, those at the bottom of the social pyramid are not able to communicate with those on top.[140] The new official Croatian language has many features of diglossia. Since the new language changes almost everyday and only the rulers know what the appropriate language of the day is, they are in a position to control the masses and delegitimise all counter-hegemonic attempts as not being Croatian enough.

A second feature of the language present in normative ideology is a clear obsession with history and a perception of the world as passing through fixed historical stages. Hence, one reads about the 'historical task'[141] that the CDC had to achieve, or how

> the entire historical experience obliged the CDC to remain on the rampart of achieved results with the hinged strength in the development of the Croatian fatherland into a country of full democracy and prosperity, for the well-being of Croatian people and all citizens of the sovereign Croatian state.[142]

One also reads of how 'in that *fatal historic moment*, it was only the CDC which offered the programme of establishing a democratic, independent and sovereign Croatian state';[143] or

> achieving all [this success] on the basis of the idea of all-Croatian harmony, the reconciliation of all strata[144] and generations of Croats that live here and abroad, and on the unity of all Croatian lands and regions, the CDC has *a historic mission* to continue the process of the political and economic renaissance of Croatia.[145]

The language is extremely dramatic and full of mystical concepts such as fate, destiny of the people,[146] civilisations or historical mission. However, the strongest and most often invoked idea is that the independence of the Croatian state was 'a thousand-year-old dream of the Croatian people'.[147]

What one sees here is the highly deterministic language of reason that formulates history as a theory or, even better, the science of development and progress. This is a universalist language that aims to explain all particular events of Croatian history with reference to some grand historical plan. All the concepts and terminology used in normative ideology, such as 'historical task' or 'historical mission', are obviously derived from this universalist theory of history.

The language of operative ideology differs completely from these ideas. The vocabulary of operative ideology does not rely on the rationality deduced from theoretically formulated concepts, but rather is instrumental in focusing on traditionalism, myths, hero-worship and delegitimisation of the enemy. The history that we encounter here is not Fukuyama's big teleological History[148] but rather the small, particularist history of Croats.

The central myth developed in textbooks and editorials is that Croatian ethnonational consciousness was uninterrupted and strong throughout the history. So we read about Croats as always being nationally conscious and showing unity and harmony at crucial moments of their history: 'by defending their rights and benefits, the Croatian nobility has set up the basis for Croatian national consciousness',[149] or 'Croats in the fatherland and abroad have homogenised their patriotism, strength, feelings and thoughts',[150] or 'a permanent and a stable bridge between domestic Croatia and Croatia abroad has received one more support'.[151] The language and arguments used in the textbooks and editorials show how this myth has been personalised and individualised by identifying concrete individual and collective actors and agents responsible for the persistence of Croatianhood. So we read about the Dubrovnik Republic as a 'long and glorious history of the free Croatian state'; or about Franciscans who 'have contributed to the Croatian people's consciousness remaining alive'.[152]

The unity of the Croats was not only historically traced, but is also believed to exist in the present. Croats are flattered as mature and strong: 'by relying on our own strength without any help from abroad but with the maturity of an entire people, we await the third anniversary of the Day of Statehood'.[153] Here again, as in the two previous cases of Yugoslavia and Serbia, the emphasis is not on conflict but on harmony and unity, projecting thus the ideal picture of reality (in history as well as in the future) to support, as Žižek would say, the existing reality.[154]

Interestingly enough, as in the Serbian case, we read not only about Croatian heroism and strength, but also about Croatian victimisation. Croats are shown as victims throughout history. They had suffered under the Austrians, Hungarians, Turks, Venetians and Germans but mainly under the Serbs. They have suffered collectively as a nation but also individually through their martyrs who were killed or forcefully assimilated by foreign oppressors. So we read about the crude 'Germanisation of the Croatian nobility by Maria Theresa';[155] or about the conspiracy to kill the Croatian national leader, S. Radić, in 1928 in the Yugoslav state parliament by the Serbian MP, P. Račić – 'it is obvious that this criminal was just an executor of an already planned crime'.[156]

This historically traced victimisation has been directly connected with the present situation, where one sees how Croats have to suffer because the international community is unable 'to stop wild Serbian imperialism',[157] or about 'the continuation of war and the ethnic cleansing that Muslim forces are committing in central Bosnia and whose victims are Croats'.[158] This principle of victimisation is personalised in the concrete, visible instances by appealing to affects. So we read about 'the little [Croatian] girl in whose head is lodged the shrapnel from a Muslim shell'.[159] The cruelty of the enemy and the pain produced by its inhuman deeds justify 'our' revenge. As one newspaper editorial clearly stated:

> in this situation it is the legitimate right and duty of every people and its political leadership to undertake all the necessary means to preserve national self-determination and the biological existence of the people.[160]

The function of this connection between victimisation and heroism in the past with the present situation is the same as in cases of Yugoslavia and Serbia. The aim is to justify externally and internally the policies of the party by blurring its historical record. The responsibility of the Croatian government for its involvement in the Bosnian war and its international condemnation had to be justified in reference to historical victimisation. The message is the following: 'As our history shows, we were always victims of our hostile neighbours and the big powers have never helped us at the critical moment. They are cynical, they did not stop "wild Serbian imperialism" and are now accusing us of being aggressors.' The responsibility of the party has again been shifted to the 'nation'. Internally the justification of the party's policies has been secured by depicting the enemy as having no human characteristics. The enemy is unscrupulous, it kills innocent little girls. The image of the little girl killed by Muslim shrapnel will also have a much more powerful effect on public attitudes to the war than the delegitimisation of the ideas that the enemy stands for.

The analysis of the strategies of enemy delegitimisation shows that they are similar to those used in the cases of Serbia and Yugoslavia. Here, too, the enemy has no real essence. Our enemies are not real human beings, they are not what they claim to be, but something artificial. They are not real Serbs, they are only Serbised Valachs and Morlocs. Thus, the authors of the textbooks speak about Orthodox, Valachs or Morlocs instead of Serbs: 'with Military Krajina the things were to become even further complicated because its inhabitants (of Orthodox faith) were to ask for autonomy for themselves'.[161] They also observe that

> on that territory [Krajina] Croats were in the majority. Besides Croats there were Italians and Orthodox who came to these territories as

conquerors; they were Turkish and Balkan Valachs – Morlocs who, under the influence of the modern Serbian state and Church propaganda from the nineteenth century, have been Serbised and assimilated into Serbs.[162]

Similarly, 'apart from the Muslim population and Orthodox Valachs who moved in during the sixteenth century, Croats have lived in today's Bosnia and Herzegovina since the sixth and seventh centuries'.[163]

The same attitude is expressed when ideas potentially damaging to the myth of strong national consciousness are discussed. We read about the Illyrian movement that was exceptionally strong among Croatian intellectuals in the nineteenth century, which aimed to unite southern Slavs under the single Illyrian name, as imposed and artificial. We are informed how 'unnatural the Illyric name' was or how 'artificial the Illyric name' was.[164] The movement was characterised as an 'Illyrian and pan-Slavic illusion'.[165]

The language of normative and operative ideologies differs sharply, as it does in the cases of Yugoslavia and Serbia. Normative ideology's terminology of reason, history and science has been translated into operative ideology as the particularist images of affect and interests. Instead of fixed stages of development and newspeak terminology through which normative ideology controls and filters its membership and potential counter-hegemonic elites, operative ideology relies on traditionalism, patriarchy, popularly shared values of heroism and victimisation as well as on villains and heroes. By invoking the images of popular and folk culture, operative ideology aims at personalising and materialising the ideas given in normative ideology. Operative ideology brings down abstract and symbolic reality to the level of concrete material reality. In this way, it serves also as a defensive moment in ideological relation trying to justify the concrete moves and actions of the party.

Counter-ideologies
As in the analysis of the cases of Yugoslavia and Serbia, one can identify the different ways in which normative and operative ideologies conceptualise the main counter-ideologies. The first noticeable difference is the degree of emphasis placed on counter-ideologies at the normative and operative levels. While normative ideology makes only sporadic reference to counter-ideologies by focusing mostly on the presentation and explanation of its own ideas, operative ideology provides an extensive description of these ideologies. This fact demonstrates again that among other functions, operative ideology serves as a defensive moment in this ideological articulation. The ideas elaborated at the normative level have a better chance of being popularly accepted if all

other hegemonic counter-projects are delegitimised. Additionally, as in the cases of Yugoslavia and Serbia, these counter-ideologies are at the operative level, formulated not through the attack on their ideas, but principally by attacking the actors as the representatives of these ideas. Here again, for a counter-ideology to be delegitimised success-fully it is necessary to personalise it and give it recognisable material features.

The second striking difference between the two levels of ideology lies in their articulation of the main counter-ideologies. While normative ideology gives only sporadic attention to the counter-ideologies of Yugoslavism, Greater Serbianism and communism, and makes no clear distinction between these counter-ideologies, opera-tive ideology clearly distinguishes between the two main counter-ideologies and gives exceptional attention to both of them. Thus, we read in the manifesto that 'the CDC has appeared at the crucial historical period for the liberation from the Yugoslav state and communist social system',[166] that 'Greater Serbia hegemonism ... intend[s] to overthrow the Croatian government and to renew Bolshevism and dictatorship',[167] that 'with the results of the first round of free elections started the final breakup of the communist, one-party system based on the planned economy',[168] and that the party intends 'to rationalise and modernise state administration, to exterminate all remains of Yugo-Unitarianism and Bolshevik bureau-cratism'.[169]

At the level of operative ideology there is no mix of these counter-ideological ideas. The textbooks and editorials make a clear, precise and elaborate distinction between the ideologies of Greater Serbia and communism. Both these counter-ideologies have been histori-cally traced and intensively delegitimised.

In the case of the ideology of Greater Serbia, the aim is to demon-strate the continuity of this idea from medieval times to the present in order to show that 'our present enemies' were 'always our enemies', and in this way justify 'our' behaviour towards 'them'. Thus, in order historically to trace the roots of the ideology of Greater Serbia, the textbooks and editorials had to differentiate it from communist ideology. Here we find that the ideology of Greater Serbian is a political project shaped in the nineteenth-century work, *Načertanije*, by Ilija Garašanin:

> With this programme, Serbia had to expand in the Balkans and unite all Serbs into a single state. To achieve this it was necessary to conquer other non-Serbian peoples. That was the first programmatic formulation of the Greater Serbia idea, the predecessor of today's Greater Serbian expansionism on the territories of the former Yugoslavia.[170]

Although the ideology of Greater Serbia starts with Garašanin's *Načertanije,* we are also instructed that

> Greater Serbianism and all-Serbian consciousness established in *Načertanije* have [deeper] roots. They go deep into Serbian history from the time of the medieval Serbian state when *Svetosavlje* wanted by force to unite heterogeneous ethnic elements in the Balkan peninsula which had been included into the Serbian state by conquest. *Svetosavlje, Načertanije* and Vuk [Karadžić's] theory about Serbs of three religions are the roots of all-Serbian consciousness and Serbo-centrism that even today, as throughout history, endangers the independence and freedom of the non-Serbian peoples in the Balkans.[171]

Hence, the sources of today's Greater Serbianism are to be found in *Svetosavlje, Načertanije* and Vuk Karadžić's theory of Serbs with three religions.

Further on we read how the idea of Greater Serbia was gaining strength at the beginning of the twentieth century with the creation of an independent Serbian state and the establishment of terrorist organisations such as 'Unification or Death' and 'Black Hand'.[172] We read that 'supporting the idea of Greater Serbia, [this organisation] will make an impact on all official factors in Serbia and outside of Serbia [and] will fight with all means against the enemies of this idea'.[173] The contemporary version of this idea is found in the *Memorandum* of the Serbian Academy of Arts and Sciences, while textbooks and editorials constantly make this parallel: 'That Greater Serbian nationalism was supported by Serbian academics (with their *Memorandum* from 1986 which was inspired mainly by Dobrica Cosić)';[174] or that 'Milošević relied on war as an extension of *Načertanije*-politics';[175] or

> what kind [of policies does the EU offer to] neutralise *Memorandum*'s project ... with what kind of surveillance programme does Europe plan to stop and eliminate future military battles when all they have done is prove themselves useful as a means for the realisation of the *Načertanije* programme.[176]

Communist ideology is also intensively discredited in textbooks and editorials. Sometimes Marxist ideas and Marxism in general are criticised from the Catholic Church's point of view:

> Practice will show that Marx and Marxists have offered to workers the wrong medicine to heal their difficult economic position. Analysing the teachings of Marxists, Pope Leo XIII rightly points out that ...

socialists impose violence on society, injustice and confusion among
different classes, that the realisation of their ideas would be an open
road to envy and conflict and that imagined equality would mean
general poverty. The prophetic ideas of Pope Leo XIII have been
confirmed in our days where we witness the economic and political
breakdown of communist systems established by force.[177]

However, more often the emphasis is placed on the delegitimisation
of the economic and political system of state socialism, thus appealing
to interests and emotions. The political systems of state socialist
societies are characterised as unsuccessful and coercive:

> all communist states were (and are) based on terror, police, military,
> one-mindedness, quasi-democratism ... The states with communists in
> power could not, on the basis of social ownership, organise successful
> production and well-being of the people'.[178]

Elsewhere it was claimed that 'socialist countries were run by a
planned economy and ruled with the political single-mindness which
has stopped their development, caused low productivity and had as a
result a low standard of life of their citizens '[179] or that 'the break up of
communist states in Europe, followed by the intensive internal conflicts
as in the case of former Yugoslavia with its tragic outcome, show all the
historical and social baselessness of communist kingdoms'.[180]

How can one explain this significant difference in the representation of counter-ideologies at the normative and operative levels? The
answer lies in the different aims of the two levels of ideology as well as
in the different audiences they address. Since normative ideology is
written for party members and its sympathisers, it has no need to elaborate on, or distinguish between, the ideas of Yugoslavism, Greater
Serbia and communism. These are basically already defeated ideas
around which there is common agreement within the party membership and hence there is no further necessity for extensive descriptions
and explanations. Yugoslavia broke up and became only a historical
reference, the Greater Serbia idea was delegitimised and defeated
during the war while the original ideas of communism were buried
for good as elsewhere in eastern Europe. The manifesto clarifies its
attitude towards these counter-ideologies, but they are really of
secondary importance here.

In contrast, these ideas are of primary importance in operative
ideology. Since operative ideology targets the masses and aims to
justify the present situation and the party's monopolistic position
within it, it has to 'exploit the revolution' as much as possible and
maintain the presence of the familiar enemy. Operative ideology

focuses on the historical basis of current relationships and the delegit-imisation of the familiar enemy by identifying the 'roots' of evil.

While the ideology of Greater Serbia and communism appear to be of little importance for normative ideology, this is certainly not the case when two other counter-ideologies are discussed – 'Islamic fundamentalism' and the ideologies of the opposition parties.

Following the war in Bosnia and Herzegovina, a new enemy ideology was proclaimed in Croatian politics which was also reflected in the CDC manifesto. This is the ideology of the Bosnian Muslim leadership whose main aim the manifesto's authors describe as 'establishing an Islamic state'[181] and who, for that purpose, attacked Croats and their territories in Bosnia and Herzegovina. Thus, we read that 'after Serbs conquered 60–65 per cent of the territory of Bosnia Herzegovina because of unprepared Muslim leadership, the Muslims are set to conquer the regions that have been marked as Croatian provinces by the Vance–Owen plan';[182] that 'the CDC rejects the creation of an Islamic state which Muslim extremists want to establish in Bosnia and Herzegovina';[183] and that 'there are 140,000 Croats besieged by Muslim forces in central Bosnia who are fighting for survival'.[184]

To understand the importance given to this counter-ideology it is necessary to take into account that the CDC's leadership was internally split over the issue of Croatia's involvement in the Bosnian war. While President Tudjman and the Herzegovinian lobby within the party were behind Croatian's intervention on the behalf of Croats living in Bosnia and Herzegovina, the party's vice-president and a few other leading members were opposed to this action.[185] Thus, in order to achieve internal homogenisation within the party leadership, the manifesto's focus was placed on the delegitimisation of ideas that stood for 'Islamic fundamentalism'. So we read also that 'under the leadership of the CDC and Croatia, the Croatian people of Bosnia Herzegovina have managed to defend themselves from Serbian, and later from Muslim aggression',[186] and that 'in the organisation of the CDC, Croats have prevented all of Bosnia Herzegovina from falling into the hands of Greater Serbia. By defending the regions where they lived, they [the Croats] came under attack from Muslim aggressors.'[187]

At the level of operative ideology, this counter-ideology is less evident than those of Greater Serbia and communism. When reference is made to this counter-ideology, ideas are again personalised in concrete individuals, so the attack was regularly made on the individuals from the Bosnian Muslim leadership. Hence, we read about 'detailed planned political action' by which 'this Muslim leadership in Sarajevo intended to move the attention of the world from the aggressive and offensive actions of their army against Croats in central

Bosnia' and about how, by 'showing themselves as so-called victims of Croatian regular army, Silajdžić, Izetbegović and their followers attempted before the world to secure moral and political backing for their own crimes'.[188] However, 'Islamic fundamentalism' is not as important a counter-ideology at the operative level as at the level of normative ideology.

Another counter-ideology present in normative ideology but almost non-existent in the operative ideology are the ideas and practices of Croatian opposition parties.[189] The opposition is mostly attacked on moral grounds. So we read in the manifesto that:

> Unification of parties with heterogeneous world-views and political programmes simply because of their greed for power harms national interests in this sensitive time of peaceful integration of the Croatian Podunavlje and realisation of the project of BH [Bosnia Herzegovina] Federation which is confronted with the difficulties caused by [Bosnian] Muslim fundamentalists.[190]

Similarly,

> provoking the crisis in Zagreb is an attempt to destabilise and remove the government in the whole of Croatia, and the united opposition, by its search for help from abroad, generates and makes it easier for international forces to put pressure on Croatia.[191]

The opposition is also patronised:

> Why do opposition parties call for the overthrow of this government which has led Croatia on the road to freedom and independence; why are they uniting their efforts for its [Croatia's] general humiliation, destabilisation and removal of the president, instead of uniting their efforts to renew destroyed and, until yesterday, occupied areas and strengthen Croatia's international position?[192]

Finally, the opposition is also accused of being communist: 'the common appearance and actions of the united left and pro-communist parties ... are spreading a false picture among the domestic and foreign public about the so-called totalitarian character of the Croatian government'.[193]

In operative ideology, opposition politics and ideas are rarely mentioned. Textbooks make no reference to the importance of other political parties and movements in the process of the State's independence. However, this fact in itself tells us enough about operative ideology. As Pareto's concept 'accords with sentiments' indicates, minimising and neglecting opposition views in the media and the educational system is the most efficient way of decreasing their influence on the public.[194] Here again one can see how operative ideology functions as a defensive moment in this process of ideology translation. As discussion with opposition ideas is important for the party membership, such ideas have to be delegitimised at that level, whereas the presence of opposition views among a public that is not so dedicated and committed to the party's ideology can be harmful. Thus, it is much better if these views are publicly ignored and the opposition silenced.

As in the cases of Yugoslavia and Serbia, the content analysis has revealed a significant difference between normative and operative ideologies in their representation of counter-ideologies. Whereas normative ideology is less focused on the delegitimisation of ideas that have already been defeated, operative ideology draws most of its strength from the depiction of the enemy who is individualised, personalised and historically traced. While normative ideology deals extensively with the potential threat of present and future counter-ideologies, operative ideology is firmly oriented towards the past, trying simultaneously to show the continuity between past and present enemies and to keep these images of the enemy alive. In this way operative ideology aims to maintain the fear of enemies and to appeal to emotion and the interests of the general public.

Conclusion

The structure and content of normative and operative ideologies in Croatia show many similarities with the normative and operative ideologies of post-World War II Yugoslavia and post-communist Serbia. Here again one can see that normative ideology is abstract, blueprint-oriented and universalist, deriving its authority from the general teachings of Christian doctrine, whereas operative ideology is particularist and pragmatist, aiming to legitimise the monopolistic position of the ruling party. For that reason the two levels of ideology differ significantly in almost every respect. The economic, political and cultural organisation of the society has been differently articulated at the two levels of ideology. While normative ideology gives exceptional attention to explanations of economic, social and political issues, grounding its arguments in the authority of Christian teachings and social science, operative ideology, for the most part, ignores these central issues and concentrates on the 'revolutionary legacy' and the role of the president and party in the establishment of an independent Croatian state. While normative ideology derives its legitimation and ideas about sovereignty, independence and civilisational circles in the 'higher' reality of a tradition shaped by the Enlightenment and Romanticism, operative ideology focuses on the depiction of various actors (mostly enemies), trying to personalise and psychologise the principles and ideas of normative ideology and deriving its strength from the authority of individual and collective personalities.

What is different between the two ideologies is that normative ideology also poses as its core values Christian democracy and Christian values while, at the level of operative ideology, these concepts are reduced almost exclusively to the Catholic Church and its teachings. Hence, instead of the universalism of Christian teachings present in normative ideology (Christian morality, Christian solidarity), we find only particularist praise for institutional Catholicism. The function of the Catholic Church and Catholicism in general serves in operative ideology only as an important element of Croatianhood. To be a Catholic in operative ideology means only to be a non-Serb, i.e. a Croat. Thus, operative ideology appeals to Catholicism solely to back the central concept of ideology – ethnonationalism. This is evident in the difference between dominant values in the internal organisation of society (especially politics, economy, culture and nation) in normative and operative ideologies. This finding also confirms that while normative ideology is more likely to appeal to universal principles, whether as the Enlightenment-shaped appeal to superior knowledge as in the case of Yugoslavia or to universal Christian ethics as in Croatia, operative ideology will draw its strength from the reference to emotional and interest-driven contents.

Hence again one can see that symbols, language, actors and events play a more important role in operative than in normative ideology. The hero and the villain are again personified in concrete individuals and groups. As Moscovici points out, the image of 'the devil is so useful and so powerful precisely because you do not meet him in the street'.[195] The complex, abstract and potentially unpopular ideas and concepts of normative ideology can be understood, accepted and followed by the general public only if transformed and translated through the images that evoke fear, desire, material or symbolic benefits. Thus, counter-ideologies are much more fully developed in operative ideology which concentrates on the primary targets and consumers of delegitimisation. While the masses are intensely threatened with the 'ghosts' of communism, Greater Serbia and Yugoslavism, the ruling party elite feels more threatened by opposition ideologies.

Here again, as in the other two case studies, the aim of operative ideology is to subsume existing differences in Croatian society under the umbrella of the 'nation'. It is the 'nation' that functions here in Lefort's term as 'the People-as-One' which, through its appeal to ethnonationalist interests and emotions, aims to achieve the absolute unity and integration of the social.

Since Croatianhood and Christianity are the two core values of dominant normative ideology in Croatia, it seems appropriate to call this ideology *ethnonationalist Christian democracy*. At the same time, the dominant operative ideology which emphasises Croatianhood and Catholicism may be described as *Catholic ethnonationalism*.

NOTES

1 As Milovan Djilas observed, if proper democratic elections had been held in 1945, a majority of Croatian voters would probably have supported the Croatian Peasant Party (HSS):

> In 1945 we [the communists] were absolutely sure that we would win the election even if there was an opposition list and if great pressure was not used (pressure would be used anyway) on voters through the election process. There would be a difference between the regions: in Macedonia everybody would vote for the CP [Communist Party] and would not allow the formation of an opposition party; it would be the same in Montenegro; but in Croatia, the HSS would probably have a majority, while in Serbia, Grol would have most supporters.

See Z. Golubović, *Kriza identiteta savremenog Jugoslovenskog društva* (Belgrade: Filip Višnjić, 1988), p. 117.

2 The agreement called *Pacta Conventa* united Hungary and Croatia under the rule of King Koloman, but as Croatian historians claim 'with this act the statehood of Croatia was legally untouched'. See F. Miroševic and F. Sanjek, *Hrvatska i svijet od V. do XVIII. stoljéca* (Zagreb: Školska knjiga, 1995), p. 154.

3 *Feral Tribune*, 10 April 1995, p. 32.

4 Ibid., 14 August 1995, p. 32.

5 I. Čolović, 'Društvo mrtvih ratnika', *Republika*, 145/146 (1996), pp. 1–4.

6 *Feral Tribune*, 10 April 1995, p. 32.

7 For more on the concept of the invention of tradition see E. Hobsbawm and T. Ranger, (eds), *The Invention of Tradition* (Cambridge: Cambridge University Press, 1983).

8 Bleiburg is a place on the Austro-Slovenian border where communist partisans allegedly massacred several thousand soldiers of the NDH (*Ustashas* and *Domobrans*).

9 Čolović, 'Društvo', p. 4.

10 Bruno Bušic was a Croatian radical nationalist killed as a very young man by the Yugoslav secret service in the 1970s. Like Ivo Lola Ribar, who was idolised under the communist regime, Bruno Bušić was perceived as a handsome romantic revolutionary figure resembling Che Guevara in his looks, political radicalism and his life style if not in his political ideology.

11 E. Gellner, *Nationalism* (London: Weidenfeld, 1997), p. 74.

12 *Feral Tribune*, 13 January 1997.

13 Like Tito, Tudjman would often unscrupulously recognise that he was above the law. For example, Tudjman would say that 'the courts were making decisions without my knowledge'. G. Uzelac, 'Franjo Tudjman's Nationalist Ideology', *East European Quarterly*, 31, 4 (1998), pp. 449–73.

14 Olujić was quickly accused of being involved in a sex scandal with an under-age girl. Although, this accusation was never proved it served its purpose. Olujić was publicly humiliated and forced to resign.

15 *Feral Tribune*, 13 January 1997.

16 I. Bićanić, 'Mjerenje veličine i promjena neslužbenog gospodarstva', *Financijska praksa*, 21, 1–2 (1997), p. 24.

17 In February 1989, Tudjman and his followers established the CDC in semi-legal conditions, expecting to be arrested at any time. See L. Silber, and A. Little, *The Death of Yugoslavia* (London: Penguin and BBC Books, 1995), p. 88.

18 Tudjman was a historian and a former YPA army general who was sacked and jailed in the former Yugoslavia on several occasions for his nationalism.

19 Tudjman would often use this phrase to emphasise the importance of his victory, although with the break up of the Yugoslav state, its army, consisting of officers and soldiers from different nationalities, was also in a state of disintegration and thus was more likely to be the twenty-fourth military force of Europe in its strength.

20 Silber and Little, *Death*, p. 90.

21 Uzelac has analysed Tudjman's speeches and among other interesting things has found that in 50 analysed speeches, Tudjman has used 35 phrases that include the term 'history' See G. Uzelac, 'Tudjman's Ideology', pp. 449–73.

22 I. Žanić, 'Navrh gore Romanije …', p. 14.

23 A. Hodžić, 'Etnocentrizam društvenih grupa i nacionalnih zajednica', in M. Lazić (ed.), *Položaj naroda i medjunacionalni odnosi u Hrvatskoj* (Zagreb: IDIS, 1991), p. 123.

24 *Feral Tribune*, 4 September 1995, p. 32.

25 Ibid., 11 September 1995, p. 32.

26 Ibid., 14 April 1997, p. 32.

27 On one such occasion Tudjman said: 'They say give us back *Dinamo*. What to give them back? Yugoslavia, Serbia, Pančevo? [Pančevo is a town in Serbia whose football team bears the name, Dinamo.] It was those from the opposition who don't know what it means to have an independent state who found a few lunatics and gave them DM 100 each to shout in the stadium'. See *Feral Tribune*, 19 May 1997, p. 32.

28 G. Gill, 'Personal Dominance and the Collective Principle: Individual Legitimacy in Marxist–Leninist Systems', in T. Rigby and F. Feher (eds), *Political Legitimation in Communist States* (London: Macmillan, 1982).

29 *Feral Tribune*, 20 March 1995, p. 32.

30 Ibid., 10 April 1995, p. 32.

31 Uzelac, *Tudjman's Ideology*, p. 463.

32 *Feral Tribune*, 21 April 1997, p. 32

33 *Program Hrvatske Demokratske Zajednice. + Povijest HDZ-a.* (Http://www.hdz.hr, 1993), p. 29.

34 Ibid.

35 Ibid.

36 Ibid., p. 21.

37 Ibid., p. 30.

38 Ibid.

39 I. Perić, *Hrvatska i svijet u XX. stoljeću* (Zagreb: Školska knjiga, 1995), p. 203.

40 *Vjesnik*, 5 October 1993, p. 1.

41 *Program HDZ*, p. 24.

42 Ibid., p. 21.

43 Ibid., p. 18.

44 Ibid., p. 21.

45 Ibid., p. 20.

46 Ibid.

47 Ibid.

48 Ibid., p. 21.

49 *Vjesnik*, 5 August 1992, p. 2.

50 Perić, *Hrvatska i svijet*, p. 21.

51 *Vjesnik*, 1 June 1993, p. 1.

52 Ibid., 5 August 1992, p. 2.

53 Ibid.

54 F. Mirošević and T. Macan, *Hrvatska i svijet u XVIII. I XIX. stoljeću* (Zagreb: Školska knjiga, 1995), p. 145.
55 Ibid., p. 146.
56 Ibid., p. 147.
57 *Program HDZ*, p. 28.
58 Ibid., p. 21.
59 Ibid., p. 28.
60 Ibid., p. 34.
61 Ibid., p. 35.
62 Mirošević and Macan, *Hrvatska i svijet*, p. 4.
63 Perić, *Hrvatska i svijet*, p. 192.
64 *Vjesnik*, 30 October 1993, p. 1.
65 Ibid., 15 January 1994, p. 1.
66 Mirošević and Macan, *Hrvatska i svijet*, p. 41.
67 Ibid., p. 44.
68 Ibid., p. 147.
69 Ibid., p. 60.
70 *Program HDZ*, p. 23.
71 Ibid., p. 22.
72 Ibid.
73 Ibid., p. 3.
74 Ibid., p. 7.
75 Ibid., p. 2.
76 Ibid., p. 5.
77 Mirošević and Sanjek, *Hrvatska i svijet*, p. 4.
78 Mirošević and Macan, *Hrvatska i svijet*, p. 28.
79 Ibid., p. 4.
80 Mirošević and Sanjek, *Hrvatska i svijet* p. 4.
81 Mirošević and Macan, *Hrvatska i svijet*, p. 27.
82 Ibid., p. 4.
83 Ibid., p. 19.
84 Perić, *Hrvatska i svijet*, p. 116.
85 Mirošević and Macan, *Hrvatska i svijet*, p. 92.
86 Ibid., p. 96.
87 Ibid., p. 26.
88 Ibid., p. 20.
89 Perić, *Hrvatska i svijet*, p. 102.
90 Ibid., p. 98.
91 Ibid., p. 179.
92 *Program HDZ*, p. 21.
93 Ibid., p. 28.
94 Ibid., p. 18.
95 Ibid., p. 1.
96 Ibid., p. 18.
97 Ibid., p. 20.
98 Mirošević and Sanjek, *Hrvatska i svijet*, pp. 5–6.
99 Mirošević and Macan, *Hrvatska i svijet*, p. 96.
100 Perić, *Hrvatska i svijet*, p. 183.
101 Ibid., pp. 213–14.
102 Ibid., p. 26.
103 Ibid., p. 190.
104 H. Tajfel, *Social Identity and Intergroup Relations* (Cambridge: Cambridge University Press, 1982).

105 See, for example, *Vjesnik,* 11 June 1994, p. 3, and 31 May 1994, p. 2.
106 Mirošević and Macan, *Hrvatska i svijet,* p. 60.
107 *Vjesnik,* 11 June 1994, p. 1.
108 Perić, *Hrvatska i svijet,* p. 178.
109 Ibid.
110 Mirošević and Macan, *Hrvatska i svijet,* p. 59.
111 Ibid., p. 147.
112 Perić, *Hrvatska i svijet,* p. 192.
113 Ibid., p. 213 (my italics).
114 Mirošević and Macan, *Hrvatska i svijet,* p. 151.
115 Perić, *Hrvatska i svijet,* p. 9.
116 Mirošević and Macan, *Hrvatska i svijet,* p. 153.
117 Perić, *Hrvatska i svijet,* p. 27.
118 Mirošević and Macan, *Hrvatska i svijet,* p. 153.
119 See Perić, *Hrvatska i svijet,* pp. 39–40.
120 Ibid., p. 40.
121 Ibid., p. 58.
122 Ibid., p. 160–1.
123 *Vjesnik,* 5 April 1994, p. 1.
124 Ibid., 5 March 1993, p. 1.
125 Ibid., 15 August 1992, p. 2.
126 Perić, *Hrvatska i svijet,* p. 212.
127 Ibid.
128 Ibid., p. 47.
129 Ibid., p. 210.
130 Mirošević and Macan, *Hrvatska i svijet,* p. 152.
131 Perić, *Hrvatska i svijet,* p. 132.
132 *Vjesnik,* 30 September 1992, p. 2.
133 Ibid.
134 Perić, *Hrvatska i svijet,* p. 106.
135 Ibid., p. 186.
136 Ibid., p. 179.
137 Ibid., p. 155.
138 Ibid., p. 190.
139 *Program HDZ,* p. 27.
140 The familiar historical examples include the position of Latin and French in medieval and eighteenth- and nineteenth-century Europe in relation to vernacular languages.
141 *Program HDZ,* p. 20.
142 Ibid.
143 Ibid., p. 18 (my italics). This statement contains elements of a certain *post facto* interpretation and thus is an *ideologem,* because a great number of Croatian parties of that period supported radical changes in the organisation of the then federal Yugoslav state, mostly in the direction of a confederation, and almost all of them supported a change in the political system. Although the the CDC was more radical than some other parties, it did not opt for independence until it was clear to all political forces in the country that no other reasonable solution was available.
144 The word that appears in the original is *stalež,* meaning estate, rank, class, and is traditionally associated with a feudal social structure.
145 *Program HDZ,* p. 20.
146 Ibid., p. 21.
147 Ibid., p. 20.
148 F. Fukuyama, *The End of History and the Last Man* (London: Hamish Hamilton, 1992).

149 Mirošević and Macan, *Hrvatska i svijet*, p. 29.
150 Perić, *Hrvatska i svijet*, p. 214.
151 *Vjesnik*, 5 July 1993, p. 1.
152 Mirošević and Macan, *Hrvatska i svijet*, p. 26.
153 *Vjesnik*, 1 June 1993, p. 1.
154 S. Žižek (ed.), *Mapping Ideology* (London: Verso, 1994).
155 Mirošević and Macan, *Hrvatska i svijet*, p. 32.
156 Perić, *Hrvatska i svijet*, p. 84.
157 *Vjesnik*, 27 June 1994, p. 3.
158 Ibid., 5 November 1993, p. 1.
159 Ibid., 15 October 1993, p. 1.
160 Ibid., 5 November 1993, p. 1.
161 Mirošević and Macan, *Hrvatska i svijet*, p. 19.
162 Ibid., p. 37.
163 Ibid., p. 40.
164 Ibid., p. 101.
165 Ibid., p. 102.
166 *Program HDZ*, p. 18.
167 Ibid., p. 4.
168 Ibid., p. 3.
169 Ibid., p. 7.
170 Mirošević and Macan, *Hrvatska i svijet*, p. 66.
171 Ibid., p. 67.
172 Perić, *Hrvatska i svijet*, p. 27.
173 Ibid.
174 Ibid., p. 199.
175 *Vjesnik*, 15 November 1993, p. 1.
176 Ibid., 30 November 1993, p. 1.
177 Mirošević and Macan, *Hrvatska i svijet*, p. 150.
178 Ibid.
179 Perić, *Hrvatska i svijet*, p. 187.
180 *Vjesnik*, 5 October 1992, p. 2.
181 *Program HDZ*, p. 8.
182 Ibid.
183 Ibid., p. 7.
184 Ibid.
185 This group was to split later on and form its own party, the Croatian Independent Democrats, which remained marginal to the political life of Croatia.
186 *Program HDZ*, p. 19.
187 Ibid., p. 8.
188 *Vjesnik*, 31 January 1994, p. 1.
189 Most of these views are related to the Zagreb Council crisis which resulted in a deadlock after the united opposition won the local elections and the Croatian president refused to confirm a new opposition party mayor.
190 *Program HDZ*, p. 14.
191 Ibid.
192 Ibid.
193 Ibid., p. 15.
194 V. Pareto, *Sociological Writings* (Oxford: Basil Blackwell, 1966).
195 C. F. Graumann and S. Moscovici (eds), *Changing Concepts of Conspiracy* (New York: Springer, 1986), p. 157.

Part III

Back to Theory

6

Ideology and Legitimacy: Back to Theory

IDEOLOGY

Inclusive definition of ideology

The results of the content analyses of normative and operative ideologies in my three case studies demonstrate that an inclusive definition of ideology is better able to deal with differently structured societies than a restrictive concept of ideology. The analysis shows that one cannot talk about a single uniform ideology at work such as capitalism, communism or nationalism, but rather about a number of differently structured and differently shaped dominant ideologies that operate at two different levels – as normative ideologies (self-management socialism, reformed democratic socialism and ethnonationalist Christian democracy) and as operative ideologies (integral nationalist self-management socialism, ethnonationalist socialism and Catholic ethnonationalism). Hence, instead of looking at particular ways of thinking, groups of people or political systems as ideological, this approach helps us to identify six different conceptual structures of ideology. At the same time, the analytic position used demonstrates that an inclusive concept of ideology does not automatically mean reducing ideology to party politics or different world-views. On the contrary, the concept has preserved the idea of ideology with its more generalising and totalising features. However, these features are not only related to one political or economic type of social organisation such as capitalism and 'its mode of production' or communism and its 'totalitarian dictatorship', but also include many different forms of society's structure. In other words, we are not only to look for how a capitalist economic system produces alienated subjects and their alienated perceptions of reality as in Marx's commodity fetishism, or how the capitalist mode of production has a direct impact on the establishment of cultural hegemony by shaping the contents of the educational system and mass media as in Gramsci and Althusser. It demonstrates rather that differently structured political and economic systems can produce the same effects, implying that there are different sources of ideological practices and different ways in which ideology operates. If ideology is conceptualised in a restrictive way, tied only to one form of society or political practice, and if an ideology-free society is conceived as possible, then one could not satisfactorily explain how ideology operates in societies with different political systems or in societies where the economy does not function as an autonomous sphere as in the three case studies under consideration.

The argument of the functionalist tradition that ideology operates as an illusion, but a socially functional illusion equally as psychoanalytic perception of ideology as an illusory wishful thinking or fantasy scenario, although applicable to an analysis of language, symbols and metaphors, reduce the general concept of ideology to social pathology. It is again assumed that one can be 'healed' from ideology. This way of thinking is also evident in Boudon who opposes science and ideology, as well as in critical theory which intends to liberate us from the Enlightenment-produced ideological concept of reason.

All these positions see ideology as a set of manipulative values and practices and claim to know what non-ideological activity is. As the case studies that I have analysed here show, one can distinguish between claims with a direct manipulative meaning (*ideologems*) and more 'mundane' statements without employing a restrictive concept of ideology. One can also distinguish between direct manipulative practices such as control of the media and education system on the one hand, and the less direct manipulative and non-manipulative impact of charismatic authority and particular traditions on the formation and dissemination of certain ideas and practices, on the other. In this way one can accept that some ideological practices are manipulative without accepting the idea that an ideology-free society is possible. Yugoslav, Serbian and Croatian elites certainly did instrumentalise and manipulate the mass media and educational system for their political purposes, but definitely not in either zero-sum or *ex nihilo* ways. The new ideas, values and practices had to be reshaped and implemented on the pattern of already existing values and practices: self-management socialism could successfully be disseminated only if conceptualised as simplified and more accessible integral nationalist self-management socialism; reformed democratic socialism could, in the context of the breakup of Yugoslavia and the fall of communist regimes in Eastern Europe, be made acceptable to the majority of the population only if framed as ethnonationalist socialism, while the Christian universalism of ethnonationalist Christian democracy could be made fully understandable to masses only if conceived as Catholic ethnonationalism.

The analysis undertaken indicates that Mannheim's paradox can be avoided by simply perceiving the concept of ideology as 'technical' and thus neutral, while at the same time preserving the idea of potential manipulation and mystification. In this way we do not treat the central claims and statements made by particular ideologies as being true or false, but rather focus on differences and similarities in their content and structure. The case studies examined here have clearly shown how three apparently very different and often opposing ideologies of communism, socialism and Christian democracy show many similarities at the operative level. All three appeal to almost identical symbols and metaphors and use almost the same type of argument and terminology and depict the main actors and counter-ideologies in a very similar way.

The inclusive definition of ideology applied here is, as previously explained, congruent with neo-Kantian, Paretian, structuralist and post-modernist positions in viewing any action-oriented and power-related coherent world-view about the structural organisation of a particular society as ideology. Although ideology was not studied here as a historically determined belief system (Mannheim), cultural system (Geertz), logical model (Barthes and Lévi-Strauss) or a set of language games (Lyotard), it demonstrated that true/false and science/non-science criteria and the attribution of ideology to particular sets of values, people and political orders are methodologically fruitless in the interpretation of different forms of ideology. Let us now take a more detailed look at each of these categories and examine in depth the results of the above content analyses.

Against true/false criteria

The case studies indicate that true/false criteria appear to be irrelevant for most of the time in the analysis of the structure, form and content of ideology. This applies equally to micro- and macro-levels of analysis.

On the micro-level most of the statements are given a priori and basically cannot be tested. They acquire their full meaning only in the specific social context of a particular ideology. Let us take a look, for example, at the following statement from the LCY manifesto:

> the progressive position of the working class comes from the fact that the working class cannot liberate itself from exploitation if it, at the same time, does not liberate the entire society from historically surpassed capitalist society and from every form of exploitation.[1]

This statement is basically circular and as such cannot be refuted or proven. It contains five a priori premises: first, capitalism is exploitative;

second, being exploitative, capitalism must be historically surpassed; third, the working class is progressive; fourth, the working class should be liberated from capitalism; and fifth, society should be liberated from capitalism. The conclusion deduced from these premises is that the working class cannot liberate itself from capitalism if it does not at the same time liberate society. Although the conclusion does not result from the premises, it cannot be refuted because the relationship between the working class and society is not established. If society is equated with the working class, and that seems to be the case in other statements, then the relationship between the statements is tautological. Therefore, if the criteria of truth and falsity are strictly applied, they tell us that most of the statements are either tautologies or cannot be tested. Either way, they do not tell us much about the structure of ideology.

It is a similar case with statements such as 'capitalism reached its final stage [in] imperialism, and Lenin gave a scientific Marxist analysis of that process'[2] or 'what defines a national minority is not its size but the fact that it refers to citizens who possess a national state outside the borders of Yugoslavia'.[3] These statements cannot be evaluated from some universal standpoint because the 'final stage of capitalism' is not specified and can extend to hundreds and thousands of years, and thus cannot be refuted, while the definition of national minority is a matter of consensus within a particular community. In this concrete case, to paraphrase Foucault, the power of definition equals the definition of power. The group that controls state institutions is in a position to define who is to be treated as a minority and who as a constitutive ethnonation in the new Yugoslav federation. In that way Montenegrins who number about 650,000 are declared to be a constitutive ethnic nation with all the privileges that accompany such a definition, while Albanians who number about 2 million are legally defined as a national minority. Here again the question of truth and untruth is not only impossible to answer, but also appears to be irrelevant for the study of ideology.

The next point against true/false criteria is that the terminology, symbols and metaphors used, which are extremely important devices of ideology, are regularly given in the form which cannot be judged by applying these criteria. 'Bourgeois element', 'imperialist hegemonism', '*Chetniks*', 'Serbo-communist aggression', 'mixed society', 'occupied territories' or 'Croatian national being' are neither true nor false since in Yugoslav, Croatian and Serbian societies these terms have different meanings and hence different definitions. By reducing them to a true/false dichotomy, one would lose the richness of their meaning and their emotional appeal for particular populations. Thus, while *Chetniks* resemble everything evil in Croatian society, in Serbian society the term would have a mainly neutral if not positive connotation. The same circumstances apply for the term 'communism' in post-World War II Yugoslav and post-1990 Croatian society, or 'decentralisation' in post-World War II Yugoslavia and post-1987 Serbia. Their truthfulness is socially and culturally bound.

However, the inadequacy of true/false criteria in the analysis of ideology can be most properly illustrated by concentrating on the macro-level. The 'images of the world' depicted in these three case studies will help us to demonstrate this inadequacy. The images of the world analysed in these three cases gave us basically three different grand narratives about the social world. These narratives are given in two forms, as the normative or official story and as the operative story that one comes across while reading newspapers and school textbooks. These interpretations of the world also differ substantially between themselves. For example, in one case, the working class is the principal subject of social change (Yugoslavia), in another, ethnic nations have that privileged position in history (Croatia), while in the third, the two concepts are combined and classes and nations identified as the driving forces of social development (Serbia). However, what is common to these three narratives, and thus to every ideological grand narrative, is the use of a conflictual paradigm. They all interpret the social world by stressing contradictions and conflicts between social groups. In the case of post-World War II Yugoslavia these contradictions are of an economic nature – history is a history of class struggle and of the economic exploitation of the underprivileged by the privileged. In the case of post-communist Serbia the conflicts emphasised are principally political in their content – one (sometimes two) mighty political power intends to establish its political hegemony in the world and to impose its will in international relations. In the case of post-communist Croatia it is cultural and civilisational contradictions that are singled out as the main feature of social history – Western Christian civilisation is opposed to the Balkans. All three narratives exhibit some form of determinism – economic (Yugoslavia), political (Serbia) and cultural (Croatia), and all view human history through evolutionary and teleological glasses. In the Yugoslav case these are historical stages of development – societies inevitably pass through 'social formations' (from slavery, feudalism and capitalism to socialism and communism). In the Croatian case, the history of the world is seen as a constant struggle between ethnically defined nations, cultures and civilisations which end up in the establishment of the independent and sovereign nation state. The Serbian case combines the two interpretations and views socialism and the nation state as the final and most progressive aim of history.

However, none of these views can be evaluated in terms of being true or false, or even of being truer than the other. These grand ideological narratives function like any consistent social and political theory that employs evolutionary schema in the explanation and interpretation of human history. Thus, Hegel's distinction between the oriental, Graeco-Roman and Germanic stages of development,[4] Spencer's view of societies as passing from hordes to military and industrial organisation and then to an ethical order,[5] Comte's theological, metaphysical and positive phases,[6] Habermas's social formations[7] or Gellner's concept of hunting/gathering, agrarian and industrial society,[8] although more complex, are equally valid with the narratives given in the ideology's images of the world.

As successfully argued on many occasions, evolutionary theory itself is given in an a priori form and its principal statements cannot be proven. As Sztompka has pointed out, evolutionism is based on three ontological assumptions – determinism (the predetermined path of development through which all societies must pass); fatalism (the path of development seen as an 'inexorable necessity'); and finalism (the predetermined stages and phases of development).[9] These three ideas of the hierarchisation of human development as well as of societies is present in both ideologies and social theory. Since the majority of ideologies draw their ideas and concepts from political and social theory, as directly in the case of self-management socialism, and indirectly in cases of reformed socialism and ethnonationalist Christian democracy, the similarity of their argument is understandable. In this way ideologies and political theories have equal ontological validity.

However, their ontological validity does not imply that all forms of knowledge are judgementally equal. As Bhaskar[10] and Brown[11] have rightly observed, accepting the idea that all knowledge emerges in a particular social and historical environment, and, as such, is shaped by that environment, does not automatically mean accepting the idea that all forms of knowledge are equally valid. The difference is made between epistemological and judgmental relativism. While epistemological relativism assumes that all knowledge is partial since the truth is always situationally or historically shaped, judgmental relativism treats all truths as equal and incomparable. Whereas judgmental relativity is absolutist and insists that 'all standards must be universal to be valid', epistemological relativity accepts the existence of alternative forms of valid knowledge. Thus what is claimed here is that narratives present in ideologies and political or social theories cannot be proven in terms of absolute, universally accepted law-like statements because the truth in itself can have multiple forms. All these narratives are ontologically and epistemologically relative. At the same time, the knowledge claims, although multiple, are often comparable and socially and politically unequal. That is why it is much more fruitful to follow Foucault and look for the 'how' instead of the 'what' of truth. As Brown puts it, 'the fear of relativism can be partly allayed by shifting from a conception of truth as discovery or product, towards a view of truth as invention or process'.[12]

Against science/non-science criteria

The idea of truth/falsity is closely linked to another dichotomy which is often employed in the study of ideology – science/non-science criteria. If applied to the analysis of these three case studies, this classical positivist principle appears to be impossible to achieve.

Some, if not the majority of ideologies, make claims to the posses-sion of ultimate knowledge just as science does. Their terminology, explanations and arguments often appear identical to the discourse of science. Self-management socialism is a typical example. This ideology sees itself as a science and speaks with the voice of science: 'this programme attempts to formulate ... general laws of socialist development'.[13] Perceiving socialism as science (Marx and Engels's scientific socialism), it sets as its aim 'to educate working people so that they can ... think and act socialistically',[14] meaning in a scientific and truthful way. This ideology also formulates its explanations in the spirit of economic science explaining, for example, the origins of monopolist capitalism by deducing state intervention from the inability of capitalist production to cope with the development of productive forces.[15]

A similar ambition is present in reformed democratic socialism. Although this ideology does not perceive itself as science, it presents its ideas as grounded in scientific discoveries. A typical example is the following statement:

> historical science will give definite analysis and evaluation of that period and its leading personalities. However, on the basis of the knowledge that science has already established ... the Socialist Party of Serbia has certain views about this period of our recent history.[16]

This ideology also uses arguments and gives explanations in the spirit of science. Thus, we learn that the unregulated market economy inevitably leads to periodic disturbances which reflect deep economic crises,[17] that capitalist relations inescapably lead to exploitation,[18] or that new technologies free workers from alienation.[19]

Even ethnonationalist Christian democracy derives its authority from the interpretation of history as science. It refers to ideas such as 'culture' or 'civilisation' and treats them as firm and unproblematic concepts. So we read that 'the Croatian people are a people of Western civilisation and democratic traditions'[20] and that the CDC follows 'the principles of Christian civilisation of the Western world to which the Croatian people have always belonged'.[21]

The ambition of these three ideologies to assume the mantle of science makes them indistinguishable from those social and political theories which have the same aim. What, for example, makes the theories of Durkheim and Parsons different from the claims made by self-management socialism and reformed democratic socialism? Not much. All of them aim to explain the social world, relationships between individuals and groups or the nature of social change in a meaningful way. Although Durkheim and Parsons use different jargon and refer to 'social facts' and 'social systems' instead of 'mixed society' and 'capitalist hegemonism', the material quality of their explanations of 'anomic suicide' and 'dedifferentiation of societies' are as distant from the laws of thermodynamics and gravity as the explanations of 'monopolist capitalism' and the 'need for state regulation in economy' offered by these three ideologies.

If this argument is pursued to its end, it inevitably leads to the conclusion that one can either treat both ideologies and social and political theories as science or, in a neo-Kantian and post-modern spirit, give up the ambition of analysing and explaining the social world in terms of the natural world. Nevertheless, this discussion can make sense only if the concept of science as given in natural and technical sciences was deemed to be firm, stable and unquestionable. As new research and discoveries in physics, chemistry and astronomy have made this less obvious, the entire discussion looses its point. As MacIntyre and Brown[22] have convincingly demonstrated, science itself, like all discourses of knowledge, has a narrative structure. Relativity, quantum and chaos theories have clearly demonstrated that the ideal of mechanistic science to find the ultimate element to which all the matter can be reduced was a pure illusion. Newtonian physics was driven with this aim to find the final particle: first, there was the molecule, then the atom, then electrons, protons and neutrons, and, finally, quarks. Nevertheless, Einstein's research showed that the aim of mechanical science could not be achieved simply because there are no eternally stable particles; on the contrary, particles compose a field with strong and weak regions that have only temporary stability. The stability of the objects that we see is not inherent in the objects themselves. As Bohm points out: 'all the forms we see in it [the universe] are abstracted by our own way of looking and thinking, which is convenient at times, helping us with our technology, for example'.[23] Quantum theory has further relativised the idea of a stable and predictable universe. It demonstrated that 'ultimately no continuous motion exists'[24] and that the motion and behaviour of particles is deeply dependent on the context in which they are treated. Quantum theory found not only that space and time are directly interrelated and basically one, but also that matter and energy have a dual nature manifested either as particles or waves depending on the type of experimental treatment. If relativity and quantum theory have undermined the whole idea of stability in the natural sciences, chaos theory has demolished the concept of predictability. Chaos theory has introduced the idea of non-linear dynamics showing how small fluctuations in their environments or their interactions may have surprisingly large effects.[25] It has demonstrated how it is possible for nearly identical entities located in identical environments to exhibit radically different behaviours. According to chaos theory, prediction and precise measurements are intrinsically impossible for dynamic systems.[26] The variety of systems which act unpredictably despite their presumable simplicity have been examined and the fact that the forces involved in this action are governed by a well-understood physical world. All these findings have significantly demolished the image of the natural sciences as firm and exact and hence indicate the pointlessness of applying scientific criteria to the analysis of ideology.

However, the crucial argument against the science/non-science dichotomy in the study of ideology is its enormous manipulative potential. In the post-Enlightenment age, science has replaced religion as the main source of legitimation. Hence, if one succeeds in establishing one's position as scientific, one is automatically in a position of power to decide which truth claims are legitimate and which are not. This is Foucault's power/knowledge unity. As Horkheimer and Adorno[27] and later Lyotard[28] have rightly identified, in order to legitimise this new post-Enlightenment scientific society, science is being used to delegitimise all other language games. Science itself cannot function as the demythologiser of grand meta-narratives since it functions as a mythical narrative itself.

Since the Enlightenment was also responsible for equating knowledge and science with happiness, and material with moral progress, the claim to possess knowledge meant also a claim to have found the road to happiness. This is precisely why all theoretical positions and ideologies struggle, sometimes fiercely, to prove their ideas and practices as scientific and those of the competing theories and ideologies as non-scientific. He who knows the road to happiness is guaranteed the power to lead.

In order to establish their scientific legacy, various theories and ideologies were obliged to represent themselves in a neutral way. They would use esoteric terminology which resembled the jargon of

Ideology, Legitimacy and the New State

science, give explanations of social reality in causal or scientific terms and would present their 'discoveries' through the same means as science – books, journals, periodicals for selected audiences, the mass media and school textbooks for the entire population. The mass media were responsible for the popular presentation of information gathered with regard to scientific 'discoveries', while the educational system was set up for the dissemination of 'pure' knowledge discovered by science among succeeding generations. Thus, people were to be taught that socialism, the State based on the *Sharia* or liberal parliamentary democracy are the best possible forms of social and political organisation, just as the laws of thermodynamics and gravity are the only true and meaningful explanations of the Earth's temperature and movement.

The three ideologies analysed in this study show the same ambition. Although their operative language might sometimes be deliberate, vulgar and evidently committed, the main impact they make is not through these 'direct' means but principally through 'scientific' and less visible ways. It is not the fact that the United States is classed as an exploitative imperialist in Yugoslav textbooks or Serbs described as murderous *Chetniks* in Croatian textbooks or, indeed, Croats as genocidal *Ustashas* in Serbian textbooks that will have a crucial impact on the internalisation of these values among succeeding generations. The pejorative and offensive attributes attached to these groups are deeply emotional, reflecting actual political conflict between these groups that can easily be forgotten as the political situation changes and as soon as new enemies are introduced into the public arena. Their effect might be very intensive but it is short-lived. What is much more important are other, non-deliberate, 'neutral' and 'scientific' ways of presentation and explanation. These are the less evident attempts scientifically to explain social phenomena using the neutral language of science.[29] They are used to demonstrate, for example, how capitalism and imperialism are inevitably connected, or how class conflict is a characteristic of all historical epochs (the Yugoslav case); how Serbian hegemonism has deep historical roots and seems to predetermine all Serbian politics; how Croatian national consciousness was a seamless phenomenon that was always equally strong (the Croatian case); how Serbian bravery, strong resistance to foreign invasions, both political and cultural, and sacrifice are cornerstones of Serbian behaviour in history, and how Croatian treachery and cowardice were present in all periods of modern history (the Serbian case).

Most of these ideas are not directly spelled out in the mass media or educational system; rather, they lead readers and pupils to develop their own conclusions in this direction. These conclusions and explanations then become knowledge that the majority of these readers and pupils will take with them for the rest of their lives. These are not just images and descriptions of different actors and events but 'scientific' explanations supported by 'facts' (selected truths), many of which will be internalised. Current and subsequent generations will not only learn but also develop their vision of the world and social reality on the basis of these 'facts' and explanations. They will acquire the knowledge which will help them orient and develop their identities in the social world they enter. These explanations are building blocks of knowledge that are always value specific and of particular political colour on which grounds one forms one's identity. On these building blocks of knowledge subsequent generations will develop the basis of their 'ontological security'.[30]

The analysis of the 'counter-ideologies' in these three cases demonstrates also how 'science' has been used for self-legitimisation and for the delegitimisation of other ideologies. Thus, normative ideologies in the Yugoslav, Serbian and Croatian cases all ground their legitimacy in science. They all refer to scientific discoveries, whether to Marxism–Leninism as in the Yugoslav case, to modern economics and political science as in the Serbian case or to Christian science and history as in the case of Croatia. Their arguments are the following: Marx and Lenin discovered the laws of human development and social history and what we (the party, society, leader) do is only to implement this knowledge in our society (Yugoslav case); or economic science has discovered that ownership is irrelevant for the efficiency of economy so it is not necessary to privatise state-run companies (Serbian case); or Christian science and the Enlightenment and Romanticism established that human beings can acquire their true human potential only through Christian solidarity via the ethnically established nation state (Croatian case). These arguments allow them to establish their position as the only truth and from there to delegitimise other concepts as erroneous. Thus, political economy as formulated in capitalism by 'bourgeois' social scientists preserves existing class relations and is therefore not scientific/truthful but intended to deceive (Yugoslav case); as scientifically proven, liberal democratic societies do not include economic democracy and are therefore not truly democratic (Serbian case); or as history and Christian science have demonstrated, class solidarity is an illusion and the only true solidarity is an ethnonational one (Croatian case).

Universality of ideology

The content analysis of dominant power-keeping ideologies in post-World War II Yugoslavia and post-Cold War Serbia and Croatia points towards the conclusion that ideology is a universal phenomenon.

Regardless of the type of society and content of dominant values, there are many common elements that confirm the idea that all ideologies have a similar structure. The vocabulary and expressions they use, the symbols they appeal to, the descriptions of different agents and their strategies of delegitimisation all suggest this idea.

As Barthes[31] and Althusser[32] have emphasised, ideology speaks with 'the voice of nature'. It offers and interprets its ideas and practices as obvious and self-evident. In Billig's terms, 'ideology comprises the habits of behaviour and belief which combine to make any social world appear to those, who inhabit it, as the natural world'.[33] Althusser has termed this process when ideology reproaches its subjects as inter-pellation or hailing. Ideology, in his view, 'interpellates concrete individuals as subjects', meaning that it actually defines them within itself as such. By addressing concrete subjects as 'Hey, you ... man, ... German, ... peasant, ... black!', ideology tells these subjects who they are, formulating them as concrete individuals.

Indeed, in the three case studies presented here, we can see how three different ideologies address their subjects in a similar way. They hail their public as 'working class', 'working people', 'Yugoslavs' (Yugoslavia), 'Serbs', 'a part of Serbdom' (Serbia) or 'Croats', 'members of Croatian national being' (Croatia). They address their subjects always as members of the particular group, of the group whose membership seems 'normal' and 'natural'. It appears as self-evident that people are and should be grouped in nations and classes. In the Yugoslav case the message is: We live in a world divided along class lines. This world has always been divided along class lines. We represent the (working) class which is the most progressive and victorious class. In the Croat-ian case the message is: we live in a world divided along cultural and civilisational lines. This world has always been divided along the lines of culture and civilisation. We represent (Croatian) culture and (Western and Christian) civilisation which is the most progressive and victorious civilisation. In the Serbian case the message is: we live in a world divided along class and political lines. This world has always been divided along class and political lines. We represent the (work-ing) class and a (Serbian) nation that is the most progressive and victorious class.

The message of ideology also relies heavily on selective collective memory or more accurately, on collective amnesia.[34] Forgetting is equally important as remembering in the acceptance of certain ideol-ogy. The 'normality' and 'obviousness' of all three of these ideologies comes from the projection of the past as directly leading to the present situation and the perception of the future only in relation to the present state. The present is depicted and functions as an eternal present. Everything that happened before 'our time' is relevant only if it fits in the context of the present, and everything that happens in the future can happen only in the direction set by present ideology. This is exactly what Lefort means when he speaks about the 'society without history'.[35] However, Lefort's exceptionally strong distinction between 'democracy' and 'totalitarianism' leads him to conclusion that 'democracy' is a historical society *par excellence* unlike 'totalitarianism' which is unhistorical. At the level of ideologies, whether one speaks of Leninist socialism, national-socialism or liberalism, this distinction is not sustainable because all ideologies aim at projecting and establishing 'society without history'. The only and important difference was that some ideologies, like Leninist socialism and national-socialism, had managed to monopolise power at the State level and to impose their values on society, while in the case of some other ideologies, such as ecologism, feminism and libertarianism, this was not yet the case.

The difference between operative and normative ideologies as shown in this study suggests that although Althusser was right in interpreting the way ideology addresses its subjects, his claim that ideology defines and shapes individuals is certainly too strong. Althusser places too much emphasis on the unconscious forces outside the individual and neglects rationality and individual 'good reasons' for accepting a particular ideology. In order successfully to disseminate a particular set of ideas, values and practices, one has to rely on already existing interests and emotions of individuals. The content analysis shows that while normative ideology formulated for the narrow circle of party members speaks in the abstract language of science, universal principles and Kantian or Christian ethics, operative ideology appeals more to the concrete utilitarian interests and emotions of the general public. Self-management socialism could not define and produce subjects as 'self-managing socialists' but only as 'Yugoslav working people'; reformed democratic socialism could not interpellate individuals as 'reformed democratic socialists' but as 'Serbian working people', and even ethnonationalist Christian democracy could not hail its subjects as 'Hey, you Croat Christian Democrat!' but only as 'Hey, you Catholic Croat!'.

Nevertheless, the most significant way by which ideology addresses its subjects is by the use of the pronouns 'we' and 'us'. So one reads in newspapers and textbooks about 'our unquestionable rights', about 'ours, only ours, and for a thousand times, our Trieste', about 'our sacrifices for the country' or 'our national duty'. This 'us' can also become eternal and is presented, as Althusser would say, as having no history. So we read about the Romans who conquered and ruled *our* land[36] without contradicting the historical record which says that 'we' inhabited these territories a couple of centuries later. The 'we' and 'us' appeal directly to the emotions and interests of the subjects being addressed. They also automatically incorporate individuals into one collective 'we', which is inclusive and exclusive at the same time. As Billig points out, analysing 'banal forms of nationalism' in the West:

> 'we' can become an ambiguous term, indicating both the particularity of 'we', the nation [class, state, etc.], and the universality of 'we', the universally reasonable world. In this way, 'our' interests – those of party, government, nation and world – can appear to coincide rhetorically, so long as 'we' do not specify what we mean by 'we' [and], instead, allow the first person plural to suggest a harmony of interests and identities'.[37]

The data in the case studies show clearly how the concepts 'working class', 'working people', 'people', 'communist party' in the Yugoslav case become one single 'we', the same as the concepts 'Serbs', 'socialists' and 'people' in the Serbian case and 'Croats', 'people' and 'Catholics' in the Croatian case.

The symbols and expressions used in these three ideologies indicate that all of them employ similar vocabularies and metaphors. At the normative level the emphasis is clearly on the delegitimisation of the ideas and values of enemy ideologies, while at the operative level, delegitimisation moves in the direction of dehumanisation and is concentrated almost exclusively on concrete individual and group actors. Thus, instead of an attack on ideas, one encounters an attack on individuals and groups. Normative ideology also uses the language of science and quasi-science (Yugoslav and Serbian cases) or pseudo-metaphysics (Croatian case), whereas operative ideology invokes familiar and comparable images and group relationships in the language of 'common sense'. In the Yugoslav case the idea of dialectics in normative ideology is often used to justify and mystify contradictions in the new socialist reality,[38] while the identical function in the Croatian and Serbian cases would have the notion of 'organic link'. Thus, conflicts that arise in the new socialist society would be explained as dialectical and not as real conflict. In a similar vein, Serbs or Croats would be depicted as conflict-free, 'organic' collective entities by minimising their political or economic differences. The appeal to emotions and interests in operative ideology is to be found in all three cases. The emphasis on the sacrifices of 'our' ancestors from where the responsibility of the young generation is implied as a duty, invokes the Durkhemian idea of 'moral community'; because Major Gavrilović and his soldiers sacrificed for 'what we have today', it is not only 'our' responsibility to do the same for 'our' community/homeland/nation, but also 'our' way of recognising that the community/homeland/

nation is sacred and worth dying for. All three ideologies also appeal to strong traditional values: face-saving, masculinity, militarism and hero-worship. Conspiracy theory is another important tool to evoke the fear of some mighty, invisible force that intends to destroy 'us'. The use of kin-like metaphors such as 'our brotherly Russian people', 'our Croatian brothers' or 'the best sons of Vojvodina' is equally intended to provoke strong emotions associated with the closest kinship ties. The ideology here speaks with the voice of 'our' mothers, fathers, daughters and sons. The nation is 'our' mother, and as Croats or workers 'we' are all brothers and sisters. The ideology does not address the ordinary individual as 'Hey, you self-managing enlightened member of the working class!' but rather as 'Hey, you, my brother, let's together defend the honourable socialist flag of our country, meaning 'the honour of our mother'.

The metaphors used provoke intense emotions. The image of the 'old Serbian fireplaces' that they had to abandon, the Soviet Union as 'the tower of light', the mystical 'Seven offensives' launched by Tito and the partisans, the 'thousand-year-old dream of the Croatian people' for an independent state all function as Žižek's fantasy scenarios.[39] They are projected outside 'the real' in order to support the existing reality. To survive the hardships of the present individuals are fed with images of imaginary places where the ideal harmony of communal life is already achieved. In the faraway country of the Soviet Union there is no pain and suffering, nobody is hungry and all help each other. The message is the following: harmony can only be achieved when we establish a society where all of us will be economically identical (Yugoslav case); harmony can only be achieved when we establish a society where all of us will be culturally identical (Croatian case); or harmony can only be achieved when we establish a society where all of us will be economically and culturally identical (Serbian case). The similarities between all these metaphors, symbols and expressions suggest that there is indeed a universal language of ideology.

It is a similar case with the depiction of counter-ideologies. Even though the three (+ three) narratives presented present conceptually different counter-ideologies, the way they are delegitimised is almost identical: enemy ideologies are aggressive and threatening to the very existence of 'our' political system, they are morally inferior and socially regressive. Thus, capitalism, bourgeois and Soviet imperialism are perceived in the Yugoslav case as constant threats to socialist development: 'capitalism and imperialism have not yet given up their plans to organise aggressive offensives against communism and socialist countries'.[40] Liberal imperialism serves the same function in the Serbian case: 'those who have blood-thirstily butchered us in two world wars for their empires and who now in the name of their new European and world order are threatening us with expulsion and force'.[41] The ideology of Greater Serbia has the same role in the case of Croatia: 'Greater Serbia hegemonism ... intends to overthrow the Croatian government and renew Bolshevism and dictatorship'.[42] Here again, the appeal and structural discourse of different ideologies is almost identical.

Modernity of ideology

The modernity of ideology cannot be identified directly. Since this is not a historical study that focuses on the transitional period from the 'Middle Ages' to the Enlightenment period, I am in no position to claim on the basis of my three case studies that ideology is a modern phenomenon. However, the analysis of the form and content of ideology can give us some indirect indicators about the relationship between ideology and modernity. Two sets of issues indicate that one has to treat ideologies as the products of modernity: the first relates to the form of argumentation and language used and the second, to the types of issues raised with regard to the organisation and functioning of (modern) society.

As Gouldner was already well aware, unlike religion in pre-modern times modern ideologies do not appreciate mass ignorance, illiteracy and misinformation.[43] On the contrary, they argue for more information and more explanation in everyday life. Ideologies need individuals who are literate and who want to be informed. For ideology to operate properly, individuals 'must be more interested in the news from this world than in the tidings from another'. Only when ideology has before itself such individuals can it function properly. As the theories of nationalism elaborated by Gellner, Anderson[44] and others[45] emphasise, without standardised vernacular languages, a mass public educational system, printing (or as Anderson would say, 'print-capitalism'), the proliferation of newspapers and novels that portray society as a sociological community and a modern bureaucratic state, ideologies can have no influence on the masses. In other words, for ideology to make an appeal to the masses it is necessary that some historical and structural preconditions exist. To be able to make an impact on the public it is necessary to have a public.

Ideologies have appeared at particular historical moments when gigantic structural changes have undermined the entire hierarchical structure of society based on the legacy of the king's divine origins. In this new situation individuals were given an option and forced by economic and political pressures to choose one among the many interpretations of the social world. Ideologies intended to replace

religion, but since there were many interpretations of the social world
on offer they had to compete between themselves for the 'souls' of
the new, soon-to-be modern citizens. To succeed in this often fierce
battle, ideologies had to legitimise themselves in terms of some
'higher' reality. For the majority of ideologies these 'higher realities'
were the ideas of rationality and progress embodied in science. For
others they were higher moral values ('justice', 'rights'), or collective
and individual interests ('freedom', 'territorially or culturally defined
community'). The 'new symbolic frames' were thus to insist on more
information, facts and explanations. These were, however, always to
be 'our' information, our 'facts' and 'our' explanations. The intention
was to convince as many potential followers as possible that 'our'
explanations and interpretations of social reality were the true ones,
and, at the same time, provide as much (mis)information as possible
about counter-ideologies to delegitimise their truths. If one does
not have citizens who are literate or willing to be informed one is not
able to disseminate one's truths. In other words, without modern
citizenry and modern means of communication ideologies can have
no influence. As such, they are modern projects.

The types of argumentation and language used in the dominant
normative ideologies of Yugoslavia, Serbia and Croatia exhibit exactly
this feature of ideology. As we have seen, Yugoslav and Serbian
normative ideologies ground their arguments in the vocabulary of
science and reason shaped by the Enlightenment, while Croatian
and, to a certain extent, Serbian normative ideology operates with a
terminology that is in many ways compatible with another modern
project that appeared as a reaction to the Enlightenment – Romanticism. Reading the manifestos of the SPS and especially the CDC, as
well as textbooks and editorials, one recognises the terminology and
concepts of Vico, Herder and Schiller. Romanticism, and especially
the philosophy of Herder, transferred the ideas of the Enlightenment, which placed individual reason at the centre of the universe, to
collective entities – communities. Herder defined these communities
as *Völker* or culturally shaped nations.[46] Unlike the Enlightenment, the
emphasis here was on emotions and feelings. *Völker* were perceived
almost as living organisms which had distinctive national souls, characters and destinies. *Völker* not individuals were the principal subjects
of history. All these ideas and concepts are mirrored in the dominant
ideologies of Serbia and Croatia. The perception of the nation as a
cultural group with inherited, stable and unchangeable characteristics whose naturalness is self-understandable is evident not only in the
cases of Serbia and Croatia but also in the operative ideology of post-
war Yugoslavia. Even there we come across many examples where
ethnically defined nations are treated as entities which possess free will

and collective consciousness ('spirit of the people'). Terms such as 'organic link between Croats abroad and those Croats in Bosnia and Herzegovina and those living in Croatia', 'Croatian national being', 'Serbian national renewal', 'all Serbdom', 'the unity of Croathood' or 'Croat national feeling', all sound as if they are taken literally from Herder's works. The deterministic and mystical language which speaks in terms of 'fate', 'historical task', 'destiny' and 'spiritual renewal' is also the language of Romanticism. This strong presence of a vocabulary and of concepts shaped by the Enlightenment and Romanticism indicates the modernity of ideology.

Another common and a modern feature of ideologies in the three cases is the way they articulate social reality. They all use totalist categories. The intention is to develop the image of a society which a particular ideology addresses as a homogeneous, organic and conflict-free community. In the words of Lefort:

> Power makes no reference to anything beyond the social; it rules as though nothing existed outside the social, as though it had no limits, it relates to a society beyond which there is nothing, which is assumed to be society fulfilling its destiny as a society produced by the people who live in it.[47]

Thus, the images that these three ideologies project are all totalist: the citizens of Socialist Federative Republic of Yugoslavia are not women and men, old and young, rich and poor, fat and skinny, blue- and brown-eyed, Beatles and Rolling Stones fans, psychologists and sailors but they are all 'Yugoslav working class'. The same image is projected on to the citizens of the new Croatian and Serbian states. We do not see different groups of people who share different interests, have different dreams and show different emotions. We do not see the people who smile at different things, who like different food and dress differently. In the eyes of ideology they are all only (Catholic) Croats and (socialist) Serbs.

For ideology there can be no plurality of voices. Different views of reality are either depicted as enemy views (counter-ideology) or, if directly threatening to power-keeping dominant ideology, completely removed from the public discourse. Pareto was already aware that ideologies/derivations make a much stronger appeal by withholding information and arguments that can be threatening to the dominant ideology than by delegitimising it directly. He defined this practice as the 'accords with sentiments'. And indeed ideologies also operate 'through silence', because 'the dominant discursive practices of a group or society define not only what is to be said, but, more importantly, what cannot be stated and what goes without saying. Regimes of truth marginalise certain kinds of knowledge and move others to centre-stage.'[48] Thus, for example, normative ideology in Croatia finds as its principal enemy Croatian oppositional ideologies and discusses them at length, whereas in operative ideology they are non-existent. Their influence on the general public is minimised by removing them from the public discourse. In operative ideology they simply do not exist.

The totalist concepts used as well as 'delegitimation through silence' are both indicators of ideology's modernity. With the breakup of feudal organisation of society and of a society based on God-given truths, individuals lost their predictable ways of living. Instead of the clear, simple and understandable message – God gave you your earthly life which you spend in hard work and suffering but you will be rewarded in your heavenly life in God's kingdom – there were now many mutually conflicting messages on offer. These included messages which declared that Nature gave you your life and you do not have to suffer but enjoy it because there is no heavenly life, or that God gave you your life but whatever you do you are already predestined for heaven or hell, or that there is no way to find out if there is a God, so you should live your life according to your free will and so on. Individuals were now to choose between these different diagnoses of the social world. By choosing one of these different sets of ideas, values and practices they automatically took the whole symbolic 'package' that went with them.[49] In such an environment competing ideologies had to present their interpretations of reality and their grand narratives as totalist concepts. Unlike religion in the medieval period, which gave a vague and simple description of heaven and hell and the rules for an earthly life, ideologies were now obliged to cover with their explanations every single aspect of social life. In times when eternal truths were not questioned there was no need for detailed explanations, but once Pandora's box was opened every new grand narrative had to prove that it was the right view. To succeed in this aim, ideologies had to pose themselves in all or nothing mode. Although individuals could rarely accept or understand the claims and propositions of the ideology, the ideology had to display the image of absolute unity. This could only be achieved through the application of totalist concepts.

To be able to replace religion as a dominant doctrine it was also necessary to demonstrate that the new ideology promised everything guaranteed by the old religion and more. It also was necessary to show that the new doctrine was realisable and in touch with everyday life. Therefore, ideologies had to offer a complete picture of the ideal society they are striving to develop, as well as offer an analysis of the present. Their political programmes, pamphlets and manifestos had to have detailed views on the economy, politics, social issues, culture, nation, international relations and even, in recent days, the environment. These views had also to be popularly recognisable at the operative level. Thus, one finds arguments about why socialist planning in economy has more advantages over a market-oriented economy or vice versa, why a parliamentary democracy of a liberal democratic type is true democracy while a state based on the *Sharia* is a dictatorship and about how to resolve social problems in a just manner. The content analysis of my three case studies shows that all three dominant power-keeping ideologies have offered interpretations and explanations in all of these areas. Thus, one finds that socialist self-management in the economy is not only the most efficient way of development but also the most just type of economy ever invented. Identical ideas and forms of argument are present in the Serbian and Croatian cases. Although both recognise the dysfunctionality of socialist planning, they are also aware of the pitfalls of the market economy, referring often to the 'mixed economy' or 'social-market economy'.

What is even more interesting here and what also indicates the modernity of ideology is the clear discrepancy between operative and normative ideologies. Although both levels of ideology deal with all these issues, there is a difference in the content and type of argument. While normative ideology extensively ('scientifically') explains why a particular route in government, economy or international relations is taken, operative ideology formulates a few central principles which appear at times to be contradictory. The contradictions between the operative and normative levels are again the result of ideology's need to speak in totalist either/or concepts. For example, in both Serbian and Croatian official ideology, awareness is shown that a completely open and uncontrolled market economy in the situation of the present economic crisis is an impossible option that would in the short run bring the majority of the population to a level of deprivation. Reference is made, therefore, at the normative level to the 'mixed' and 'social-market' economy. On the other hand, in order to delegitimise the previous political order and to emphasise the difference with the *ancien régime*, it is necessary at the level of operative ideology to speak about a 'pure market economy'. In the vocabulary of operative ideology there is no place for 'something in between' even if that is the only reasonable option. The economy, like all other aspects of society, has to be defined in totalist terms.

Materiality of ideology

Although ideology is traditionally associated with ideas, values, systems of thought and belief, it is its material form that is central to its

functioning. To have an impact on a large group of people it is necessary, as Gramsci was already aware, to have control over the institutional means that secure cultural hegemony. In Althusser's theory
these institutional forms of ideology dissemination have acquired the
precise name – ideological state apparatuses (ISA). Among all the
ISA, the educational ideological apparatus is for Althusser the most
important for ideology reproduction in every modern society. It is
universal school-transmitted education that becomes central for the
internalisation of particular ideas, values and beliefs. Gouldner's
theory, despite its different scope and ambitions, contributes further,
although indirectly, to the perception of ideology as a material force.
Gouldner emphasises the importance of the mass media in the
dissemination of ideology in all modern societies. The central place
that the mass media have acquired in the post-Enlightenment period
comes from their position as a mediator of primary reality. This is
distant from the individual's sensory experience but at the same time
is highly important for the post-Enlightenment citizen who is exposed
to the second order reality, given and formulated by the mass media
as the 'news' and 'information'. The image of the world that the public
receives from the 'news' is necessarily fragmented and selective and
this opens a large space for manipulation. Therefore these two systems
or apparatuses, educational and informational, are the main channels
of ideology dissemination in every modern society.

   Let us now analyse the structure of the relationship between these
two apparatuses and dominant power-keeping ideology in our three
case studies. The degree and type of differences and similarities
between normative and operative ideologies are the best indicators of
ideology's materiality. In order to prove that Gramsci, Althusser or
Gouldner are right, one would have to demonstrate that official and
operative ideology are congruent if not identical. Although in the
case of liberal democratic societies one has to put more effort into
showing that this is the case, as Miliband,[50] or Herman and Chomsky[51]
have tried to, in state socialist societies as well as in post-1990 Croatia
and Serbia where the State had a monopoly over both of these two
institutions this is not difficult to demonstrate. The content analysis
of school textbooks and the government-controlled mass media
clearly shows similarities in form with the ideas and values promoted
in the ruling party's manifestos. We can see similarities and even some
identity between normative and operative ideologies. The similarities
exist in the main principles of ideology, in the economic and political
organisation of society, in culture and nation, in the depiction of
counter-ideologies and even in the definition of the main actors.
Nevertheless, the content analysis has shown that official and operative
ideologies also differ extensively in almost all these elements. We see

that the language, expressions and symbols used in narative and operative ideologies are regularly different and indicate more similarities
among the three operative ideologies themselves than between
particular normative and operative ideologies. It is also evident that
enemy actors are portrayed much more directly in operative ideology,
which attacks their 'personality qualities' rather than the ideas for which
they are supposed to stand. The concept, definition and presence of
the nation is also significantly different in official and operative
ideologies, the ethnically and/or territorially defined nation being
the central issue in all three operative ideologies. Even the formulation
of counter-ideologies differs, emphasising the territorial and cultural
threat in operative ideology instead of the conflict of ideas as in
normative ideology. The content analysis suggests that although
ideology is certainly material since it operates through educational
and information systems, the relationship between these state apparatuses and official ideology is more complex than suggested by
Marxists and critical theorists.

First, the analysis of the case studies leads us to the conclusion that
ideology dissemination is not necessarily connected to the economic
organisation of society or to capitalist modes of production. The
cultural hegemony achieved in these three cases could not result from
the particular mode of production simply because the economy did
not exist as an autonomous sphere in these three societies. The relationship between individuals in these three societies is not determined
by their specific position in relation to the means of production
because the dominant type of ownership is not private. In post-World
War II Yugoslavia there was state ownership until 1950 and thereafter,
'social ownership', while in post-1990 Croatia and Serbia the dominant
type of ownership is often referred to as 'public', meaning, in fact,
state ownership. As the private ownership of the means of production
is central for the existence of Marx's 'commodity fetishism', Gramsci's
'organic ideology' and 'hegemony', and Althusser's 'ideological state
apparatuses', one might come to conclusion that this concept of
ideology's materiality is not applicable to non-capitalist societies and
thus is not universal. To talk about a universal concept of ideology it
is necessary to broaden the notion of ideology's materiality from its
narrow economistic formulation to the political conceptualisation of
materiality. As some observers have already noted,[52] power relations
include economic relations because 'economic power is an integral
part of political power'. Thus, in order to study ideology as a material
force, one has to move from economic to political materialism. In
theoretical terms that means to move from Marx, Gramsci or Althusser
to, for example, Pareto, Weber or Foucault and to study power as
universal and decisive for all social relationships.

Second, as these case studies show the dissemination of ideology is never achieved in a one-way fashion. One cannot manipulate the masses *ex nihilo*. An ideology can be disseminated only if it can 'awaken' and channel emotions and interests that are already there. As both Pareto and Boudon were aware, an ideology is more likely to succeed if it presents its ideas through images already familiar to masses, appealing directly to their individual interests and already existing affects. The counter-ideology of 'bourgeois capitalism' and 'Soviet revisionism' would certainly remain an abstract, distant and inaccessible concept for the majority of the post-war Yugoslav public if it were not reformulated in operative ideology as the historically familiar idea of 'rich or powerful countries which intend to enslave and exploit us'. It is identical with concepts such as 'new world order', and 'liberal imperialism' in the case of Serbia, and 'Yugoslav unitarism' and 'Bolshevism' in case of Croatia. These concepts are translated into operative ideology as more direct statements, such as 'Germany which intends to establish a fourth Reich', 'America which aims to conquer our proud country' or 'Serbia which wants to convert us all to Ortho-doxy and turn us all into Serbs'. Operative ideology manipulates historical fears that are embedded deeply in the collective memory. The opposing ideologies that one encounters in normative ideology are first transformed into concrete collective actors (Americans, Germans, Russians, Serbs, Croats, Muslims) and then quickly delegit-imised either by appealing to their weak personality traits (cowards, traitors) or depicting them as the destroyers of social norms upon which the particular society is based (terrorists, murderers, exploitative profiteers).

However, the appeal is made not only in regard to counter-ideologies and enemy actors, but also to the already existing dominant moral values of society. Although communist ideas were in many ways in direct opposition to the traditional ethics and patriarchal values of post-war Yugoslavia, the ruling elite (who themselves originated from this culture) had no intention of eradicating these values. On the contrary, state socialism was built by relying heavily on these traditional values. This is evident not only in the terminology used in operative ideology, for example, the concept of honour, 'father of the nation', 'prominent masters of the house', and historically rooted egalitarian values and respect for authority, but also in the crucial idea of moral purity as reflected in the concept of the 'new man'. The new socialist man was to be built as an ethically pure individual in an ethically pure and thus superior community/society. This is the individual that is hard-working, patriotic, socially conscious, honest and brave, a loving father and husband, physically and mentally strong and healthy, beautiful and, above all, committed to the realisation of some higher and divine aim beyond everyday reality – the aim of achieving total harmony in the perfect proletarian society. This is basically a very Christian idea and a religious concept of morality already present in the popular psyche of the Yugoslav masses. As such it was not diffi-cult for the public to accept this image. Instead of pure Christians there were pure Socialists or Workers; instead of God's kingdom there was Communism. Serbian and Croatian dominant ideologies are formulated in a similar way. Here again one sees the aim of building a new, morally superior individual in a new, organic and morally superior community. While in the Croatian case the new man is to be an ethically and culturally pure Croat, in the Serbian case, in addition to his Serbian moral purity, he is to be a pure socialist as well. Although Croatian dominant ideology depicts itself as Christian at the normative level, operative ideology suggests that it is perfect Croathood itself that is the final aim of the new man. The Catholicism which appears in the media and textbooks is only there to distinguish Croats from Serbs (and Bosnian Muslims) and to provide strong support for the idea of a unique ethnonation of Croats. In all three cases the Christian concept of an ethically clean, harmonic and conflict-free society that will achieve salvation is preserved, regardless of enormous differences in the three official ideologies.

Therefore, the importance of the educational system and the mass media in the dissemination of dominant ideologies remains crucial for the statement of ideology's materiality. Nevertheless, to identify the materiality of ideology one has to operate with the political rather than the economic concept of materialism and recognise that ideology dissemination is never a one-way process.

Rationality of ideology

As already discussed, the rationality of ideology can be observed and analysed at three different levels by focusing on the aims of ideology, by studying the mass perception and reception of ideology and by concentrating on the dissemination of ideology. It was also stated, following Weber and Boudon, that the concept of rationality is three-dimensional, so that one can talk about utilitarian, axiological and situated rationality. Although ideology appears to have principally rational characteristics on all three levels, there is also an important emotional dimension present in the explanation of ideology dissemi-nation. Let us look at how rationality operates at these three levels in the case studies analysed here.

Although it may at first sound paradoxical, the practical aims of self-management socialism, reformed democratic socialism and ethnonationalist Christian democracy are basically the same. All three ideologies are interest- or power-driven, and hence grounded in utilitarian rationality. This is clearly evident from the type of appeal they make at the operative level. In fact, one of the main purposes of this 'translation' from the normative to the operative level is to secure the support of individuals who might not originally subscribe to these ideologies. That is why ideologies instrumentalise already existing and commonly familiar values, concepts and images and omit those ideas that would be too abstract or in clear contradiction with already existing dominant values. So, for example, the post-war Yugoslav ruling elite intentionally preserved ethnic categories and ethnic mythologies in operative ideology even though they were in clear contradiction with the 'cosmopolitan' ideas promoted by normative ideology. This is even more evident in the extensive emphasis in operative ideology on pan-Slavic unity and pan-Slavic mythologies, instead of the distant, abstract and popularly unrecognisable ideas of socialist internationalism and socialist solidarity with the Soviet Union and other east European countries. A similar situation is present in the description of clericalism in the Serbian case. While in normative ideology one observes a deeply negative attitude towards religion's influence on society and strong support for secular politics and secular education including all religious denominations, in operative ideology this unpopular idea has been 'translated' into a struggle against non-Serbian Orthodox denominations – Catholicism and Islam. Finally, the Croatian case gives us a number of examples of ideology's utilitarian aims. For example, there is a clear tension between the ideas promoted by operative ideology which justify the establishment of the ethnically defined Croatian independent state in opposition to 'Yugoslav unitarism', 'Serbian hegemony' or 'Serbian backward Bolshevism' and the ideas of European integration where the concept of the ethnically defined nation state is perceived as outdated. Here both normative and operative ideologies have a difficult task of bridging two contradictory ideas, with the single aim of persuading all those who would support Croatian independence, as an escape from 'Bolshevik' and 'backward' Serbia into the EU, and those who would support Croatian independence regardless of whether the new state was authoritarian or liberal.

The rationality of ideology's aims is also evident in the values and ideas promoted by the ideologies of Yugoslavia, Serbia and Croatia. All of them are conceptualised as rational projects that aim to realise particular blueprints. Their normative ideologies give us detailed, consistent and systematic formulations in all the important spheres of social life (economy, politics, international relations) and they all set for themselves particular rational goals they intend to achieve: for self-management socialism that final goal is a society of absolute economic harmony – communism; for ethnonationalist Christian democracy that goal is a society of absolute ethnocultural harmony – the ethnically pure Croatian state; and for reformed democratic socialism the two aims are combined to realise economic and ethno-cultural harmony – the ethnosocialist Serbian state. The rationality of their projects is also visible from the terminology and arguments used (scientific reasoning, ethical principles, individual and collective interests).

The perception of ideology and its reception by masses and elites is another level where the rationality of ideology can be observed. The differences between normative and operative ideologies suggest that the elite's concept of dominant ideology differs significantly from the one formulated for and acquired by the masses. Although I have not studied individual actions and motives for the acceptance of particular ideologies, it is possible indirectly to demonstrate that the rationality of the elites and the masses differs in terms of how they perceive the dominant ideology. While neither differs significantly in terms of its individual utilitarian rationality, since as rational individuals they all aim to realise individual interests, there is a significant difference in the way their axiological and situated rationality works. Sartori's point about the distinct belief systems of the elite (rich, articulate and constraining value system) and the masses (poor, inarticulate and unconstraining value system) makes sense.[53] Having different aims and possessing different degrees and types of knowledge, these two groups will exhibit different forms of rationality. Thus, political elites which possess what Bourdieu would call larger cultural and symbolic capital,[54] and which aim to maintain or acquire state power positions, would act differently from the masses whose 'amount and type' of knowledge as well as the structural obstacles facing them would force them to act rationally in terms of their everyday interests. Thus, mass behaviour would often appear irrational to the outsider, much as today Westerners would perceive Iraqis or Cubans, and citizens of the former Soviet Union would regard the working classes of capitalist countries. However, all these would represent cases of situated and axiological rationality. The different function and meaning of ratio-nality can be also observed in the case studies under examination here. One could see that the form and content of normative ideology was shaped at a more theoretical level by applying abstract concepts and complex terminology and grounding the main ideas in some 'higher reality' (scientific discoveries in economics, social and politi-cal theories, Christian teachings). Since these normative or official ideologies were written for the elites to justify their actions in the eyes of potential or existing counter-elites, they had to be formulated not only in esoteric ways, but also with programmes by which the elites could prove that they were the true interpreters of the 'sacred thing'. So, for example, Yugoslav communists had to demonstrate with their manifesto that they were following the only true path to communism and that their interpretation of Marx, Engels and Lenin was the right one, unlike that of Soviet and, later, Chinese revisionism. By introducing concepts such as 'self-management' and 'delegate system', Yugoslav communists aimed to delegitimise not only Soviet and Chinese interpretations of the 'great teachers' but also to establish unity within the elite, that is, within the party central committee. It is a very similar case with Serbian and Croatian normative ideologies. The SPS and CDC elites had to prove that they were the true interpreters of the 'national thing', unlike the opposition parties. That is why in the analysis of manifestos one finds fierce debate with the opposition ideas and programmes, while in operative ideology these are either marginalised or non-existent. Here again, the delegitimisation of internal counter-ideologies aims to undermine the opposition and unite the ruling elite. At the same time all these issues appear to be irrelevant to and not understandable by the broader public.

However, one of the most interesting questions for this study is how axiological or value rationality operates so that a certain degree of ideological unity in society is achieved. In these three case studies one can see that concepts such as 'socialism' or the 'national state' were equally present in both normative and operative ideologies, and, as explained previously, were seen by the majority of the population as the most advanced forms of how their societies should be organised. Although the great majority of the population could not understand the true and complex meaning behind the ideas and theories of the 'dictatorship of proletariat', 'participatory democracy', 'sovereignty', derived from Marx, Montesquieu, Locke, Rousseau or Vico, there was still ideological agreement on the central values of society. This ideological unity is achieved primarily through the instrumentalisation of axiological rationality, when the masses are mobilised along the common political project. What is important to emphasise at this stage is that the perception and reception of ideology among both elites and masses had clearly rational origins, meaning that ideology was rationally conceived. The question of how elites have managed to 'convince the public' that they are all ideologically identical will be more extensively elaborated in the following section of this chapter.

Before we move on to an explanation of this complex relationship between axiological rationality, masses, elites, legitimacy and ideology, it is necessary to interpret the third level of ideology's rationality analysis – the dissemination of ideology. This is the only segment where ideology operates by combining utilitarian and axiological rationality with emotional appeal. As shown in the case studies, official ideology is 'translated' into operative ideology in a way that is recognisable to the public. Instead of ideas, values and concepts shaped by the Enlightenment as in normative ideology, one finds direct appeal to already existing and commonly internalised emotions as well as to individual and collective interests.

It has already been demonstrated how official ideology transforms its language of reason into the operative language of metaphors, symbols and fantasy scenarios, and how abstract theories, concepts and ideas are translated into familiar images of the 'old and recognisable' enemy. Although, both normative and operative ideology operate with what Lévi-Strauss calls binary oppositions between characters and events,[55] there is a visible difference between the two. While the grand narratives of normative ideology show more complexity and strive to justify their ideas in terms of their superiority (whether of knowledge, justice or rights), operative ideologies are formulated as folk-tales, as the stories of good and evil, with heroes, villains, demons and martyrs. The structure of these tales is just the same as those analysed by Wright[56] and Eco,[57] who studied the structure of Hollywood westerns and James Bond films, respectively. What one finds in operative ideologies studied here is a triangle consisting of society, villain and hero, where society appears to be passive, weak and torn between heroes and villains who are strong and powerful and, unlike society, have a will of their own. As evident from the case studies, the heroes and villains in ideology are often collective actors who in the eyes of ideology behave as individuals with their personalities: cowardly and genocidal Croats, aggressive Americans or canny and plotting Serbs. If villains, they are regularly shown as demonic personalities who are the real threat to society. The stronger and more dangerous the villians are, the weaker and more unprotected the society. At the same time, the heroes become important and their role meaningful. This is exactly why operative ideology places so much emphasis on actors and particular events.

The potential fear must be projected onto a concrete group and, sometimes, individual actors. Formerly, these were capitalists, bourgeoisie, imperialists or fascists in Yugoslavia, while today they are hegemonists, Bolsheviks, communists or simply Serbs in Croatia, or traitors paid by Western powers, Vatican crusaders, Islamic fundamentalists or Croats in Serbia. While the groups outside of society are easily delegimitised and often dehumanised,[58] more effort has to be put into delegitimising 'the enemy within'. Among those who are most threatening are the intellectual counter-elites. Thus it becomes necessary to distinguish between loyal intellectuals and those depicted as traitors. So in our three case studies one finds that terms such as 'honest intelligentsia' (Yugoslavia), 'state-building intelligentsia' (Croatia) and 'patriotic intelligentsia' (Serbia) carry the same meaning in the three operative ideologies. On the other hand, the unity of society in the presence of a villain is also regularly emphasised. So we read how and why the unity of the working class is needed: 'the working class is disunited ... and needs at least as much unity as various factions of the bourgeoisie'.[59] Similarly, with the Serbs: 'in the situation when Serbian people have again to fight for their survival, it is necessary to gather all national forces and foster all kinds of solidarity and help from the Serbs in diaspora'.[60] And for the Croats: 'on the basis of historical experience for Croatian people and the Croatian state ... it is especially important to continue to work on the preservation of the Croatian people's unity'.[61]

All these messages are given by making an appeal to emotions and utilitarian interests. The masses are afraid of the villain and thus will support the hero who will rescue them, but the masses will also individually and collectively benefit from the support of the hero's ideology. What is needed now is to explain the relationship between the dominant rationality of ideology and its particular appeal to the emotions. To analyse the relationship between rationality and affectivity in ideology we have to move to the analysis of the relationship between ideology and legitimacy. Since ideology is conceptualised here in very materialist terms as modern, rational, and universal, it is also necessary to explain how one can relate this idea to Weberian concepts of charismatic authority and to the axiological or value rationality which are typically seen as 'irrational' or 'idealist' explanations of social action. Another question related to the rationality of ideology that also needs an answer is why and how nationalism always appears to be the dominant force of operative ideology?

IDEOLOGY, LEGITIMACY AND THE NEW STATE: THE
IDEOLOGISATION OF CHARISMA

The analysis of legitimacy types of these three case studies indicates that there is a high degree of similarity between them. In all three cases the concept of legal rationality appeared as an important source of the regimes' legitimacy. All three, Yugoslavia, Serbia and Croatia, were built as complex, hierarchical, bureaucratic and rationally conceptualised societies. All three were developing along the lines of particular blueprints: for Yugoslav society it was the concept of scientific socialism, for Croatian society it was the ethnically conceptualised nation state, whereas for Serbian society it was some form of ethnically formulated socialism. However, the persistence of clientism, nepotism and the extremely weak and sometimes non-existent separation between the public and private spheres, as well as the clear domination of discretion over the law, confirmed that this type of legitimate domination was very far from being the central source of the regimes' legitimacy in all three cases. On the contrary, it demonstrated that traditionalism plays a more important role in the process of the legitimation. Both old and new traditions, including values of heroism, manliness, victimisation, self-sacrifice and face-saving, were extremely important devices to secure legitimacy. More-over, the regimes extensively exploited traditionalism via folk culture and mythology in everyday life. Nevertheless, the strong presence and use of traditions did not automatically mean that these societies derived their political legitimacy principally from traditionalism. Analysts such as Heller[62] and even Lane,[63] who define these societies in terms of traditional legitimacy, make the mistake of conflating a traditional type of authority with ritualism and ritualist practices that are present in every society. Thus, for example, the 'American way of life' and the cult of the flag in the United States, like the cult of the royal family and 'imperial values' in Britain, are traditions with ritual-istic features. In this way, Yugoslav, Serbian and Croatian societies are no different from US or British society. They all rely extensively on ritualism and some traditional values.

However, the main argument against the idea that traditionalism is the dominant type of legitimate authority comes from the revolution-ary origins and nature of these three societies. All three societies emerged in parallel with or immediately after the structures of the old states had collapsed. The citizens of these societies were also engaged in wars that resulted in the establishment of new political entities – new independent states. Thus, the changes that occurred were revo-lutionary and radical, and in many ways affected the entire structure of the society. As we learn from Weber, the only type of legitimate domination compatible with a revolutionary form of society is charis-matic legitimacy. It is charismatic authority that results from unusual political circumstances and especially from radical changes in the political structure and organisation of society. In Weber's words: 'in a revolutionary and sovereign manner, charismatic domination trans-forms all values and breaks all traditional and rational norms: "It has been written ..., but I say unto you ...".'[64] In exactly the same way, all three cases show that charismatic authority is central to an under-standing of the dominant sources of a regime's legitimacy. Tito's authority in post-war Yugoslavia is the same as Milošević's authority in Serbia and Tudjman's in Croatia. The charisma of each leader was the cornerstone of his regime's legitimacy. All three of them are perceived by the masses as prophetic leaders who set themselves to realise millenarian targets: communism (Tito), uniting all Serbs into a single ethnonational state (Milošević) and establishing an independent Croatian state (Tudjman). They have also produced miracles in the eyes of the public: against all the odds Tito succeeded in liberating and uniting the country with a handful of followers; Milošević united Serbia and has come very close to uniting all Serbs into single state; while Tudjman made 'the thousand-year-old dream' come true by establishing an independent Croatian state.

Nonetheless, more important still in the process of legitimation is that the public themselves in all three societies have expressed deep and sincere devotion to the charismatic authority. The masses have seen their leaders as 'natural', God-given leaders, who can deliver their promises and realise these miracles. Their emotions towards the charismatic authority have been real and true. The great majority of the public would gather to see and listen to their leaders, they would feel deeply attached to the leader's ideas, they would be overjoyed when the leader praises them, they would be sincerely sad when the leader was sick and they would also be ready to sacrifice their lives for their leaders. Even though these cults of personality were to a great deal dependent on the regime's well-planned and elaborate propaganda machine, as is more than evident from the analysis of newspaper editorials and school textbooks, the dimension and intensity of popular support for the charismatic authority show that the feelings of devotion on the part of the majority of population were sincere. People really did cry and felt desperate when Tito died. They joined voluntary army units in the late 1980s to 'defend' Serbs in Kosovo in response to Milošević's indirect call. They would also spend their last savings and travel long distances just to see and listen to Tudjman. Examples from other, especially state socialist, societies show that a regime's propaganda alone can never achieve this degree of popular devotion to the authority. Although the post-1956 Hungarian government, like the post-1968 Czechoslovak government and the Polish government of the 1980s, employed more intensive propaganda machines aimed at developing new personality cults, these attempts quickly failed as they found no popular support. Unlike traditional and bureaucratic authority which impose themselves from outside ('from without'), charismatic legitimacy, as Weber explains, has to come 'from within'. This process that Weber calls *metanoia*[65] (change) is a characteristic only of charismatic authority. While bureaucratic rationalisation revolutionises with technical means, charismatic authority revolutionises individuals from the inside. Instead of changing the material and social order first and then the people through this order, charismatic power, by resting on the belief in revelation and heroism, shapes first the people and then the 'material and social conditions according to its revolutionary will'. Thus, although it can be supported by propaganda, charismatic devotion cannot be generated from the outside. To function as charismatic domination it has to originate from the inside.

However, since charismatic authority is intrinsically unstable and is the strongest anti-routine and anti-economic force, it is doomed to a short life; to benefit from its strength, one has to institutionalise or routinise charisma. The transformation of charismatic authority into 'a permanent possession of everyday life' is, as Weber explains, 'desired usually by the master, always by his disciples, and most of all by his charismatic subjects'.[66] In Weber's theory there are two principal ways through which charisma is routinised: by becoming traditionalised or by becoming bureaucratised. In both cases personal authority is transformed into institutional authority. The regime is publicly accepted as legitimate because it derives its authority either from the established will of a (deceased) charismatic person (hereditary charisma) or by establishing its legitimate domination from the institutions/offices set up by the charismatic personality. However, two issues need to be raised here. First, Weber concentrates almost exclusively on the impact of charismatic authority on the masses and gives no proper explanation of why and how the masses are introduced and persuaded to new ideas and values. The second issue, connected to the first, is the question of how the charismatic leader and his disciples manage to retain popular support when the miracle is achieved or when an attempt to perform a miracle fails. Although Weber's response to this second issue is that the leader either loses his charismatic power or routinises his charisma into traditional or bureaucratic form, there is another, I believe more persuasive, explanation. Both these issues are resolved when one takes into account the fourth concept of legitimate authority – axiological or value rationality.

As has already been explained, legitimacy based on value rationality is derived from the popular belief that values promoted by the authority in power are identical to those shared by the population. The masses have trust in the regime simply because they perceive the regime as 'theirs', as being ethnically, culturally, politically and ideologically identical to them. The relationship between charismatic authority and value-rational legitimacy provides us with an explanation of both these issues. A charismatic authority does not make an impact on the masses only through his personality but also through the ideas and values that he promotes. 'The gift of grace' is secured only when both the personality and the ideas appear to appeal to the masses. The religious leaders to which Weber often alludes could establish their charisma only when the ideas they preached found fertile ground among the masses. If Jesus had promoted the idea that Romans were racially superior to Jews, he would not, despite all his miracles and prophetic qualities, have succeeded in establishing himself as a charismatic figure. This applies even more to contemporary charismatic rulers.

It is necessary to take this fact into account to understand how charismatic authority operates. Charisma is supported by both a personality and ideas. This means that when a charismatic personality starts to lose its power, legitimacy can be preserved only through the ideas and values to which the charismatic authority appealed. When these ideas are commonly accepted and popularly perceived as the central ideas on which society is based, it becomes possible to talk about value-rational legitimacy. Thus, the central question here is when and how charismatic authority is transformed into value–rational authority.

As I have tried to show in these three case studies, this is achieved through the *ideologisation of charisma*. The new regime in power will derive its main source of legitimacy from charismatic authority (initially more from the personality than from the ideas promoted). It will also rely on some traditionalist values and ritualism as well as on a number of legal–rational principles and rules which will gradually transform the power of personality into the power of ideas, values and practices, that is, into axiological or value rationality.

The charismatic personalities of Tito, Milošević and Tudjman were thus always accompanied by a particular set of values that were initially new, different and often contradictory and threatening to the already existing dominant ideology. Nevertheless, within a few years these values were to become the dominant values of these societies. The citizens of monarchist Yugoslavia, as election results showed on many occasions, were very far from being supportive of communist ideals, while these same citizens in just a few years became strong supporters of the new communist regime. In the case of the dominant values and ideas of Yugoslavia in the 1980s the outcome was similar. All reliable surveys and public polls conducted in that period[67] showed that the values of ethnic nationalism and ethnic distance towards other Yugoslav nationalities were supported and expressed by a minority of the population, while within a couple of years of the change of regime, as new surveys show,[68] these values became the dominant values of these societies. How could this happen?

This striking change can be most adequately explained through the 'ideologisation of charisma'. In all three cases one can identify extraordinary socio-political circumstances, such as wars, the breakup of the larger state and the revolutionary change of economic and political systems. In the situation of these radical changes, individuals (the citizens of these countries) were, on the one hand, physically and emotionally threatened and looking for some form of security and stability, and, on the other, forced to make quick individual and group choices in accordance with their immediate interests. In this way they were looking for a concrete individual leader whose personality and strength would guarantee individual and collective safety and some form of predictability. The guarantee that an individual has these qualities could only be evident from his deeds. Hence Tito, Milošević and Tudjman each provided a miracle and established themselves as charismatic authorities.

As soon as they succeeded in establishing their 'gifts of grace', all three leaders were in a position to instrumentalise their charismatic auras by introducing new values and ideas among the public. These ideas, values and practices could only be gradually introduced to and accepted in a step-by-step manner by the general population. They were also much more often accepted through the redirection and reformulation of existing ideas and values than through their presentation as completely new concepts. With the help of the education system and the mass media, which were firmly controlled in each of the three cases, the ideas promoted by the charismatic authority were now disseminated to the masses. Nevertheless, to realise this aim successfully one has to approach the general public in a way that will be commonly acceptable. That means that the ideas and values promoted have to be formulated through already familiar images, symbols, language, metaphors and actors. This is achieved through a peculiar 'translation' of normative or official ideology into its operative form. The charismatic authority and his disciples have, as demonstrated in these three case studies, reconceptualised normative ideology in the form of popular folk-tales with heroes vs. villains, with good guys vs. bad guys, with 'us' vs. 'them'. In this way a particular ideology becomes recognisable to, and accepted by, a large majority of the population and soon these values and ideas are perceived as central for the society's existence. As these values become identified as 'our' values, the promoters of these ideas come to be seen as identical to the public but also more competent in their interpretation of these ideas than the rest of society. This is how charismatic power is transformed into and reinforced by value-rational authority. The relationship between the two becomes circular when the new authority draws its legitimacy from the dominant values and the dominant ideology is legitimised through the charismatic personality.

Nevertheless, how can one reconcile the impact of charismatic authority and value–rational values with the instrumentality of operative ideology? The answer is the following: the legitimacy of these three regimes is initiated by and starts with a clearly irrational (affective) impulse – a charismatic force. This force or authority is further grounded and supported by relying on traditionalist values of which the most important are those of a ritualistic nature. The regime also appeals to and makes use of some legal–rational principles. However, the most significant source of mass support comes from popular perceptions of value rationality which is articulated through the operative ideology. Although the dominant ideologies of each society are nominally shaped by drawing their justification from a 'higher' ethical or scientific reality (normative ideology), they basically gain their legitimacy from an appeal to utilitarian, axiological and situated rationality. Hence, even though the initial source is irrational, both legitimacy and dominant ideology operate principally in a rational way and through rational means. This is the process of the ideologisation of charisma.

However, it is important to emphasise that even charismatic authority, no matter how irrational it initially might be, has to ground itself in some symbolic or material promise. As one reads in Weber, the charismatic personality 'must work miracles, if he wants to be a prophet' and 'perform heroic deeds, if he wants to be a warlord'. However, some form of reward is needed to motivate the masses to follow the messiah: 'Most of all, his divine mission must prove itself by *bringing well-being* to his faithful followers; if they do not fare well, he obviously is not the god-sent master'.[69] Thus, charismatic authority does not follow from mere irrationality: it also promises economic and political well-being. Even here legitimacy works through axiological rationality; an appeal is made to material and symbolic benefits.

Another question that remains unanswered is why and how nationalism is, in all three cases, the dominant operative ideology. As the analysis of the case studies demonstrates, while normative ideology is more or less congruent with the principles and teachings of particular political theories and the doctrines they support (Leninist socialism, reformed socialism, Christian democracy), operative ideologies in all three cases combine some of these ideas and values with the peculiar nationalist concepts and ideas. Hence, if the dominant normative ideology in Yugoslavia could be characterised as the 'red ideology', its operative form was not 'red' but rather 'red–brown'; the same might be said of Serbia where the operative ideology was, let us say, 'pink' whereas the normative one was 'pink–brown', or of Croatia where operative ideology was 'grey' and its operative variant was 'grey–brown'.

In order to explain this difference it is necessary to raise two points. First, as Hall,[70] Guibernau,[71] Jenkins[72] and others have convincingly argued, there is no one form of nationalism. Both in historical and socio-political terms one has to talk about nationalisms. The historical record shows us that nationalism has had many different forms: post-absolutist nationalism of the French and the American revolutions, Risorgimento nationalism as developed in the nineteenth century in the Czech lands and Italy, the Nazi type of integral nationalism characteristic of 1930s Germany, anti-colonial nationalism of the 'Third World countries' from the mid-twentieth century and post-Cold War nationalism in eastern Europe and the former Soviet Union.[73] All these nationalisms differed in their particular doctrines and aims (some being inclusive and some exclusive), in the public they were addressing (mono-ethnic or multi-ethnic, peasants, middle class or intellectuals) in the type of appeal they made (Enlightenment-oriented, romanticist or neo-traditionalist), as well as in the means they used (wars, revolutions, institutional means).

This is equally evident in socio-political terms. One can identify conservative nationalism, liberal nationalism, ethnic nationalism, civic nationalism, fascist nationalism, socialist/Marxist nationalism and so on. This flexibility of nationalisms has often led to the conclusion that nationalism in itself is 'insufficient as a programme for political action'[74] or even that nationalism, unlike liberalism, socialism or conservatism, is not a political ideology at all.[75] This is justified with the idea that, unlike liberalism or conservatism, nationalism has a dual character, being simultaneously a political doctrine and a source of identity. Although it is certainly true that nationalism can take many forms and is largely dependent on some other ideology, as has also been demonstrated in this study, this does not mean that nationalism is not an ideology. Nationalism might be more flexible and more adaptable than some other political doctrines, but nationalism has all the features of political ideology and is in this respect no different from liberalism or socialism. Although nationalism might be less theoretically developed and less grounded in social or political theory, it, too, has its prophets (such as Mazzini, List and even Hegel), its blueprints and utopias, its dominant actors of social change, its enemies, its images of the world, its theoretical concepts and its own esoteric language.

Furthermore, just as nationalism is never 'alone' but accompanied by some other doctrines, the same applies to any other ideology. There is no 'pure' liberalism or socialism, nor can they act 'alone'. Every ideology if it intends to become and operate as a dominant ideology has to be syncretic. While liberalism or conservatism might be less flexible, they cannot have an influence on the population if not supported and 'supplemented' by some other ideology, of which the most common is nationalism. In addition, all these political ideologies (liberalism, conservatism, socialism) serve, like nationalism, both as political doctrines and as sources of individual and group identity. As social identity theory convincingly demonstrates,[76] situational factors determine whether an individual will identify more strongly as a member of the German nation or as a socialist, Protestant, an engineer, a women or a 'white' person.

Nationalism, therefore, is a political ideology that exists in different shapes and can be articulated differently by being formulated, supported and 'supplemented' with some other political ideology. Our three case studies show how this is the case here. To be able to make an appeal to the public it was necessary for the three normative ideologies to be shaped as nationalist: the integral nationalist self-management socialism, ethnonationalist socialism and Catholic ethnonationalism. The content of these particular nationalisms differs as much as their normative ideologies. However, their form, the type of appeal they make, is similar if not identical.

The second point one needs to make is that nationalism, whether ethnic, civic, integral, economic, cultural, political, regional, liberal, socialist, conservative, communist or fascist, is the principal form of legitimation in all modern societies. Nationalism is not a doctrine that can only be attributed to some social movements and marginal right wing political groups nor is it an irrational and extreme feeling of 'pathological' groups and individuals. As Gellner and Hobsbawm have demonstrated, nationalism, like other political ideologies, is a modern phenomenon. It was only in the latter half of the eighteenth and the beginning of the nineteenth century that this doctrine, which linked group identification with the State, acquired popular support. As Weber[77] and Connor[78] have well documented, we cannot talk of the existence of nationalism before the French Revolution because the majority of the population did not conceive themselves as members of a 'nation' but rather in terms of their region, district, village or religion. In addition, the discrepancy between the feudal elite (aristocracy and clergy) and the masses (peasants) within medieval societies was not only economic and political, but also cultural. Different regions and villages spoke mutually incomprehensible vernaculars, and the distance between 'high' and 'low' culture, to use Gellner's terminology, was as great as, for example, that between 'French' and 'English' 'high' culture. If loyalty existed and was expressed, it could only be a loyalty towards the monarch whose legitimacy rested on his 'divine origins'. With the French Revolution, Enlightenment and later Romanticism, the monopoly of the 'king's divine origins' was replaced by numerous ideologies out of which nationalism succeeded in establishing itself as the dominant one. Why nationalism became the dominant ideology of the modern age is a complex question that cannot be extensively dealt with here. Whether nationalism appeared as a form of secular millenarianism that replaced religion as a key to salvation,[79] or whether it originated from the need of modern societies to operate in a culturally homogeneous environment,[80] or whether it was simply an invention of political elites in the centuries of tremendous political changes,[81] or even whether it was the rise of the modern bureaucratic state that was crucial for the development and centrality of nationalist ideology,[82] is not a question that one can answer here. What one can only do is to relate this point to the cases of Yugoslavia, Serbia and Croatia. Hence, we can see that, as in all modern states, these regimes had to ground their legitimacy and dominant ideology in some form of nationalism. Since the nation state is the dominant and only legitimate political and territorial entity in the modern world, the monopoly over the definition of the nation and what 'our' nation stands for or who is to be regarded as a member of the nation means not only the monopoly of identity articulation, but also a monopoly over the structures of power. As Billig rightly points out, 'the battle for nationhood is a battle for hegemony'.[83] The nature of the modern world is that 'society' stops at the boundaries of the nation state. Thus, citizenship in a particular state automatically means membership in a particular society where citizens develop feelings of 'deep horizontal comradeship'.[84] They perceive their nation/state/society not only as an 'imagined political community',[85] but also as a culturally homogeneous unit. Having been socialised in the world of the nation state and having internalised these values, the public always expects their rulers to stand for the values, ideas and interests of the 'nation'. As already explained, the legitimacy of the regime will thus derive from the popular perception of seeing the rulers as culturally, politically or ideologically identical to the public. This axiological or value rationality in more exceptional cases, such as the establishment of a new state, would have to be initiated by the charismatic 'impulse'. It is the charismatic authority that will make an impact on the articulation of a particular nationalism. The influence of the charismatic personality in power will, as already explained, be gradually 'supplemented' and, in the longer run, be transformed into a value-rational type of authority where it will be articulated as an operative ideology. The principal way through which this operative ideology will function is by appealing to the interests and emotions of the general public, which will now recognise its particular nationalist appeal as 'their values', as the values around which their society is built and on which it is based. These values now become binding on individuals in a sense that they themselves perceive them as such. As Weber emphasises, 'it is only in cases where human action is motivated by the fulfilment of such unconditional demands that it will be called value-rational'.[86] And this is indeed how the ideologisation of charisma works.

NOTES

1 *Program Saveza Komunista Jugoslavije* (henceforth *Program SKJ*) (Belgrade: Komunist, 1958/ 1977), p. 113.
2 Ibid., p. 12.
3 *Korak u novi vek: Osnove programa Socijalističke Partije Srbije* (henceforth *Program SPS*) (Belgrade: GO SPS, 1992), p. 27.
4 G. F. Hegel, *The Philosophy of History* (Buffalo, NY: Prometheus, 1991).
5 H. Spencer, *The Factors of Organic Evolution* (London: Williams & Horgate, 1887).
6 A. Comte, *August Comte and Positivism: The Essential Writings* (Chicago, IL: University of Chicago Press, 1975).
7 J. Habermas, *Legitimation Crisis* (London: Heinemann, 1976).
8 E. Gellner, *Plough, Sword and Book: The Structure of Human History* (London: Paladin Grafton Books, 1991).
9 P. Sztompka, *The Sociology of Social Change* (Oxford: Blackwell, 1993), p. 181.
10 R. Bhaskar, *The Possibility of Naturalism: A Critique of the Contemporary Human Science* (Brighton: Harvester Press, 1979).
11 R. H. Brown, 'Reconstructing Social Theory after the Postmodern Critique', in H. Simons and M. Billig (eds), *After Postmodernism* (London: Sage, 1994).
12 Brown, 'Reconstructing', p. 29.
13 *Program SKJ*, p. 7.
14 Ibid., p. 122.
15 Ibid., p. 95.
16 *Program SPS*, p. 9.
17 Ibid., p. 126.
18 Ibid., p. 127.
19 Ibid., p. 44.
20 *Program Hrvatske Demokratske Zajednice. + Povijest HDZ-a.* (henceforth *Program HDZ*) (http:www.hdz.hr, 1993) p. 21.
21 Ibid., p. 20.
22 Brown, 'Reconstructing', p. 21.
23 D. Bohm, 'Postmodern Science and a Postmodern World', in D. Griffin (ed.), *The Reenchantment of Science: Postmodern Proposals* (Albany, NY: State University of New York Press, 1988), p. 346.
24 Bohm, 'Postmodern Science', p. 347.
25 P. Nijkamp and A. Reggiani, *Interaction, Evolution and Chaos in Space* (Berlin: Springer Verlag, 1992).
26 J. B. Rosser, *From Catastrophe to Chaos: A General Theory of Economic Discontinuities* (Amsterdam: Kluwer Academic Publishing, 1992).
27 T. Adorno and M. Horkheimer, *Dialectic of Enlightenment* (London: Allen Lane, 1973).
28 F. Lyotard, *The Postmodern Condition: A Report on Knowledge* (Manchester: Manchester University Press, 1984).
29 The language of science used in the textbooks certainly does not exclude its simultaneous appeal to the interests and emotions of the pupils.
30 A. Giddens, *Modernity and Self-Identity: Self and Society in the Late Modern Age* (Cambridge: Polity Press, 1991), pp. 36–46.
31 R. Barthes, *Roland Barthes* (Basingstoke: Macmillan, 1977), p. 47.
32 L. Althusser, 'Ideology and Ideological State Apparatuses', in S. Žižek (ed.), *Mapping Ideology* (London: Verso, 1994), pp. 129–30.
33 M. Billig, *Banal Nationalism* (London: Sage, 1997), p. 37.
34 E. Renan and E. Gellner also point out the importance of shared amnesia in the formation of modern nationalism. See E. Renan, 'What is a nation?', in H. Bhabha (ed.), *Nation and*

Narration (London: Routledge, 1990) and E. Gellner, *Culture, Identity and Politics* (Cambridge: Cambridge University Press, 1987), p. 6.

35 C. Lefort, *Democracy and Political Theory* (Oxford: Basil Blackwell, 1988), p. 16.

36 Lj. Čubrilović, S. Živković and M. Popović, *Istorija za VI razred osmogodišnje škole i II razred gimnazije* (Belgrade: Znanje, 1952), pp. 55–6.

37 Billig, *Banal Nationalism*, p. 90.

38 See, for example, *Program SKJ*, p. 8. As Sesardić shows, even Marx himself was aware of the manipulative feature of his concept. In one of his letters to Engels where he comments on his prediction about the English withdrawal from India he says the following: 'It is possible that I will expose myself to blame. However, I can always help myself with a bit of dialectics. My postulates are formulated in the way that I am right in the opposite case as well.' N. Sesardić, *Iz analitičke perspektive: Ogledi o filozofiji, znanosti i politici* (Zagreb: SDH, 1991), p. 212.

39 S. Žižek (ed.), *Mapping Ideology* (London: Verso, 1994).

40 *Program SKJ*, p. 72.

41 *Dnevnik*, 1 May 1992, p. 1.

42 *Program HDZ*, p. 4.

43 A. Gouldner, *The Dialectic of Ideology and Technology: The Origins, Grammar and Future of Ideology* (London: Macmillan, 1976).

44 E. Gellner, *Nations and Nationalism* (Oxford: Basil Blackwell, 1983) and B. Anderson, *Imagined Communities* (London: Verso, 1983).

45 See, for example, J. Breuilly, *Nationalism and the State* (Manchester: Manchester University Press, 1992) and E. Hobsbawm, *Nations and Nationalism since 1780* (Cambridge: Cambridge University Press, 1992).

46 J. Penrose and J. May, 'Herder's Concept of Nation and its Relevance to Contemporary Ethnic Nationalism', *Canadian Review of Studies in Nationalism*, 18, 1–2 (1991), p. 168.

47 Lefort, *Democracy*, pp. 13–14.

48 Brown, 'Reconstructing', p. 24.

49 However, as Marx would say, individuals were not only to choose as they please but they were to choose according to their interests and structural constraints.

50 R. Miliband, *The State in Capitalist Society* (London: Weidenfeld & Nicolson, 1973).

51 E. S. Herman and N. Chomsky, *Manufacturing Consent: The Political Economy of the Mass Media* (London: Vintage, 1994).

52 See A. Cohen, *Two-Dimensional Man: An Essay on the Anthropology of Power and Symbolism in Complex Society* (London: Routledge & Kegan Paul, 1974), p. 122.

53 G. Sartori, 'Politics, Ideology and Belief Systems', *American Political Science Review*, 63 (1969), pp. 398–411.

54 P. Bourdieu, *The Field of Cultural Production: Essays on Art and Literature* (Cambridge: Polity Press, 1993).

55 C. Lévi-Strauss, *The Raw and the Cooked* (New York: Harper & Row, 1975).

56 W. Wright, *Six Guns and Society: A Structural Study of the Western* (Berkeley, CA: University of California Press, 1975).

57 U. Eco, *Travels in Hyper-Reality* (London: Picard, 1987).

58 For a more detailed analysis of dehumanisation strategies applied during the war in the former Yugoslavia, see S. Malešević, '*Ustashas* and *Chetniks*: Delegitimisation of an Ethnic Enemy in Serbian and Croatian War-Time Cartoons', in C. Lowney (ed.), *Identities: Theoretical Considerations and Case Studies* (Vienna: IWM, 1998).

59 *Program SKJ*, p. 56.

60 *Program SPS*, p. 85.

61 *Program HDZ*, p. 22.

62 A. Heller, 'Phases of Legitimation in Soviet-Type Societies', in T. Rigby and F. Feher (eds), *Political Legitimation in Communist States*. (London: Macmillan, 1982).

63 C. Lane, 'Legitimacy and Power in the Soviet Union Through Socialist Ritual', *British Journal of Political Science*, 14 (1984), pp. 207–17.

64 M. Weber, *Economy and Society* (New York: Bedminster Press, 1968), Vol. 1, p. 1115.

65 Ibid., p. 1117.

66 Ibid., p. 1121.

67 See, for example, V. Katunarić, 'Sistem moći, socijalna struktura i nacionalno pitanje', *Revija za Sociologiju*, 16, 1–4 (1986), pp. 75–89; V. Katunarić, 'Dimenzije etničke distance u Hrvatskoj', in M. Lazić (ed.), *Položaj naroda i medjunacionalni odnosi u Hrvatskoj* (Zagreb: IDIS, 1991); I. Šiber, *Psihologijski aspekti medjunacionalnih odnosa* (Zagreb: KPSH, 1988); and D. Pantić, 'Karakteristike socijalne distance kod zaposlenih u društvenom sektoru SFRJ', *Sociologija*, 29, 4 (1987), pp. 559–603.

68 See, for example, D. Pantić, *Promene vrednosnih orijentacija mladih u Srbiji* (Belgrade: IDN, 1990); V. Katunarić, 'Exotic Friends and Real Enemies: The Impact on the War and the Image of Others in Croatia', in B. Cvjetičanin (ed.), *Dynamics of Communication and Cultural Change: The Role of Networks* (Zagreb: IRMO, 1996); and S. Malešević and G. Uzelac, 'Ethnic Distance, Power and War: The Case of Croatian Students', *Nations and Nationalism*, 3, 2 (1997), pp. 291–8.

69 Weber, *Economy and Society*, p. 1114.

70 J. A. Hall, 'Nationalisms: Classified and Explained', *Daedalus*, 122, 3 (1993), pp. 1–28.

71 M. Guibernau, 'Images of Catalonia', *Nations and Nationalism*, 3, 1 (1997), pp. 89–111.

72 R. Jenkins, *Rethinking Ethnicity: Arguments and Explorations* (London: Sage, 1997).

73 Hall, 'Nationalisms', pp. 1–28.

74 Guiberneau, 'Images', p. 90.

75 See A. Finlayson, 'Ideology, Discourse and Nationalism', *Journal of Political Ideologies*, 3, 1 (1998), pp. 99–118, and M. Freeden, *Ideologies and Political Theory: A Conceptual Approach* (Oxford: Clarendon Press, 1996).

76 See H. Tajfel, *Social Identity and Intergroup Relations* (Cambridge: Cambridge University Press, 1982) and R. Jenkins, *Social Identity* (London: Routlege, 1996).

77 E. Weber, *Peasants into Frenchmen: The Modernisation of Rural France, 1870–1914* (Stanford, CA: Stanford University Press, 1976).

78 W. Connor, 'When is Nation?', *Ethnic and Racial Studies*, 13, 1 (1990), pp. 92–103.

79 E. Kedourie, *Nationalism* (London: Hutchinson, 1960).

80 Gellner, *Nations and Nationalism*.

81 Hobsbawm, *Nations and Nationalism since 1780*.

82 See J. Breuilly, *Nationalism and the State* and A. Smith, *The Ethnic Revival in the Modern World* (Cambridge: Cambridge University Press, 1981).

83 Billig, *Banal Nationalism*, p. 27.

84 Anderson, *Imagined Communities*.

85 Ibid.

86 Weber, *Economy and Society*, p. 25.

Conclusion

One of the leading contemporary theoreticians of ideology, T. Eagleton, while arguing for the preservation of a 'critical edge' approach in the study of ideology claims that

> the 'sociological' view that ideology provides the 'cement' of a social formation, or the 'cognitive map' which orientates its agents to action, is too often depoliticising in effect, voiding the concept of ideology of conflict and contradiction.[1]

The approach I have tried to develop in this study is aimed at exactly the opposite – to void the concept of ideology from conflict and contradiction as much as possible. Taking into account that the politicising effects of ideology have often even much worse effects (as the implementation of *What Is To Be Done?* and *Mein Kampf* has demonstrated), I attempted to develop and operate with a concept of ideology that would be as free of normative standards as possible. To achieve this aim it was first of all necessary to demonstrate that the concept of ideology can be a useful sociological tool even if removed from its Marxist focus on the 'economics of untruth'. In other words, my intention was to escape the hegemony of the Marxist concept of hegemony and the equation of ideology with mystification and manipulation. On the other hand, I did not want to identify ideologies solely with world-views or party politics and thus lose the analytic strength of this concept. To succeed in both these aims (at a first sight in contradiction with one another), it was necessary to shift the emphasis in the study of ideology from its function to its form and content. Hence, by focusing primarily on the form and content of ideology I first developed an operational definition of ideology which made a strong distinction between the normative/official and operative levels of ideology and identified six segments of ideology structure along which the content analysis was undertaken for both official and operative levels of ideology. The analyses of the form and content of normative and operative ideologies helped us to establish indirectly arguments for an analytic concept of ideology. Thus, hypothetical claims put forward in the introductory and theoretical part of this study about the inclusive definition of ideology, rejection of true/false and science/non-science criteria, as well as about the universality, modernity, materiality and rationality of ideology found their confirmation in the analysis of the case studies. However, these findings and especially the generalisations made on their basis are not to be taken as attempts to develop yet another 'jealous' and 'take-it-or-leave-it' grand meta-narrative. My aim was rather to show that if we concentrate on similarities and differences between various ideologies, on their language, symbols and metaphors, on their descriptions and types of their enemies, their perceptions of the internal organisations of society, their 'images of the world', their sources of self-justification and dominant actors involved in the presentation of ideology, we can come to more fruitful and sociologically interesting results. In other words, ideologies themselves give us so much material that speaks on its own. What we have to do is just to reorganise that material in a meaningful way to be able to make comparisons with other ideologies and their forms and contents. In this way we can escape sterile and basically irrelevant discussions about which ideas, theories and views are ideological and which truthful, sincere and scientific. In this way statements such as 'Weber and Schumpeter are agents of the bourgeoisie because their theories provide justification for the capitalist system' and 'There is no other God than Allah' can be treated at the same level. They are to be analysed not as right or wrong, good or bad, but solely on the grounds of their contents: what kind of language they use, what kind of appeal they make, who they address, how they function in the wider context of particular ideology, and so on.

As repeatedly argued in this study, an ideology is not to be perceived in an a priori manner as necessarily bad or good, manipulative or instrumental. Since all ideologies, as relatively coherent systems of thought and practice, are power-oriented, they can all become manipulative and instrumental. However, this is not to say that power-keeping and power-seeking ideologies have the same means of persuasion and exercise the same degree of influence on the masses. As this study tried to demonstrate, being in control of the two central pillars of 'ideology dissemination', information and the education system, means having an institutionally shaped monopoly on truth and an ability permanently to influence the public. However, since individuals in society are not just obedient and submissive puppets, an ideology has to be made accessible and appealing for it to make a decisive impact. Thus, as has been shown in this study, official or normative ideologies that were shaped to make an appeal to science, morality, universal humanistic values or some other 'higher' reality were regularly 'translated' at the level of operative ideology as popular folk-tales with precisely defined heroes, villains, demons and angels by appealing to individual and collective interests, gains and material or symbolic benefits as well as to the emotions and affects of the public. Regardless of how ideationally and conceptually different, and often opposing, dominant normative ideologies are, at the level of operative ideology they all become similar. They all speak in the same language of 'nature' and dress in the same mantle (with perhaps different buttons and collar) of nationalism.

As this study has tried to demonstrate, it is in extraordinary situations such as wars, revolutions, the breakup of old state structures and the establishment of new states that one dominant ideology is replaced by another. To achieve this 'ideology transition' successfully, the new elite in power have to rely on some new, powerful mechanism of self-legitimation. Thus, since all modern mass societies require a certain degree of self-justification in terms of their system-functionality, rationality of rules and practices, bureaucratic administration or institutional hierarchisation, the new rulers must also derive part of their and the regime's legitimation from the idea that they are building the most rational and most efficient societal community, that is to say, establishing a legal–rational type of authority. The regime also needs to, and is always able to, rely on many traditional values and practices. The old myths, rituals and popular traditions are preserved or slightly reshaped to support, or at least not contradict, the new dominant ideology. The core traditional values such as 'face saving' or 'manliness' are also to be retained if the new leaders seek wider support. Thus, traditionalism will always be an important segment of the system's legitimation. However, as argued in this study, the newly established state/society, especially if it originates from a successfully conducted revolution, will base a great deal of its legitimacy initially in charismatic authority. The superior and unique features of leaders, their heroic deeds, miracles and superhuman qualities will make an impact on the values of the majority of the population in that particular society. In a chaotic and unpredictable environment the strong, firm and uncompromising leader will guarantee as much certainty as possible. The new prophetic leader will thus become the symbol of the new society. To maintain and extend his charismatic power, the new leader and his disciples will engage in the process of identifying the leader's 'gift of grace' with the new soon-to-be dominant values of society by connecting them with already existing images in the collective memory of the public. When successful in this project, the new leader and new ruling elite are in a position to be perceived as ideologically identical to the public and hence able to speak and rule in the name of the society. To sum up, the new regime begins by legitimising itself with an irrational impulse (charismatic force), then relies on traditionalism and partially on legal–rational principles, but in the long run operates through value rationality (articulated through operative ideology) which, although nominally shaped as a higher ethical or scientific reality (normative ideology), basically appeals to utilitarian, axiological and situational rationality. This process of the legitimation of the new society is called the *ideologisation of charisma.*

In this study I have tried theoretically to formulate this concept of the ideologisation of charisma as well as to develop an analytic model of ideology. These two were then operationally connected and applied to the analysis of empirical data with the aim of identifying, classifying, locating and indirectly explaining dominant ideologies and modes of legitimation in post-World War II Yugoslavia and post-communist Serbia and Croatia. Although I have offered an interpretation and explanation of these three case studies, I do not pretend that this is a complete and final explanation for these or any other cases. On the other hand, even though I developed a model of ideology and legitimacy whose aim is, as it is of any sociological model, to be generalisable, I cannot pretend that the three cases I have analysed here are typical or representative of all modern new states. However, as I have constantly repeated in this study, my aim was not to develop a universal and all-encompassing theory of ideology that would be applicable for every situation and for every society, nor do I think that this is possible to achieve. This was even less of the case with regard to the theory of legitimacy. What I wanted was simply to formulate an outline for a conceptual model of ideology that would, by focusing on the form and content of ideology, serve as an open hypothetical framework on the basis of which one could test some more generalisable claims about the nature of ideology. I have applied this framework to the analysis of the form and content of ideology in three societies whose official ideologies are commonly believed to be not only very different but also incompatible. To refute, or support further, the hypothetical claims developed and tested here, one should continue with the application of this model to other societies and other dominant ideologies. If the results of similar studies show that the approach and research strategy developed here can function as useful research tools, then this study has achieved much more than its original aim.

NOTES

1. T. Eagleton, *Ideology: An Introduction* (London: Verso, 1991), p. 222.

References

Books and Articles

Abercrombie, N., Hill, S. and Turner, B., 'The Dominant Ideology Thesis' *British Journal of Sociology*, 29 (1978), pp. 149–70.
Abercrombie, N., Hill, S. and Turner, B., *Dominant Ideology Thesis* (London: Unwin Hyman, 1980).
Abercrombie, N., Hill, S. and Turner, B., *Dictionary of Sociology* (London: Penguin, 1984).
Abercrombie, N., 'Popular Culture and Ideological Effects', in N. Abercrombie, S. Hill and B. Turner (eds), *Dominant Ideologies* (London: Unwin Hyman, 1990).
Adorno, T. and Horkheimer, M., *Dialectic of Enlightenment* (London: Allen Lane, 1973).
Adorno, T., *Negative Dialectics* (London: Routledge & Kegan Paul, 1973).
Althusser, L., *For Marx* (London: Allen Lane, 1969).
Althusser, L., 'Ideology and Ideological State Apparatuses', in S. Žižek (ed.), *Mapping Ideology* (London: Verso, 1994).
Anderson, B., *Imagined Communities* (London: Verso, 1983).
Arendt, H., *The Origins of Totalitarianism* (New York: HBJ, 1973).
Aron, R., *The Opium of the Intellectuals* (London: Greenwood, 1977).
Barrett, M., *The Politics of Truth: From Marx to Foucault* (Cambridge: Polity Press, 1991).
Barker, R., *Political Legitimacy and the State* (Oxford: Clarendon Press, 1990).
Barthes, R., *Roland Barthes* (London: Macmillan, 1977).
Barthes, R., *Mythologies* (London: Vintage, 1993).
Baudrillard, J., *Selected Writings* (Cambridge: Polity Press, 1988).
Beetham, D., *The Legitimation of Power* (Atlantic Highlands, NJ: Humanities Press International, 1991).
Bejaković, P., 'Procjena veličine neslužbenog gospodarstva u izabranim gospodarstvima', *Financijska praksa*, 21, 1–2 (1997), pp. 91–124.
Bell, D., *The End of Ideology* (New York: Free Press, 1962).
Bendix, R., 'Review Essay: Economy and Society by Max Weber', *American Sociological Review*, 34 (1969), pp. 555–8.
Bennett, C., *Yugoslavia's Bloody Collapse* (London: Hurst, 1995).

Bernstein, E., *The Preconditions of Socialism* (Cambridge: Cambridge University Press, 1993).

Bhaskar, R., *The Possibility of Naturalism: A Critique of the Contemporary Human Science* (Brighton: Harvester Press, 1979).

Bićanić, I., 'Mjerenje veličine i promjena neslužbenog gospodarstva', *Financijska praksa*, 21, 1–2 (1997), pp. 15–28.

Billig, M. *et al.*, *Ideological Dilemmas: A Social Psychology of Everyday Thinking* (London: Sage, 1988).

Billig, M., *Banal Nationalism* (London: Sage, 1997).

Blau, P., 'Critical Remarks on Weber's Theory of Authority', *American Political Science Review*, 67 (1963), pp. 305–23.

Bohm, D., 'Postmodern Science and a Postmodern World', in D. Griffin (ed.), *The Reenchantment of Science: Postmodern Proposals* (Albany, NY: State University of New York Press, 1988).

Boudon, R., 'The Individualistic Tradition in Sociology', in J. Alexander, B. Giesen, R. Munch and N. Smelser (eds), *The Micro–Macro Link* (Berkeley, CA: University of California Press, 1987).

Boudon, R., *The Analysis of Ideology* (Cambridge: Polity Press, 1989).

Bourdieu, P., *The Field of Cultural Production: Essays on Art and Literature* (Cambridge: Polity Press, 1993).

Breuilly, J., *Nationalism and the State* (Manchester: Manchester University Press, 1992).

Brown, R. H., 'Reconstructing Social Theory after the Postmodern Critique', in H. Simons and M. Billig (eds), *After Postmodernism* (London: Sage, 1994).

Brzeziniski, Z. and Friedrich, C., *Totalitarianism, Dictatorship and Autocracy* (New York: Praeger, 1961).

Campbell, C., 'Action as Will-Power', *The Sociological Review*, 47, 1 (1999), pp. 48–61.

Cohen, A., *Two-Dimensional Man: An Essay on the Anthropology of Power and Symbolism in Complex Society* (London: Routledge & Kegan Paul, 1974).

Cohen, L., *Broken Bonds: The Disintegration of Yugoslavia* (Boulder, CO: Westview Press, 1993).

Coleman, J., and Fararo, T. (eds), *Rational Choice Theory: Advocacy and Critique* (London: Sage, 1992).

Čolović, I., 'Društvo mrtvih ratnika', *Republika*, 145/146 (1996), pp. 1–4.

Čolović, I., *Politika simbola* (Belgrade: Radio B92, 1997).

Comte, A., *August Comte and Positivism: The Essential Writings* (Chicago, IL: University of Chicago Press, 1975).

Connor, W., 'When is Nation?', *Ethnic and Racial Studies*, 13, 1 (1990), pp. 92–103.

Constitution of the Socialist Federal Republic of Yugoslavia (Belgrade: DDU, 1974).

Coole, D., 'Phenomenology and Ideology in the Work of Merleau-Ponty', in N. O'Sullivan (ed.), *The Structure of Modern Ideology* (Aldershot: Edward Elgar, 1989), pp. 122–50.

Davies, N., *Europe: A History* (Oxford: Oxford University Press, 1996).

Dedijer, V., Božić, I. Ćirković, S., and Ekmečić, M., *The History of Yugoslavia* (New York: McGraw Hill, 1974).

DeJasay, A., *The State* (Oxford: Oxford University Press, 1985).
Denitch, B., *The Legitimation of a Revolution: The Yugoslav Case* (New Haven, CT: Yale University Press, 1976).
Denitch, B. (ed.), *The Legitimation of Regimes* (London: Sage, 1979).
Durkheim, E., *The Rules of Sociological Method* (Chicago, IL: Chicago University Press, 1938).
Durkheim, E., *The Division of Labour in Society* (Glencoe, NJ: Free Press, 1964).
Durkheim, E., *The Elementary Forms of the Religious Life* (New York: Macmillan, 1964).
Dyker, D., *Yugoslavia: Socialism, Development and Debt* (London: Routledge, 1990).
Eagleton, T., *Ideology: An Introduction* (London: Verso, 1991).
Eatwell, R. (ed.), *European Political Cultures: Conflict or Convergence* (London: Routledge, 1997).
Eco, U., *Travels in Hyper-Reality* (London: Picard, 1987).
Elster, J. (ed.), *Rational Choice* (Oxford: Basil Blackwell, 1986).
Elster, J., *Nuts and Bolts for the Social Science* (Cambridge: Cambridge University Press, 1990).
Feyerabend, P., *Against Method* (London: New Left Books, 1975).
Finlayson, A., 'Ideology, Discourse and Nationalism', *Journal of Political Ideologies*, 3, 1 (1998), pp. 99–118.
Fowler, R., Hodge, B., Kress, G. and Trew, T., *Language and Control* (London: Routledge & Kegan Paul, 1979).
Freeden, M., *Ideologies and Political Theory: A Conceptual Approach* (Oxford: Clarendon Press, 1996).
Freud, S., *The Future of an Illusion* (London: Hogarth Press, 1961).
Freud, S., *Totem and Taboo* (London: Hogarth Press, 1961).
Friedrich, C., *Tradition and Authority* (London: Macmillan, 1972).
Foucault, M., *Discipline and Punish: The Birth of the Prison* (London: Allen Lane, 1977).
Foucault, M., *Power/Knowledge* (Brighton: Harvester, 1980).
Foucault, M., *The Foucault Reader: An Introduction to Foucault Thought*, P. Rabinow (ed.) (London: Penguin, 1984).
Fukuyama, F., *The End of History and the Last Man* (London: Hamish Hamilton, 1992).
Gallie, W. B., 'Essentially Contested Concepts', *Proceedings of the Aristotelian Society*, 56 (1956), pp. 167–97.
Geertz, C., 'Ideology as a Cultural System', in D. Apter (ed.), *Ideology and Discontent* (New York: Free Press, 1964).
Geertz, C., *The Interpretation of Cultures* (New York: Basic Books, 1973).
Gellner, E., *Nations and Nationalism* (Oxford: Basil Blackwell, 1983).
Gellner, E., *Culture, Identity and Politics* (Cambridge: Cambridge University Press, 1987).
Gellner, E., *Plough, Sword and Book: The Structure of Human History* (London: Paladin Grafton, 1991).
Gellner, E., *Nationalism* (London: Weidenfeld, 1997).
Georgeoff, J., 'Nationalism in the History Textbooks of Yugoslavia and Bulgaria', *Comparative Education Review*, 10 (1966), pp. 442–50.

Giddens, A., *Capitalism and Modern Social Theory: An Analysis of the Writings of Marx, Durkheim and Max Weber* (Cambridge: Cambridge University Press, 1971).

Giddens, A., 'Four Theses on Ideology', in A. Kroker and M. Kroker (eds), *Ideology and Power in the Age of Lenin in Ruins* (New York: St Martin's Press, 1991).

Giddens, A., *Modernity and Self-Identity: Self and Society in the Late Modern Age* (Cambridge: Polity Press, 1991).

Gill, G., 'Political Myth and Stalin's Quest for Authority in the Party', in T. Rigby, A. Brown and P. Reddaway (eds), *Authority, Power and Policy in the USSR* (London: Macmillan, 1980).

Gill, G., 'Personal Dominance and the Collective Principle: Individual Legitimacy in Marxist–Leninist Systems', in T. Rigby and F. Feher (eds), *Political Legitimation in Communist States* (London: Macmillan, 1982).

Godelier, M., *The Mental and the Material – Thought Economy and Society* (London: Verso, 1986).

Goldmann, L., *The Hidden God* (London: Routledge, 1955).

Golubović, Z., *Kriza identiteta savremenog jugoslovenskog društva* (Belgrade: Filip Visnjic, 1988).

Gouldner, A., *The Dialectic of Ideology and Technology: The Origins, Grammar and Future of Ideology* (London: Macmillan, 1976).

Grafstein, R., 'The Failure of Weber's Conception of Legitimacy: Its Causes and Implications', *Journal of Politics*, 43 (1981), pp. 456–72.

Gramsci, A., *Selections from the Prison Notebooks* (London: Lawrence & Wishart, 1971).

Graumann, C. F. and Moscovici, S. (eds), *Changing Concepts of Conspiracy* (New York: Springer, 1986).

Guibernau, M., 'Images of Catalonia', *Nations and Nationalism*, 3, 1 (1997), pp. 89–111.

Gurr, T., *Why Men Rebel* (Princeton, NY: Princeton University Press, 1970).

Habermas, J., *Towards a Rational Society* (London: Heinemann, 1970).

Habermas, J., *Knowledge and Human Interests* (London: Heineman, 1972).

Habermas, J., *Legitimation Crisis* (London: Heinemann, 1976).

Habermas, J., *The Philosophical Discourse of Modernity* (Cambridge: Polity Press, 1987).

Habermas, J., *Communication and the Evolution of Society* (Cambridge: Polity Press, 1991).

Hall, J.A., 'Nationalisms: Classified and Explained', *Daedalus*, 122, 3 (1993), pp. 1–28.

Hegel, G. F., *The Philosophy of History* (Buffalo, NY: Prometheus, 1991).

Heller, A., 'Phases of Legitimation in Soviet-Type Societies', in T. Rigby and F. Feher (eds), *Political Legitimation in Communist States* (London: Macmillan, 1982).

Herman, E.S. and Chomsky, N., *Manufacturing Consent: The Political Economy of the Mass Media* (London: Vintage, 1994).

Hindess, B. and Hirst, P., *Modes of Production and Social Formation: An Auto-Critique of 'Pre-Capitalist Modes of Production'* (London: Macmillan, 1977).

Hirst, P., *On Law and Ideology* (London: Macmillan, 1979).

Hobsbawm, E. and Ranger, T. (eds), *The Invention of Tradition* (Cambridge: Cambridge University Press, 1983).

Hobsbawm, E., *Nations and Nationalism since 1780* (Cambridge: Cambridge University Press, 1992).

Hodžić, A., 'Etnocentrizam društvenih grupa i nacionalnih zajednica', in M. Lazić (ed.), *Polozaj naroda i medjunacionalni odnosi u Hrvatskoj* (Zagreb: IDIS, 1991).

Humphreys, A. J., *New Dubliners: Urbanization and the Irish Family* (London: Routledge, 1966).

Huntington, S., *Political Order in Changing Societies* (Yale: Yale University Press, 1968).

Jenkins, R., *Social Identity* (London: Routlege, 1996).

Jenkins, R., *Rethinking Ethnicity. Arguments and Explorations* (Sage: London, 1997).

Jugoslavija 1945–1985: Statistički prikaz (Belgrade: Savezni Zavod za Statistiku, 1986).

Kardelj, E., *Problemi naše socialističke izgradnje* (Belgrade: Kultura, 1960).

Kardelj, E., *Izbor iz dela, I–VII* (Belgrade: Komunist, 1979).

Kateb, G., 'On the "Legitimization Crisis"', *Social Research*, 4 (1979), pp. 695–727.

Katunarić, V., 'Sistem moći, socijalna struktura i nacionalno pitanje', *Revija za Sociologiju*, 16, 1–4 (1986), pp. 75–89.

Katunarić, V., 'Dimenzije etničke distance u Hrvatskoj', in M. Lazić (ed.), *Položaj naroda i medjunacionalni odnosi u Hrvatskoj* (Zagreb: IDIS, 1991).

Katunarić, V., 'Exotic Friends and Real Enemies: The Impact on the War and the Image of Others in Croatia', in B. Cvjetičanin (ed.), *Dynamics of Communication and Cultural Change: The Role of Networks* (Zagreb: IRMO, 1996).

Kedourie, E., *Nationalism* (London: Hutchinson, 1960).

Keohane, K., 'Central Problems in the Philosophy of the Social Sciences after Post-Modernism: Reconciling Consensus and Hegemonic Theories of Epistemology and Political Ethics', *Philosophy and Social Criticism*, 19, 2 (1993), pp. 145–69.

Kuhn, T., *The Structure of Scientific Revolutions* (Chicago, IL: University of Chicago Press, 1965).

Laclau, E. and Mouffe, C., *Hegemony and Socialist Strategy* (London: Verso, 1985).

Lane, C., 'Legitimacy and Power in the Soviet Union Through Socialist Ritual', *British Journal of Political Science*, 14 (1984), pp. 207–17.

Larrain, J., *The Concept of Ideology* (London: Hutchinson, 1979).

Larrain, J., *Marxism and Ideology* (London: Hutchinson, 1983).

Larrain, J., *Ideology and Cultural Identity* (Cambridge: Polity Press, 1994).

Lazić, M. and Sekelj, L., 'Privatisation in Yugoslavia (Serbia and Montenegro)', *Europe–Asia Studies*, 49, 6 (1997), pp. 1057–71.

Lefort, C., *Democracy and Political Theory* (Oxford: Basil Blackwell, 1988).

Lévi-Strauss, C., *The Raw and the Cooked* (New York: Harper & Row, 1975).

Lévi-Strauss, C. *Strukturalna antropologija 2* (Zagreb: Skolska knjiga, 1988).

Lewins, F., 'Recasting the Concept of Ideology: A Content Approach', *British Journal of Sociology*, 40, 4 (1989), pp. 678–93.

Lipset, S. M., *Political Man* (London: Heinemann, 1960).

Lipset, S. M., 'Social Conflict, Legitimacy, and Democracy', in W. Connoly (ed.), *Legitimacy and the State* (Oxford: Basil Blackwell, 1984).

Lukacs, G., *History and Class Consciousness* (London: Merlin Press, 1971).

Lukes, S., *Individualism* (Oxford: Basil Blackwell, 1973).

Lyotard, F., *The Postmodern Condition: A Report on Knowledge* (Manchester: Manchester University Press, 1984).

Machiavelli, N., *The Prince* (Cambridge: Cambridge University Press, 1988).

Magnusson, K., 'Secularisation of Ideology: The Yugoslav Case', in C. Arvidsson and L. E. Blomqvist (eds), *Symbols of Power: The Esthetics of Political Legitimation in the Soviet Union and Eastern Europe* (Stockholm: Almqvist & Wiksell International, 1987), pp. 73–84.

Malešević, S., 'Utopia and Dystopia After Communism: Visions of an Ideal Society Among Zagreb University Students', *East European Quarterly*, 30, 2 (1996), pp. 251–69.

Malešević, S., 'Ustashas and Chetniks: Delegitimisation of an Ethnic Enemy in Serbian and Croatian War-Time Cartoons', in C. Lowney (ed.), *Identities: Theoretical Considerations and Case Studies* (Vienna: IWM, 1998).

Malešević, S., 'Ethnicity and Federalism in Communist Yugoslavia and its Successor States', in Y. Ghai (ed.), *Autonomy and Ethnicity: Negotiating Competing Claims in Multi-Ethnic States* (Cambridge: Cambridge University Press, 2000).

Malešević, S. and Uzelac, G., 'Ethnic Distance, Power and War: The Case of Croatian Students', *Nations and Nationalism*, 3, 2 (1997), pp. 291–8.

Malinowski, B., *Myth in Primitive Psychology* (Westport, CT: Negro Universities Press, 1926).

Manning, D., 'Ideology and Political Reality', in N. O'Sullivan (ed.), *The Structure of Modern Ideology* (Aldershot: Edward Elgar, 1989), pp. 54–88.

Mannheim, K., *Ideology and Utopia* (London: Routledge & Kegan Paul, 1936).

Mannheim, K., *Essays on the Sociology of Knowledge* (London: Routledge, 1957).

Marcuse, H., *One-Dimensional Man* (Boston, MA: Beacon Press, 1971).

Markus, G., 'Concepts of Ideology in Marx', in A. and M. Kroker (eds), *Ideology and Power in the Age of Lenin in Ruins* (New York: St Martin's Press, 1991).

Marx, K., *Capital: A Critical Analysis of Capitalist Production* (Moscow: Foreign Languages Publishing House, 1954).

Marx, K., *Selected Writings* (Oxford: Oxford University Press, 1977).

Marx, K. and Engels, F., *The German Ideology* (London: Lawrence & Wishart, 1977).

McLellan, D., *Ideology* (London: Open University Press, 1991).

McLennan, G., 'Post-Marxism and the "Four Sins" of Modernist Theorising', *New Left Review*, 218 (1996), pp. 53–75.

Merton, R., *Social Theory and Social Structure* (New York: Free Press, 1957).

Mežnarić, S. 'The Rapist's Progress: Ethnicity, Gender and Violence', *Revija za Sociologiju*, 24, 3–4 (1993), pp. 119–26.

Mihailović, S., 'Izbori 90: Mnijenje gradjana Srbije', in S. Mihailović *et al.*, *Od izbornih rituala do slobodnih izbora* (Belgrade: IDN, 1991).

Miliband, R., *The State in Capitalist Society* (London: Weidenfeld & Nicolson, 1973).

Mirowsky, J., Ross, C. and Van Willigen, M., 'Instrumentalism in the Land of Opportunity: Socio-Economic Causes and Emotional Consequences', *Social Psychology Quarterly*, 59, 4 (1996), pp. 322–37.

Mommsen, W., *The Age of Bureaucracy* (Oxford: Blackwell, 1974).

Mosca, G., *The Ruling Class* (New York: McGraw Hill, 1939).

Murvar, V., *Theory of Liberty, Legitimacy and Power: New Directions in the Intellectual and Scientific Theory of Max Weber* (London: Routledge & Kegan Paul, 1985).

Nietzche, F., *The Will to Power* (New York: Vintage Books, 1968).

Nijkamp, P. and Reggiani, A., *Interaction, Evolution and Chaos in Space* (Berlin: Springer Verlag, 1992).

Offe, C., *Contradictions of the Welfare State* (London: Hutchinson, 1984).

O' Kane, J., 'Against Legitimacy', *Political Studies*, 16 (1993), pp. 471–87.

O'Sullivan, N. (ed.), *The Structure of Modern Ideology* (Aldershot: Edward Elgar, 1989).

Oxford Advanced Learner's Dictionary (Oxford: Oxford University Press, 1995).

Pakulski, J., 'Legitimacy and Mass Compliance: Reflections on Max Weber and Soviet-type Societies', *British Journal of Political Science*, 16, 1 (1986), pp. 45–63.

Pantić, D., 'Karakteristike socijalne distance kod zaposlenih u društvenom sektoru SFRJ', *Sociologija*, 29, 4 (1987), pp. 559–603.

Pantić, D., *Promene vrednosnih orijentacija mladih u Srbiji* (Belgrade: IDN, 1990).

Pareto, V., *Sociological Writings* (Oxford: Basil Blackwell, 1966).

Parsons, T., *Social System* (New York: Free Press, 1951).

Parsons, T., *Politics and Social Structure* (New York: Free Press, 1969).

Parsons, T., *The System of Modern Societies* (Engelwood Cliffs, NJ: Prentice Hall, 1971).

Parsons, T., 'A Tentative Outline of American Values', in R. Robertson and B. S. Turner (eds), *Talcot Parsons – Theorist of Modernity* (London: Sage, 1991).

Parsons, T. and White, W., 'Commentary on the Mass Media and the Structure of American Society', *Journal of Social Issues*, 16, 3 (1960), pp. 67–77.

Parsons, T. and White, W., 'The Link between Character and Society', in S. M. Lipset and K. Lowenthal (eds), *Culture and Social Character* (New York: Free Press, 1961).

Penrose, J. and May, J., 'Herder's Concept of Nation and its Relevance to Contemporary Ethnic Nationalism', *Canadian Review of Studies in Nationalism*, 18, 1–2 (1991), pp. 165–78.

Pitkin, H., *Wittgenstein and Justice* (Berkeley, CA: University of California Press, 1972).

Pilić-Rakić, V., *Siva ekonomija* (Belgrade: Nauka i Društvo, 1997).

Popović, D., *Knjiga o Milutinu* (Belgrade: Prosveta, 1986).

Reich, W., *The Mass Psychology of Fascism* (London: Penguin, 1975).

Renan, E., 'What is a Nation?', in H. Bhabha (ed.), *Nation and Narration* (London: Routledge, 1990).

Rigby, T. A., 'The Conceptual Approach to Authority, Power and Policy in the Soviet Union', in T. Rigby, A. Brown and P. Reddaway (eds), *Authority, Power and Policy in the USSR* (London: Macmillan, 1980).

Rigby, T., 'Introduction: Political Legitimacy, Weber and Communist Mono-Organisational Systems', in T. Rigby and F. Feher (eds), *Political Legitimation in Communist States* (London: Macmillan, 1982).

Rosser, J. B., *From Catastrophe to Chaos: A General Theory of Economic Discontinuities* (Amsterdam: Kluwer Academic Publishing, 1992).

Salecl, R., 'The Crisis of Identity and the Struggle for New Hegemony in the Former Yugoslavia', in E. Laclau (ed.), *The Making of Political Identities* (London: Verso, 1994).

Sarantakos, S., *Social Research* (London: Macmillan, 1993).

Sartori, G., 'Politics, Ideology and Belief Systems', *American Political Science Review*, 63 (1969), pp. 398–411.

Schaar, J., 'Legitimacy in the Modern State', in W. Connoly (ed.), *Legitimacy and the State* (Oxford: Basil Blackwell, 1984).

Schopenhauer, A., *The World as Will and Representation* (New York: Dover Publishers, 1969).

Seliger, M., *Ideology and Politics* (London: Allen & Unwin, 1976).

Sesardić, N., *Iz analitičke perspektive: Ogledi o filozofiji, znanosti i politici* (Zagreb: SDH, 1991).

Šezdeset godina Saveza Komunista Jugoslavije (Sarajevo: MSCC CK SK BIH, 1979).

Shils, E., 'The Concept and Function of Ideology', *International Encyclopaedia of the Social Sciences*, 7 (1968), pp. 66–76.

Shlapentokh, V., 'The Study of Values as a Social Phenomenon: The Soviet Case', *Social Forces*, 61, 4 (1982), pp. 403–17.

Šiber, I., *Psihologijski aspekti medjunacionalnih odnosa* (Zagreb: KPSH, 1988).

Silber, L. and Little, A., *The Death of Yugoslavia* (London: Penguin/BBC Books, 1995).

Sinclair, J. and Coulthard, R. *Towards an Analysis of Discourse: The English Used by Teacher and Pupils* (Oxford: Oxford University Press, 1975).

Smith, A., *The Ethnic Revival in the Modern World* (Cambridge: Cambridge University Press, 1981).

Sorel, G., *Reflections on Violence* (Cambridge: Cambridge University Press, 1999).

Spencer, H., *The Factors of Organic Evolution* (London: Williams & Horgate, 1887).

Sztompka, P., *The Sociology of Social Change* (Oxford: Blackwell, 1993).

Tajfel, H., *Social Identity and Intergroup Relations* (Cambridge: Cambridge University Press, 1982).

Tarifa, F., 'The Quest for Legitimacy and the Withering Away of Utopia', *Social Forces*, 76, 2 (1997), pp. 437–74.

Taylor, C., 'Foucault on Freedom and Truth', in *Philosophy and the Human Sciences* (Cambridge: Cambridge University Press, 1985).

Therborn, G., *The Ideology of Power and the Power of Ideology* (London: New Left Books, 1980).

Thompson, J., *Studies in the Theory of Ideology* (Cambridge: Polity Press, 1984).
Uzelac, G., 'Franjo Tudjman's Nationalist Ideology', *East European Quarterly*, 31, 4 (1998), pp. 449–73.
Wallerstein, I., 'The Challenge of Maturity: Whither Social Science?, *Review*, 15, 1 (1992), pp. 1–7.
Weber, E., *Peasants into Frenchmen: The Modernisation of Rural France, 1870–1914* (Stanford, CA: Stanford University Press, 1976).
Weber, M., *Economy and Society, I–II* (New York: Bedminster Press, 1968).
Weber, M., *The Protestant Ethic and the Spirit of Capitalism* (London: Allen & Unwin, 1976).
Wright, W., *Six Guns and Society: A Structural Study of the Western* (Berkeley, CA: University of California Press, 1975).
Yin, R., *Case Study Research: Design and Methods* (Newbury Park: Sage, 1991).
Žanić, I., 'Navrh gore Romanije ...', *Erasmus*, 6 (1994), pp. 13–22.
Žižek, S. (ed.), *Mapping Ideology* (London: Verso, 1994)
Županov, J., *Sociologija i samoupravljanje* (Zagreb: Školska knjiga, 1977).

Manifestos

Program Saveza Komunista Jugoslavije (Belgrade: Komunist, 1958/1977).
Korak u novi vek: Osnove programa Socijalističke Partije Srbije (Belgrade: GO SPS, 1992).
Program Hrvatske Demokratske Zajednice. Povijest HDZ-a. (Http:www.hdz.hr, 1993).

Newspapers

Borba (1945–50)
Dnevnik (1990–96)
Vjesnik (1990–96)
Feral Tribune
Naša Borba
Književne Novine
Vreme

School textbooks

Yugoslavia

Čubrilović, Lj., Živković, S. and Popović, M., *Istorija za VI razred osmogodišnje škole i II razred gimnazije* (Belgrade: Znanje, 1952).
Čulinović, F., *Stvaranje nove Jugoslavenske države* (Zagreb: Grafički Zavod Hrvatske, 1959).
Solarić, G., *Istorija za VIII razred osmogodišnje škole i IV razred gimnazije* (Belgrade: Znanje, 1952).
Teodosić, R., Stanojević, M., Bajalica, M. and Vuković, R., *Zemljopis za III razred osnovne škole* (Belgrade: Prosveta, 1946).

Serbia

Danilović, D. and Danilović, B., *Poznavanje društva za 4. razred osnovne škole* (Belgrade: Zavod za udžbenike i nastavna sredstva, 1993).

Gaćeša, N., Živković, D. and Radović, L. J., *Istorija za III razred gimnazije prirodno-matematičkog smera i IV razred gimnazije opšteg i društveno-jezičkog smera* (Belgrade: Zavod za udžbenike i nastavna sredstva, 1996).

Gaćeša, N., Mladenović-Maksimović, Lj. and Živković, D. *Istorija za 8. razred osnovne škole* (Belgrade: Zavod za udžbenike i nastavna sredstva, 1997).

Mihaljčić, R., *Istorija za 6. razred osnovne škole* (Belgrade: Zavod za udžbenike i nastavna sredstva, 1993).

Croatia

Mirošević, F. and Macan, T., *Hrvatska i svijet u XVIII. I XIX. stoljeću* (Zagreb: Školska knjiga, 1995).

Mirošević, F. and Sanjek, F., *Hrvatska i svijet od V. do XVIII. stoljeća* (Zagreb: Školska knjiga, 1995).

Perić, I., *Hrvatska i Svijet u XX. stoljeću* (Zagreb: Školska knjiga, 1995).

Index